TAKING SIDES

Clashing Views on Controversial
Issues in World Politics

TENTH EDITION

Selected, Edited, and with Introductions by

John T. Rourke
University of Connecticut

McGraw-Hill/Dushkin
A Division of The McGraw-Hill Companies

For my son and friend—John Michael

Cover image: © 2002 by PhotoDisc, Inc.

Cover Art Acknowledgment
Charles Vitelli

Manufactured in the United States of America

Tenth Edition

123456789BAHBAH5432

Library of Congress Cataloging-in-Publication Data
Main entry under title:
Taking sides: clashing views on controversial issues in world politics/selected, edited, and with introductions by John T. Rourke.—10th ed.
Includes bibliographical references and index.
1. World Politics—1989–. I. Rourke, John T., *comp.*
909.82

0-07-248050-5
ISSN: 1094-754X

Printed on Recycled Paper

Preface

In the first edition of *Taking Sides*, I wrote of my belief in informed argument:

> [A] book that debates vital issues is valuable and necessary. . . . [It is impor-
> tant] to recognize that world politics is usually not a subject of absolute
> rights and absolute wrongs and of easy policy choices. We all have a re-
> sponsibility to study the issues thoughtfully, and we should be careful to
> understand all sides of the debates.

It is gratifying to discover, as indicated by the success of *Taking Sides* over
nine editions, that so many of my colleagues share this belief in the value of a
debate-format text.

The format of this edition follows a formula that has proved successful
in acquainting students with the global issues that we face and generating discussion of those issues and the policy choices that address them. This book
addresses 18 issues on a wide range of topics in international relations. Each
issue has two readings: one pro and one con. Each is accompanied by an issue *introduction*, which sets the stage for the debate, provides some background
information on each author, and generally puts the issue into its political context. Each issue concludes with a *postscript* that summarizes the debate, gives
the reader paths for further investigation, and suggests additional readings that
might be helpful. I have also provided relevant Internet site addresses (URLs)
in each postscript and on the *On the Internet* page that accompanies each part
opener. At the back of the book is a listing of all the *contributors to this volume*,
which will give you information on the political scientists and commentators
whose views are debated here.

I have continued to emphasize issues that are currently being debated
in the policy sphere. The authors of the selections are a mix of practitioners,
scholars, and noted political commentators.

Changes to this edition   The dynamic, constantly changing nature of the
world political system and the many helpful comments from reviewers have
brought about significant changes to this edition. Of the 36 readings in this
edition, 33, or 92 percent, are new, with only 3 readings being carried over
from the previous edition.

The kaleidoscopic dynamism of the international system is also evident in
the high turnover in issues from one edition to the next of this reader. Only 2
(11 percent) of the 18 issues are carried over in toto from the previous edition.
In contrast, 10 issues (56 percent) are completely new. They are: *Should Greater
Global Governance Be Resisted?* (Issue 2); *Will State Sovereignty Survive Globalism?*

(Issue 3); *Should the United States Seek Global Hegemony?* (Issue 4); *Is China an Expansionist Power?* (Issue 6); *Should Sanctions Against Iraq Be Continued?* (Issue 8); *Is the Capitalist Model for Third World Development Destructive?* (Issue 9); *Does the International Monetary Fund Do More Harm Than Good?* (Issue 10); *Is There a Great Danger From Chemical or Biological Terrorism?* (Issue 12); *Did the NATO Military Action Against Yugoslavia Violate Just War Theory?* (Issue 14); and *Is Violence as a Form of Protest on International Political Issues Always Wrong?* (Issue 17).

Another 6 issues have been recast to reflect changes in the specific concerns related to general topics that were included in the last edition. These "semi-new" debates are: *Is Economic Globalism a Positive Trend?* (Issue 1); *Is Russia Likely to Become an Antagonistic Power?* (Issue 5); *Should Israel Take a Hard Line With the Palestinians?* (Issue 7); *Should U.S. Military Spending Be Increased?* (Issue 11); *Should the United Nations Be Given Stronger Peacekeeping Capabilities?* (Issue 13); and *Is Dangerous Global Warming Occurring?* (Issue 18).

It is important to note that the changes to this edition from the last should not disguise the fact that most of the issues address enduring human concerns, such as global political organization, arms and arms control, justice, development, and the environment. Also important is the fact that many of the issues have both a specific and a larger topic. For instance, Issue 13 is about the specific topic of strengthening the UN's peacekeeping (or peacemaking) ability, but it is also about more general topics. These include whether or not international organizations should be given supranational powers; the propriety of interventionism using UN, NATO, or international forces; and the argument by some small countries that there is a growing neocolonialism in the world today.

A word to the instructor An *Instructor's Manual With Test Questions* (multiple-choice and essay) is available through the publisher for instructors using *Taking Sides* in the classroom. A general guidebook, *Using Taking Sides in the Classroom,* which discusses methods and techniques for integrating the pro-con approach into any classroom setting, is also available. An online version of *Using Taking Sides in the Classroom* and a correspondence service for *Taking Sides* adopters can be found at http://www.dushkin.com/usingts/.

Taking Sides: Clashing Views on Controversial Issues in World Politics is only one title in the Taking Sides series. If you are interested in seeing the table of contents for any of the other titles, please visit the Taking Sides Web site at http://www.dushkin.com/takingsides/.

A note especially for the student reader You will find that the debates in this book are not one-sided. Each author strongly believes in his or her position. And if you read the debates without prejudging them, you will see that each author makes cogent points. An author may not be "right," but the arguments made in an essay should not be dismissed out of hand, and you should work at remaining tolerant of those who hold beliefs that are different from your own.

There is an additional consideration to keep in mind as you pursue this debate approach to world politics. To consider divergent views objectively does not mean that you have to remain forever neutral. In fact, once you are informed, ought to form convictions. More important, you should try to influence international policy to conform better with your beliefs. Write letters to policymakers; donate to causes you support; work for candidates who agree with your views; join an activist organization. *Do* something, whichever side of an issue you are on!

Acknowledgments I received many helpful comments and suggestions from colleagues and readers across the United States and Canada. Their suggestions have markedly enhanced the quality of this edition of *Taking Sides*. If as you read this book you are reminded of a selection or an issue that could be included in a future edition, please write to me in care of McGraw-Hill/Dushkin with your recommendations.

My thanks go to those who responded with suggestions for the tenth edition:

Francis Adams
Old Dominion University

Scott Bennett
Pennsylvania State University

Lewis Brownstein
SUNY College at New Paltz

Michael DeMichele
University of Scranton

Gary Donato
Three Rivers Community Technical College

June Teufel Dreyer
University of Miami

Roger Durham
Aquinas College

Timothy L. Elliot
Brigham Young University

Kevin Ellsworth
Arizona State University

Tahmineh Entessar
Webster University

Marc Genest
University of Rhode Island

Monir Saad Girgis
Edinboro University of Pennsylvania

Donald Grieve
Northwood University

Mark Griffith
University of West Alabama

Kenneth Hall
Ball State University

Dennis Hart
Kent State University

Ngozi C. Kamalu
Fayetteville State University

Wei-chin Lee
Wake Forest University

Guioli Liu
College of Charleston

Nelson Madore
Thomas College

Timothy Nordstrom
Pennsylvania State University

Arnold Oliver
Heidelberg College

Peter Sanchez
Loyola University

John Seitz
Wofford College

Zhe Sun
Ramapo College of New Jersey

Melvin M. Vuk
New Mexico State University

Christopher Van Aller
Winthrop University

Jutta Weldes
Kent State University

I would also like to thank Ted Knight, list manager for the Taking Sides series, and David Brackley, senior developmental editor, for their help in refining this edition.

John T. Rourke
University of Connecticut

Contents In Brief

Contents

PART 2   REGIONAL   57

Robert Kagan, senior associate at the Carnegie Endowment for International Peace, contends that the United States has proved to be a relatively benevolent hegemon and that continued American dominance of the international system is necessary in order to preserve a reasonable level of international peace and prosperity. Charles William Maynes, president of the Eurasia Foundation, argues that promoting American global hegemony is not worth the costs. Ultimately it will fail, he asserts, and we will lose the opportunity to establish a new, less power-based international system.

Ariel Cohen, a research fellow in Russian and Eurasian studies at the Heritage Foundation in Washington, D.C., argues that the current Russian government espouses a nationalist agenda that seeks to reestablish Russia as a great world power and to undermine U.S. leadership. Anatol Lieven, a senior associate at the Carnegie Endowment for International Peace in Washington, D.C., contends that the negative view of Russia inherited from the cold war era leads to bad policies.

Professor of politics Aaron L. Friedberg depicts China as wanting to become the dominant power in Asia, replacing the United States as the preeminent power in the region. Nicholas Berry, a senior analyst at the Center for Defense Information in Washington, D.C., contends that China will not seek regional hegemony and that Americans who see China as the new imperialist power need to review the historical record.

Daniel Pipes, director of the Middle East Forum, a policy analysis center in Philadelphia, Pennsylvania, contends that Israel should not give up any of its existing advantages in the face of Arab intransigence and outside pressure. Herbert C. Kelman, director of the Program on International Conflict Analysis and Resolution at Harvard University, contends that to move the Middle East peace process forward, Israel and the Palestinians have to commit to a solution that includes, among other things, the creation of a Palestinian state.

Walter B. Slocombe, who was undersecretary of defense for policy at the time of his statement before the Committee on Armed Services, argues that the complete unwillingness of Iraq to comply with UN inspections means that sanctions should continue. Sophie Boukhari, a journalist for the *UNESCO Courier,* maintains that the sanctions are causing unconscionable suffering among the Iraqi people and should be ended.

Vandana Shiva, director of the Research Foundation for Science, Technology and Ecology in New Delhi, India, asserts that development that follows the capitalist model more often than not destroys the environment, the livelihoods, and the cultures of Third World communities. Bill Emmott, editor of *The Economist,* contends that places in the Third World that have followed capitalist principles to guide their development have prospered much more than those that have followed socialism and other models.

John Cavanagh, director of the Institute for Policy Studies in Washington, D.C.; Carol Welch, an international policy analyst at Friends of the Earth USA; and Simon Retallack, managing editor of *The Ecologist*, charge that the International Monetary Fund (IMF) has consistently elevated the need for financial and monetary stability above any other concerns. Michel Camdessus, managing director of the IMF (1987–2000), in an interview conducted by Moisés Naím, editor of *Foreign Policy*, contends that there is extraordinary confusion behind the criticism of the IMF.

Henry H. Shelton, a general in the U.S. Army and chairman of the Joint Chiefs of Staff, argues that the United States, its citizens, and its interests are threatened in many places in the world and across a wide range of issues. He contends that while the dangers may not seem as menacing as they did during the cold war, it is prudent to invest in force modernization in the near term to ensure razor-sharp forces for the long haul. Carl Conetta, director of the Project on Defense Alternatives at the Commonwealth Institute in Cambridge, Massachusetts, contends that U.S. military overspending derives from a lack of realism in threat assessment, an unnecessarily ambitious post–cold war military strategy, and failure to adapt to the specific challenges of the new era.

James K. Campbell, a terrorism expert and a commander in the United States Navy assigned to the Defense Intelligence Agency, testifies before the U.S. Congress that terrorists can acquire and use lethal chemical, biological, and radiological weapons. Jonathan B. Tucker, a visiting fellow of the Hoover Institution at Stamford University, argues that the threat of chemical and biological terrorism is not great enough to warrant a massive effort to prepare for and defend against an attack.

Introduction

World Politics and the Voice of Justice

John T. Rourke

Some years ago, the Rolling Stones recorded "Sympathy With the Devil." If you have never heard it, go find a copy. It is worth listening to. The theme of the song is echoed in a wonderful essay by Marshall Berman, "Have Sympathy for the Devil" (*New American Review*, 1973). The common theme of the Stones' and Berman's works is based on Johann Goethe's *Faust*. In that classic drama, the protagonist, Dr. Faust, trades his soul to gain great power. He attempts to do good, but in the end he commits evil by, in contemporary paraphrase, "doing the wrong things for the right reasons." Does that make Faust evil, the person-ification of the devil Mephistopheles among us? Or is the good doctor merely misguided in his effort to make the world better as he saw it and imagined it might be? The point that the Stones and Berman make is that it is important to avoid falling prey to the trap of many zealots who are so convinced of the truth of their own views that they feel righteously at liberty to condemn those who disagree with them as stupid or even diabolical.

It is to the principle of rational discourse, of tolerant debate, that this reader is dedicated. There are many issues in this volume that appropriately excite passion—for example, Issue 7 on whether or not Israel should follow a hard-line policy toward the Palestinians or Issue 12, which examines the degree of danger from chemical or biological terrorism. Few would deny, for example, that a danger from terrorism exists. But what is not clear is whether or not the degree of danger warrants a crash program to prevent chemical and biological (and nuclear) terrorism and to react to such an attack if it were to happen. Are scenarios such as those portrayed in the 1998 film *The Siege* in our future?

In other cases, the debates you will read do diverge on goals. In Issue 2 Mark Leonard argues that the world will be better off if countries accept greater governance from international organizations and law. Therefore, Leonard fa-vors working toward the goal of greater global governance. Marc A. Thiessen disagrees vigorously and is dedicated to the goal of maintaining national sovereignty by resisting global governance.

As you will see, each of the authors in all the debates strongly believes in his or her position. If you read these debates objectively, you will find that each side makes cogent points. They may or may not be right, but they should not be dismissed out of hand. It is also important to repeat that the debate format does not imply that you should remain forever neutral. In fact, once you are informed, you *ought* to form convictions, and you should try to act on those convictions and try to influence international policy to conform better with your beliefs. Ponder the similarities in the views of two very different leaders, a very young president in a relatively young democracy and a very old emperor in a very old country: In 1963 President John F. Kennedy, in recalling the words of the author of the epoch poem *The Divine Comedy* (1321), told a West German audience, "Dante once said that the hottest places in hell are reserved for those who in a period of moral crisis maintain their neutrality." That very same year, while speaking to the United Nations, Ethiopia's emperor Haile Selassie (1892–1975) said, "Throughout history it has been the inaction of those who could have acted, the indifference of those who should have known better, the silence of the voice of justice when it mattered most that made it possible for evil to triumph."

The point is: Become Informed. Then *do* something! Write letters to policymakers, donate money to causes you support, work for candidates with whom you agree, join an activist organization, or any of the many other things that you can do to make a difference. What you do is less important than that you do it.

Approaches to Studying International Politics

As will become evident as you read this volume, there are many approaches to the study of international politics. Some political scientists and most practitioners specialize in *substantive topics,* and this reader is organized along topical lines. Part 1 (Issues 1 through 3) features a series of related debates on the evolution of the international system in the direction of greater globalization. The most pronounced changes have been in the economic sphere, and the staff of the International Monetary Fund and Scott Marshall engage in a debate about whether or not increasing global economic interdependence is a positive trend. Issue 2 takes up the relatively less advanced but still important aspect of globalization represented by the growth in the importance of international organizations and international law. The final topic in Part 1 engages Stephen D. Krasner and Kimberly Weir in a debate over whether countries will continue to maintain their sovereignty in the future or become at least partially subordinate to regional and global organizations.

Part 2 (Issues 4 through 8) focuses on country-specific issues, including the role of the United States in the international system, the future diplomatic postures of Russia and China, relations between Israel and the Palestinians, and UN sanctions on Iraq. Part 3 (Issues 9 and 10) deals with specific concerns of the international economy, a topic introduced more generally in Issue 1. With the United States and other wealthy capitalist countries dominating the international system, there is great pressure on less developed countries to follow the capitalist model in trying to better their economies. In Issue 9, Vandana Shiva, an analyst in India, maintains that the capitalist model of development is often destructive. Bill Emmott, who edits the well-known British publication *The Economist,* takes the opposite point of view and says that capitalism is the surest and fastest path to development for the Third World. Then, in Issue 10, the debate turns to the International Monetary Fund (IMF), one of the international financial institutions that, among other things, strongly promotes the capitalist model. In this issue, a trio of authors condemn the IMF for doing more harm than good, while the former head of the IMF defends the institution's policies.

Part 4 (Issues 11 and 12) examines military security. Defense expenditures by the United States far outstrip those of any other country, yet both Al Gore and George W. Bush, the primary candidates for president in 2000, advocated increased military spending. Issue 11 debates whether current and projected threats warrant increased spending or, alternatively, might allow significant cuts in the U.S. defense budget. This debate is followed by the focus in Issue 12 on the growing concern over what is known as "asymmetrical" warfare, or the use of terrorism to attack countries that are relatively invulnerable to conventional military attack, such as the United States. The use of biological, chemical, and nuclear weapons of mass destruction is of particular concern. James Campbell and Jonathan Tucker both recognize the threat, but they disagree on how acute the danger is.

Part 5 (Issues 13 through 15) addresses controversies related to international law and organizations. The ability of the United Nations to deploy effective peacekeeping forces is severely constrained by a number of factors, and in Issue 13, Lionel Rosenblatt and Larry Thompson contend that enhancing the strength of UN peacekeepers would represent progress. John Hillen disputes this view, arguing that the UN was never intended to have a powerful military arm and that it would be an error to create such a capability. There are also a number of important controversies surrounding the application of international law in world politics. Issue 14 takes up one of these, exploring whether the U.S.-led NATO intervention in Yugoslavia was just. The two authors, one a colonel in the U.S. Marine Corps, the other the president of the United States, disagree over whether or not both the reasons for the intervention and the manner in which the war was waged met the test of just war theory. The issue on the law of war flows into the debate in Issue 15, which evaluates the wisdom of establishing a permanent international criminal court to punish those who violate the law of war. It is easy to advocate such a court as long as it is trying and sometimes punishing alleged war criminals from other countries. But one has to understand that one day a citizen of one's own country could be put on trial.

Part 6, which includes Issues 16 through 18, takes up global moral, social, and environmental issues. There can be little doubt that national and international politics have historically been dominated by males. There can also be little doubt that women are more frequently playing larger roles in the world by, among other things, holding such positions as president, prime minister, and foreign secretary. Issue 16 considers the potential impact of the growing role of women on the level of violence in the world. Certainly, equity demands that women have the same opportunity as men to achieve leadership positions. But will that equity also promote a decrease in world violence? Therein lies the debate. The focus in Part 6 then switches to political activism. One would be hard-pressed to find any serious analyst today who would disagree with the proposition that political activism by citizens is good, even necessary to the survival of democracy. The boundaries of that activity are debated in Issue 17, with Satish Kumar and Jake Bowers differing over whether or not there is a legitimate role for political violence. Finally, the environment is addressed in Issue 18, which focuses on the degree of danger posed by global warming.

Political scientists also approach their subject from differing *methodological perspectives*. We will see, for example, that world politics can be studied from different *levels of analysis*. The question is, What is the basic source of the forces that shape the conduct of politics? Possible answers are world forces, the individual political processes of the specific countries, or the personal attributes of a country's leaders and decision makers. Various readings will illustrate all three levels.

Another way for students and practitioners of world politics to approach their subject is to focus on what is called the realist versus the idealist debate. Realists tend to assume that the world is permanently flawed and therefore advocate following policies in their country's narrow self-interests. Idealists take the approach that the world condition can be improved substantially by following policies that, at least in the short term, call for some risk or self-sacrifice. This divergence is an element of many of the debates in this book.

Dynamics of World Politics

The action on the global stage today is vastly different from what it was a few decades ago, or even a few years ago. *Technology* is one of the causes of this change. Technology has changed communications, manufacturing, health care, and many other aspects of the human condition. Technology has given humans the ability to create biological, chemical, and nuclear compounds and other material that in relatively small amounts have the ability to kill and injure huge numbers of people. Issue 12 frames a debate over whether or not we humans have created a monster that constitutes a dire threat. Another negative byproduct of technology may well be global warming, which is caused by the vastly increased discharges of carbon dioxide and other "greenhouse" gases into the atmosphere that have resulted from industrialization, the advent of air conditioning, and many other technological advances. These effects are taken up in Issue 18.

Another dynamic aspect of world politics involves the *changing axes* of the world system. For about 40 years after World War II ended in 1945, a bipolar system existed, the primary axis of which was the *East-West* conflict, which pitted the United States and its allies against the Soviet Union and its allies. Now that the cold war is over, one broad debate is over what role the United States should play. A related issue is whether or not there are potential enemies to the United States and its allies and, if so, who they are. The advocates on either side of Issue 4 disagree about whether or not the United States should try to dominate international politics. As for potential rivals to U.S. hegemony, Issues 5 and 6 deal with Russia and China, two cold war antagonists of the United States. Some people believe that one or both of these countries, or even both of them in alliance, could pose a threat in the future. As such, the two debates, beyond the specific issues involved in them, also deal with how to interact with former and potential enemies. Issue 11 takes an even broader look at the future of U.S. security, with two analysts debating whether the approximately $300 billion the United States spends annually on its military should be increased or decreased.

Technological changes and the shifting axes of international politics also highlight the *increased role of economics* in world politics. Economics have always played a role, but traditionally the main focus has been on strategic-political questions—especially military power. This concern still strongly exists, but it now shares the international spotlight with economic issues. One important change in recent decades has been the rapid growth of regional and global markets and the promotion of free trade and other forms of international economic interchange. As Issue 1 on economic interdependence indicates, many people support these efforts and see them as the wave of the future. But there are others who believe that free economic interchange undermines sovereignty and the ability of governments to control their destinies. One topic related to control, which is taken up in Issue 9, is whether or not the developed countries should insist that less developed countries follow a capitalist development model. That topic is addressed in even greater depth in Issue 10, which examines the policies of the International Monetary Fund and asks whether the IMF is making a contribution or using the desperation of needy countries to impose alien and often destructive standards on those countries.

Another change in the world system has to do with the main *international* actors. At one time states (countries) were practically the only international actors on the world stage. Now, and increasingly so, there are other actors. Some actors are regional. Others, such as the United Nations, are global actors. At the broadest level, Issue 2 takes up the governance role of these actors. This is followed by Issue 3, which examines the future of countries as the principal and sovereign actors in the international system. Turning to the most notable international organization, Issue 13 examines the call for strengthening the peacekeeping and peacemaking capability of the United Nations by establishing a permanent UN military force. And Issue 15 focuses on whether or not a supranational criminal court should be established to take over the prosecution and punishment of war criminals from the domestic courts and ad hoc tribunals that have sometimes dealt with these cases in the past.

Perceptions Versus Reality

In addition to addressing the general changes in the world system outlined above, the debates in this reader explore the controversies that exist over many of the fundamental issues that face the world.

One key to these debates is the differing *perceptions* that protagonists bring to them. There may be a reality in world politics, but very often that reality is obscured. Many observers, for example, are alarmed by the seeming rise in radical actions by Islamic fundamentalists. However, the image of Islamic radicalism is not a fact but a perception; perhaps correct, perhaps not. In cases such as this, though, it is often the perception, not the reality, that is more important because policy is formulated on what decision makers *think*, not necessarily on what *is*. Thus, perception becomes the operating guide, or *operational reality*, whether it is true or not. Perceptions result from many factors. One factor is the information that decision makers receive. For a variety of reasons, the facts and analyses that are given to leaders are often inaccurate or represent only part of the picture. The conflicting perceptions of Israelis and Palestinians, for example, make the achievement of peace in Israel very difficult. Many Israelis and Palestinians fervently believe that the conflict that has occurred in the region over the past 50 years is the responsibility of the other. Both sides also believe in the righteousness of their own policies. Even if both sides are well-meaning, the perceptions of hostility that each holds means that the operational reality often has to be violence. These differing perceptions are a key element in the debate in Issue 7.

A related aspect of perception is the tendency to see oneself differently than some others do. The tendency is to see oneself as benevolent and to perceive rivals as sinister. This reverse image is partly at issue in the debates over U.S. defense expenditures (Issue 11) and China's future (Issue 6). Most Americans, especially those who favor increased defense expenditures, see U.S. policy as benign and the U.S. military as purely defensive. Americans are apt to see the recent changes in China, which include a more active regional role and increased military spending, as threatening. Most analysts in China see a reverse image, picturing themselves as arming to defend China against a United States with hegemonic intentions. Perceptions, then, are crucial to understanding international politics. It is important to understand objective reality, but it is also necessary to comprehend subjective reality in order to be able to predict and analyze another country's actions.

Levels of Analysis

Political scientists approach the study of international politics from different levels of analysis. The most macroscopic view is *system-level analysis*. This is a top-down approach that maintains that world factors virtually compel countries to follow certain foreign policies. Governing factors include the number of powerful actors, geographic relationships, economic needs, and technology. System analysts hold that a country's internal political system and its leaders do not have a major impact on policy. As such, political scientists who work from this perspective are interested in exploring the governing factors, how they cause policy, and how and why systems change.

After the end of World War II, the world was structured as a *bipolar* system, dominated by the United States and the Soviet Union. Furthermore, each superpower was supported by a tightly organized and dependent group of allies. For a variety of reasons, including changing economics and the nuclear standoff, the bipolar system has faded. Some political scientists argue that the bipolar system is being replaced by a *multipolar* system. In such a configuration, those who favor *balance-of-power* politics maintain that it is unwise to ignore power considerations.

State-level analysis is the middle and most common level of analysis. Social scientists who study world politics from this perspective focus on how countries, singly or comparatively, make foreign policy. In other words, this perspective is concerned with internal political dynamics, such as the roles of and interactions between the executive and legislative branches of government, the impact of bureaucracy, the role of interest groups, and the effect of public opinion. The dangers of global warming, which are debated in Issue 18, extend beyond rarified scientific controversy to important issues of public policy. Should the United States and other industrialized countries adopt policies that are costly in economic and lifestyle terms to significantly reduce the emission of greenhouse gases? This debate pits interest groups against one another as they try to get the governments of their respective countries to support or reject the Kyoto Treaty and other efforts to reduce greenhouse gas emissions. To a large degree, it is the environmentalists versus the business groups.

A third level of analysis, which is the most microscopic, is *human-level analysis*. This approach focuses, in part, on the role of individual decision makers. This technique is applied under the assumption that individuals make decisions and that the nature of those decisions is determined by the decision makers' perceptions, predilections, and strengths and weaknesses. Human-level analysis also focuses on average citizens, and Issue 17 explores whether or not those who disagree with policy and who find that they cannot change it though peaceful means are ever justified in resorting to violence as a political tool.

Realism Versus Idealism

Realism and idealism represent another division among political scientists and practitioners in their approaches to the study and conduct of international relations. *Realists* are usually skeptical about the nature of politics and, perhaps, the nature of humankind. They tend to believe that countries have opposing interests and that these differences can lead to conflict. They further contend that states (countries) are by definition obligated to do what is beneficial for their own citizens (national interest). The amount of power that a state has will determine how successful it is in attaining these goals. Therefore, politics is, and ought to be, a process of gaining, maintaining, and using power. Realists are apt to believe that the best way to avoid conflict is to remain powerful and to avoid pursuing goals that are beyond one's power to achieve. "Peace through strength" is a phrase that most realists would agree with.

Idealists disagree with realists about both the nature and conduct of international relations. They tend to be more optimistic that the global community is capable of finding ways to live in harmony and that it has a sense of collective, rather than national, interest. Idealists also maintain that the pursuit of a narrow national interest is shortsighted. They argue that, in the long run, countries must learn to cooperate or face the prospect of a variety of evils, including nuclear warfare, environmental disaster, and continuing economic hardship. Idealists argue, for example, that armaments cause world tensions, whereas realists maintain that conflict requires states to have weapons. Idealists are especially concerned with conducting current world politics on a more moral or ethical plane and with searching for alternatives to the present pursuit of nationalist interests through power politics.

Many of the issues in this volume address the realist-idealist split. Realists and idealists differ over whether or not states can and should surrender enough of their freedom of action and pursuit of self-interest to cooperate through and, to a degree, subordinate themselves to international organizations. This is one basis of disagreement in Issue 13, which contemplates a permanent UN military force. Realists and idealists also disagree on whether or not moral considerations should play a strong role in determining foreign policy. What constitutes morality is the focus of debate between realist William DeCamp III and Bill Clinton in Issue 14. Issue 15 then takes up who should sit in judgment of those accused of violating just war theory and other standards of international law and morality. The Lawyer's Committee for Human Rights argues that the proposed International Criminal Court is the proper vehicle to dispense justice; John Bolton rejects that view.

The Political and Ecological Future

Future *world alternatives* are discussed in many of the issues in this volume. Abraham Lincoln once said, "A house divided against itself cannot stand." One suspects that the 16th president might say something similar about the world today if he were with us. Issue 1, for example, debates whether or not growing economic interdependence is a positive or negative trend. The debate in Issue 2 on whether increased global governance should be encouraged or resisted is about how we establish laws and norms and at what level (international, national, or local) policies should be implemented. There can be little doubt that the role of global governance is growing; that reality is the spark behind the debate in Issue 3 over whether or not the traditional sovereignty of states will persist in a time of increasing globalization. More specific debates about the future are taken up in many of the selections that follow this triad of debates in Part 1. Far-reaching alternatives to a state-centric system based on sovereign countries include international organizations taking over some (or all) of the sovereign responsibilities of national governments, such as peacekeeping and peacemaking (Issue 13) or the prosecution of international war criminals (Issue 15). The global future also involves the ability of the world to prosper economically while, at the same time, not denuding itself of its natural resources or destroying the environment. This is the focus of Issue 18 on global warming.

The Axes of World Division

It is a truism that the world is politically dynamic and that the nature of the political system is undergoing profound change. As noted, the once-primary axis of world politics, the East-West confrontation, has broken down. Yet a few vestiges of the conflict on that axis remain.

In contrast to the moribund East-West axis, the *North-South axis* has increased in importance and tension. The wealthy, industrialized countries (North) are on one end, and the poor, less developed countries (LDCs, South) are at the other extreme. Economic differences and disputes are the primary dimension of this axis, in contrast to the military nature of the East-West axis.

Issues 9 and 10 explore these differences and debate the terms under which the North should give economic aid to the South.

The North-South division is one of the outstanding issues in the debate over global warming and the Kyoto treaty in Issue 18. The poorer countries of the South have won an exemption from the requirement to cut down greenhouse gas emissions. Their argument is that they give off much less of such gases than the industrialized countries do. Moreover, the countries of the South say that they will not be able to achieve industrialization if they are required to curtail their economic activity. Some in the North, especially in the economic sector, argue that saddling the North with restrictions and not applying them to the South will not solve the problem (because increased emissions in the South will offset declining emissions in the North) and will also result in unacceptable economic burdens to the North.

Then there is the question of what, if anything, will develop to divide the countries of the North and replace the East-West axis. The possibility for tension is represented in several issues. Some believe that the remnants of the USSR, especially Russia, will one day again pose a threat to the rest of Europe. That concern is the backdrop to Issue 5. A provocative idea of political scientist Samuel Huntington is that cultures will be the basis of a new, multiaxial dimension of global antagonism. If that comes to pass, then it might be that most of what Huntington calls the Western countries will be one step in the formation of one part of the axis. One cultural group that Huntington projects to be an antagonist of the West centers on China, as discussed in Issue 6.

Increased Role of Economics

As the growing importance of the North-South axis indicates, economics are playing an increased role in world politics. The economic reasons behind the decline of the East-West axis is further evidence. Economics have always played a part in international relations, but the traditional focus has been on strategic-political affairs, especially questions of military power.

Political scientists, however, are now increasingly focusing on the international political economy, or the economic dimensions of world politics. International trade, for instance, has increased dramatically, expanding from an annual world exports total of $20 billion in 1933 to $6.5 trillion in 1997. The impact has been profound. The domestic economic health of most countries is heavily affected by trade and other aspects of international economics. Since World War II there has been an emphasis on expanding free trade by decreasing tariffs and other barriers to international commerce. In recent years, however, a downturn in the economies of many of the industrialized countries has increased calls for more protectionism. Yet restrictions on trade and other economic activity can also be used as diplomatic weapons. The intertwining of economies and the creation of organizations to regulate them, such as the World Trade Organization, is raising issues of sovereignty and other concerns. This is a central matter in the debate in Issue 1 over whether or not the trend toward global economic integration is desirable.

Conclusion

Having discussed many of the various dimensions and approaches to the study of world politics, it is incumbent on this editor to advise against your becoming too structured by them. Issues of focus and methodology are important both to studying international relations and to understanding how others are analyzing global conduct. However, they are also partially pedagogical. In the final analysis, world politics is a highly interrelated, perhaps seamless, subject. No one level of analysis, for instance, can fully explain the events on the world stage. Instead, using each of the levels to analyze events and trends will bring the greatest understanding.

Similarly, the realist-idealist division is less precise in practice than it may appear. As some of the debates indicate, each side often stresses its own standards of morality. Which is more moral: defeating a dictatorship or sparing the sword and saving lives that would almost inevitably be lost in the dictator's overthrow? Furthermore, realists usually do not reject moral considerations. Rather, they contend that morality is but one of the factors that a country's decision makers must consider. Realists are also apt to argue that standards of morality differ when dealing with a country as opposed to an individual. By the same token, most idealists do not completely ignore the often dangerous nature of the world. Nor do they argue that a country must totally sacrifice its short-term interests to promote the betterment of the current and future world. Thus, realism and idealism can be seen most accurately as the ends of a continuum —with most political scientists and practitioners falling somewhere between, rather than at, the extremes. The best advice, then, is this: think broadly about international politics. The subject is very complex, and the more creative and expansive you are in selecting your foci and methodologies, the more insight you will gain. To end where we began, with Dr. Faust, I offer his last words in Goethe's drama, *"Mehr licht,"* . . . More light! That is the goal of this book.

The Ultimate Political Science Links Page

Under the editorship of Professor P. S. Ruckman, Jr., at Rock Valley College in Rockford, Illinois, this site provides a gateway to the academic study of not just world politics but all of political science. It includes links to journals, news, publishers, and other relevant resources.

http://www.rvc.cc.il.us/faclink/pruckman/PSLinks.htm

Poly-Cy: Internet Resources for Political Science

This is a worthwhile gateway to a broad range of political science resources, including some on international relations. It is maintained by Robert Duval, director of graduate studies at West Virginia University.

http://www.bomis.com/rings/politicalscience/2

The WWW Virtual Library: International Affairs Resources

Maintained by Wayne A. Selcher, professor of international studies at Elizabethtown College in Elizabethtown, Pennsylvania, this site contains approximately 2,000 annotated links relating to a broad spectrum of international affairs. The sites listed are those that the Webmaster believes have long-term value and that are cost-free, and many have further links to help in extended research.

http://www.etown.edu/vl/

Commission on Global Governance

Insofar as the study of international law is also about the larger subject of creating a more integrated system of world governance, a good place to view the argument for this direction is the Web site of the Commission on Global Governance, an organization that promotes the creation and strengthening of global measures and institutions to make the world a better place.

http://www.cgg.ch

PART 1

Global Trends

*T*he most significant change that the international system is experiencing is the trend toward globalization. Countries are becoming interdependent, the number of international organizations and their power is increasing, and global communications have become widespread and almost instantaneous. As reflected in the issues that make up this part, these changes and others have led to considerable debate about the value of globalization and what it will mean with regard to human governance.

- Is Economic Globalism a Positive Trend?

- Should Greater Global Governance Be Resisted?

- Will State Sovereignty Survive Globalism?

ISSUE 1

Is Economic Globalism a Positive Trend?

YES: International Monetary Fund/Michael W. Bell, from "Globalization: Threat or Opportunity?" *International Monetary Fund Issue Brief* (April 12, 2000)

NO: Scott Marshall, from "Imperialist Globalization," *Political Affairs* (July 2000)

ISSUE SUMMARY

YES: The staff of the International Monetary Fund (IMF), with Michael W. Bell at the point, argue that the best way to promote global prosperity is to ensure that all people in all countries have access to the benefits of globalization.

NO: Scott Marshall, a contributing editor to *Political Affairs*, maintains that globalization is a destructive process that capitalist corporations and countries are using to exploit workers globally.

O ne of the most important political and economic changes during the twentieth century has been the rapid growth of economic globalization (or interdependence) among countries. The impact of international economics on domestic societies has expanded rapidly as world industrial and financial structures have become increasingly intertwined. Foreign trade wins and loses jobs, for example, and people in most countries depend on petroleum and other imported resources to fuel cars, homes, and industries. Inexpensive imports into industrialized countries from less economically developed countries also help to keep inflation down and the standard of living up. It is likely that the very clothes you are wearing and the television you watch were made in another country. In fact, global exports grew from $53 billion in 1948 to $7.7 trillion in 2000.

In addition to trade, the trend toward globalization also includes factors such as the growth of multinational corporations (MNCs), the flow of international investment capital, and the increased importance of international exchange rates. There are now at least 40,000 MNCs that conduct business (beyond just sales) in more than one country. Of these, just the 50 largest global corporations in 1997 had assets of $8.8 trillion, produced $2.7 trillion in goods and services, and employed over 8 million workers. Foreign investment is also immense and growing. In 1990 the total new flow of foreign investment was $199 billion; that figure shot up to $619 billion in 1999.

The issue here is whether this economic globalization and integration is a positive or negative trend. For about 60 years, the United States has been at the center of the drive to open international commerce. The push to reduce trade barriers that occurred during and after World War II was designed to prevent a recurrence of the global economic collapse of the 1930s and the war of the 1940s. Policymakers believed that protectionism had caused the Great Depression, that the ensuing human desperation provided fertile ground for the rise of dictators who blamed scapegoats for what had occurred and who promised national salvation, and that these fascist dictators had set off World War II. In sum, policymakers thought that protectionism caused economic depression, which caused dictators, which caused war. They believed that free trade, by contrast, would promote prosperity, democracy, and peace.

Based on these political and economic theories, American policymakers took the lead in establishing a new international economic system. As the world's dominant superpower, the United States played the leading role at the end of World War II in establishing the International Monetary Fund (IMF), the World Bank, and the General Agreement on Tariffs and Trade (GATT). The latest GATT revision talks were completed and signed by 124 countries (including the United States) in April 1994. Among the outcomes was the establishment of a new coordinating body, the World Trade Organization (WTO).

The movement during the entire latter half of the twentieth century toward economic globalization has been strong, and there have been few influential voices opposing it. Most national leaders, business leaders, and other elites continue to support economic interdependence. The people in various countries have largely followed the path set by their leaders. In the following selection, Michael W. Bell and the rest of the staff of the IMF, an international organization that was set up in the 1940s to promote the international monetary stability necessary for extensive global economic interchange, take the view that the movement toward globalization remains beneficial.

More recently, the idea that globalization is either inevitable or necessarily beneficial has come under increasing scrutiny and has met increasing resistance. The strongest critique of globalization as it is occurring comes from analysts who are often referred to as "economic structuralists." They believe that the way global politics work is a function of how the world is organized economically. Structuralists contend that countries are divided between "haves" and "have-nots" and that the world is similarly divided between have and have-not countries. Moreover, structuralists believe that both domestically and internationally, the wealthy haves are using globalization to keep the have-nots weak and poor in order to exploit them. To change this, economic structuralists, a group that includes Scott Marshall, the author of the second selection, favor a radical restructuring of the economic system designed to end the uneven distribution of wealth and power.

International Monetary
Fund/Michael W. Bell

 **YES**

Globalization: Threat or Opportunity?

Introduction

The term "globalization" has acquired considerable emotive force. Some view it as a process that is beneficial—a key to future world economic development —and also inevitable and irreversible. Others regard it with hostility, even fear, believing that it increases inequality within and between nations, threatens employment and living standards and thwarts social progress. This brief offers an overview of some aspects of globalization and aims to identify ways in which countries can tap the gains of this process, while remaining realistic about its potential and its risks.

Globalization offers extensive opportunities for truly worldwide development but it is not progressing evenly. Some countries are becoming integrated into the global economy more quickly than others. Countries that have been able to integrate are seeing faster growth and reduced poverty. Outward-oriented policies brought dynamism and greater prosperity to much of East Asia, transforming it from one of the poorest areas of the world 40 years ago. And as living standards rose, it became possible to make progress on democracy and economic issues such as the environment and work standards.

By contrast, in the 1970s and 1980s when many countries in Latin America and Africa pursued inward-oriented policies, their economies stagnated or declined, poverty increased and high inflation became the norm. In many cases, especially Africa, adverse external developments made the problems worse. As these regions changed their policies, their incomes have begun to rise. An important transformation is underway. Encouraging this trend, not reversing it, is the best course for promoting growth, development and poverty reduction.

The crises in the emerging markets in the 1990s have made it quite evident that the opportunities of globalization do not come without risks—risks arising from volatile capital movements and the risks of social, economic, and environmental degradation created by poverty. This is not a reason to reverse direction, but for all concerned—in developing countries, in the advanced countries, and of course investors—to embrace policy changes to build strong economies and a stronger world financial system that will produce more rapid growth and ensure that poverty is reduced.

From International Monetary Fund/Michael W. Bell, "Globalization: Threat or Opportunity?" *International Monetary Fund Issue Brief* (April 12, 2000). Copyright © 2000 by The International Monetary Fund. Reprinted by permission. Notes omitted.

How can the developing countries, especially the poorest, be helped to catch up? Does globalization exacerbate inequality or can it help to reduce poverty? And are countries that integrate with the global economy inevitably vulnerable to instability? These are some of the questions covered in the following sections.

What Is Globalization?

Economic "globalization" is a historical process, the result of human innovation and technological progress. It refers to the increasing integration of economies around the world, particularly through trade and financial flows. The term sometimes also refers to the movement of people (labor) and knowledge (technology) across international borders. There are also broader cultural, political and environmental dimensions of globalization that are not covered here.

At its most basic, there is nothing mysterious about globalization. The term has come into common usage since the 1980s, reflecting technological advances that have made it easier and quicker to complete international transactions—both trade and financial flows. It refers to an extension beyond national borders of the same market forces that have operated for centuries at all levels of human economic activity—village markets, urban industries, or financial centers.

Markets promote efficiency through competition and the division of labor —the specialization that allows people and economies to focus on what they do best. Global markets offer greater opportunity for people to tap into more and larger markets around the world. It means that they can have access to more capital flows, technology, cheaper imports, and larger export markets. But markets do not necessarily ensure that the benefits of increased efficiency are shared by all. Countries must be prepared to embrace the policies needed, and in the case of the poorest countries may need the support of the international community as they do so.

Unparalleled Growth, Increased Inequality: 20th Century Income Trends

Globalization is not just a recent phenomenon. Some analysts have argued that the world economy was just as globalized 100 years ago as it is today. But today commerce and financial services are far more developed and deeply integrated than they were at that time. The most striking aspect of this has been the integration of financial markets made possible by modern electronic communication.

The 20th century saw unparalleled economic growth, with global per capita GDP [gross domestic product] increasing almost five-fold. But this growth was not steady—the strongest expansion came during the second half of the century, a period of rapid trade expansion accompanied by trade—and typically somewhat later, financial—liberalization.... [Between World War I and World War II] the world turned its back on internationalism—or globalization as we now call it—and countries retreated into closed economies, protectionism and pervasive capital controls. This was a major factor in the devastation of this period, when per capita income growth fell to less than 1 percent during 1913–1950. For the rest of the century, even though population grew at an unprecedented pace, per capita income growth was over 2 percent, the fastest pace of all coming during the post-World War boom in the industrial countries.

The story of the 20th century was of remarkable average income growth, but it is also quite obvious that the progress was not evenly dispersed. The gaps between rich and poor countries, and rich and poor people within countries, have grown. The richest quarter of the world's population saw its per capita GDP increase nearly six-fold during the century, while the poorest quarter experienced less than a three-fold increase. Income inequality has clearly increased. But, as noted below, per capita GDP does not tell the whole story.

Developing Countries: How Deeply Integrated?

Globalization means that world trade and financial markets are becoming more integrated. But just how far have developing countries been involved in this integration? Their experience in catching up with the advanced economies has been mixed.... [I]n some countries, especially in Asia, per capita incomes have been moving quickly toward levels in the industrial countries since 1970. A larger number of developing countries have made only slow progress or have lost ground. In particular, per capita incomes in Africa have declined relative to the industrial countries and in some countries have declined in absolute terms. [One] part of the explanation [is that] the countries catching up are those where trade has grown strongly....

The special case of the economies in transition from planned to market economies—they too are becoming more integrated with the global economy—is not explored in much depth here. In fact, the term "transition economy" is losing its usefulness. Some countries (e.g. Poland, Hungary) are converging quite rapidly toward the structure and performance of advanced economies. Others (such as most countries of the former Soviet Union) face long-term structural and institutional issues similar to those faced by developing countries.

Does Globalization Increase Poverty and Inequality?

During the 20th century, global average per capita income rose strongly, but with considerable variation among countries. It is clear that the income gap between rich and poor countries has been widening for many decades. The most recent *World Economic Outlook* studies 42 countries (representing almost 90 percent of world population) for which data are available for the entire 20th century. It reaches the conclusion that output per capita has risen appreciably but that the distribution of income among countries has become more unequal than at the beginning of the century.

Figure 1

Twentieth Century World Income Trends

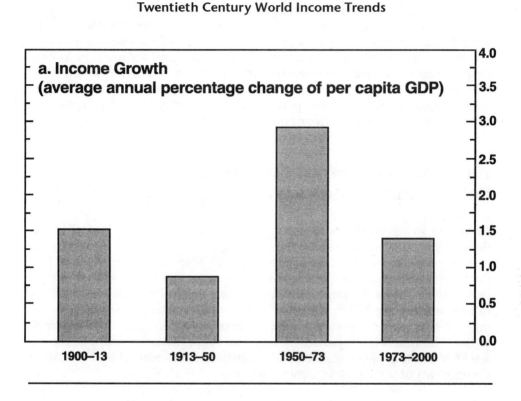

But incomes do not tell the whole story; broader measures of welfare that take account of social conditions show that poorer countries have made considerable progress. For instance, some low-income countries, e.g. Sri Lanka, have quite impressive social indicators. One recent paper finds that if countries are compared using the UN's Human Development Indicators (HDI), which take education and life expectancy into account, then the picture that emerges is quite different from that suggested by the income data alone.

Indeed the gaps may have narrowed. A striking inference from the study is a contrast between what may be termed an "income gap" and an "HDI gap". The (inflation-adjusted) income levels of today's poor countries are still well below those of the leading countries in 1870. And the gap in incomes has increased. But judged by their HDIs, today's poor countries are well ahead of where the leading countries were in 1870. This is largely because medical advances and improved living standards have brought strong increases in life expectancy.

But even if the HDI gap has narrowed in the long-term, far too many people are losing ground. Life expectancy may have increased but the quality of life for many has not improved, with many still in abject poverty. And the spread of AIDS through Africa in the past decade is reducing life expectancy in many countries.

This has brought new urgency to policies specifically designed to alleviate poverty. Countries with a strong growth record, pursuing the right policies, can expect to see a sustained reduction in poverty, since recent evidence suggests that there exists at least a one-to-one correspondence between growth and poverty reduction. And if strongly pro-poor policies—for instance in well-targeted social expenditure—are pursued then there is a better chance that growth will be amplified into more rapid poverty reduction. This is one compelling reason for all economic policy makers, including the IMF, to pay heed more explicitly to the objective of poverty reduction.

How Can the Poorest Countries Catch Up More Quickly?

Growth in living standards springs from the accumulation of physical capital (investment) and human capital (labor), and through advances in technology (what economists call total factor productivity). Many factors can help or hinder these processes. The experience of the countries that have increased output most rapidly shows the importance of creating conditions that are conducive to long-run per capita income growth. Economic stability, institution building, and structural reform are at least as important for long-term development as financial transfers, important as they are. What matters is the whole package of policies, financial and technical assistance, and debt relief if necessary. Components of such a package might include:

- Macroeconomic stability to create the right conditions for investment and saving;
- Outward oriented policies to promote efficiency through increased trade and investment;
- Structural reform to encourage domestic competition;
- Strong institutions and an effective government to foster good governance;
- Education, training, and research and development to promote productivity;
- External debt management to ensure adequate resources for sustainable development.

All these policies should be focussed on country-owned strategies to reduce poverty by promoting pro-poor policies that are properly budgeted —including health, education, and strong social safety nets. A participatory approach, including consultation with civil society, will add greatly to their chances of success.

Advanced economies can make a vital contribution to the low-income countries' efforts to integrate into the global economy:

- By promoting trade. One proposal on the table is to provide unrestricted market access for all exports from the poorest countries. This should help them move beyond specialization on primary commodities to producing processed goods for export.
- By encouraging flows of private capital to the lower-income countries, particularly foreign direct investment, with its twin benefits of steady financial flows and technology transfer.
- By supplementing more rapid debt relief with an increased level of new financial support. Official development assistance (ODA) has fallen to 0.24 percent of GDP (1998) in advanced countries (compared with a UN target of 0.7 percent). As Michel Camdessus, the former Managing Director of the IMF put it: "The excuse of aid fatigue is not credible—indeed it approaches the level of downright cynicism—at a time when, for the last decade, the advanced countries have had the opportunity to enjoy the benefits of the peace dividend."

The IMF supports reform in the poorest countries through its new Poverty Reduction and Growth Facility. It is contributing to debt relief through the initiative for the heavily indebted poor countries.

An Advanced Country Perspective: Does Globalization Harm Workers' Interests?

Anxiety about globalization also exists in advanced economies. How real is the perceived threat that competition from "low-wage economies" displaces workers from high-wage jobs and decreases the demand for less skilled workers? Are the changes taking place in these economies and societies a direct result of globalization?

Economies are continually evolving and globalization is one among several other continuing trends. One such trend is that as industrial economies mature, they are becoming more service-oriented to meet the changing demands of their population. Another trend is the shift toward more highly skilled jobs. But all the evidence is that these changes would be taking place—not necessarily at the same pace—with or without globalization. In fact, globalization is actually making this process easier and less costly to the economy as a whole by bringing the benefits of capital flows, technological innovations, and lower import prices. Economic growth, employment and living standards are all higher than they would be in a closed economy.

But the gains are typically distributed unevenly among groups within countries, and some groups may lose out. For instance, workers in declining older industries may not be able to make an easy transition to new industries.

What is the appropriate policy response? Should governments try to protect particular groups, like low-paid workers or old industries, by restricting trade or capital flows? Such an approach might help some in the short-term, but ultimately it is at the expense of the living standards of the population at large. Rather, governments should pursue policies that encourage integration into the global economy while putting in place measures to help those adversely affected by the changes. The economy as a whole will prosper more from policies that embrace globalization by promoting an open economy, and, at the same time, squarely address the need to ensure the benefits are widely shared. Government policy should focus on two important areas:

- education and vocational training, to make sure that workers have the opportunity to acquire the right skills in dynamic changing economies; and
- well-targeted social safety nets to assist people who are displaced.

Are Periodic Crises an Inevitable Consequence of Globalization?

The succession of [economic] crises in the 1990s—Mexico, Thailand, Indonesia, Korea, Russia, and Brazil—suggested to some that financial crises are a direct and inevitable result of globalization. Indeed one question that arises in both advanced and emerging market economies is whether globalization makes economic management more difficult.

Clearly the crises would not have developed as they did without exposure to global capital markets. But nor could these countries have achieved their impressive growth records without those financial flows.

These were complex crises, resulting from an interaction of shortcomings in national policy and the international financial system. Individual governments and the international community as a whole are taking steps to reduce the risk of such crises in future.

At the national level, even though several of the countries had impressive records of economic performance, they were not fully prepared to withstand the potential shocks that could come through the international markets. Macroeconomic stability, financial soundness, open economies, transparency, and good governance are all essential for countries participating in the global markets. Each of the countries came up short in one or more respects.

At the international level, several important lines of defense against crisis were breached. Investors did not appraise risks adequately. Regulators and supervisors in the major financial centers did not monitor developments sufficiently closely. And not enough information was available about some international investors, notably offshore financial institutions. The result was that markets were prone to "herd behavior"—sudden shifts of investor sentiment and the rapid movement of capital, especially short-term finance, into and out of countries.

The international community is responding to the global dimensions of the crisis through a continuing effort to strengthen the architecture of the international monetary and financial system. The broad aim is for markets to operate with more transparency, equity, and efficiency. The IMF has a central role in this process....

Conclusion

As globalization has progressed, living conditions (particularly when measured by broader indicators of well being) have improved significantly in virtually all countries. However, the strongest gains have been made by the advanced countries and only some of the developing countries.

That the income gap between high-income and low-income countries has grown wider is a matter for concern. And the number of the world's citizens in abject poverty is deeply disturbing. But it is wrong to jump to the conclusion that globalization has caused the divergence, or that nothing can be done to improve the situation. To the contrary: low-income countries have not been able to integrate with the global economy as quickly as others, partly because of their chosen policies and partly because of factors outside their control. No country, least of all the poorest, can afford to remain isolated from the world economy. Every country should seek to reduce poverty. The international community should endeavor—by strengthening the international financial system, through trade, and through aid—to help the poorest countries integrate into the world economy, grow more rapidly, and reduce poverty. That is the way to ensure all people in all countries have access to the benefits of globalization.

The author, a staff member of the International Monetary Fund, is indebted to several Fund staff colleagues who commented on drafts of this paper. The opinions expressed are those of the author, and do not necessarily reflect the views of the IMF.

Scott Marshall

Imperialist Globalization

There is a clear trend in the fight against capitalist globalization. Around the world, and in the U.S. labor is stepping up to the front lines. While still in the early stages, many diverse and powerful anti-monopoly, anti-corporate coalitions are developing.

Much of the development of these movements so far has been spontaneous. Capitalist globalization has hurt so many people that it produces angry victims with many diverse concerns—workers, farmers, environmentalists, peace activists, women, youth and students, religious, small businesses, independent mass media, cultural workers and scientists.

Unity and mass action so far has been based on identifying a common enemy. Every group can agree that the WTO [World Trade Organization], the IMF [International Monetary Fund] and the World Bank are harmful to their interests. However, most have differing and even contradictory views on what should be done with them.

Already, a series of mass demonstrations, from Seattle to Geneva, and from Washington D.C. to Singapore, have backed up the multinationals and forced serious debate in the ranks of global capitalist organizations. . . .

Where Do We Go From Here?

In the heat of battle, unions and the mass movements are asking themselves, "What's next?" A healthy debate is taking place and people are asking: Should we demand the abolishment of the WTO? Doesn't someone have to regulate trade worldwide? How can trade unions effectively fight multinational corporations spread all over the globe? What is the role of nation-states in the new global economy?

In many ways, all these questions boil down to a very basic question: How will these movements arrive at a positive program of demands and actions to curb or even roll back capitalist globalization? We need reform demands to grab on to.

What About the Left?

For... the... left there is even a greater challenge. Most of these coalitions, especially with labor, have a decided left-center character. Strong left-center ties are being built on bonds of common action and common militancy against corporate domination.

... [L]eft forces have a critical part to play. Not having all the answers or even all the questions, the need to produce popular Marxist critiques of capitalism, imperialism and globalization is more than evident. One thing is clear, there is no real and lasting solution to capitalist globalization that leaves the multinational corporations in charge. This is why socialism is necessary.

V.I. Lenin pointed out in his famous book, *Imperialism, the Highest Stage of Capitalism,* that imperialism and globalization are not just "bad policies" of the capitalist class. They are rather the "natural" development of capitalism, unchecked and unregulated. They are developments of the capitalist system itself and thus are not subject to change simply by changed policies. The system itself must be changed.

And this knowledge imposes that most difficult of all tasks, what Lenin called, "patiently to explain." One should add for today's usage, patiently to question, to probe and discuss with others in an open, frank and friendly way.

Imperialism or Globalization or Both?

Lenin wrote in *Imperialism* the following:

> Railways are a summation of the basic capitalist industries, coal, iron and steel; a summation and the most striking index of the development of world trade and bourgeois-democratic civilization. How the railways are linked up with large-scale industry, with monopolies, syndicates, cartels, trusts, banks and the financial oligarchy is shown in the proceeding chapters of this book. The uneven distribution of railways, their uneven development—sums up as it were, modern monopolist capitalism on a worldwide scale.

It is tempting to just substitute the word "computer" for the word "railways" in the quote above. Of course, it's not so simple. The quote does illustrate that much has changed in the specifics of imperialism and world capitalism. But we can recognize enough that is the same to show that each new situation and subsequent creative development of Marxist analysis must be built on solid basics that have come before.

Perhaps the most revealing sentence in the paragraph is: "How the railways are linked up with large-scale industry, with monopolies, syndicates, cartels, trusts, banks and the financial oligarchy is shown in the proceeding chapters of this book." It indicates the tremendous importance Lenin placed on rigorous examination of facts and figures, of study of the exact situation.

Is globalization just a new name for the imperialism that Lenin described? Or is it a new stage or level of capitalism? And what real difference does it make how we answer those questions? What are some of the new features of globalization?

The Sheer Size of It All

In Lenin's *Imperialism* he spoke of the U.S. having about 51 million German marks in direct overseas investments. According to the Department of Commerce's Bureau of Economic Analysis, in 1998 the U.S. had direct overseas investments of approximately $2 trillion, 140 billion, 582 million in market value. That compares to about $72.9 billion U.S. direct investment overseas in 1966. This is an increase in scale that could not have been imagined in Lenin's time.

The Production Process

This illustrates that both Marx and Lenin were correct in their projections that capitalism and imperialism would result in ever larger monopoly concentrations of capital, wealth and power. But they could not have foreseen just how behemoth these concentrations could become. At some point it's no longer just more of the same. And certainly basic industry has expanded far beyond coal, iron and steel, railways and the other mass production industries of the early century.

In *Imperialism* Lenin describes how capitalism, in the era of imperialism, was being concentrated into larger and larger factories and workplaces. It took huge outlays of capital to make effective use of the then new science and technology of electricity and machinery. Production processes were huge and required large concentrations of workers to make them effective and productive.

Today the trend is in the opposite direction. Science and technology is making huge factories obsolete. The mechanics of production and micro circuitry are shrinking production facilities. Where once all aspects of production needed to be right at hand and physically and mechanically integrated today, computers and modular production processes, combined with much greater control over faster and more sophisticated transportation and communications systems make for the fracturing and decentralization of production into smaller and smaller units, often spread out to all corners of the globe.

For just a taste of how transportation has changed try buying a product online over the Internet. Most often you are given a tracking number that can tell you on a minute by minute basis, where your package is and when it is due to arrive at your doorstep. It is easy to see the implications of such precision in organizing complex and diverse worldwide production processes.

The Working Class Is Bigger

At the same time, new technology has considerably reshaped the kinds of skills needed for production. Many skills have migrated off the shop or production floor into offices, changing the face of the work force and somewhat blurring the distinction between what was known as blue-collar and white-collar work. At the same time, whole new industries like electronics, chips and robots, pharmaceuticals, and many others have grown up.

Millions have been brought into the working class through a raft of new services that are the result of continued socialization of production and daily life. Today the working class is numerically, and as a percentage of the population, bigger than ever before. This has profound implications for those who see the revolutionary role of labor and the working class.

Finance Capital

Lenin pointed to the growth and parasitic nature of finance capital in the era of imperialism. He would be astounded at where this has developed in the era of globalization. In the first place the scale would be unrecognizable; secondly, the computer technology that makes it all possible was not dreamed of in his time. Just a few facts from the UN's Human Development Report of 1999 will illustrate the point. In the 1970s the daily turnover in foreign exchange markets was about $10 to $20 billion. In 1998 it reached $1.5 trillion a day. International bank lending grew from $265 billion in 1975 to $4.2 trillion in 1994 in just under 20 years. And finally, between 1983 and 1993 cross-border sales of U.S. Treasury bonds increased from $30 to $500 billion.

Finance capital, which Lenin and Marx both described as parasitic and dead and as its most reactionary and predatory section, is a much larger percentage of world capital. Lenin began to describe in *Imperialism* how finance capital is inextricably tied to industrial and all other forms of capital.

Today that is even more so. Globalization, export and import trade, shifting manufacturing, improvements in transportation and communications, the new technologies, including biotechnologies, are all tightly bound to finance capital. Nothing in the global economy is built, exported or imported, insured, financed or moved without a slice off the top for finance capital. Today, finance capital is qualitatively more the "mover and shaper," the "command and control" of globalization and development than ever before.

When Lenin wrote, a large share of direct overseas investment was in the plundering of natural resources of colonial countries. Today, even though direct foreign investment has grown seven times on a world scale since the 1970s, the bulk (58 percent) is invested in the industrial capitalist countries. Only 37 percent is invested in developing countries with the rest (5 percent) invested in the former socialist countries in Russia and Eastern Europe. This includes the fact that capitalists in many developing countries, like South Africa, invest their profits heavily in industrial countries instead of their own economies. Much of this is speculative capital or to speak bluntly—just plain gambling.

This investment pattern of globalization has tremendous significance for the labor movements in America and the other developed capitalist countries. The UN report on Human Development points out that less than a tenth of the job loss in America can be attributed to U.S. capital flight to Third World or underdeveloped countries.

Once this is understood it's easier to see that General Motors, U.S. Steel and General Dynamics are the real enemies of working families, not the workers of Mexico and China. More jobs are lost to the mergermania of conglomeration than in export of capital to developing countries. To be sure, global capital pursues cheap labor in the "race to the bottom," but there is a lot more going on here, especially with finance capital's role.

Mergermania

Deregulation and the weakening of anti-trust laws, especially in the arena of banking and finance, has led to an unpredicted orgy of mergers and acquisitions. This has been particularly the case with the multinationals. Global megamergers like Daimler Chrysler, Exxon-Mobil and world banking mergers like Bank One and First Chicago set the pace.

A totally new feature of globalization is the tremendous domination of news, information, media and culture by giant multinational conglomerates; Warner ate Time, Time Warner ate CNN, America Online ate Time Warner or was it the other way around? Anyway you get the picture.

"From 1990 to 1997 the annual number of mergers and acquisitions more than doubled from 11,300 to 24,600. Cross-border mergers and acquisitions accounted for $236 billion in 1997," according to UN figures. A chart in Forbes magazine shows corporations like General Motors, Ford, Mitsubishi, Shell, Exxon, WalMart, and many others have gross sales that exceed the GDP of many countries.

World Trade

World exports have now reached an astounding $7 trillion a year. That is about 21 percent of the world's Gross Domestic Product (GDP) in the 1990s. That compares to 17 percent of a much smaller GDP in the 1970s. World exports of goods and services almost tripled between the 1970s and 1997 in real adjusted dollars. According to the UN report, "the top fifth of the world's people in the richest countries enjoy 82 percent of the expanding export trade and 68 percent of foreign direct investment—the bottom fifth, barely more than 1 percent."

Rising and Savage Inequalities

World inequalities have been rising steadily for the last century. They are accelerating today. In world income distributions between rich and poor countries the pattern is thus: In 1820, the ratio of rich to poor countries was about 3 to 1, that is rich countries had about 3 times the assets and wealth of poor countries. In the 1950, it was 35 to 1. In 1973, it rose to 44 to one and in 1992 it had risen to a ratio of 72 to 1.

Here are some startling statistics on the poverty that imperialism and globalization leave in its wake: Nearly 1.3 billion people on this planet have no access to clean water. One child in seven of primary school age is not in school. More than 840 million people are malnourished with a very high percentage being women and children. The UN estimates that 1.3 billion people live on incomes of less than a $1 a day.

In the industrial countries, though often hidden, human poverty and exclusion are also on the rise. In the eight richest countries, one out of every eight people is stricken by one of more of the main poverty indicators: long-term un-employment, under 60 years life expectancy, an income below the national poverty line or illiteracy. Wage inequality, that is, the gap between the highest and lowest wages has continued to widen except in Germany and Italy.

Racism, National Chauvinism, and Gender Inequality

Many of these statistics do not illustrate well enough the extra cutting edge caused by racism and national oppression. Any map that illustrates the patterns of global investments, or that charts the poverty ratios of the world will make the point. There are more than enough statistics available in the U.S. to prove the impact of racism and chauvinism on poverty, unemployment, lack of health care, lack of decent housing. What is not so apparent to many is the conscious role of imperialism and globalization in fostering and creating these extra burdens of inequality.

Take the debates in the WTO itself. It was clear in Seattle that one factor in the failure of those talks, besides the mass pressure outside, was the dissatisfaction of delegates from the underdeveloped countries. Delegates said that seeing the resistance to the WTO in the streets emboldened them to stand up. They cited unfair and exploitative trade rules and policies being forced on them. Many also pointed to the totally secret closed-door governing committee comprised of the architects of globalization.

According to the UN report, foreign investment has meant an increase in women in the work force. But they note that for many women this amounts to extending their workday by eight to ten hours when allowing for unpaid work that many women perform. In addition they point out that much of the increase in women's employment in the last few years has been in the "informal economy." These jobs are most often very substandard and frequently part-time, home-work situations,—most are also "off the books," making for easy cheating on wages and hours.

When Lenin wrote *Imperialism,* a world socialist system was coming into being. Today, while some of that system still exists, it is greatly weakened. This relative lack of a socialist counterbalance has emboldened capitalism to new heights of globalization and savagery. The 1990s saw a worldwide offensive to weaken labor, to privatize and destroy the public sector, to demolish social programs and to turn back the clock on freedom and equality struggles.

... [I]t is clear that even a "one world superpower" with unchallenged military superiority does not mean an end to war dangers. We only need to look at the military destruction rained down on the Balkans, the continued bombing of Iraq or Vieques to see the danger.

This unbridled U.S. power is a totally new feature of globalization. While it is most clear in the military arena, U.S. domination of globalization is apparent in trade and in the institutions of global governance like the WTO, the IMF and the World Bank. This in no way means an end to the contradictions between imperial powers but it does give the deadening appearance of power so great as to be unchangeable.

Some Tentative Conclusions

In... Africa, [anti-globalization] activists speak of fighting TINA, an acronym for "There Is No Alternative." This is clearly the mass line of globalization. All their think tanks and all their apologists for imperialism work overtime to try and convince the working people of the world that capitalist globalization is the end of history. And they are very keen on trying to convince the left that only modest reforms of the system are possible.

One of Lenin's greatest contributions in *Imperialism* is the idea that imperialism cannot be fought in little pieces. It is not enough to fight only against this or that manifestation of imperialism or globalization. It must be fought by Communists and the left in particular as a system of relations.

This is what some might call fighting the big picture. To put it another way, while we have to be deeply involved in every fight, against every aspect of capitalist globalization, we have to constantly show those we fight with the system of imperialism and that can't be done effectively without presenting an alternative: socialism.

This isn't a call for breast-beating or holding up signs that read socialism now. But it does mean that how we introduce the question of socialism as the only alternative to capitalist globalization is a critical task right now. Ultimately we cannot defeat TINA without it. There are no effective stages here. We have to bring the courage of our convictions into the mix of our allies and coalition partners fighting globalization. It we don't, cynicism, detours, and disillusionment are bound to follow.

Boldly Search for Struggles That Target the Multinationals

We need, with our coalition partners and allies, to think big and bold. We know many of the demands that begin to make up an anti-globalization program:

- Curbs and taxes on capital exports: how about the requirement that corporations invest $5 at home for every $1 they invest overseas. In the U.S. just closing investment tax loopholes on foreign investments would bring hundreds of millions of dollars in new revenues that could be spent on public works and job creation. This must include full taxation on overseas U.S. corporate profits made by foreign branches, subsidiaries and subcontractors.
- Abolish the WTO and instead deal with trade issues and trade treaties through the International Labor Organization (ILO) and the UN. These are far more democratic international organizations that already include the participation of labor and other public interest Non-Governmental Organizations (NGOs).

- The U.S. Congress should immediately ratify the six core labor conventions of the ILO that they have refused to confirm, including the right to collective bargaining, the right to organize against all forms of racial, national and gender discrimination, against child labor, and against forced and slave labor.
- Cancel the debt of developing countries and fully fund the UN Development agencies. The U.S. government should immediately live up to its financial responsibilities and pay up its dues.
- Develop a corporate code of conduct, enforceable by Congress on U.S. corporations abroad that include the right to organize, collective bargaining and minimum wage, health and safety, and environmental standards.

Importantly, one of the demands put forward by the UN Report on Human Development calls for "a world anti-monopoly authority to monitor the activities of multinational corporations and ensure that markets are competitive."

One Last Point

There is nothing about globalization that makes it above the laws of capitalist development presented by Marx and Engels, rather it confirms them.

For one, the basic contradiction between the social and cooperative nature of work versus private profit is intensified. The socialization process has now intensified across borders in an unprecedented way. Today an auto worker in Detroit knows a lot more about the conditions of an autoworker in Mexico than previous generations and vice versa.

In the *Communist Manifesto* Marx remarked,

> This union (of workers) is helped by the improved means of communication that are created by modern industry, and that place the workers in different localities in contact with one another. It was just this contact that was needed to centralize the numerous local struggles, all of the same character, into one national struggle between classes.

What prophetic words for today's struggles against capitalist globalization. Marching in Seattle, marching in Singapore, marching in Johannesburg, striking in Ohio, striking in Osaka, sitting in at the University of Wisconsin, sitting in Indonesia, these are just the contacts we need to centralize numerous national struggles into one international struggle against capitalist globalization.

POSTSCRIPT

Is Economic Globalism a Positive Trend?

There can be no doubt that the global economy and the level of interdependence have grown rapidly since World War II. To learn more about this, read Robert Gilpin and Jean M. Gilpin, *Global Political Economy: Understanding the International Economic Order* (Princeton University Press, 2001).

For most of the period since the 1940s, the drive to create ever freer international economic interchange sparked little notice, much less opposition. That has changed, and one of the most remarkable shifts in political momentum in recent years has been the marked increase in the resistance to globalization. Not long ago, meetings of international financial organizations such as the IMF and the WTO once used to pass unnoticed by nearly everyone other than financiers, scholars, and government officials. Now their meetings often occasion mass protests, such as the riots that broke out in Seattle, Washington, in 1999 at a meeting of the WTO. Similarly, when the leaders of the Western Hemisphere met in Quebec, Canada, in 2001 to discuss the formation of the Free Trade Area of the Americas (FTAA), officials in the host country were so worried about protesters that they deployed 6,700 police officers and 1,200 troops to keep order, and they built a 10-foot-high, 2.5-mile-long fence around the conference site.

One of the oddities about globalization, economic and otherwise, is that it often creates a common cause between those of marked conservative and marked liberal views. More than anything, conservatives worry that their respective countries are losing control of their economies and, thus, a degree of their independence. Echoing this view, arch-conservative 2000 presidential candidate Patrick Buchanan warns that unchecked globalism threatens to turn the United States into a "North America province of what some call The New World Order."

Conservatives also worry that increased economic interdependence can endanger national security. If, for example, a country becomes dependent on foreign sources for vehicles, then it may well have no ability to produce its own military vehicles in times of peril if cut off from its foreign supplier or, worse, if that supplier were to become an international antagonist.

Some liberals share the conservatives' negative views of globalization but for difference reasons. This perspective is less concerned with sovereignty and security; it is more concerned with workers and countries being exploited and the environment being damaged by MNCs that shift their operations to other countries to find cheap labor and to escape environmental regulations. Referring to the anti-WTO protests in 1999, U.S. labor leader John J. Sweeney told reporters, "Seattle was just the beginning. If globalization brings more inequality, then it will generate a violent reaction that will make Seattle look tame."

For a view that globalization needs to be restrained, consult William Greider, *The Manic Logic of Global Capitalism* (Simon & Schuster, 1997).

For all these objections, the continued thrust among governments—with strong support in business, among economists, and from other influential groups—is to continue to promote expanded globalism. "Turning away from trade would keep part of our global community forever on the bottom. That is not the right response," President Bill Clinton warned just before leaving office.

For now, the upsurge of feelings against globalism have had the effect of pressing policymakers and analysts to consider what reforms are necessary to continue globalization, while instituting reforms that will help quiet the opposition. For one such view, see economist Dani Rodrik's *New Global Economy and Developing Countries: Making Openness Work* (Overseas Development Council, 1999), in which Rodrik argues, "Globalization can succeed and be sustained only if appropriate domestic policy measures are undertaken to cushion the impact on groups that are adversely affected and, even more important, to equip all sectors of society to take advantage of the benefits of globalization rather than be undermined by it."

ISSUE 2

Should Greater Global Governance Be Resisted?

YES: Marc A. Thiessen, from "When Worlds Collide," *Foreign Policy* (March/April 2001)

NO: Mark Leonard, from "When Worlds Collide," *Foreign Policy* (March/April 2001)

ISSUE SUMMARY

YES: Marc A. Thiessen, who serves on the majority staff of the U.S. Senate Committee on Foreign Relations, contends that globalists want to undermine the national independence of the world's countries but that doing so would be a mistake.

NO: Mark Leonard, director of the Foreign Policy Centre in London, United Kingdom, maintains that all countries will benefit if each increasingly cooperates with multilateral organizations and adheres to international laws, rules, and norms.

Countries, which political scientists refer to as "states," have been the most important actors in the international system for more than five centuries. States are political units that exercise ultimate internal authority within a defined territory and that recognize no legitimate external authority over them. This characteristic of not being willingly or legally subject to any outside authority is called "sovereignty."

Sovereignty does not mean that states never cooperate with one another; they often do. And states may also follow rules that they have agreed to within treaties and international organizations. But in these cases the state has either specifically agreed to a certain rule in a treaty or voluntarily abides by rules established by international organizations.

Sovereignty also does not mean that countries never do things unwillingly because of external pressure. Power is a key element of the international system, and powerful countries regularly press and even force less powerful countries to take certain actions. When the United States did not like certain things that were occurring in Panama in 1989, for example, it invaded the much smaller country, toppled the government, and changed Panamanian policy. The key point is that the unilateral use of force by one country against another in such cases is not legitimate and, thus, violated Panamanian sovereignty.

This long-standing principle of state sovereignty is beginning to weaken, however. Increasingly, international laws and rules made by international organizations are beginning to be viewed by some as superceding national rules and policy. To the degree that an international organization has such rule-making power, it can be said to be exercising "supranational authority." That means legitimate authority over states, with states being subordinate.

There are many examples that demonstrate that the world community is beginning to reject sovereignty. For instance, the principle of sovereignty was not tolerated as a defense for South Africa's mistreatment of its nonwhite citizens during the era of apartheid. The United Nations condemned South Africa, countries imposed sanctions on South Africa, and eventually the country's white government agreed to share political power with the country's black citizens.

Many other examples of the diminution of sovereignty exist. Some involve forceful outside interventions, such as the air assault in 1999 by the U.S.-led North Atlantic Treaty Organization (NATO) on Yugoslavia because of that country's alleged ethnic-cleansing campaign againt ethnic Albanians in Kosovo, a province of Yugoslavia.

Less noticeable, but no less important, there has been a rapid expansion of international organizations that make rules that apply to member countries and, arguably, also sometimes apply to all countries, whether or not they have agreed to those rules. These organizations may have units and processes to decide who is right when two or more countries are in a dispute. The World Trade Organization (WTO), for one, regularly decides cases when countries disagree over an interpretation of the WTO's trade rules.

Some people believe that the world would be better off if states surrendered at least some of their sovereignty and conceded legitimate rule-making authority to international organizations. Those who advocate this approach believe that international organizations ought to have real authority to address those problems that states cannot or will not resolve. Within this general approach, the degree of change that people support varies greatly. It can range from believing in gradual, relatively limited grants of legitimate rule-making power to international organizations to believing that a world government should be formed and that states should be subordinate to it. Within this range of approaches, the second of the following selections by Mark Leonard falls at the more limited, gradualist end of the continuum. In it, Leonard argues that multilateralism, as he calls it, is about "rescuing, not destroying" states.

The idea of surrendering even a shred of sovereignty brings a sharp negative response by many people. Moreover, as the number and authority of international organizations has grown, the warnings of peril have become stronger from those who are alarmed by what they see as an unwarranted and dangerous undermining of the principle of sovereignty. Marc A. Thiessen, in the first of the following selections, is among those who reject the notion that their country will be better off if it gives up some of its sovereignty.

Marc A. Thiessen  **YES**

When Worlds Collide

Out With the New

A transformation is taking place in the world of a magnitude unseen since the Protestant Reformation and the creation of the modern nation-state almost 500 years ago. Nations that jealously guarded their sovereignty for five centuries are now willingly ceding it to a plethora of new regional and global supranational institutions, which are being given the authority to sit in judgment of nation-states, their citizens, and their leaders.

Speaking to the United Nations General Assembly [in 2000], Secretary-General Kofi Annan declared that all nations must come to accept that state sovereignty is superseded by what he calls individual sovereignty—"the human rights and fundamental freedoms enshrined in our [U.N.] Charter"—and that the U.N. has a mandate from "the peoples, not the governments, of the United Nations" to protect those rights. He is far from alone in this view. Polish Foreign Minister Bronislaw Geremek has declared that "in the 21st century . . . relations between states can no longer be founded on respect for sovereignty—they must be founded on respect for human rights." Czech President Vaclav Havel announced that "in the next century I believe that most states will begin to change from cult-like entities charged with emotion into far simpler, less powerful . . . administrative units," while power moves "upward to regional, transnational and global organizations." Former U.S. Deputy Secretary of State Strobe Talbott went so far as to say that the ultimate end is the end of the nation-state itself. Just months before joining the Clinton administration, Talbott declared: "All countries are basically social arrangements . . . no matter how permanent or even sacred they may seem at one time, in fact they are all artificial and temporary. Within the next hundred years, nationhood as we know it will be obsolete; all states will recognize a single global authority."

These are not the idle musings of bored intellectuals. They are statements of people with their hands on the levers of power. With the active encouragement of international nongovernmental and human rights organizations, these globalist leaders are laying the foundations of a new system of supranational authority.

Ironically, the drive for this new order is coming principally from Europe, the cradle of the nation-state. Regionally, European leaders are submitting their domestic laws to the scrutiny of supranational courts. In September of [2000], the European Court of Human Rights in Strasbourg, France, struck down a British law barring gays in the military. Earlier that same month, the court struck down another British law (on the books since 1861) on corporal punishment, declaring in effect that the spanking of unruly children by their parents is an internationally recognized abuse of human rights. Great Britain formalized its acceptance of the supremacy of European law when it codified the European Convention on Human Rights, replacing with the stroke of a pen the entire body of English common law dating back to the Magna Carta. Now, if a British law conflicts with European law, British courts will issue a "declaration of incompatibility" that gives Parliament the option of either amending the offending statute— or having it done for them in Strasbourg.

It is not just the European democracies that have come under supranational judicial scrutiny. Earlier [in 2001], when the United States permitted NATO [North Atlantic Treaty Organization] to answer a written interrogation by the Yugoslav War Crimes Tribunal for alleged allied war crimes during the Kosovo campaign, Washington essentially gave a supranational court jurisdiction over U.S. armed forces.

This exception notwithstanding, to the consternation of our European friends, Americans remain stubbornly attached to self-government. While it may be commonplace for Europeans to have their national courts overruled —and their citizens tried—by supranational courts, for most Americans the idea is unthinkable. Indeed, most Americans know little about this globalist movement or its aspirations for them. The creation of an International Criminal Court (ICC) that could try and imprison American citizens without the consent of their government has gone virtually unreported in the U.S. press and unnoticed by the American public. And that is just how the globalists want it.

Why? Because the globalist project is the work of intellectuals impatient with the constraints of participatory democracy. The impulse is dictatorial. Rather than doing the hard work of gaining public support for their agenda, they wish to impose it from above. And so we have the spectacle of the French presidency of the European Union (EU) recently announcing a goal of admitting 50 to 75 million new immigrants into Europe by 2050 with the bizarre and paternalist declaration: "Public opinion must be told clearly that Europe, a land of immigration, will become a place where cross-breeding occurs."

In a democracy, public opinion is not "told clearly" what will happen.

But the new global order is fundamentally undemocratic. It represents a massive concentration of power in the hands of unelected bureaucrats who preside over unaccountable institutions that are further and further removed from the people affected by their decisions. With all due respect to Secretary-General Annan, he was elected not by the "peoples of the United Nations" but by the General Assembly of the United Nations, less than half of whose members are full-fledged democracies, and almost one in four of whom are outright dictatorships. As for the EU, its only directly elected institution is the European Parliament, which is a toothless farce—a legislature with no legislative powers. All real power in the European Union rests in the hands of unelected commissioners, judges, and an appointed permanent bureaucracy.

The globalists object that their motives are pure: All they want to do is create a world with institutions that ensure human rights are universally protected. No doubt the globalists have the best of intentions. But their intentions are irrelevant. The effect of their campaign will be the establishment of unaccountable institutions that will trample, rather than protect, individual liberty.

Worse, these institutions are doomed to fail. The way to promote human rights is not by policing dictators from above; it is by replacing them from below. So long as there are dictators in the world, they will abuse their people, commit summary executions, jail dissidents, trample religious freedom, and commit genocide. An International Criminal Court cannot change that. Communism and fascism were not defeated by an international legal framework. Supranational institutions have not fueled the dramatic expansion of human freedom in the last 20 years. What has inspired and enabled the spread of individual liberty is the principled projection of power by the world's democracies and the audacity of oppressed peoples around the world to rise up and demand sovereignty and freedom.

Today, that principled projection of power is all that prevents dictators from rolling back democratic advances. What stops communist China from invading and annexing democratic Taiwan? What prevents 1 million North Korean troops from swarming over the demilitarized zone into South Korea? Fear of United Nations censure and war-crimes prosecution? Or fear of the United States military?

The answer is obvious. But the globalists want to constrain U.S. power and popular sovereignty. They insist, against all available evidence and experience, that the only way to advance human rights is to subject all nations—be they democracies or dictatorships—to supranational laws enforced by supranational institutions. They ignore history. We cannot afford to let them.

Don't Tread on U.S.

So, Mr. Leonard and his globalist cohorts are here to rescue the nation-state! Thanks all the same, but we'll take a pass.

Ah, but in the new international order, passing is not an option. There are "universal standards" that must be enforced, and every nation (be it a dictatorship or democracy) must be subject—like it or not.

Mr. Leonard confuses international cooperation with global governance. It is one thing for sovereign states to agree voluntarily to cooperate through "peacetime alliances," something the United States does all the time without ceding sovereignty. It is quite another for a group of nations to impose their vision of "global" moral standards on citizens of a sovereign democracy.

Take the proposed International Criminal Court, for instance. The Rome Treaty insists that this court will have the authority to indict, try, and imprison American citizens, whether or not the United States has ratified the treaty. I demand to know: By what authority?

This kind of supranational diktat is precisely what causes Americans to resist and reject the globalist agenda—and that drives the globalists crazy. Consider their indignation at the U.S. Senate's rejection [in 2000] of the Comprehensive Test Ban Treaty (CTBT), which a majority of senators determined would undermine the safety and reliability of our nuclear deterrent. Editorial writers across Europe howled like children who had never been told "no" before. How dare the Americans resist!

But we do resist, because the international order the globalists wish to visit upon us is inimical to our democratic standards. In the very same breath, Mr. Leonard insists that the new global order is fully democratic, but then declares that it is OK for a supranational court to overrule Britain's domestic laws banning gays in the military. Why? Because said law is "offensive." Who says the law is offensive? The British people? Was there a referendum I missed? Did their elected representatives vote in Parliament to repeal the law? No, they did not. Strasbourg made the decision for them.

If Mr. Leonard believes the law is offensive, good for him; as a British citizen living (for the moment) in a free society, he is at liberty to launch a campaign in Britain to repeal it. Ah, but he does not want to go through the difficult process of convincing his compatriots and rallying them to his cause. Much easier to go to Strasbourg and convince a panel of foreign judges. What other issues will be so decided?

Mr. Leonard credits globalization with the spread of democracy. He confuses correlation with causation. No serious person—certainly not in Prague, Warsaw, Budapest, or Berlin—will tell you that globalization liberated Central Europe from Soviet domination; and, sorry, they won't credit the U.N. either. Most will credit the efforts of the United States and the Western democracies, which challenged and defeated Soviet communism.

International law had nothing to do with it. To the contrary, time and again during the Cold War, "international law" was used to impede America's defense of freedom. The International Court of Justice declared U.S. mining of Nicaraguan harbors and support of the contra freedom fighters a violation of international law. The U.N. General Assembly condemned our invasion of Grenada as another violation of international law (by a wider margin than it condemned the Soviet invasion of Afghanistan). We defeated communism despite the globalists' best efforts to constrain us.

As for the EU, Mr. Leonard declares that it is fully democratic since "national governments control Europe." He must have missed the EU's summit in Nice, France, last December [2000], where Britain gave up its national veto on more than 30 issues and barely resisted pressure to give vetoes up on taxes and a host of other categories. No matter—the Eurocrats will put those issues on the agenda of the next summit. The abolition of Britain is, after all, a process, not an event.

In the United States, our Founding Fathers had the wisdom to require two-third majorities in both houses of Congress and two thirds of the state legislatures to change our constitution. By contrast, European nations are handing over their sovereignty to Brussels in a series of referendums often decided by razor-thin margins—what our founders called a "tyranny of the majority." And that is when a referendum is even permitted.

Ronald Reagan once said that the most frightening words in the English language are, "I'm from the government, and I'm here to help." The same promise is even more chilling coming from a nascent world government. Mr. Leonard says we need "a broader conception of democracy." Here in America, we like the conception in our Constitution and Declaration of Independence just fine, thank you.

World Pax, Not World Pacts

I am not exactly sure what "unilateralist double-think" is, but it appears to mean that anyone who opposes Mr. Leonard's brand of globalism must also be opposed to air traffic control and international mail. That is absurd.

Mr. Leonard is effectively arguing that to receive the benefits of safe air travel and worldwide postal service, America must also accept the presumed authority of an International Criminal Court to try our citizens without the consent of the American people. He can't seem to accept that those of us who reject his global vision are not opposed to international cooperation to address common problems and challenges. In fact, we support not only postal cooperation but a lot of other cooperation as well: everything from the Gulf War coalition that expelled Saddam Hussein from Kuwait to international adoption, tax, investment, and mutual legal assistance pacts, to the expansion of the NATO alliance. The U.S. Senate ratified 52 bilateral and multilateral treaties in the last Congress alone.

But there is a difference between international cooperation and supranational imposition. And while Mr. Leonard argues that multilateralism does not "subject" and "impose," the facts increasingly speak otherwise.

Mr. Leonard asserts, for example, that there is nothing undemocratic about European nations "pooling their sovereignty" to accomplish common objectives. We could have a long debate on the democratic deficiencies of the EU, but for the sake of argument, let's accept his premise: The EU is legitimate to the extent that it is based on "voluntary" cooperation by "elected leaders" acting by the "will of its citizens." How then does he justify an International Criminal Court, which imposes its jurisdiction on Americans involuntarily, without the consent of our elected leaders, and against the will of our citizens? Mr. Leonard still refuses to answer my question: By what authority do the nations that framed the ICC assert the power to try Americans even if the U.S. refuses to ratify the Rome Treaty?

Mr. Leonard says "believing in the rules doesn't mean going soft" on the likes of Saddam Hussein and Slobodan Milosevic. What, then, does he say to Kofi Annan, who has declared that the U.N. Security Council is "the sole source of legitimacy on the use of force" in the world? Does Mr. Leonard agree? If so, he must surely have opposed the Kosovo war, since NATO neither sought nor received Security Council approval for that intervention (for fear of Russian or Chinese veto).

Following Mr. Leonard's so-called rules would have left us powerless to stop Milosevic's genocide. But at NATO's 50th anniversary summit [in 1999], the French, German, and Belgian governments discussed amending NATO's "Strategic Concept" to bar the alliance from ever again taking any military action, save defense of territory, without the express consent of the Security Council.

The globalist framework Mr. Leonard champions—where U.N. approval is needed to project force and an unaccountable global court can try American soldiers—is a recipe for "going soft." This is why a dozen current and former senior U.S. officials (including Henry Kissinger, Zbigniew Brzezinski, and Donald Rumsfeld) recently issued a statement declaring that the ICC would "chill decision-making within our government, and could limit the willingness of our national leadership to respond forcefully to acts of terrorism, aggression and other threats to American interests." That must not be allowed to happen. The projection of American military power is what guarantees regional stability and prevents North Korea from marching on Seoul or China from invading Taiwan—not obeisance to some international norm against the use of force. And the only thing that has ever worked to curb China's weapons proliferation is the projection of American economic power through the threat or imposition of sanctions.

In the long term, however, policing dictatorships from above—be it to respect human rights or reduce carbon emissions—is not the answer. The answer lies in promoting political and economic freedom from below. Developed free-market democracies do not invade their neighbors or pollute their environment, because they must answer to their citizens. Mr. Leonard would have us sacrifice this democratic accountability and concentrate power in supranational institutions further and further removed from the people.

Yes, multilateral institutions have their place and can sometimes help states work together to coordinate collective action and address "transnational" problems. But they are means—not ends themselves. Because the United States has unique responsibilities, we cannot afford to ratify flawed treaties like the Ottawa Convention banning land mines (which would have left our forces in South Korea unprotected in the face of a million North Korean troops), the CTBT (which would undermine our nuclear deterrent) or the ICC (which would expose American soldiers to politicized prosecutions).

We cannot afford to join Mr. Leonard in Utopia, because America has real responsibilities back in the real world. That is not projecting the U.S. ego; it is protecting the Pax Americana that makes possible an increasingly liberal world order where future Milosevics are confronted, where free enterprise and individual liberty are the norm, and where an expanding community of sovereign democracies can work together to address common problems without sacrificing their independence.

Mark Leonard  **NO**

When Worlds Collide

Soybeans and Security

I think [Marc A. Thiessen and I] agree that something dramatic is afoot: the end of a foreign policy driven by the balance of power between a few strong nation-states. But before we jump to extreme conclusions, a few facts.

It was domestic politics, not an internationalist political project, that killed the balance of power. That system relied on a particular conception of the state—with clearly defined borders, a monopoly on legitimate violence, and highly centralized systems of administration and service provision—which has been in decline since the middle of the 20th century. Multilateralism is about rescuing, not destroying, the nation-state. In the past, the principle of noninterference was sacrosanct because the territorial state provided us with security, prosperity, and democracy; all threats came from other countries. Today, the threats to our citizens are less likely to come from invading armies than climate change, drug trafficking, terrorism, population movements, or the erratic flow of the $1.5 trillion traded daily in foreign-exchange markets. These problems demand multilateral agreements, not military action. Even when military action can help, it will be difficult to persuade skeptical citizens to go along with missions that are not designed to defend territory or natural resources.

That is why we are forming peacetime alliances to govern everything from chemical weapons to currencies: so that we can resolve disputes in the courts rather than on the battlefield or through economic sanctions. And, paradoxically, we guarantee security by opening ourselves up to mutual surveillance with agreements like the nuclear non-proliferation treaty and interfering in each other's domestic affairs, right down to the genetic composition of soybeans. You are right that this kind of world will sometimes mean changing our own laws. But supranational agreements are not random codes plucked out of thin air—they are signed by democratically elected governments, and they embody universal values such as human rights or free trade. The fact that discriminatory laws have longevity (such as Great Britain's ban on gays in the military) doesn't make them any less offensive to the norms of our time; and the fact that protectionist behavior is supported by interest groups within your country doesn't make it any less of a barrier to the free trade your government is pushing for.

[Mr. Thiessen] think[s] that this globalism is a threat to democracy, but the most dramatic consequence of globalization has been the spread of democracy. It is not just the number of democracies that has risen—121 free or partially free countries in 1998 compared to 76 in 1972. Citizens are better educated, better informed, and more assertive, challenging old elites and old ways of doing things. And these democratic instincts are expanding into the international realm. When Europeans are concerned about genetically modified organisms and hormones, U.S. farmers feel the pain. Sometimes unrepresentative pressure groups will skew the global agenda as they did in Seattle. But the solution to these new tensions is surely to create new ways of involving people and new kinds of institutions governed by clear rules such as a transatlantic food-standard agency or a World Environmental Organization, rather than retreating into trade wars.

We now need a broader conception of democracy. No international institution needs an 18th-century model of national democracy, because no international institution asks people to risk their lives or pay taxes. Each institution will need to be legitimized in a different way—some by their effectiveness in meeting certain goals, such as low inflation and high employment for the European Central Bank; others, such as the United Nations, by their accountability to international charters; and still others, such as the European Parliament, by direct elections. Almost all will have to be legitimized by the controlling involvement of national governments.

And that is what the EU [European Union]—which [Mr. Thiessen] seem[s] to have totally misunderstood—is about. [He says] that all real power rests in the hands of unelected bureaucrats. In fact, national governments control Europe. They are showing how transnational systems can improve national democracy. Peer review of national policies, protecting individual rights through the court of justice, elections to a European parliament, and the involvement of national parliamentarians in European decisions all create new types of accountability. This model is no United States of Europe (which would be a betrayal of people's democratic choice), but rather a network of states that cooperate to create the largest single market in the world and solve cross-border challenges, while competing the rest of the time.

None of that renders the principled projection of power obsolete. But it does suggest that projection is more effective within a multilateral framework. History shows that the old rules brought the world to the brink of destruction. It is not a coincidence that the most prosperous, peaceful, and successful period has coincided with the rise of international law.

A Declaration of Interdependence

... [Mr. Thiessen] should focus on real issues instead of taking down straw men.

By presenting multilateralism as something that "subjects" and "imposes," [he] offer[s] people a false choice between national governments that are democratic but cannot deliver solutions to key problems, and a global government that is undemocratic but able to deal with cross-border difficulties. What is undemocratic about elected governments freely deciding to pool their sovereignty with others to achieve goals that are close to their voters' hearts? European Union measures to boost prosperity and fight pollution and international crime are clearly not unwelcome impositions forced "against the will of its citizens."

[Mr. Thiessen] insist[s] on talking about "supranational diktats" and treating all multilateral institutions as embryonic states or attempts at global government. In fact, multilateral institutions only have legitimacy insofar as they enforce the common standards and objectives agreed upon by sovereign states. In the EU, member states obey the rules not because they fear the threat of force, but because they see how a rule-based system will benefit everyone in the long term—even if they don't always get their way in the short term. Although multilateral organizations may adopt some of the trappings of statehood (a flag or an anthem, for example), no multilateral regime has any of the core functions of a state, such as large welfare budgets, direct taxation systems, or a monopoly on legitimate violence. Nor will they in the future.

Of course, no intergovernmental organization is perfect. All could be run more efficiently and all must find new ways of connecting in an age of accountability. But that hardly means we should scrap them and retrench to uniquely national solutions in an age of transnational problems and opportunities.

[Mr. Thiessen's] unilateralist double-think requires [him] to blank out the innumerable ways you depend on multilateralism every day. To post a letter, get on a plane, buy clothes, drink water, or watch a film you rely on a web of hidden multilateral institutions and agreements governing everything from air traffic control and food safety to intellectual property and pollution. By adopting international standards we have agreed upon common norms that work for everyone. The Lockerbie trial [of Libyans accused of planting a bomb on PanAm flight 103 in 1988] is just one example of a situation where compromise and multilateralism are delivering where ego-driven national inflexibility would have failed. The families of the victims—who had been in limbo for a dozen years—wanted details such as the venue of the trial to be conceded in return for the guarantee of justice.

The only way to promote an open and democratic world order today is to set clear rules to govern the system. [Mr. Thiessen] quote[s] Reagan ("I'm from the government, and I'm here to help.") to illustrate the dangers of over-regulation. However, free trade is simply impossible without some domestic governance; look at the lessons of Russian reform, where capitalism without rules has halved the country's gross domestic product (GDP) and driven it back to a barter economy in just 10 years. Those lessons are even more evident at the international level.

At the moment, less than 1 billion of the world's 6 billion people live in countries that subscribe to the multilateral, liberal democratic principles that British diplomat Robert Cooper calls the postmodern order. "Modern" countries like China and India still live with a balance-of-power mind-set. Even more challenging are "premodern" states such as Somalia, Rwanda, Bosnia, and, in some respects, Russia, which have very little power to contain their own problems, let alone live up to international obligations. We must help and encourage these countries to join the multilateral system—and the most powerful way to do it is to lead by example.

Believing in the rules doesn't mean going soft. We must never be afraid to intervene militarily when dictators such as Saddam Hussein and Slobodan Milosevic threaten the international order we are trying to promote. However, unless this brute force is combined with a framework for long-term peace and prosperity—which must be based on multilateralism—the results will not be sustainable.

As for [the] United States, [Mr. Thiessen] seem[s] to confuse defending U.S. interests with projecting the U.S. ego. It is ironic that the United States, which sought to introduce idealism into what it saw as the cynical power politics of Europe, should now have so much to learn from its former pupil.

I hope the above helps separate real disagreements from rhetorical ones. Perhaps [Mr. Thiessen] could use [his] next contribution to explain how [he] will get China and India to cut their carbon emissions, respect international agreements on non-proliferation, and promote regional stability if the Bush administration follows [his] strictures and refuses to commit itself to international norms.

Rules for Global Living

[Mr. Thiessen's] position simply does not stack up. If [he] admit[s], as [he] seem[s] to . . ., that we need multilateral solutions to transnational problems, then you also must be ready to negotiate in order to establish common standards. What is frustrating for Europeans is the schizophrenic attitude America adopts: On the one hand, the 52 bilateral and multilateral treaties [he] mention[s] have brought the United States a multitude of benefits; on the other hand, America sometimes seems all too ready to threaten such gains by willfully disregarding the rules that it helped to establish.

The fundamental flaw running through [Mr. Thiessen's] remarks is a pathological fear of supranational imposition. [His] arguments about the ICC are a complete red herring. American citizens are already subject to the national laws of other countries when they live or travel abroad, including all the international agreements that country may have signed. It is due to this long-established principle that U.S. nationals can be tried in the ICC. Similarly, European citizens who travel to the United States can be tried and punished in American courts even though our governments have not ratified [his] Constitution. We do not denounce this authority as a "jurisdictional imposition." If you want to avoid other countries' jurisdictions there is a simple answer: Give up international travel.

[Mr. Thiessen's] opposition to the court places [him] in pretty inauspicious company. China, Iraq, and Serbia are the only other states that see the protection of human rights as potentially "against the will of our citizens." This stance is all the more baffling since [he] seem[s] to agree that we have a duty beyond a narrowly conceived "national interest" to prevent the violation of human rights.

At least that's what I understood when [Mr. Thiessen wrote] that the international community had a moral responsibility to stop the genocide in Kosovo. Yet [he does] not support any means to bring Milosevic and his cohorts to justice. I find it odd that the United States—staunch defender of liberty, justice, and the rule of law—feels it cannot acknowledge that some human depravities are always beyond the pale. Why can [Mr. Thiessen] not agree that genocide is wrong, whatever flag the perpetrators serve under?

On the United Nations some of [his] skepticism is valid. The General Assembly often descends into a chamber for grandstanding and the Security Council is held back by the balance-of-power mind-sets of some of its members. Reform must be high on the agenda. However, it does not follow that operating by a set of rules would have left us powerless to stop Milosevic's genocide. The genocide was a clear breach of international peace and security, and the use of force was therefore justified under Chapter Seven of the U.N. Charter. The real threat lies in intervention without rules, a precedent that can be abused by regimes that use ethical language as a cover for brutal internal repression. At the same time, intervention without rules can provoke accusations of renewed Western imperialism and foster antidemocratic sentiment. Such interventions are also no real deterrent against future abuses, since they are largely arbitrary and short-term. One of the toughest challenges facing us is to settle on internationally agreed regulations that will legitimize future interventions.

In [Mr. Thiessen's] final flourish, [he] set[s] up a false conflict between winning hearts and minds "from below" and the importance of having rules to govern the international order. The two are not mutually exclusive but rather strongly complement each other. Indeed, the Central and East European countries that [he] cite[s] overthrew communism and embraced political and economic reform in large part due to their desire to become eligible for membership in the EU. And [his] blithe assertion that "developed free markets do not pollute or invade their neighbors, because they answer to their citizens" is hardly borne out by U.S. behavior at successive climate change conferences. Democracies are not always beyond reproach: The persecution of ethnic Albanians in Kosovo was carried out with the support of a vociferous majority.

[Mr. Thiessen] invoke[s] the responsibilities of the real world while prescribing a mind-set that is irresponsible. Certainly we need to be ready to defend our peace and security against numerous enemies. However, consider again a point I made earlier, which [he] singularly failed to address: Unless we ourselves are willing to obey the rules, we will never be able to convince others to join us. That is the choice we face today. Unless the United States takes the plunge and firmly embraces multilateralism, we will all lose out.

POSTSCRIPT

Should Greater Global Governance Be Resisted?

However Thiessen and Leonard may disagree on the issue of undiminished sovereignty, they and other careful observers agree that "something dramatic is afoot," as Leonard puts it. What is "afoot" is that the level of global interactions are rising rapidly. International organizations have been established to deal with the myriad aspects of globalization. And these organizations are establishing rules to regulate the interactions within their realm of activity. It is at this juncture that Thiessen and Leonard part company. The former believes that the trend toward global governance is threatening; the latter analyst welcomes the trend.

Discussing the idea of surrendering sovereignty and accepting global governance may sound fanciful, but it is not. Europe, which was the scene of numerous warring, sovereign states until fairly recently, has been undergoing a momentous change. The European Union (EU) has gone a long way toward becoming a supranational government. Certainly, France, Germany, and the other states of Europe that are members of the EU still possess sovereignty, but that sovereignty is much less extensive than it was just 50 years ago.

The things "afoot" on which Thiessen and Leonard agree mean that what you will almost certainly see in the years ahead is ongoing tension between traditional state sovereignty and its advocates, on the one hand, and the alternative of increased global governance and its advocates, on the other hand. The United Nations, the World Trade Organization, the International Monetary Fund, and numerous other international organizations will become the battleground as their roles and authority are advanced and resisted.

There are numerous books and articles that examine the issue of global governance. One book that you would profit from reading is *The Politics of Global Governance: International Organizations in an Interdependent World* by Paul F. Diehl (Lynne Rienner, 1996). Also, your local library may subscribe to the aptly titled journal *Global Governance,* the 2001 editions of which include such articles as "Intervention and State Sovereignty: Breaking New Ground," by Gareth Evans and Mohamed Sahnoun (vol. 7, no. 2) and "Human Security and Global Governance: Putting People First," by Lloyd Axworthy (vol. 7, no. 1).

To learn more from one of the organizations that favors vastly increased authority for international organizations, go to the Web site of the Commission on Global Governance at http://www.cgg.ch, which includes the report *Our Global Neighbourhood*. There are also numerous groups who take a distinctly negative approach to diminished sovereignty. One example is the Concerned Women for America (CWA). You can learn about the CWA's views on this issue at http://www.cwfa.org/library/nation/.

ISSUE 3

Will State Sovereignty Survive Globalism?

YES: Stephen D. Krasner, from "Sovereignty," *Foreign Policy* (January/February 2001)

NO: Kimberly Weir, from "The Waning State of Sovereignty," An Original Essay Written for This Volume (2002)

ISSUE SUMMARY

YES: Professor of international relations Stephen D. Krasner contends that the nation-state has a keen instinct for survival and will adapt to globalization and other challenges to sovereignty.

NO: Kimberly Weir, a doctoral student in political science, maintains that the tide of history is running against the sovereign state as a governing principle, which will soon go the way of earlier, now-discarded forms of governance, such as empire.

There are political, economic, and social forces that are working to break down the importance and authority of states and that are creating pressures to move the world toward a much higher degree of political, economic, and social integration. Whatever one may think of international organizations and their roles, the increasing number and importance of them provide evidence of the trend toward globalization.

Many have questioned whether or not the growth of international law and norms, international organizations, and other transnational phenomena are lessening the sovereignty of states. The debate concerning this issue takes the discussion over the international political system yet another step by asking what the future holds for states. Will the state persist as the principal actor in the international system or be eclipsed?

To grasp this debate it is crucial to understand that countries (states) are not a natural political order. Instead, there are two things to bear in mind. One is that states as we know them have not always existed as a form of political organization. Logically, this means that states need not always exist. Second, states, or any form of governance, are best regarded as tools. They are vehicles to serve the interests of their citizens and arguably only deserve loyalty as long as they provide benefits.

The modern state is largely a Western creation. For almost a millennium after the universalistic Roman Empire fell in 476, political power rested at two levels of authority—one universal, the other local. On the universal level authority existed in the form of the Roman Catholic Church in an era when kings and other secular leaders were subordinate in theory, and often in practice, to popes. Later, the broad authority of the Catholic Church was supplemented and, in some cases, supplanted by the Holy Roman Empire and other multi-ethnic empires that exercised control over many different peoples. Most of the people within these empires had little if any sense of loyalty to the empire.

The second level was local feudal authority in principalities, dukedoms, baronies, and other such fiefdoms in political units that were smaller than most modern states. Here, too, the common people were not citizens, as we know the concept today. Instead, the minor royalty came close to owning the peasantry.

For a variety of economic, military, and other reasons, this old system failed, and a new system based on territorially defined sovereign states slowly evolved.

States came to dominate the international system not because of any ideological reason but simply because they worked better than the models of governance that had failed or any of the other models (such as a rebirth of city-states like Venice) that were tried. The Treaty of Westphalia (1648), which divided Europe into Catholic and Protestant states and marked the end of the pan-European dominance of the Holy Roman Empire, is often used to symbolize the establishment of the state. The treaty was certainly important, but, in fact, that establishment of the state and the growth of the concept of citizenry and patriotism evolved over centuries.

Once this occurred, all of the basic parameters for the modern state that exists today were in place. Yet in the ceaseless ebb and flow of world forces, pressures were beginning to build that would work to undermine the modern states. Those economic, military, and other forces have, in the view of some, built up rapidly since the mid-twentieth century and cast doubt on the future role, even existence, of states as sovereign entities at the center of the international system.

There are some observers who contend that globalization of trade, communications, and other processes do not and should not threaten the existence of the state as a fundamental political unit. Analysts of this persuasion believe that countries can, will, and should continue to exist as the sovereign entities they are today. Stephen D. Krasner takes this point of view in the following selection.

Other analysts believe that states have run their course as a model for governance and are becoming outmoded in a world that is increasingly interdependent. They note that the world has changed greatly since the rise of the state to political dominance centuries ago. The analysts ask whether or not it is reasonable to assume that a model of governance that worked hundreds of years ago is the best model for the future. Their answer is no. Kimberly Weir represents this view in the second of the following selections.

 **YES**

Sovereignty

The idea of states as autonomous, independent entities is collapsing under the combined onslaught of monetary unions, CNN, the Internet, and non-governmental organizations [NGOs]. But those who proclaim the death of sovereignty misread history. The nation-state has a keen instinct for survival and has so far adapted to new challenges—even the challenge of globalization.

The Sovereign State Is Just About Dead

Very wrong Sovereignty was never quite as vibrant as many contemporary observers suggest. The conventional norms of sovereignty have always been challenged. A few states, most notably the United States, have had autonomy, control, and recognition for most of their existence, but most others have not. The polities of many weaker states have been persistently penetrated, and stronger nations have not been immune to external influence. China was occupied. The constitutional arrangements of Japan and Germany were directed by the United States after World War II. The United Kingdom, despite its rejection of the euro, is part of the European Union [EU].

Even for weaker states—whose domestic structures have been influenced by outside actors, and whose leaders have very little control over transborder movements or even activities within their own country—sovereignty remains attractive. Although sovereignty might provide little more than international recognition, that recognition guarantees access to international organizations and sometimes to international finance. It offers status to individual leaders. While the great powers of Europe have eschewed many elements of sovereignty, the United States, China, and Japan have neither the interest nor the inclination to abandon their usually effective claims to domestic autonomy.

In various parts of the world, national borders still represent the fault lines of conflict, whether it is Israelis and Palestinians fighting over the status of Jerusalem, Indians and Pakistanis threatening to go nuclear over Kashmir, or Ethiopia and Eritrea clashing over disputed territories. Yet commentators nowadays are mostly concerned about the erosion of national borders as a consequence of globalization. Governments and activists alike complain that multilateral institutions such as the United Nations, the World Trade Organization, and the International Monetary Fund overstep their authority by promoting universal standards for everything from human rights and the environment to monetary policy and immigration. However, the most important impact of economic globalization and transnational norms will be to alter the scope of state authority rather than to generate some fundamentally new way to organize political life.

Sovereignty Means Final Authority

Not anymore, if ever When philosophers Jean Bodin and Thomas Hobbes first elaborated the notion of sovereignty in the 16th and 17th centuries, they were concerned with establishing the legitimacy of a single hierarchy of domestic authority. Although Bodin and Hobbes accepted the existence of divine and natural law, they both (especially Hobbes) believed the word of the sovereign was law. Subjects had no right to revolt. Bodin and Hobbes realized that imbuing the sovereign with such overweening power invited tyranny, but they were predominately concerned with maintaining domestic order, without which they believed there could be no justice. Both were writing in a world riven by sectarian strife. Bodin was almost killed in religious riots in France in 1572. Hobbes published his seminal work, *Leviathan,* only a few years after parliament (composed of Britain's emerging wealthy middle class) had executed Charles I in a civil war that had sought to wrest state control from the monarchy.

This idea of supreme power was compelling, but irrelevant in practice. By the end of the 17th century, political authority in Britain was divided between king and parliament. In the United States, the Founding Fathers established a constitutional structure of checks and balances and multiple sovereignties distributed among local and national interests that were inconsistent with hierarchy and supremacy. The principles of justice, and especially order, so valued by Bodin and Hobbes, have best been provided by modern democratic states whose organizing principles are antithetical to the idea that sovereignty means uncontrolled domestic power.

If sovereignty does not mean a domestic order with a single hierarchy of authority, what does it mean? In the contemporary world, sovereignty primarily has been linked with the idea that states are autonomous and independent from each other. Within their own boundaries, the members of a polity are free to choose their own form of government. A necessary corollary of this claim is the principle of nonintervention: One state does not have a right to intervene in the internal affairs of another.

More recently, sovereignty has come to be associated with the idea of control over transborder movements. When contemporary observers assert that the sovereign state is just about dead, they do not mean that constitutional structures are about to disappear. Instead, they mean that technological change has made it very difficult, or perhaps impossible, for states to control movements across their borders of all kinds of material things (from coffee to cocaine) and not-so-material things (from Hollywood movies to capital flows). Finally, sovereignty has meant that political authorities can enter into international agreements. They are free to endorse any contract they find attractive. Any treaty among states is legitimate provided that it has not been coerced. . . .

Universal Human Rights Are an Unprecedented Challenge to Sovereignty

Wrong   The struggle to establish international rules that compel leaders to treat their subjects in a certain way has been going on for a long time. Over the centuries the emphasis has shifted from religious toleration, to minority rights (often focusing on specific ethnic groups in specific countries), to human rights (emphasizing rights enjoyed by all or broad classes of individuals). In a few instances states have voluntarily embraced international supervision, but generally the weak have acceded to the preferences of the strong: The Vienna settlement following the Napoleonic wars guaranteed religious toleration for Catholics in the Netherlands. All of the successor states of the Ottoman Empire, beginning with Greece in 1832 and ending with Albania in 1913, had to accept provisions for civic and political equality for religious minorities as a condition for international recognition. The peace settlements following World War I included extensive provisions for the protection of minorities. Poland, for instance, agreed to refrain from holding elections on Saturday because such balloting would have violated the Jewish Sabbath. Individuals could bring complaints against governments through a minority rights bureau established within the League of Nations.

But as the Holocaust tragically demonstrated, interwar efforts at international constraints on domestic practices failed dismally. After World War II, human, rather than minority, rights became the focus of attention. The United Nations Charter endorsed both human rights and the classic sovereignty principle of nonintervention. The 20-plus human rights accords that have been signed during the last half century cover a wide range of issues including genocide, torture, slavery, refugees, stateless persons, women's rights, racial discrimination, children's rights, and forced labor. These U.N. agreements, however, have few enforcement mechanisms, and even their provisions for reporting violations are often ineffective.

The tragic and bloody disintegration of Yugoslavia in the 1990s revived earlier concerns with ethnic rights. International recognition of the Yugoslav successor states was conditional upon their acceptance of constitutional provisions guaranteeing minority rights. The Dayton accords established externally controlled authority structures in Bosnia, including a Human Rights Commission (a majority of whose members were appointed by the Western European states). NATO [North Atlantic Treaty Organization] created a de facto protectorate in Kosovo.

The motivations for such interventions—humanitarianism and security—have hardly changed. Indeed, the considerations that brought the great powers into the Balkans following the wars of the 1870s were hardly different from those that engaged NATO and Russia in the 1990s.

Globalization Undermines State Control

No   State control could never be taken for granted. Technological changes over the last 200 years have increased the flow of people, goods, capital, and ideas—but the problems posed by such movements are not new. In many ways, states are better able to respond now than they were in the past.

The impact of the global media on political authority (the so-called CNN effect) pales in comparison to the havoc that followed the invention of the printing press. Within a decade after Martin Luther purportedly nailed his 95 theses to the Wittenberg church door, his ideas had circulated throughout Europe. Some political leaders seized upon the principles of the Protestant Reformation as a way to legitimize secular political authority. No sovereign monarch could contain the spread of these concepts, and some lost not only their lands but also their heads. The sectarian controversies of the 16th and 17th centuries were perhaps more politically consequential than any subsequent transnational flow of ideas.

In some ways, international capital movements were more significant in earlier periods than they are now. During the 19th century, Latin American states (and to a lesser extent Canada, the United States, and Europe) were beset by boom-and-bust cycles associated with global financial crises. The Great Depression, which had a powerful effect on the domestic politics of all major states, was precipitated by an international collapse of credit. The Asian financial crisis of the late 1990s was not nearly as devastating. Indeed, the speed with which countries recovered from the Asian flu reflects how a better working knowledge of economic theories and more effective central banks have made it easier for states to secure the advantages (while at the same time minimizing the risks) of being enmeshed in global financial markets.

In addition to attempting to control the flows of capital and ideas, states have long struggled to manage the impact of international trade. The opening of long-distance trade for bulk commodities in the 19th century created fundamental cleavages in all of the major states. Depression and plummeting grain prices made it possible for German Chancellor Otto von Bismarck to prod the landholding aristocracy into a protectionist alliance with urban heavy industry (this coalition of "iron and rye" dominated German politics for decades). The tariff question was a basic divide in U.S. politics for much of the last half of the 19th and first half of the 20th centuries. But, despite growing levels of imports and exports since 1950, the political salience of trade has receded because national governments have developed social welfare strategies that cushion the impact of international competition, and workers with higher skill levels are better able to adjust to changing international conditions. It has become easier, not harder, for states to manage the flow of goods and services.

Globalization Is Changing the Scope of State Control

Yes   The reach of the state has increased in some areas but contracted in others. Rulers have recognized that their effective control can be enhanced by walking away from issues they cannot resolve. For instance, beginning with the Peace of Westphalia [1648 treaty often cited as the political big bang that created the modern system of autonomous states], leaders chose to surrender their control over religion because it proved too volatile. Keeping religion within the scope of state authority undermined, rather than strengthened, political stability. Monetary policy is an area where state control expanded and then ultimately contracted. Before the 20th century, states had neither the administrative competence nor the inclination to conduct independent monetary policies. The mid-20th-century effort to control monetary affairs, which was associated with Keynesian economics, has now been reversed due to the magnitude of short-term capital flows and the inability of some states to control inflation. With the exception of Great Britain, the major European states have established a single monetary authority. Confronting recurrent hyperinflation, Ecuador adopted the U.S. dollar as its currency in 2000.

Along with the erosion of national currencies, we now see the erosion of national citizenship—the notion that an individual should be a citizen of one and only one country, and that the state has exclusive claims to that person's loyalty. For many states, there is no longer a sharp distinction between citizens and noncitizens. Permanent residents, guest workers, refugees, and undocumented immigrants are entitled to some bundle of rights even if they cannot vote. The ease of travel and the desire of many countries to attract either capital or skilled workers have increased incentives to make citizenship a more flexible category.

Although government involvement in religion, monetary affairs, and claims to loyalty has declined, overall government activity, as reflected in taxation and government expenditures, has increased as a percentage of national income since the 1950s among the most economically advanced states. The extent of a country's social welfare programs tends to go hand in hand with its level of integration within the global economy. Crises of authority and control have been most pronounced in the states that have been the most isolated, with sub-Saharan Africa offering the largest number of unhappy examples.

NGOs Are Nibbling at National Sovereignty

To some extent   Transnational nongovernmental organizations (NGOs) have been around for quite awhile, especially if you include corporations. In the 18th century, the East India Company possessed political power (and even an expeditionary military force) that rivaled many national governments. Throughout the 19th century, there were transnational movements to abolish slavery, promote the rights of women, and improve conditions for workers. The number of transnational NGOs, however, has grown tremendously, from around 200 in

1909 to over 17,000 today. The availability of inexpensive and very fast communications technology has made it easier for such groups to organize and make an impact on public policy and international law—the international agreement banning land mines being a recent case in point. Such groups prompt questions about sovereignty because they appear to threaten the integrity of domestic decision making. Activists who lose on their home territory can pressure foreign governments, which may in turn influence decision makers in the activists' own nation.

But for all of the talk of growing NGO influence, their power to affect a country's domestic affairs has been limited when compared to governments, international organizations, and multinational corporations. The United Fruit Company had more influence in Central America in the early part of the 20th century than any NGO could hope to have anywhere in the contemporary world. The International Monetary Fund and other multilateral financial institutions now routinely negotiate conditionality agreements that involve not only specific economic targets but also domestic institutional changes, such as pledges to crack down on corruption and break up cartels.

Smaller, weaker states are the most frequent targets of external efforts to alter domestic institutions, but more powerful states are not immune. The openness of the U.S. political system means that not only NGOs, but also foreign governments, can play some role in political decisions. (The Mexican government, for instance, lobbied heavily for the passage of the North American Free Trade Agreement [NAFTA].) In fact, the permeability of the American polity makes the United States a less threatening partner; nations are more willing to sign on to U.S.-sponsored international arrangements because they have some confidence that they can play a role in U.S. decision making.

Sovereignty Blocks Conflict Resolution

Yes, sometimes   Rulers as well as their constituents have some reasonably clear notion of what sovereignty means—exclusive control within a given territory—even if this norm has been challenged frequently by inconsistent principles (such as universal human rights) and violated in practice (the U.S.- and British-enforced no-fly zones over Iraq). In fact, the political importance of conventional sovereignty rules has made it harder to solve some problems. There is, for instance, no conventional sovereignty solution for Jerusalem, but it doesn't require much imagination to think of alternatives: Divide the city into small pieces; divide the Temple Mount vertically with the Palestinians controlling the top and the Israelis the bottom; establish some kind of international authority; divide control over different issues (religious practices versus taxation, for instance) among different authorities. Any one of these solutions would be better for most Israelis and Palestinians than an ongoing stalemate, but political leaders on both sides have had trouble delivering a settlement because they are subject to attacks by counterelites who can wave the sovereignty flag.

Conventional rules have also been problematic for Tibet. Both the Chinese and the Tibetans might be better off if Tibet could regain some of the autonomy it had as a tributary state within the traditional Chinese empire. Tibet had extensive local control, but symbolically (and sometimes through tribute payments) recognized the supremacy of the emperor. Today, few on either side would even know what a tributary state is, and even if the leaders of Tibet worked out some kind of settlement that would give their country more self-government, there would be no guarantee that they could gain the support of their own constituents.

If, however, leaders can reach mutual agreements, bring along their constituents, or are willing to use coercion, sovereignty rules can be violated in inventive ways. The Chinese, for instance, made Hong Kong a special administrative region after the transfer from British rule, allowed a foreign judge to sit on the Court of Final Appeal, and secured acceptance by other states not only for Hong Kong's participation in a number of international organizations but also for separate visa agreements and recognition of a distinct Hong Kong passport. All of these measures violate conventional sovereignty rules since Hong Kong does not have juridical independence. Only by inventing a unique status for Hong Kong, which involved the acquiescence of other states, could China claim sovereignty while simultaneously preserving the confidence of the business community.

The European Union Is a New Model for Supranational Governance

Yes, but only for the Europeans   The European Union (EU) really is a new thing, far more interesting in terms of sovereignty than Hong Kong. It is not a conventional international organization because its member states are now so intimately linked with one another that withdrawal is not a viable option. It is not likely to become a "United States of Europe"—a large federal state that might look something like the United States of America—because the interests, cultures, economies, and domestic institutional arrangements of its members are too diverse. Widening the EU to include the former communist states of Central Europe would further complicate any efforts to move toward a political organization that looks like a conventional sovereign state.

The EU is inconsistent with conventional sovereignty rules. Its member states have created supranational institutions (the European Court of Justice, the European Commission, and the Council of Ministers) that can make decisions opposed by some member states. The rulings of the court have direct effect and supremacy within national judicial systems, even though these doctrines were never explicitly endorsed in any treaty. The European Monetary Union created a central bank that now controls monetary affairs for three of the union's four largest states. The Single European Act and the Maastricht Treaty provide for majority or qualified majority, but not unanimous, voting in some issue areas. In one sense, the European Union is a product of state sovereignty because it has been created through voluntary agreements among its member states. But, in another sense, it fundamentally contradicts conventional understandings of sovereignty because these same agreements have undermined the juridical autonomy of its individual members.

The European Union, however, is not a model that other parts of the world can imitate. The initial moves toward integration could not have taken place without the political and economic support of the United States, which was, in the early years of the Cold War, much more interested in creating a strong alliance that could effectively oppose the Soviet Union than it was in any potential European challenge to U.S. leadership. Germany, one of the largest states in the European Union, has been the most consistent supporter of an institutional structure that would limit Berlin's own freedom of action, a reflection of the lessons of two devastating wars and the attractiveness of a European identity for a country still grappling with the sins of the Nazi era. It is hard to imagine that other regional powers such as China, Japan, or Brazil, much less the United States, would have any interest in tying their own hands in similar ways. (Regional trading agreements such as Mercosur and NAFTA have very limited supranational provisions and show few signs of evolving into broader monetary or political unions.) The EU is a new and unique institutional structure, but it will coexist with, not displace, the sovereign-state model.

 **NO**

The Waning State of Sovereignty

Those who think that the sovereign state will reign supreme forever in the international system have been fooled. Like a torrential downpour, a multitude of things—ranging from the industrial revolution to the inception of the Internet, from the end of colonialism to the formation of the European Union [EU] —are at work eroding state sovereignty. Although they will try to weather the storm, states will eventually go the way of the Holy Roman Empire.

The Sovereign State Is Just About Dead

No, but they are dying. The state as a political unit is not on its immediate deathbed, but states are outdated institutions that have difficulty meeting the needs of their citizens. One argument is that states are too big to do the small things. The size of states and the scope of their governments leave many people complaining about "big government," where the multiple layers of bureaucracy complicate accomplishing any task. Securing a passport can take months, and implementing a new social welfare program can take years to get through the system.

It can also be said that states are too small to do the big things. We live in an era of global problems. Just a few of the concerns that affect the Earth and which are difficult or impossible for any state to address alone include: global warming; the depletion of the ozone layer; the increase of nuclear, biological, and chemical weapons of mass destruction which can be delivered intercontinentally by missiles or terrorists; the movement of trade, investment capital, and money across borders; transnational communications and travel; and the global spread of AIDS and other diseases. Can states any longer truly protect the health, wealth, and very lives of their citizens? The answer in many cases is, "not very well."

Then there is the problem of small states. Microstates are on the increase as more and more people seek national self-determination. Too often what that means, however, is the creation of sovereign entities that more resemble a small city than a country. Nauru is a good example. With a territory that is but eight square miles, a population of barely 10,000, and an economy that depends on the export of guano (seabird droppings) for fertlizer, Nauru is a sham state. Yes, it may take only a day to obtain a Nauruan passport, but no, Nauru cannot provide a secure future for its population.

In 1648, the Treaty of Westphalia marked the birth of the modern state. The states that formed and survived did so because at that time they were the most available means to provide people with security and resources. A competition ensued between the states that formed in Europe. They sought to secure trade relations and to stake claims on territories throughout the world to create empires. This process continued until World War II. The atrocities brought about by the fascist ideology driving the conflict pushed the victors of the war towards working to preserve human dignity and identity. To facilitate this goal of self-determinism, the colonial empires were broken up, and the former colonies were granted their independence and recognized as states. As a result, the number of states increased exponentially during the mid-twentieth century. It was expected that through a process of decolonization, the former empires would endow the colonies with the institutions they needed to become successful and independent states. Instead, a division has emerged between the wealthy North (most of the former imperial countries) and poor South (most of the former colonies) that structures the international system. The geographical description of these countries does not fully illustrate the economic, political, social, and ecological disparities that separate these states.

Indeed many factors have contributed to the developmental problems encountered by the former colonies. Not the least of these is rather abstractly-drawn political borders that failed to take into consideration the indigenous settlements established long before colonization. The intrastate (internal) ethnic conflict that now plagues the majority of all developing states—particularly in Africa, the region most randomly dissected—constitutes the majority of all conflict in the post–cold war era.

One of the main functions of the state is that it is supposed to provide security for its citizens. Yet the millions of people who have been killed as a result of conflict since the formation of states raises questions as to the ability of states to provide security. Considering that weapons are increasingly powerful, and that biological, chemical, and weapons of mass destruction know no political boundaries, the state does not appear to be a very effective means of protection. In most cases, it is the state that incites war and violence. Furthermore, there are countless examples where states even do this against their own citizens who [are] the very ones the state is supposed to protect.

Those who argue that states are still strong sovereign units are missing the reality of state existence. In theory, all states are equal. Any state recognized as sovereign by the international community earns the same status as other states. This is true regardless of the state's resources, its level of development, or its ability to sustain itself and its population. International recognition also almost automatically earns the state a seat in the United Nations (UN) General Assembly, gives the state the opportunity to make treaties with other states, and otherwise gives the state legal standing as one among equals with other states. This theory is largely fiction, however. According all states the same status masks the reality of the situation. It appears that states possess all of the qualities necessary to act as sovereign units, when, indeed, many states fail to provide economic security for their own citizens. Many people in such states would suffer without international assistance offered by nongovernmental organizations (NGOs) and intergovernmental organizations (IGOs).

So, those who argue that state sovereignty is not in decline ignore the fact that a majority of the states have very limited sovereignty to begin with. Recognizing the inconsistencies between the entities collectively called states prompted scholar Robert Jackson to coin the term 'quasi-state' to refer to states that are recognized as sovereign, yet do not meet the criteria for actual statehood. Even more discouraging is the fact that Jackson was also moved to coin the term 'failed-state' to describe states like Somalia, Chad, Liberia, and Afghanistan, whose infrastructures have disintegrated almost beyond repair. Despite their inability to function, however, these states continue to be recognized as legitimate actors because the international system does not permit states to "quit" or decide they are no longer going to be states.

Sovereignty Means Final Authority

Not anymore, if ever.   Many, even most, states have never been free to [do] whatever they want, and some small states with powerful neighbors have been on very short leashes. That continues to occur. Furthermore, most developing states still struggle to lay the foundation necessary to hold free and fair elections, keep government corruption in check, and maintain a state of order sufficient enough to withstand meddling by other states and the international community.

Though having sovereign recognition gives states the ability to enter into agreements and treaties, enables them to become members of IGOs, makes them eligible for international aid, and is supposed to protect states from unwanted foreign intervention, these "benefits" also compromise state authority. A closer look at sovereignty reveals that it is not necessarily what it appears to be.

While no government wants to relinquish any of its sovereignty and most claim that no other authority supersedes its own, the international system is pushing states more and more to abide by decisions made by IGOs. Membership in an international organization necessarily requires a state to relinquish at least some of its authority for the organization to function effectively. Changes in the international system (the rising importance, number, and influence of NGOs, emergent transnational issues, and the increasing number of overall actors) have required states and other actors to cooperate through international organizations. The primary incentive for states to cooperate is to minimize the effects of the changes and the challenges to state sovereignty. China took considerable heat during talks over its application for admission to the World Trade Organization (WTO) from the United States and the European Union (EU) because of its human rights record. And the WTO members, including both the powerful and less powerful members alike, have been subject to rulings by the

WTO that require these states to change their domestic policies to be consistent with those at the international level.

Most states attempting to meet the basic needs of their citizens require international assistance. However, that aid usually has stipulations attached, ranging from revamping state budgets to downsizing bureaucracy size to requiring that states adopt a democratic form of government. States are then evaluated on a regular basis and may have their aid withdrawn if they are noncompliant.

While the notion of nonintervention is considered sacred in the international community, the reality of the situation is that intervention, both overt and covert, happens regularly. Instances abound, from the justifiable drive to end apartheid in South Africa to the equally understandable wish to end ethnic cleansing in Kosovo, where the international community, as well as individual states, have interfered in one or another state's domestic affairs.

Universal Human Rights Are an Unprecedented Challenge to Sovereignty

Indeed they are. The Universal Declaration of Human Rights, as negotiated by the UN member-states in 1948 following the atrocities of World War II, invites interference in states' domestic affairs in the name of humanitarian intervention. In the post–cold war era, the number of conflicts throughout the world has exploded, and the Somalias, Bosnias, Rwandas, Yugoslavias, and Haitis of the world have prompted the international community to intervene for humanitarian reasons. However, the sovereignty of these states is depleted as foreigners intervene in the internal affairs of these countries. This is not to say that the massacre and violence taking place is justified, but rather that events are indicators of how states have become obsolete.

Not only is the sovereignty of domestic states diminished by the Universal Declaration of Human Rights, but the authority of Eastern states is undermined by the Western-oriented values that are the foundation of this so-called universal declaration. The difference is that the Western idea of rights is individually-based while the Eastern concept of rights is communally-based. Many Eastern cultures feel that Western values predominated in defining what a "universal" set of human rights should encompass. Thus, states like China are constantly criticized for violating the Universal Declaration of Human Rights, even though their practices coincide with their own values of the good of the community taking precedence over that of the individual.

Although some argue that UN agreements regarding the various human rights issues are often ineffective, more people are now conscious of these issues. Oppression, hate, slavery, abuse, and violence have not been wiped out by these agreements, but international agreements have spread awareness about these issues. Furthermore, the establishment of international war crime tribunals now provides a way to evaluate and determine whether or not actions warrant punishment. For those found guilty of unnecessarily inhumane practices during a time of war, the international system now has a means for seeking retribution. NGOs such as Amnesty International and WorldWatch monitor state action as well as lobby, protest, and boycott states that violate human rights. At least, their efforts have put states' human rights violations in the spotlight. Their perseverance has helped to push countries to amend their policies, with South Africa as the most stark example of a state's authority being undermined because of its human rights violations.

Globalization Undermines State Control

Yes.   While states undeniably remain significant actors in the international system, the effects of globalization are steadily eroding away at state authority. Trade, communications, technology, and travel all serve to undermine state control.

The increase in international trade has had devastating effects throughout various sectors of economically advanced economies. One does not have to see [the film] *The Full Monty* to be reminded of the power that MNCs [multinational corporations] wield over states. A visit to Bethlehem, Pennsylvania, or Birmingham, England, finds huge factories abandoned, houses vacant due to bank foreclosures, and unemployment rates through the sky. Whole cities have lost their main source of jobs when MNCs decided to utilize cheap foreign labor and have moved abroad, leaving both blue-collar workers and middle-managers jobless. Consider that U.S. labor union members—fighting to keep jobs at home —constituted the largest number of protestors at the Seattle Millennium Round of the WTO talks in 1999.

States have been forced into devising social welfare strategies in attempts to salvage their economies from the effects of globalization. Indeed, it would appear that developing countries benefit from the industry losses of the industrially advanced countries. Instead, however, studies indicate that in most cases the high trade-offs, such as land, tax incentives, and capital, for developing countries offer only a few small returns. In the end, it is the MNCs that both contribute to and benefit from waning state sovereignty.

Communications have been chipping away at the state since the printing press was invented. Since that time, countless communications innovations, from Radio Free Europe to televised satellite broadcasts, have whittled away at government control. Undoubtedly the most recent of these is the Internet. Despite the many opportunities and convenience it brings, surfing the web diminishes state control. Citizens are moving from interacting with one another in civil society to virtual reality. The more time citizens spend alone at home in front of their computers, the less likely they are to take part in community or civic activities, play on a softball team, or sing in the church choir. Furthermore, the Internet provides the freedom to move beyond political boundaries. People have endless opportunities to voice their points of view or network globally to challenge states' authority on issues like environmental practices or human rights records. States, including China and Singapore, have attempted to regulate Internet access in order to preserve their authority. But, it has been an uphill battle as more people gain access to information outside of what their governments report.

Just as traditional forms of terrorism challenge a state's authority over its territory and/or nationals, cyberterrorism also undermines state control. The number of cyberterrorist attacks increases daily, with infiltrators planting viruses that destroy entire databanks, as has happened in the United States, or posting slanderous information, as occurred in Japan. As governments increasingly rely on the Internet to disseminate information and to process passports, driver's licenses, and welfare benefits, states open themselves to cyberterrorist attacks.

There is yet another way that technology presents problems for governments, especially those that do not have it. The increasing technology gap between the North and South only serves to undermine the authority of developing states as they struggle to advance. Falling farther behind the cutting edge of technology decreases job opportunities, chances for development, and hopes for improving living standards. As people become frustrated with the lack of services provided by the state, the possibility for social unrest increases tremendously.

The technological advances of the agricultural industry also affect state sovereignty. Though genetically modified organisms (GMOs) are touted for the fortified grains and vegetables that can be produced and the plants genetically encoded with built-in pesticides, there is a downside to altering genes. Biotech companies can also produce seeds that do not reproduce, forcing poor countries to buy new seeds every season, rather than storing seeds from the last crop for the next year. GMOs undermine state development programs by keeping poor countries dependent upon international aid to feed their people.

More efficient travel presents a plethora of problems for the state. To begin, travel facilitates terrorist activities. It provides terrorists with an easy way to enter a foreign country or to take hostage a country's nationals who are traveling abroad. Transportation also moves migrants. Consider the effect of the break-up of Yugoslavia and the consequent conflict. Tens of thousands of people abandoned their homes, seeking refuge. They spread across Europe, only to be faced with neofascist movements protesting their arrival. More affordable travel also undermines state sovereignty because it carries people abroad where, for any number of reasons, they choose to remain illegally. In many cases, these people rely on the social welfare of their host country to help to meet their needs, thus depleting the state's resources. Finally, more efficient travel means more efficient spread of disease. Thanks to mobility, AIDS has spread like wildfire across Africa, now threatening into Asia. The situation has become so horrific that many states now consider AIDS to be a threat to their national security because states cannot guarantee their citizens' protection from this threat.

Globalization Is Changing the Scope of State Control

Yes. Globalization is forcing states to alter their authority. States have not voluntarily changed the amount or level of control they hold. Rather, the nature of the Global Village requires states to change if they want to remain players in the international system. This argument, however, diminishes the fact that the world is not a static thing and that, as Darwin concluded, all things must evolve if they are to survive. It is not enough to argue that state sovereignty is not waning but just trying to survive by transforming. Instead, what needs to be considered is that the significance of the state to its people is in decline, regardless of the changes that happen to a state as an evolving entity.

States are being challenged by international organizations. These include both the intergovernmental bodies that the states created and are members [of] and the myriad private membership nongovernmental organizations (NGOs) that have sprung up. If states did not concede at least some of their authority to the international organizations they formed, it would defeat the purpose of creating them, i.e., to facilitate relations between them.

NGOs Are Nibbling at National Sovereignty

To a large extent.   This is especially if, as is appropriate, one considers corporations to be NGOs.

MNCs have power, mobility, and resources. They are very mobile; if a state is not willing to grant incentives to MNCs to set up or to stay, corporations will move. In a global business environment where states compete for industries that provide revenue and jobs, MNCs have the upper hand over many small developing economies. MNCs seek out places like the *maquiladoras* (factories near the U.S. border) in Mexico that draws in businesses because of the low cost of labor, or havens in the Caribbean that attract banks with lax financial regulations. And it is not just developing states that are willing to bargain away their control over tax and environmental regulations to entice businesses to build new factories in their backyards; indeed developed states are just as tenacious in offering enticements and incentives with hopes of boosting their economies.

Big businesses are not the only NGOs that nibble on states. The recent growth spurt of private citizen organizations can be attributed to a phenomenon called "post-materialism" by Professor Ronald Inglehart. Enough citizens of the North have achieved sufficient economic security that they are willing to spend time and money on substantive issues like the environment and human rights. These post-materialist trends have brought people with similar concerns together to create, join, and support NGOs. The result is people uniting across political boundaries to form transnational networks that challenge state authority. Many of the groups that protested the Seattle Millennium Round of the WTO or the United Nations Council on Trade and Development (UNCTAD) in Bangkok are NGOs that demonstrated to press governments to make responsible decisions regarding enforcement of stricter environmental codes or labor regulations. Their efforts at the WTO talks have recently been rewarded, as the major IGO that determines and governs trade policy between states is now trying to work with NGOs rather than exclude them, as had previously been the case.

As the overall number of NGOs increases, so does the number of NGOs moving into developing countries in need of assistance. In many instances, these groups provide essential social welfare services that struggling economies and fractured governments cannot supply. Increasingly, industrially advanced states and IGOs are using NGOs to distribute aid and evaluate progress because they have a local knowledge of the situation. Though countless people benefit from these services, the consequence is that the legitimacy of these developing states is even further undermined because people come to depend on the NGOs, rather than the states. The net effect is to put the NGOs in a position of power over those governments.

Sovereignty Blocks Conflict Resolution

Increasingly less. It appears that conflict resolution is based more on issues of self-identity and expression than on preserving state sovereignty. Before Lebanon crumbled to pieces, the Jews, Christians, and Arabs lived peaceably together under a well-functioning government. But Lebanon was eventually affected by neighboring religious conflict. As long as each of these ethnically diverse groups was recognized, the state prospered. When groups attempted to oppress one another, conflict broke out.

A majority of conflict occurring in the post–cold war era is a result of ethnic intrastate clashes in developing countries. Oppressing minorities without fair representation chips away at state sovereignty. Rwanda's Tutsi population was massacred as a result of ethnic hatred. Somalia is still divided by clan rivalries. Kurds throughout Turkey, Iran, and Iraq are persecuted daily. Though they express their desires in very different ways, the Zapatista rebels in the southern Mexican state of Chiapas and many of the French-heritage Quebecois in Canada continue to fight for separation seeking representation.

When the international community does intervene in these conflicts, most efforts are channeled through regional organizations and IGOs. The North Atlantic Treaty Organization (NATO) member-states as well as the UN forces intervened in the Balkans in attempts to save Yugoslavia from itself because of ethnic intrastate differences.

The European Union Is a New Model for Supranational Governance

Yes. It provides a model of what is likely to come.

Given the success of the EU, particularly in the global market, it is not only desirable, but also necessary for other countries to emulate its success. Though the laws of capitalism are based on competition, cooperation has proven to be successful for the member-countries of the EU. The strengthening of the EU has even prompted other industrially advanced countries like the United States to join trade groups like the North American Free Trade Agreement (NAFTA) and seek even larger multilateral trade organizations, such as the Free Trade

Agreements of the Americas that, if it comes into being as planned, will include virtually all the countries in the Western Hemisphere.

Globalization is pressuring individual states into regional blocs in order to compete with other regionally based economic organizations that have formed. Across the globe, few states do not belong to at least one regional economic organization. Despite resistance to external political and economic forces, even previously closed countries such as Burma/ Myanmar have realized the benefits of regional cooperation.

Stephen Krasner argues that expanding the EU to include more Central and Eastern European countries would make it difficult to "move toward a political organization that looks like a conventional sovereign state." But, that's the point—the conventional states are becoming obsolete as regional and international organizations supplant them by providing more of what citizens need. The formation and relative success of the EU provided the inspiration for other regional economic organizations, such as MERCOSUR (the Southern Cone Common Market in South America), the Association of Southeast Asian Nations (ASEAN), and the Southern Africa Development Community (SADC), that hope to emulate the EU's successes. By joining together within regions, member-states have already increased their potential in terms of a larger market for their products and possibilities for joint ventures, such as the hydroelectric plants being built in the Southern Cone region. Rather than competing against international powerhouses in a highly heterogeneous international market, Latin American, Asian, and African states open their markets regionally, thus exponentially increasing the size of their markets for their domestic businesses by targeting similarly situated consumers and economies. Just as the EU started out with joint economic ventures, these regional economic organizations have begun to lay the same foundations that have proven successful for the advancement of the EU.

What Can We Conclude About the Future of the Sovereign State?

Its prospects are poor.   Stephen Krasner is whistling past the proverbial graveyard of states. The growth of separatist movements and the general rising tide of frustration that people feel about the national governments are evidence that states have gotten too big to tend efficiently to the needs of their people. States also cannot hope to deal with global pollution, the spread of weapons of mass destruction, the rocketing level of economic interdependence, and a host of other problems that ignore national borders.

Those who cannot see the end of the state coming also seem oblivious to the impact that rapid international travel, almost instantaneous international communications, the Internet, the increasing homogenization of culture, and a host of other transnational trends are having on obliterating national distinctions. "What is now must always be," may seem comforting, but it is self-delusion.

POSTSCRIPT

Will State Sovereignty Survive Globalism?

Many people find it difficult to debate the issue of the survival of the sovereign state. Nationalism, the identity link between people and their country, is such a powerful force that some find it almost treasonous to suggest that their country—whether the United States, Canada, Zimbabwe, or any other country—is destined to at least be eclipsed and perhaps to cease to exist as the dominant unit of the international political system.

Yet it could happen. Since states as we know them did not always exist as a political unit, there is little reason to believe that they will necessarily persist. Instead, as economic, military, and other factors change, it is reasonable to suspect that the form of governance best suited to address these new realities will also change. It may be that just as feudal units once proved to be economically nonviable, states may also fail to meet the tests of a global economy. So, too, just as small units could not provide adequate security amid new weapons and tactics, critics say that states provide little protection from weapons of mass destruction (WMDs) and terrorism. Sohail H. Hashmi provides a review of the history of the concept of sovereignty in his edited volume *State Sovereignty: Change and Persistence in International Relations* (Pennsylvania State University Press, 1997). For a general view of the role of states in the contemporary international system, see Walter C. Opello, Jr., and Stephen Rosow, *The Nation-State and Global Order: A Historical Introduction to Contemporary Politics* (Lynne Rienner, 1999).

Krasner and Weir both make thoughtful arguments, but it is unclear which scholar the verdict of history will ultimately uphold on the question of whether or not states should continue to dominate the political system and to be the principal focus of political identity. Clearly, states continue to exercise great political strength and remain most people's main focus of political identification. But it is also the case that states exist in a rapidly changing political environment and that, ultimately, they need to adapt and serve the needs of their people. As Spruyt puts it, "History sides with no one.... [The] lesson to be drawn [from the rise and evolution of states] is that all institutions are susceptible to challenges" and that the sustainability of existing institutions depends in substantial part on whether or not they provide "efficient responses to such challenges."

For other views on the future of states, read Frederick C. Turner and Alejandro L. Corbacho, "New Roles for the State," *International Social Science Journal* (Winter 2000) and Linda Weiss, *The Myth of the Powerless State* (Cornell University Press, 1988).

On the Internet ...

DUSHKIN ONLINE

Country Indicators for Foreign Policy (CIFP)

Hosted by Carlton University in Canada, the Country Indicators for Foreign Policy project represents an ongoing effort to identify and assemble statistical information conveying the key features of the economic, political, social, and cultural environments of countries around the world.

`http://www.carleton.ca/cifp/`

U.S. Department of State

The information on this site is organized into categories based on countries, topics, and other criteria. "Background Notes," which provide information on regions and specific countries, can be accessed through this site.

`http://www.state.gov/index.cfm`

PART 2

Regional

*T*he issues in this section deal with countries that are major regional powers. In this era of interdependence among nations, it is important to understand the concerns that these issues address and the actors involved because they will shape the world and will affect the lives of all people.

- Should the United States Seek Global Hegemony?

- Is Russia Likely to Become an Antagonistic Power?

- Is China an Expansionist Power?

- Should Israel Take a Hard Line With the Palestinians?

- Should Sanctions Against Iraq Be Continued?

ISSUE 4

Should the United States Seek Global Hegemony?

YES: Robert Kagan, from "The Benevolent Empire," *Foreign Policy* (Summer 1998)

NO: Charles William Maynes, from "The Perils of (and for) an Imperial America," *Foreign Policy* (Summer 1998)

ISSUE SUMMARY

YES: Robert Kagan, senior associate at the Carnegie Endowment for International Peace, contends that the United States has proved to be a relatively benevolent hegemon and that continued American dominance of the international system is necessary in order to preserve a reasonable level of international peace and prosperity.

NO: Charles William Maynes, president of the Eurasia Foundation, argues that promoting American global hegemony is not worth the costs. Ultimately it will fail, he asserts, and we will lose the opportunity to establish a new, less power-based international system.

The international system is composed of multiple factors: the actors (e.g., countries, international organizations), the economic realities (trade patterns, resources, etc.), values, and the distribution of power among the major actors. Major power centers, whether they consist of a single country or a group of allied countries, are called *poles,* and many political scientists believe that the number of poles and, in general, the status of power in the international system have a great deal to do with whether or not the system is relatively peaceful or relatively unstable.

Most political scientists would use the term *multipolar* to describe the distribution of power during the nineteenth and twentieth centuries through World War II. Some great powers, such as France, Germany, Great Britain, and Russia (and the Soviet Union), persisted throughout this period. Other great powers, such as the Austro-Hungarian Empire and the Ottoman Empire in Turkey, collapsed. Japan and the United States rose to the ranks of the great powers. Whomever the specific actors were, though, the system had four or more poles and, thus, constituted a multipolar system.

What followed World War II was a bipolar system, bifurcated into two antagonistic camps: the United States and its allies, and the Soviet Union and its allies. The system's bipolarity was never absolute, however. Some countries remained neutral, and there were strains within both of the two supposedly unified camps. The last vestiges of bipolarity vanished with the collapse of the Soviet Union in late 1991.

Most political scientists believe that the international system is returning to multipolarity. Within that multipolarity, however, there is, for now at least, one dominant power: the United States.

A hegemon is the single pole in a unipolar system. The Roman Empire during its zenith would come close to unipolarity in the Western world as it was known then. More modestly, some have described Great Britain as being the hegemonic power during the late eighteenth and early nineteenth centuries. The example of Great Britain is important because, to the degree that it was the hegemonic power, it was so within a multipolar system. The British used power unilaterally to their own ends, and they also tipped the balance one way or another by siding with a less powerful pole in times of conflict.

The United States is in a similar position today. It would be too strong to say that the system is unipolar. Other countries, even cold war allies, such as Germany, Great Britain, and Japan, do not answer to the United States. Furthermore, other countries, such as China, are often at odds with U.S. policy. Yet there can be little doubt that the United States is by far the dominant power.

The two readings that follow question whether or not the United States should seek to solidify its position as the hegemonic power. The controversy exists at two levels. At one level the debate involves whether or not continued American hegemony would be good for the world. There are those who argue that the promotion abroad of democracy, free enterprise, and other elements of the "American way" will make the world a better place. Others contend that the United States has not been and would not be a benevolent hegemon and that it has often tolerated dictators, human rights abuses, and other unsavory practices to further its own interests.

The second level of the debate about hegemony involves whether or not maintaining global dominance would be beneficial to the United States. One school of thought holds that trying to be hegemonic is a dangerous goal that will lead the United States to expend its resources foolishly in places and situations that are not vital to the national interest. This, critics charge, will lead to a decline in U.S. fortunes.

This "declinist" view is rejected by those who argue that the United States should try to maintain its dominance. They argue that the United States benefits in many ways from its preeminent position in the world. Moreover, those who favor a powerful U.S. role contend that U.S. hegemony is necessary to maintain peace and economic stability in the system.

In the following selections, Robert Kagan takes a positive view of the impact of American hegemony on both the international system and the United States. Charles William Maynes argues that both the world and the United States will be better off if Americans give up any thought of trying to achieve hegemony.

Robert Kagan

 **YES**

The Benevolent Empire

Not so long ago, when the Monica Lewinsky scandal first broke in the global media, an involuntary and therefore unusually revealing gasp of concern could be heard in the capitals of many of the world's most prominent nations. Ever so briefly, prime ministers and pundits watched to see if the drivewheel of the international economic, security, and political systems was about to misalign or lose its power, with all that this breakdown would imply for the rest of the world. Would the Middle East peace process stall? Would Asia's financial crisis spiral out of control? Would the Korean peninsula become unsettled? Would pressing issues of European security go unresolved? "In all the world's trouble spots," the *Times* of London noted, leaders were "calculating what will happen when Washington's gaze is distracted."

Temporarily interrupting their steady grumbling about American arrogance and hegemonic pretensions, Asian, European, and Middle Eastern editorial pages paused to contemplate the consequences of a crippled American presidency. The liberal German newspaper *Frankfurter Rundschau,* which a few months earlier had been accusing Americans of arrogant zealotry and a "camouflaged neocolonialism," suddenly fretted that the "problems in the Middle East, in the Balkans or in Asia" will not be solved "without U.S. assistance and a president who enjoys respect" and demanded that, in the interests of the entire world, the president's accusers quickly produce the goods or shut up. In Hong Kong, the *South China Morning Post* warned that the "humbling" of an American president had "implications of great gravity" for international affairs; in Saudi Arabia, the *Arab News* declared that this was "not the time that America or the world needs an inward-looking or wounded president. It needs one unencumbered by private concerns who can make tough decisions."

The irony of these pleas for vigorous American leadership did not escape notice, even in Paris, the intellectual and spiritual capital of antihegemony and "multipolarity." As one pundit (Jacques Amalric) noted wickedly in the left-leaning *Liberation,* "Those who accused the United States of being overbearing are today praying for a quick end to the storm." Indeed, they were and with good reason. As Aldo Rizzo observed, part in lament and part in tribute, in Italy's powerful *La Stampa*: "It is in times like these that we feel the absence of a power, certainly not [an] alternative, but at least complementary, to America, something which Europe could be. Could be, but is not. Therefore, good luck to Clinton and, most of all, to America."

This brief moment of international concern passed, of course, as did the flash of candor about the true state of world affairs and America's essential role in preserving a semblance of global order. The president appeared to regain his balance, the drivewheel kept spinning, and in the world's great capitals talk resumed of American arrogance and bullying and the need for a more genuinely multipolar system to manage international affairs. But the almost universally expressed fear of a weakened U.S. presidency provides a useful antidote to the pervasive handwringing, in Washington as well as in foreign capitals, over the "problem" of American hegemony. There is much less to this problem than meets the eye.

The commingled feelings of reliance on and resentment toward America's international dominance these days are neither strange nor new. The resentment of power, even when it is in the hands of one's friends, is a normal, indeed, timeless human emotion—no less so than the arrogance of power. And perhaps only Americans, with their rather short memory, could imagine that the current resentment is the unique product of the expansion of American dominance in the post–Cold War era. During the confrontation with the Soviet Union, now recalled in the United States as a time of Edenic harmony among the Western allies, not just French but also British leaders chafed under the leadership of a sometimes overbearing America. As political scientist A.W. DePorte noted some 20 years ago, the schemes of European unity advanced by French financial planner Jean Monnet and French foreign minister Robert Schuman in 1950 aimed "not only to strengthen Western Europe in the face of the Russian threat but also—though this was less talked about—to strengthen it vis-à-vis its indispensable but overpowering American ally." Today's call for "multipolarity" in international affairs, in short, has a history, as do European yearnings for unity as a counterweight to American power. Neither of these professed desires is a new response to the particular American hegemony of the last nine years.

And neither of them, one suspects, is very seriously intended. For the truth about America's dominant role in the world is known to most clear-eyed international observers. And the truth is that the benevolent hegemony exercised by the United States is good for a vast portion of the world's population. It is certainly a better international arrangement than all realistic alternatives. To undermine it would cost many others around the world far more than it would cost Americans—and far sooner. As Samuel Huntington wrote five years ago, before he joined the plethora of scholars disturbed by the "arrogance" of American hegemony: "A world without U.S. primacy will be a world with more violence and disorder and less democracy and economic growth than a world where the United States continues to have more influence than any other country shaping global affairs."

The unique qualities of American global dominance have never been a mystery, but these days they are more and more forgotten or, for convenience' sake, ignored. There was a time when the world clearly saw how different the American superpower was from all the previous aspiring hegemons. The difference lay in the exercise of power. The strength acquired by the United States in the aftermath of World War II was far greater than any single nation had ever possessed, at least since the Roman Empire. America's share of the world economy, the overwhelming superiority of its military capacity—augmented for a time by a monopoly of nuclear weapons and the capacity to deliver them— gave it the choice of pursuing any number of global ambitions. That the American people "might have set the crown of world empire on their brows," as one British statesman put it in 1951, but chose not to, was a decision of singular importance in world history and recognized as such. America's self-abnegation was unusual, and its uniqueness was not lost on peoples who had just suffered the horrors of wars brought on by powerful nations with overweening ambitions to empire of the most coercive type. Nor was it lost on those who saw what the Soviet Union planned to do with *its* newfound power after World War II.

The uniqueness persisted. During the Cold War, America's style of hegemony reflected its democratic form of government as much as Soviet hegemony reflected [Josef] Stalin's approach to governance [in the USSR, 1924–1953]. The "habits of democracy," as Cold War historian John Lewis Gaddis has noted, made compromise and mutual accommodation the norm in U.S.-Allied relations. This approach to international affairs was not an example of selfless behavior. The Americans had an instinctive sense, based on their own experience growing up in a uniquely open system of democratic capitalism, that their power and influence would be enhanced by allowing subordinate allies a great measure of internal and even external freedom of maneuver. But in practice, as Gaddis points out, "Americans so often deferred to the wishes of allies during the early Cold War that some historians have seen the Europeans—especially the British—as having managed *them.*"

Beyond the style of American hegemony, which, even if unevenly applied, undoubtedly did more to attract than repel other peoples and nations, American grand strategy in the Cold War consistently entailed providing far more to friends and allies than was expected from them in return. Thus, it was American *strategy* to raise up from the ruins powerful economic competitors in Europe and Asia, a strategy so successful that by the 1980s the United States was thought to be in a state of irreversible "relative" economic decline—relative, that is, to those very nations whose economies it had restored after World War II.

And it was American *strategy* to risk nuclear annihilation on its otherwise unthreatened homeland in order to deter attack, either nuclear or conventional, on a European or Asian ally. This strategy also came to be taken for granted. But when one considers the absence of similarly reliable guarantees among the various European powers in the past (between, say, Great Britain and France in the 1920s and 1930s), the willingness of the United States, standing in relative safety behind two oceans, to link its survival to that of other nations was extraordinary.

Even more remarkable may be that the United States has attempted not only to preserve these guarantees but to expand them in the post–Cold War era. Much is made these days, not least in Washington, of the American defense budget now being several times higher than that of every other major power. But on what is that defense budget spent? Very little funding goes to protect national territory. Most of it is devoted to making good on what Americans call their international "commitments."

Even in the absence of the Soviet threat, America continues, much to the chagrin of some of its politicians, to define its "national security" broadly, as encompassing the security of friends and allies, and even of abstract principles, far from American shores. In the Gulf War, more than 90 percent of the military forces sent to expel Iraq's army from Kuwait were American. Were 90 percent of the interests threatened American? In almost any imaginable scenario in which the United States might deploy troops abroad, the primary purpose would be the defense of interests of more immediate concern to America's allies—as it has been in Bosnia. This can be said about no other power.

Ever since the United States emerged as a great power, the identification of the interests of others with its own has been the most striking quality of American foreign and defense policy. Americans seem to have internalized and made second nature a conviction held only since World War II: Namely, that their own well-being depends fundamentally on the well-being of others; that American prosperity cannot occur in the absence of global prosperity; that American freedom depends on the survival and spread of freedom elsewhere; that aggression anywhere threatens the danger of aggression everywhere; and that American national security is impossible without a broad measure of international security.

Let us not call this conviction selfless: Americans are as self-interested as any other people. But for at least 50 years they have been guided by the kind of enlightened self-interest that, in practice, comes dangerously close to resembling generosity. If that generosity seems to be fading today (and this is still a premature judgment), it is not because America has grown too fond of power. Quite the opposite. It is because some Americans have grown tired of power, tired of leadership, and, consequently, less inclined to demonstrate the sort of generosity that has long characterized their nation's foreign policy. What many in Europe and elsewhere see as arrogance and bullying may be just irritability born of weariness.

If fatigue is setting in, then those nations and peoples who have long benefited, and still benefit, from the international order created and upheld by American power have a stake in bolstering rather than denigrating American hegemony. After all, what, in truth, are the alternatives?

Whatever America's failings, were any other nation to take its place, the rest of the world would find the situation less congenial. America may be arrogant; Americans may at times be selfish; they may occasionally be ham-handed in their exercise of power. But, *excusez-moi*, compared with whom? Can anyone believe that were France to possess the power the United States now has, the French would be less arrogant, less selfish, and less prone to making mistakes? Little in France's history as a great power, or even as a medium power, justifies such optimism. Nor can one easily imagine power on an American scale being employed in a more enlightened fashion by China, Germany, Japan, or Russia. And even the leaders of that least benighted of empires, the British, were more arrogant, more bloody-minded, and, in the end, less capable managers of world affairs than the inept Americans have so far proved to be. If there is to be a sole superpower, the world is better off if that power is the United States.

What, then, of a multipolar world? There are those, even in the United States, who believe a semblance of international justice can be achieved only in a world characterized by a balance among relative equals. In such circumstances, national arrogance must theoretically be tempered, national aspirations limited, and attempts at hegemony, either benevolent or malevolent, checked. A more evenly balanced world, they assume, with the United States cut down a peg (or two, or three) would be freer, fairer, and safer.

A distant, though unacknowledged cousin of this realist, balance-of-power theory is the global parliamentarianism, or world federalism, that animates so many Europeans today, particularly the French apostles of European union. (It is little recalled, especially by modern proponents of foreign policy "realism," that [political science scholar] Hans Morgenthau's seminal work, *Politics Among Nations*, builds slowly and methodically to the conclusion that what is needed to maintain international peace is a "world state.") In fact, many of today's calls for multipolarity seem to spring from the view, popular in some Washington circles but downright pervasive in European capitals, that traditional measures of national power, and even the nation-state itself, are passé. If Europe is erasing borders, what need is there for an overbearing America to keep the peace? America's military power is archaic in a world where finance is transnational and the modem is king.

We need not enter here into the endless and so far unproductive debate among international-relations theorists over the relative merits of multipolar, bipolar, and unipolar international "systems" for keeping the peace. It is sufficient to note that during the supposed heyday of multipolarity—the eighteenth century, when the first "Concert of Europe" operated—war among the great powers was a regular feature, with major and minor, and global and local, conflicts erupting throughout almost every decade.

We should also not forget that utopian fancies about the obsolescence of military power and national governments in a transnational, "economic" era have blossomed before, only to be crushed by the next "war to end all wars." The success of the European Union, such as it is, and, moreover, the whole dream of erasing boundaries, has been made possible only because the more fundamental and enduring issues of European security have been addressed by the United States through its leadership of NATO, that most archaic and least utopian of institutions. Were American hegemony really to disappear, the old European questions—chiefly, what to do about Germany—would quickly rear their hoary heads.

But let's return to the real world. For all the bleating about hegemony, no nation really wants genuine multipolarity. No nation has shown a willingness to take on equal responsibilities for managing global crises. No nation has been willing to make the same kinds of short-term sacrifices that the United States has been willing to make in the long-term interest of preserving the global order. No nation, except China, has been willing to spend the money to acquire the military power necessary for playing a greater role relative to the United States

Figure 1

"The Sun Never Sets..." Global Deployment of U.S. Forces

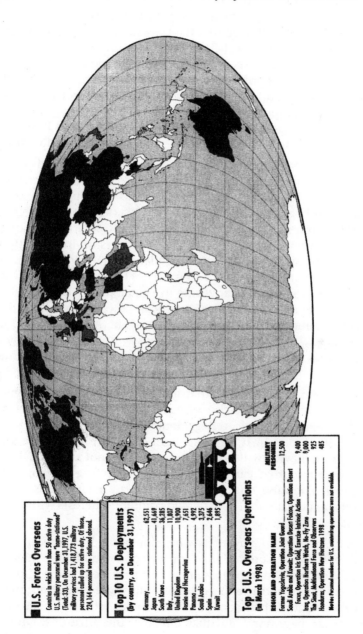

Note: This map excludes personnel who were on U.S. ships in the Pacific Ocean (13,029), off the European coast (4,466), along the Near East and South Asian coasts (8,750), off the Americas (134), and "undistributed" and classified assignments (2,020).

Source: Department of Defense.

—and China's military buildup has not exactly been viewed by its neighbors as creating a more harmonious environment.

If Europeans genuinely sought multipolarity, they would increase their defense budgets considerably, instead of slashing them. They would take the lead in the Balkans, instead of insisting that their participation depends on America's participation. But neither the French, other Europeans, nor even the Russians are prepared to pay the price for a genuinely multipolar world. Not only do they shy away from the expense of creating and preserving such a world; they rightly fear the geopolitical consequences of destroying American hegemony. Genuine multipolarity would inevitably mean a return to the complex of strategic issues that plagued the world before World War II: in Asia, the competition for regional preeminence among China, Japan, and Russia; in Europe, the competition among France, Germany, Great Britain, and Russia.

[Political scientist] Kenneth Waltz once made the seemingly obvious point that "in international politics, overwhelming power repels and leads other states to balance against it"—a banal truism, and yet, as it happens, so untrue in this era of American hegemony. What France, Russia, and some others really seek today is not genuine multipolarity but a false multipolarity, an honorary multipolarity. They want the pretense of equal partnership in a multipolar world without the price or responsibility that equal partnership requires. They want equal say on the major decisions in global crises (as with Iraq and Kosovo) without having to possess or wield anything like equal power. They want to increase their own prestige at the expense of American power but without the strain of having to fill the gap left by a diminution of the American role. And at the same time, they want to make short-term, mostly financial, gains, by taking advantage of the continuing U.S. focus on long-term support of the international order.

The problem is not merely that some of these nations are giving themselves a "free ride" on the back of American power, benefiting from the international order that American hegemony undergirds, while at the same time puncturing little holes in it for short-term advantage. The more serious danger is that this behavior will gradually, or perhaps not so gradually, erode the sum total of power that can be applied to protecting the international order altogether. The false multipolarity sought by France, Russia, and others would reduce America's ability to defend common interests without increasing anyone else's ability to do so.

In fact, this erosion may already be happening. In the recent case of Iraq, America's ability to pursue the long-term goal of defending the international order against President Saddam Hussein was undermined by the efforts of France and Russia to attain short-term economic gains and enhanced prestige. Both these powers achieved their goal of a "multipolar" solution: They took a slice out of American hegemony. But they did so at the price of leaving in place a long-term threat to an international system from which they continue to draw immense benefits but which they by themselves have no ability to defend. They did not possess the means to solve the Iraq problem, only the means to prevent the United States from solving it.

This insufficiency is the fatal flaw of multilateralism, as the Clinton administration learned in the case of Bosnia. In a world that is not genuinely multipolar—where there is instead a widely recognized hierarchy of power—multilateralism, if rigorously pursued, guarantees failure in meeting international crises. Those nations that lack the power to solve an international problem cannot be expected to take the lead in demanding the problem be solved. They may even eschew the exercise of power altogether, both because they do not have it and because the effective exercise of it by someone else, such as the United States, only serves to widen the gap between the hegemon and the rest. The lesson President Bill Clinton was supposed to have learned in the case of Bosnia is that to be effective, multilateralism must be preceded by unilateralism. In the toughest situations, the most effective multilateral response comes when the strongest power decides to act, with or without the others, and then asks its partners whether they will join. Giving equal say over international decisions to nations with vastly unequal power often means that the full measure of power that can be deployed in defense of the international community's interests will, in fact, not be deployed.

Those contributing to the growing chorus of antihegemony and multipolarity may know they are playing a dangerous game, one that needs to be conducted with the utmost care, as French leaders did during the Cold War, lest the entire international system come crashing down around them. What they may not have adequately calculated, however, is the possibility that Americans will not respond as wisely as they generally did during the Cold War.

Americans and their leaders should not take all this sophisticated whining about U.S. hegemony too seriously. They certainly should not take it more seriously than the whiners themselves do. But, of course, Americans are taking it seriously. In the United States these days, the lugubrious guilt trip of post-Vietnam liberalism is echoed even by conservatives, with William Buckley, Samuel Huntington, and James Schlesinger all decrying American "hubris," "arrogance," and "imperialism." Clinton administration officials, in between speeches exalting America as the "indispensable" nation, increasingly behave as if what is truly indispensable is the prior approval of China, France, and Russia for every military action. Moreover, at another level, there is a stirring of neo-isolationism in America today, a mood that nicely complements the view among many Europeans that America is meddling too much in everyone else's business and taking too little time to mind its own. The existence of the Soviet Union disciplined Americans and made them see that their enlightened self-interest lay in a relatively generous foreign policy. Today, that discipline is no longer present.

In other words, foreign grumbling about American hegemony would be merely amusing, were it not for the very real possibility that too many Americans will forget—even if most of the rest of the world does not—just how important continued American dominance is to the preservation of a reasonable level of international security and prosperity. World leaders may want to keep this in mind when they pop the champagne corks in celebration of the next American humbling.

Charles William Maynes

 **NO**

The Perils of (and for) an Imperial America

In their public discourse, Americans have come to the point where it is hard to find a foreign-policy address by any prominent figure in either party that does not make constant reference to the United States as the indispensable nation, the sole superpower, the uniquely responsible state, or the lone conscience of the world. William Kristol and Robert Kagan, editors at the conservative *Weekly Standard*, have unabashedly called upon the United States to take the lead in establishing a "benevolent global hegemony"—though how benevolent it would be is unclear since they propose to attain it through a massive increase in U.S. defense spending. Likewise, former national security advisor [in the Carter administration] Zbigniew Brzezinski, in his new book, *The Grand Chessboard*, speaks openly of America's allies and friends as "vassals and tributaries." He urges, only slightly tongue-in-cheek, an imperial geostrategy designed "to prevent collusion and maintain security dependence among the vassals, to keep tributaries pliant and protected, and to keep the barbarians from coming together." In the pages of this very magazine, David Rothkopf, a former senior member of the Clinton administration, expressed this mood of national self-satisfaction in a form that would be embarrassing to put into print, were it not so ardently felt: "Americans should not deny the fact that of all the nations in the world, theirs is the most just and the best model for the future." ...

The taproot of this growing geopolitical delirium, of course, is the extraordinary range of America's current position internationally. Probably not since classic Rome or ancient China has a single power so towered over its known rivals in the international system: Today, only the U.S. military retains the ability to reach into any region in the world within mere hours. The U.S. economy has become the envy of the world. Others continue to copy our political system, hiring our media handlers and campaign strategists to work in countries whose languages and cultures they barely understand. Finally, the "soft" power of U.S. culture reigns supreme internationally. For what it is worth, few foreign pop stars can rival America's Madonna or Michael Jackson, and American cinema smothers all foreign competitors.

From Charles William Maynes, "The Perils of (and for) an Imperial America," *Foreign Policy*, no. 111 (Summer 1998). Copyright © 1998 by The Carnegie Endowment for International Peace. Reprinted by permission of *Foreign Policy*.

Another characteristic of U.S. power deserves mention: The price America exacts from its "vassals" is more tolerable than the one previous imperial powers extracted from their subjects. The United States imposes extraordinarily light military burdens on its allies. Britain and France made their colonies fight for the motherland in World Wars I and II, and the colonies provided many of the soldiers that policed their empires. In the Korean, Vietnam, and Gulf Wars, America permitted its Japanese and European allies to watch largely as bystanders, while American troops did most of the fighting. In a post–Cold War world, the United States remains willing to pick up a totally disproportionate share of the expense of maintaining the common defense for the indefinite future. By some estimates, the costs for NATO expansion could run as high as $125 billion by 2012, prompting European commentators, such as former German defense planner Walther Stuetzle, to declare that the United States must be prepared to "pick up the tab." What other imperial power would have remained silent while its allies made it clear by statements and actions that they would not pay a single extra penny for a common alliance objective such as NATO expansion?

Former imperial powers also made sure their colonies served the economic interests of the metropole, which maintained a monopoly in key industries and enforced schemes of imperial preference to favor the home economy. In contrast, America's imperial strategy has evolved over the years into that of importer and financier of last resort. The United States has without much debate assumed the role of world economic stabilizer, often adversely affecting its own interests. America's political tradition of constitutional democracy, much more secure after the civil rights movement, also makes it difficult for Washington to follow a harsh imperial policy, even if it were so inclined. With their belief in the "white man's burden" or "*la mission civilatrice*," the European powers—and America for that matter in the conquest of the Philippines—were able to display, when necessary, extraordinary cruelty in the pursuit of stability. Now, in its recent imperial wars, America has been concerned about press reports of a few civilian casualties.

Ironically, of all the burdens the United States now imposes on its foreign subjects and vassals, Madonna may be the heaviest. Few foreigners accept the American position that market forces alone should dictate cultural patterns —that if the citizens want to buy it, the priests and professors should retire to their monasteries and libraries and let it happen. Many foreigners secretly sympathize with the French or Russian or Israeli position that they have the duty to protect their admittedly great cultures, even if doing so occasionally violates some of the finer points of free trade or speech. Indeed, one wonders whether American officials would cling so ardently to their own position regarding international free trade in cultural goods if it turned out that market forces were in fact overwhelming the United States with, say, the culture of the Middle East or Latin America. The number of Spanish-speaking immigrants arriving in the country, and their desire to hold on to their culture and language, represent a clear market test, yet Americans become very disturbed when these new entrants insist on maintaining their use of Spanish. The "English only" movement or the race to install V-chips in home television sets to control what minors may view each suggests that many Americans harbor some of the same concerns about preserving their culture as the French and others.

The cultural issue apart, American hegemony is benign by historical standards. Therefore, it is fair to ask, as Kagan has in several earlier articles: Why not entrench that hegemony for the betterment of all humankind? After all, one can acknowledge that one's own country is not always as principled, consistent, benign, or wise as the national self-image persistently requires that its leaders regularly affirm, yet still reach the conclusion that while American hegemony may not be the best of all possible worlds, it may be the best of all likely worlds. In other words, American hegemony may be better than any alternative hegemonic arrangement, and, historically, hegemony has proved preferable to chaos.

The Case Against U.S. Hegemony

What then is the case against Kagan's call for American hegemony? It can be summed up in the following manner: domestic costs, impact on the American character, international backlash, and lost opportunities.

Domestic Costs

Many like Kagan who support a policy of world hegemony often assert that the domestic cost of such a policy is bearable. They point out that the percentage of GNP [gross national product] devoted to American defense, around 3 percent, is the lowest it has been since Pearl Harbor, and the country is now much richer. True, the United States still spends more for defense than all the other major powers combined, but it is hard to argue that it would be unable to continue carrying this burden or even to increase it.

What proponents of this school of thought fail to point out is that the defense spending to which we are now committed is not terribly relevant to the policy of global hegemony that they wish to pursue. In an unintended manner, this point emerged during the last presidential campaign. Senator Robert Dole, the Republican nominee, publicly complained that his old unit, the 10th Mountain Division, had carried the brunt of America's post–Cold War peacekeeping responsibilities in places such as Haiti and Bosnia, and its men and women had gone months without rest or home leave.

He was, of course, right in his complaint. But the Clinton administration could not do much to reduce the burden placed on the 10th Mountain Division, for the United States has very few other units available for peacekeeping duty. If America is to strive to be the world's hegemon, in other words, not only will the U.S. defense effort have to be radically restructured, but the costs incurred will mount exponentially unless we are willing to cut existing sections of our military, a point on which the new hegemonists are largely silent. The U.S. commitment in Bosnia provides a glimpse into the future. The burden of U.S. involvement, initially estimated at $1.5 billion, surpassed $7 billion in April 1998 and will continue to grow for years to come.

Before the manipulation of budget estimates started in connection with the effort to gain Senate ratification of NATO expansion, even the most conservative estimates suggested that American taxpayers would be compelled to contribute $25 billion to $35 billion per year over the next 10 to 12 years to pay for NATO expansion. The true costs may well be much higher. And NATO expansion is just one of the expensive building blocks required to pursue a policy of hegemony.

There is no clear geographical limit to the obligations that a quest for hegemony would impose. The American desire to remain the dominant security power in Europe drove Washington, against its will, to establish, much like the Austrians or the Turks at the beginning of this century, an imperial protectorate over the former Yugoslavia. Now, as officials spot disorder in other important parts of the globe, there is official talk of using NATO troops in northern or central Africa, if necessary. Corridor chatter has even begun among some specialists about the need to send troops to the Caspian area to secure the oil there. Where will the interventionist impulse end? How can it end for a power seeking global hegemony?

The costs of hegemony will not just be military. Modern-day advocates of hegemony have lost sight of one of the crucial characteristics of the golden age of American diplomacy: From 1945 to 1965, America's dominant image rested more on the perception of its role as the world's Good Samaritan than as the world's policeman. Nearly 60 years ago, Henry Luce, the founder of *Time* magazine, issued one of the most famous calls for American dominance internationally. He understood that a quest for world leadership requires more than a large army. In his famous essay "The American Century," Luce urged his fellow citizens to spend at least 10 percent of every defense dollar in a humanitarian effort to feed the world. He recognized that to dominate, America must be seen not only as stronger but better. The United States needs to do its share internationally in the nonmilitary field and now, as the sad state of the foreign affairs budget demonstrates, it frankly does not. But is the country willing to pick up the nonmilitary costs of a quest for global hegemony?

With their neglect of this issue, today's new hegemonists are almost a parody of the Kaiser and his court at the beginning of this century. Like their German cousins, the new hegemonists are fascinated by military might, intoxicated by the extra margin of power America enjoys, and anxious to exploit this moment to dominate others. They want to reverse almost completely the direction American foreign policy has taken for most of the period following World War II. America's goal has always been to lift others up. Now, it will be to keep them down. In Kagan's own words, American power should be deployed to control or prevent the "rise of militant anti-American Muslim fundamentalism in North Africa and the Middle East, a rearmed Germany in a chaotic Europe, a revitalized Russia, a rearmed Japan in a scramble for power with China in a volatile East Asia."

His choice of words is instructive. America's goal would be not simply to protect this country and its citizens from actions that militant Islam might direct against American interests but to prevent the very rise of militant Islam. We would not only stand up to Russia were it to become hostile to U.S. interests but would try to prevent the very revival of the Russian people and state. And we would attempt to control the spread of "chaos" in the international system. All these tasks would require the United States to intervene in the internal affairs of other states to a degree not seen since the immediate postwar period, when the United States and the Soviet Union stationed their vast land armies on the soil of former enemy territories.

One of the most bitter lessons of the Cold War was that when American and Soviet soldiers sought to impose a political order on populations (or at least resolute parts of them) that resisted such efforts—namely in Afghanistan, Korea, and Vietnam—casualties began to mount. If the United States attempts a policy of global hegemony, Kagan and other proponents cannot claim it will incur low costs by citing the size of the current defense budget or referring only to the dollars spent. The character of that budget will have to change, and the price will be not only in dollars spent but in bloodshed. Is the country prepared for that, particularly when those asked to die will be told it is in the name of hegemony, not national defense? Will Americans be comfortable with an image of their country as the power always brandishing the clenched fist and seldom extending the helping hand?

Impact on the American Character

A quest for hegemony would have a corrosive effect on the country's internal relations. The United States could carry out such a quest only by using the volunteer army, which fills its ranks predominately with people who come from a segment of America that is less internationally minded than those who wish to use the U.S. military for geopolitical purposes. Former secretary of labor Robert Reich, among others, has pointed out that America is developing into two societies—not so much black versus white but cosmopolitan versus national, or between those who have directly, even extravagantly, reaped the benefits in recent years from the new globalized economy and those who have paid its price in terms of military service, endangered jobs, and repressed wages. The former may represent between 15 to 25 percent of the population. Its representatives travel widely, speak foreign languages (or at least can afford to hire a translator), and feel as at home in Rome or Tokyo as they do in New York. Almost none of their sons and daughters serve in the U.S. military. Facing them are the vast majority of citizens who will no doubt be asked to pay the price of their country's policy of hegemony.

Can America embark on a quest for global primacy with those responsible for pursuing this course paying almost no price for its execution? Will American democracy permit a situation like that of ancient Rome, where the rich sit in the stands to watch the valiant exertions of those less fortunate below?

In the early days of the post–Cold War period, it was not at all uncommon to hear foreign-policy practitioners refer to the American military in terms that suggested they were modern Hessians, available for deployment to any corner of the globe that policymakers wished to pacify or control. Ironically, prominent among the new interventionists were a number of humanitarian-aid officials—who are normally not enthusiastic about military deployments abroad—arguing that since the U.S. army consisted of volunteers who had accepted the king's shilling and, after all, had little to do in a post–Cold War world, they should be ready to serve in humanitarian missions, even if these were not related to core American security concerns.

The ease of victory in the Gulf War contributed to this new enthusiasm for the use of military force. If Iraq, with one of the most powerful armies in the world, could be so easily subdued, how could there be much danger or pain in deploying U.S. troops into the growing number of ethnic or religious conflicts emerging around the world? After the disaster in Somalia, one heard less of such talk. But empires need to have either Hessians or a populace anxious to march off to war. Fortunately, America has neither. Not to understand this fundamental point risks causing a major political explosion domestically at some unexpected moment in the future. Of course, the argument that the United States should not seek global hegemony does not mean America should not work with others to develop a shared response to some of the new challenges on the international agenda . . . but that is a different subject and article.

International Backlash

Suppose, despite all of these obstacles, a quest for world hegemony could succeed. We still should not want it. As Henry Adams warned in his autobiography, the effect of power on all men is "the aggravation of self, a sort of tumor that ends by killing the victim's sympathies." Already the surplus of power that America enjoys is beginning to metastasize into an arrogance toward others that is bound to backfire. Since 1993, the United States has imposed new unilateral economic sanctions, or threatened legislation that would allow it do so, 60 times on 35 countries that represent over 40 percent of the world's population.

Increasingly, in its relations even with friends, the United States, as a result of the interplay between administration and Congress, has begun to command more and listen less. It demands to have its way in one international forum after another. It imperiously imposes trade sanctions that violate international understandings; presumptuously demands national legal protection for its citizens, diplomats, and soldiers who are subject to criminal prosecution, while insisting other states forego that right; and unilaterally dictates its view on UN reforms or the selection of a new secretary general.

To date, the United States has been able to get away with these tactics. Nevertheless, the patience of others is shortening. The difficulty the United States had in rounding up support, even from its allies, in the recent confrontation with Iraqi president Saddam Hussein was an early sign of the growing pique of others with America's new preemptive arrogance. So was the manner in which the entire membership of the European Union immediately rallied behind the French in the controversy over a possible French, Malaysian, and Russian joint investment in the Iranian oil industry that would violate America's unilaterally announced sanctions policy against Iran. In March 1998, while reflecting on President Bill Clinton's visit to South Africa, President Nelson Mandela strongly rejected a trade agreement with the United States that would limit transactions

Figure 1

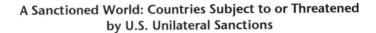

A Sanctioned World: Countries Subject to or Threatened by U.S. Unilateral Sanctions

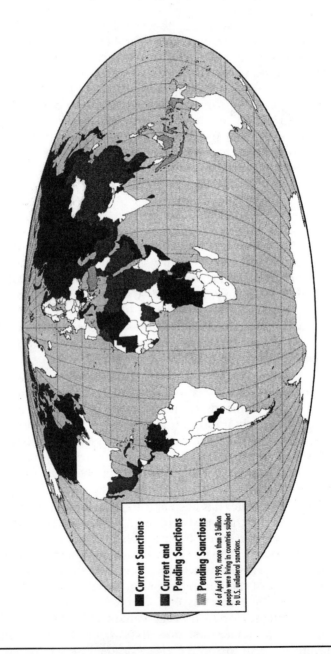

Source: For tracking of U.S. federal sanctions. *Unilateral Economic Sanctions: A Review* (Washington: President's Export Council, June 1997). U.S. state and local sanctions are tracked on the Web site of the Organization for International Investment. Sanctions pending in the U.S. Congress are reported on the Web site of USA*Engage. Map is derived from April 1998 data.

with any third country, declaring that "we resist any attempt by any country to impose conditions on our freedom of trade."

Lost Opportunities

Perhaps the biggest price Americans would pay in pursuing world hegemony is the cost in lost opportunities. Even those who propose such a policy of hegemony acknowledge that it cannot succeed over the longer run. As Kagan himself has written, we cannot "forget the truism that all great powers must some day fall." One day, in other words, some country or group of countries will successfully challenge American primacy.

There is an alternative. We could use this unique post–Cold War moment to try to hammer out a new relationship among the great powers. Today, the most inadequately examined issue in American politics is precisely whether or not post–Cold War conditions offer us a chance to change the rules of the international game.

Certainly, there is no hope of changing the rules of the game if we ourselves pursue a policy of world hegemony. Such a policy, whether formally announced or increasingly evident, will drive others to resist our control, at first unsuccessfully but ultimately with effect. A policy of world hegemony, in other words, will guarantee that in time America will become outnumbered and overpowered. If that happens, we will once and for all have lost the present opportunity to attempt to change the rules of the game among the great powers.

Why should we believe there could be an opportunity to alter these rules? There are at least three reasons:

- War no longer pays for the great powers. For most of history, wars have paid. The victor ended up with more land and people. Over time, almost all of the latter accepted the sway of the new occupier. That is how most of the great nations of the world were built. With the rise of modern nationalism, however, it has become more and more difficult to absorb conquered territories without ethnic cleansing. Successful recent examples of seizing territory include the Russian, Polish, and Czech border changes after World War II, which involved brutal exchanges of populations. Unsuccessful examples of seizing territory include those in which the indigenous populations have remained, such as Israel's occupation of the West Bank, Indonesia's occupation of East Timor, and India's incorporation of Kashmir. Moreover, although ethnic cleansing does still take place today in a number of locations worldwide, those carrying out such practices are not the great powers but countries still in the process of nation-building along nineteenth-century lines. For most of the great states, in other words, war is not an option for power or wealth seeking. War is reserved for defense.
- Instead of seeking international power and influence through external expansion, most established powers now seek both through internal development. Postwar Germany and Japan have confirmed that these are more reliable paths to greater international prominence than the

ones pursued since 1945 by Britain and France, both of which have relied on military power to hold their place in the international system only to see it decline.

- The behavior of great states in the international system that have lost traditional forms of power in recent decades has been remarkably responsible. Postwar Germany and Japan, as well as post–Cold War Russia, have all accepted being shorn of territories with notably few repercussions. A principal reason was the treatment of the first two by their rivals and the hope of the third that the rest of the world would not exploit its weaknesses so as to exclude Russia from the European system, but would instead take aggressive steps to incorporate it. In this regard, a policy of hegemony sends exactly the wrong message, particularly if one of our purposes is to prevent Russia from ever "reviving" in a way that threatens us.

Regrettably, as we approach the millennium, we are almost at the point of no return in our post–Cold War policy. We are moving along a path that will forsake the chance of a lifetime to try to craft a different kind of international system. Like France at the beginning of the nineteenth century, Britain in the middle, and Germany at the end, the United States does much to influence international behavior by the model it sets. It is still not too late to make a real effort to write a new page in history. If we pass up this opportunity, history will judge us very harshly indeed.

POSTSCRIPT

Should the United States Seek Global Hegemony?

$\mathbf{D}$ean G. Acheson, secretary of state under President Harry S. Truman, entitled his memoirs *Present at the Creation* (W. W. Norton, 1987). Acheson's title reflected his belief that he had witnessed the end of the old, pre–World War II international system and the advent of a new, post–World War II world. Moreover, Acheson believed that the United States had been and would continue to be an active participant in the new international system.

Certainly Acheson was correct about the role of the United States during his term of service. It was the dominant power in the aftermath of the war. Although the Soviet Union and its allies posed a military and perhaps an ideological threat during the cold war period, the United States nevertheless remained the undisputed leader of the far wealthier, technologically advanced, and militarily superior Western bloc. The United States was the lead player in establishing the United Nations, the International Monetary Fund, the World Bank, the General Agreement on Tariffs and Trade, and most of the other key international organizations. American values have played a strong role in the spreading democratization of the world and the increase in the importance of human rights on the international agenda. Even American culture has spread worldwide: blue jeans, T-shirts, and sneakers are worn everywhere, and English has become the lingua franca of the Internet, global business, and transnational communications.

The United States remains the global hegemon. In some ways its power has diminished as former allies like Germany and Japan have gained strength. In other ways, U.S. power has increased as its former opponents, especially the Soviet Union, have collapsed. Whatever the exact balance sheet, however, it can be said confidently that no other single power can rival the United States.

Hegemony has its benefits. Much more than any other country, the United States has a commanding say in how the world operates. There is also the view that the world is most stable when there is a hegemonic power. For more on this, see William C. Wohlforth, "The Stability of a Unipolar World," *International Security* (Summer 1999).

Hegemony also has its burdens. Others are reluctant to act unless the United States leads. The Europeans, for example, could have intervened unilaterally in Kosovo in 1999, but U.S. leadership and participation were required. Many believe, however, that the United States has overextended itself and that overextension can sap U.S. power. The best exposition of this view is Paul M. Kennedy, *The Rise and Fall of the Great Powers* (Random House, 1988).

ISSUE 5

Is Russia Likely to Become an Antagonistic Power?

YES: Ariel Cohen, from "Putin's Foreign Policy and U.S.–Russian Relations," *Heritage Foundation Backgrounder* (January 18, 2001)

NO: Anatol Lieven, from "Against Russophobia," *World Policy Journal* (Winter 2000/2001)

ISSUE SUMMARY

YES: Ariel Cohen, a research fellow in Russian and Eurasian studies at the Heritage Foundation in Washington, D.C., argues that the current Russian government espouses a nationalist agenda that seeks to reestablish Russia as a great world power and to undermine U.S. leadership.

NO: Anatol Lieven, a senior associate at the Carnegie Endowment for International Peace in Washington, D.C., contends that the negative view of Russia inherited from the cold war era leads to bad policies.

$\mathbf{R}$ussia has experienced two momentous revolutions during the twentieth century. The first began in March 1917. After a brief moment of attempted democracy, that revolution descended into totalitarian government, with the takeover of the Bolshevik Communists in November and the establishment of the Union of Soviet Socialist Republics (USSR).

The second great revolution arguably began in 1985 with the elevation of reform-minded Mikhail S. Gorbachev to leadership in the USSR. The country was faced with a faltering economic system because of its overcentralization and because of the extraordinary amount of resources being allocated to Soviet military forces. Gorbachev's reforms, including *perestroika* (restructuring, mostly economic) and *glasnost* (openness, including limited democracy), unleashed strong forces within the USSR. The events of the next six years were complex, but suffice it to say that the result was the collapse of the Soviet Union. What had been the USSR fragmented into 15 newly independent countries. Of these former Soviet republics (FSRs), Russia is by far the largest, has the biggest population, and is potentially the most powerful. Russia also retained the bulk of the Soviet Union's nuclear weapons and their delivery systems.

When Russia reemerged in the aftermath of the collapse of the USSR, its president, Boris Yeltsin, offered the hope of strong, democratic leadership. His resolute defense of Russia (then a Soviet republic) was the most visible symbol of democratic defiance, which had defeated a last-minute attempt by old-guard Soviet officials to seize power. There was great hope for a better future for Russia within the country, and there was an equally great hope around the world that the "new" Russia would be a peaceful and cooperative neighbor.

The domestic and international euphoria that occurred in the aftermath of the collapse of the Soviet Union soon faded, however, amid Russia's vast problems. The country's economy fell into shambles, with Russia's gross domestic product (GDP) declining precipitously throughout most of the 1990s and with rampant inflation ravaging the economic welfare of nearly all Russians, leaving 22 percent of them below the poverty level.

Russia's travails prompted the country to follow a relatively passive policy; it did not have the economic and military resources to assert itself. And even to the degree that Moscow might have wished to take a policy direction that would have displeased Washington and its allies, the Russians could not risk doing so because they desperately needed financial assistance from the United States and other industrialized countries and from the International Monetary Fund (IMF), which those countries control.

Arguably, Russia began to recover from its woes just as the new millennium came into being. In a stunning event, Prime Minister Vladimir Putin became president when Yeltsin resigned on December 31, 1999. The change brought to Russia's presidency an individual who spent most of his professional career in the KGB, the Soviet secret police, and who headed its successor, Russia's Federal Security Service (FSB). The new president expressed his determination to regain strong control internally, to reassert Russia's world position, and to rebuild the country's economy.

For good or ill, Putin has brought a level of stability to Russia. Slowly, Russia's economy has steadied itself. Many would consider it an overstatement to say that the economy has shown marked improvement, but at least economic conditions have stopped their decline, and some aspects of the economy have inched upwards. Moreover, with a well-educated populace, vast mineral and energy resources, and a large (if antiquated) industrial base, Russia has great economic potential.

Similarly, while Russian military forces fell into disarray in the 1990s, the country's large population, its weapons manufacturing capacity, and its huge land mass make it likely that the breakdown of Russia's conventional military capabilities and geostrategic importance will only be temporary.

The question is, then, What are the chances that the country will once again become antagonistic toward the United States and its allies? In the following selections, Ariel Cohen asserts that the United States now faces a more determined, disciplined, and organized Russian government that has marked policy differences with Washington. Anatol Lieven contends that ungrounded hostility toward Russia could become a self-fulfilling prophecy, which could drive Russia to becoming the antagonistic power we imagine it to be but which it does not have to become.

Ariel Cohen  **YES**

Putin's Foreign Policy and U.S.–Russian Relations

President... George W. Bush has inherited his predecessor's troubled relations with Russia. President Bill Clinton often overlooked Russia's transgressions, such as a recently reported political treaty with Beijing, massive arms sales to Iran and China, and pervasive money laundering. He also sought to accommodate Russian opposition to a U.S. national missile defense system, demonstrating an unwavering commitment to the Cold War view of arms control and ignoring the need to counter the growing threat of ballistic missiles from rogue states.

Russian President Vladimir Putin and his administration espouse a nationalist agenda that seeks to re-establish Russia as a great world power and to offset America's global leadership position. Putin and his security team have issued a series of documents that call the United States, and the "unipolar world order" it allegedly promotes, a major threat to the Russian state. Clearly, relations with Russia will pose serious policy challenges for the new American President.

... President... Bush must issue a clear statement about relations with Russia. Indeed, such a statement would appeal to Russian policymakers and experts, who have expressed their preference for clear-cut statements that define America's priorities with regard to Russia. The Russians respected President Ronald Reagan for his forthrightness, for example, even when he called the Soviet Union the "evil empire" and demanded that Mikhail Gorbachev "tear down this [Berlin] Wall." Clear statements of national security objectives and firm implementation of foreign policy decisions provide a measure of predictability that would help Russian leaders navigate the shoals of the global strategic environment.

However, in establishing the tenets of his foreign policy, it is vital that President... Bush impress upon his Russian counterpart the extent and limits of cooperation. For example, while such transgressions as arms sales to Iran and Iraq and support for rogue leaders like Saddam Hussein will not be tolerated, Putin can expect cooperation in such areas as strategic arms reduction, economic development, space exploration, and the fight against international crime and terrorism. To demonstrate his desire for better relations, the President... should invite Putin to a summit in Washington..., or offer to meet with him at the summit of the G-8 countries to be held in Genoa, Italy.... Such a summit would give the leaders an opportunity to initiate a new chapter in U.S.–Russian relations, one that seeks to ensure national and global security—a strategic objective for both countries.

Putin and Russia's New Agenda

Russia occupies a unique geopolitical position. It abuts most of the important regions of the Eastern Hemisphere, including Western Europe and the oil-rich Middle East. It is a prime exporter of the arms and energy many of these regions desire. Such a position enables President Putin to focus his foreign policies on ways to increase Russia's prestige and power. While abroad, Putin speaks about advancing economic reform and attracting foreign investment; at home, he talks about the "dictatorship of law" and strengthening the Russian state. As Michael McFaul of the Carnegie Endowment points out, Putin wears two hats: one when he speaks to the Russian people and another when he addresses foreign audiences. It is an ability that must not be underestimated by the new Bush Administration.

Vladimir Putin began a whirlwind foreign policy offensive to improve Russia's status in the region and the world even before he became president of Russia on May 7, 2000. After becoming prime minister in August 1999, for example, he met with President Clinton five times. As acting president, he met with British Prime Minister Tony Blair in St. Petersburg on March 11, 2000. Since becoming president, he has visited the major Western European countries, including Great Britain, Germany, France, Italy, and Spain. He has visited China, Japan, Mongolia, and the two remaining Marxist-Leninist countries, North Korea and Cuba. And he has made appearances in the Central Asian states of Uzbekistan, Turkmenistan, and Kazakhstan, hoping to enhance Russia's status in this energy-rich region. This is an impressive itinerary for Putin's first year in office. This initiative extends to officials within his administration as well, as the recent meetings in Moscow of high-ranking national security officials from Russia with similar officials from Iran and Iraq show.

Putin's effort to enhance Russia's position includes a promise to increase substantially the sales of Russian oil, natural gas, and electricity to Europe. Moreover, to gain a louder voice in European security policy, the Putin administration has broached the idea of joining the controversial European Security and Defense Policy (ESDP) initiative, a joint military structure for the European Union (EU) that some countries hope will counterbalance America's role in European security in the North Atlantic Treaty Organization (NATO).

Putin is using arms sales to boost Russia's influence as well, signing large deals in 2000 with China, India, and Iran that total almost $10 billion. Weapons sales generate revenue for Moscow to use in the strategic modernization of Russia's aging military forces; they also strengthen Russia's influence in important (and volatile) areas such as the Taiwan Strait, the Kashmir region between India and Pakistan, and the Persian Gulf. While Putin has announced plans to reduce Russia's nuclear forces significantly to between 1,000 and 1,500 warheads, either in a negotiated treaty or in tandem with the United States, he strongly opposes the deployment of a national missile defense (NMD) system for America.

To strengthen his position as a global leader, Putin made appearances at the G-8 summit in Okinawa and the Millennium Summit at the United Nations in September 2000, the summits of the Commonwealth of Independent States (CIS) in Moscow and Yalta, a bilateral summit with the EU in Paris, and the Asia-Pacific Economic Cooperation (APEC) forum in Brunei in November. During these trips, his public relations team carefully orchestrated moves that would garner media attention. In Japan, for example, he allowed a 10-year-old Japanese girl to throw him on a mat, which charmed the Japanese public. At the G-8 summit in Okinawa, he gave the other leaders an "intelligence briefing" on North Korea based on his personal meeting with Kim Jong-Il and recommended that they stay in touch by e-mail.

Behind this public relations effort is a steely commitment to Russia's re-emergence in the "major league" of nations. The focus on Russia's strategic and economic interests covers up the inherent weakness in this approach: the Russian economy, which is based on obsolete industries and a rapidly aging population and which has contracted by more than 50 percent since the collapse of the Soviet Union. Putin and his administration seek an external opponent—similar to what Great Britain was for imperial Russia in the 19th century during their "Great Game" for control of Central Asia and the Caucasus—that enables them to make a show of Russia's strengths. It appears, from Russia's actions and national security and foreign policy documents, that the opponent it has chosen is the United States. Putin is campaigning for allies in this effort by making deals with states like China and India. The implications of this offensive for U.S.-Russian policy in the future can be found in the fronts on which Putin's campaign is being waged.

Geopolitics and the Two-Headed Eagle

Russia fittingly adopted the Byzantine Empire's two-headed eagle as the state symbol in the 15th century, but it is also appropriate today. It symbolizes Russia's past efforts to expand its territory both to the East and the West. Rather than territorial aggrandizement, Russia is looking in the 21st century to strengthen its ties to its neighbors to the East and West and to create alternative foci of power to offset the global leadership position of the United States.

Russia's elites are preoccupied with advancing "Eurasianism," which sees Russia as the "ultimate World-Island state" apart from, and hostile to, the maritime and commercial Euro-Atlantic world. Russian analysts such as Yu. V. Tikhonravov argue that the nation holds a special place in the Eastern Hemisphere as a counterbalance to the "globalist" U.S.-led hegemony; their works are now part of the college curriculum approved by the Ministry of Higher Education. Because the West is so often portrayed as materialistic and corrupt, many Eurasianists advocate closer cooperation with China, the Arab world, and Iran while espousing anti-Turkic rhetoric.

Indeed, since the fall of the Soviet Union, Russia has become the major arms supplier for China and India. On a recent trip to New Delhi, Russian representatives signed arms and nuclear deals worth an estimated $3 billion, including cooperation in nuclear and missile areas.

Russia and China are in the process of negotiating a Treaty of Friendship and Cooperation, which they are expected to sign when Chinese President Jiang Zemin visits Moscow in mid-2001. Analysts have suggested that the treaty may have secret appendices outlining the conditions for a common defense, military cooperation in space, cooperation on military technologies, and new weapons sales. Russia is already selling nuclear weapons blueprints, multiple warhead (MIRV) technology, Sukhoi-27 fighter jets, and, most recently, $1 billion worth of A-50 Beriev AWACS early warning planes to China that will make it possible for the People's Liberation Army to coordinate its air, surface, and naval operations in areas like the Taiwan Strait. Russia supports China's claims regarding Taiwan, and China supports Moscow's activities in Chechnya. Finally, both Russia and China have vociferously opposed Washington's plans to deploy an NMD system.

Restoring ties with Europe has become a personal objective for Putin, who has cultivated a friendship with Prime Minister Tony Blair [of Great Britain] and also has carefully strengthened Moscow's ties to Chancellor Gerhardt Schroeder of Germany. As France and Germany have sought to strengthen the European Union and offset European military reliance on the United States, Moscow has begun to express an interest in joining the ESDP [European Security and Defense Policy discussions], which would drive a wedge between Europe and the United States. Russia's offer to construct a common missile defense with the EU may have been made with the same strategic goal in mind. However, Putin, who had suggested in March 2000 that Russia may one day be interested in joining the NATO alliance, later disavowed this possibility.

Russia's increasing activities in the Mediterranean, the Persian Gulf, and the Middle East are causing concern in Washington. Since 1991, Russia has sold Middle Eastern countries $6.9 billion worth of modern weapons, including almost $3 billion in sales to Iran alone. Aided by its multibillion-dollar missile, military technology, and civilian nuclear reactor deals with Russia, this unstable Islamic state is emerging as the predominant military power in the Gulf.

Moscow recently announced that it had annulled a secret memorandum signed by Vice President Al Gore and Prime Minister Victor Chernomyrdin in June 1995, which acknowledged that Russia had sold Iran such conventional arms as submarines, anti-ship missiles, and tanks. The agreement between the two officials made it clear that the United States would do nothing about the arms sales if Moscow promised to cease these activities by 1999. The weapons sales continue. Moreover, the secret agreement may have been in violation of the 1992 Iran-Iraq Arms Nonproliferation Act cosponsored by then-Senator Gore (D-TN), which stipulates that the United States would impose sanctions on Russia if it persisted in selling weapons of this type to Iran or Iraq.

Moscow disclosed that, in summer and fall 2000, it shipped 325 shoulder-launched anti-aircraft SA-16 missiles to Tehran, part of a deal totaling 700 missiles worth $1.75 billion. Because Tehran is known for re-exporting weapons to Islamic radicals in the Middle East, such as the Lebanon-based Hezbollah movement, it is only a matter of time before these latest missiles find their way to Hezbollah terrorists or the Islamic Jihad. U.S. objections over this sale were met with terse advice from Russian Foreign Minister Igor Ivanov:

> The issue is that Russia, when it comes to military cooperation with Iran as well as with other countries, does not consider itself constrained by any special obligations in spheres which are not restricted by international obligations.

Since 1992, Congress has attempted to impose sanctions on countries and companies that contribute to the proliferation of weapons of mass destruction (WMD), especially to rogue states. The provisions of the Arms Export Control Act, the Iran-Iraq Non-Proliferation Act, and the Iran Non-Proliferation Act of 1999 call for imposing sanctions against Russia. However, these sanctions have not worked in Iran or Iraq. Saddam continues to acquire WMD and the technology to deliver them. Moreover, Russia ignored its obligations as a member of the Nuclear Supplier Group Agreement and Missile Technology Control Regime (MTCR) and continued proliferating weapons and weapons technology to Iraq. The Clinton Administration failed to uphold the law and impose the sanctions.

Moscow is also boosting its ties with Iraq to break U.S. domination in the Persian Gulf and to recover some of the Soviet-era Iraqi debt of approximately $7 billion. In violation of the U.N. sanctions against Iraq, Russia began supplying it with high-tech military spare parts, such as gyroscopes for its Scud missiles, and equipment for the production of bacteriological weapons. Its efforts to rebuild the once-strong relationship between Iraq and Moscow include exchanges between the pro-Putin Unity party of Russia and Saddam's Ba'ath party.

Public Support for Putin's Approach

Russia's frustration with America's global preeminence began escalating under former Prime Minister Primakov and has continued escalating since Putin's ascent. An increase in nationalist sentiment and a substantial decrease in support for the United States have been reported by pollsters since 1993. Representative polling by a reliable Russian public opinion institute demonstrates how quickly attitudes about the United States have deteriorated under Putin. In December 1998, 67 percent of those polled characterized their attitude toward America as "very positive" or "basically positive." By May 1999, at the height of the NATO bombardment of Serbia, which Russia opposed, less than a third of respondents subscribed to this view, and the number of those who said their attitude was "very negative" or "generally negative" shot up from 23 percent to 52 percent. The shift is even more dramatic considering that in 1993, according to the United States Information Agency (USIA), 70 percent of Russians felt favorable toward America.

During Kosovo, it should be recalled, Russian officials encouraged the Russian people to demonstrate in front of the U.S. embassy in Moscow. Serbian diplomats provided Moscow State University students (who were bussed to the demonstrations by city authorities) with eggs and tomatoes to throw at the U.S. embassy. In the heat of these demonstrations, a Russian vigilante fired a shoulder-launched missile at the embassy. Clearly, the intention of the government is to increase anti-American sentiments.

An examination of current Russian TV programming and media content demonstrates how anti-American and anti-Western that content has become. Television moderators and reporters covering last November's vote count problems in Florida, for example, expressed glee over the "deep crisis" of the "overrated" American democracy. Such anti-Americanism, rarely heard since the early 1980s, is very troubling to Russia experts and policymakers in the United States. Yet the Clinton Administration did little of substance to counter this trend.

Institutional Support for Putin's Approach

The most disturbing development under Putin is the extent to which Russia's national security and diplomatic institutions attempt to sway public opinion against the United States and its policies. These institutions include not only the Putin administration, but also the Security Council, the foreign and defense ministries, the general staff of the armed forces, and the intelligence services, such as the Foreign Intelligence Service (SVR) and the successor to the KGB secret police, the Federal Security Service (FSB).

For example, during the Kosovo operation, the Russian military accused NATO of preparing a full-scale attack on Russia. It advocated rearmament and war in Chechnya as Russia's response to the NATO operation against Slobodan Milosevic. Marshal Igor Sergeev went so far as to accuse the United States of provoking the war in Chechnya. The commander of the Russian air force, General Anatoly Kornukov, who was responsible for downing a Korean passenger jumbo jet in 1983, recently boasted about a surprise flight made by Russian Su-24 reconnaissance planes over the U.S. aircraft carrier Kitty Hawk. The Russian military has also blamed U.S. and British submarines for the Kursk submarine disaster, despite offers from the United States and other countries to lend assistance in rescuing the crew.

During the 1990s, the FSB arrested environmental activist Alexander Nikitin, military journalist Grigory Pasko, and scientist Vladimir Soifer for treason or other alleged transgressions, such as disclosing serious environmental pollution by the Russian military. This included burying over two dozen burned-out nuclear submarine reactors on the ocean floor without taking any precautions to prevent radiation seepage. The FSB accused Igor Sutyagin, an arms control researcher at the Institute for USA-Canada, of spying for Canada. It prosecuted Radio Liberty journalist Andrey Babitsky, ostensibly for passport violations, and confiscated the passport of Al Decie, a Western assistance worker. Although American businessman Edmond Pope was convicted of espionage in December, Putin later pardoned him. These cases demonstrate the increasing power of the internal security services, while the Yeltsin and Putin administrations did nothing to re-establish the rule of law.

Energy Exports as a Foreign Policy Tool

One of Putin's primary tools in implementing his foreign policy has been energy and commodity exports. For example, Putin has resurrected the Soviet-era plans to build a gas pipeline from the Arctic Yamal peninsula into the heart of Europe through Belarus and Poland, bypassing Ukraine. Such a route will weaken Ukraine by denying Kiev tariff revenue from the pipeline and will prevent unauthorized siphoning off of Russian gas. Russia's natural gas monopoly, Gazprom, is supporting this proposal. Some Russian officials are also demanding that the government seize control of the Ukrainian natural gas distribution network and other industrial enterprises to repay the existing $1.2 billion Ukrainian debt to Russia for past supplies. In addition, the government and Gazprom's subsidiary Itera are behind the interruption in the natural gas supply to Georgia, plunging its capital, Tblisi, into darkness on New Year's Day. Critics believe such interruptions in supply are designed to force Georgia to side with Moscow over such issues as Chechnya and the direction of the pipelines through the Caspian Sea region.

Meanwhile, the energy-hungry EU countries are concerned about the current instability in the Middle East and would like to increase their imports of Russian natural gas. Russia is already planning to sell electricity to Europe and Japan, and possibly to China. But history shows that energy trade is often linked to security cooperation. Political instability or policy differences can threaten energy exports and thereby force the dependent country to mute its concerns. For example, Europe, especially France, is already toning down criticism of Russia's actions in Chechnya. Poland is decreasing its support for Ukraine. Thus, with higher dependency on energy from Russia, the EU may become even less critical of Russia's assertive foreign policies.

Russia is already exporting a large amount of its natural resources and industrial goods to emerging markets in Asia. As economic growth continues in China and the Asia-Pacific region, these markets will likely become more important to Russia's economy than the markets in Europe. China alone offers Russia a large market where it can sell goods ranging from grain to nuclear reactors and AWACS planes, though Beijing cannot reciprocate with investment dollars or new technology. Therefore, while Russia improves its relations with Asian states like China, Korea, and Japan, it will continue to seek U.S. investment.

Putin's Multipolar World View

Even before Vladimir Putin ascended to his country's highest office, as the head of the National Security Council, director of the FSB, and then acting prime minister, he presided over the formulation of four important government documents that articulate Russia's foreign and defense policy. These documents, taken together, explain the new "Putin Doctrine" for Russian national security in the 21st century and demonstrate Moscow's step back to more traditional Russian and Soviet threat assessments. The documents include:

- A Defense Doctrine, published in draft form in October 1999 and reissued by presidential decree on April 21, 2000;

- A National Security Concept unveiled in January 2000;
- The Foreign Policy Concept adopted on July 30, 2000; and
- The Information Security Concept adopted in August 2000.

Following the themes first espoused by former Prime Minister Primakov, these documents decry the emergence of a unipolar world dominated by the United States. They lay claim to a sphere of influence that encompasses most of the Eastern Hemisphere. The National Security Concept, for example, names Europe, the Trans-Caucasus, Central Asia, the Asia-Pacific region, and the Middle East as spheres of influence for Russia. It also names the expanding NATO alliance as a danger to the Russian homeland and condemns the use of force by NATO under U.S. leadership as both a violation of international law and a dangerous security trend.

More important, for the first time since the end of the Cold War, the Kremlin calls the United States a major threat to the Russian state. This represents a radical departure from Yeltsin's foreign policy documents, which proclaimed that Russia has no external enemies and that the main danger to the Russian state stems from such domestic concerns as crime, corruption, and political extremism.

The National Security Doctrine broadly defines threats to the Russian state, including the establishment of foreign military bases in proximity to Russian borders. Not only does it warn against proliferation of weapons of mass destruction and their delivery systems, but it envisages the first use of nuclear weapons by Russia if it is attacked by non-nuclear weapons of mass destruction, such as chemical warheads or biological weapons, or by an overwhelming conventional force. It brands as threatening the weakening of the integrative processes in the Commonwealth of Independent States (CIS). It cautions about claims to Russian territory and warns that conflicts close to Russia-CIS borders could escalate.

In the Foreign Policy Concept, Russia for the first time has made an open claim to the need to dominate its neighbors. The Foreign Policy Concept adopted by presidential decree on June 28, 2000, calls for the establishment of a belt of good neighbors around Russia's perimeter. As "the strongest Eurasian power," Russia asserts in the Concept that "the [U.S.] strategy of unilateral action may destabilize the world, because the use of force represents the basis for international conflict."

The Information Security Concept signed by Putin in August 2000 articulates the view that television, mass media, and the Internet are avenues that threaten Russian security and must therefore be controlled by the state. The document calls upon the Federal Security Service to monitor all e-mail traffic; it also stipulates registration and control of Web sites and all national TV channels. This same strategy was taught in the Soviet-era KGB academies.

These documents reflect the military, KGB, and Communist Party mindset, training, and education of Russia's current national security and foreign policy elites. Each one is also larded with rhetoric about peace and appeals for cooperation from other foreign governments that support international fora such as the United Nations. These appeals are an attempt to offset Russia's conventional military weakness, especially in regions where it currently lacks power projection capabilities. Despite these appeals, each document is an obvious rallying cry to countries that resent America's power and military dominance. Clearly, Russia is seeking international support for its efforts to become an alternative power center to challenge the United States.

A New Chapter in U.S.–Russian Relations

While a more confident and anti-American Russia is emerging under Putin's leadership, this does not mean that the new Bush Administration should fear that a conflict with Moscow is either imminent or necessary. However, it does mean that the United States will need to reformulate its policy approach toward Russia.

Some experts in Russia have suggested a "grand bargain" that balances U.S. acceptance of deeper strategic arms cuts and Russian foreign debt rescheduling with Moscow's acceptance of U.S. deployment of a national missile defense system and a significant reduction in military cooperation with China and Iran. But as Russia's cancellation of the secret Gore-Chernomyrdin deal and the $3 billion arms deal with Tehran signed by the Russian Defense Minister show, it is becoming more difficult to rely on Moscow's promises to curtail proliferation. Moreover, the Kremlin has shown little flexibility on U.S. national missile defense plans, and the economic outlook for Russia's economy hardly justifies debt rescheduling.

In addition to rescheduling parts of its $58 billion sovereign debt to the Paris Club, Russia wants Western help in its effort to accede to the World Trade Organization (WTO) and cooperation on fighting radical Islamic terrorism. Economic growth in Russia would help to make Moscow's policies more trade-friendly and less security-oriented.

The new Bush Administration must design its Russia policy around a core set of priorities: deploying a national missile defense; limiting, to the extent possible, strategic cooperation between China and Russia; preventing Iran from increasing its nuclear weapon and ballistic missile capabilities; containing Saddam Hussein and Iraq; and keeping Eurasian countries from falling exclusively under a Russian sphere of influence.

To this end, President... George W. Bush should offer to meet with Vladimir Putin at a summit to address the issues of concern.... During this summit, the Bush Administration should:

- Pursue Russia's acceptance of the deployment of a national missile defense system for America. The Administration should emphasize that such a system is not aimed at eliminating Russia's potential for deterrence. The system would be designed, first and foremost, to shield the American people against missile attack by rogue states that possess small numbers of weapons or by terrorist groups. Moscow has already expressed an interest in joint development of boost-stage interceptors for theater missile defense. Such cooperation could open the door to Russia's agreement on a U.S. national missile defense system.

Further incentives could include an offer to purchase more of Russia's uranium from its dismantled weapons, to be blended into nuclear reactor fuel at energy-generating facilities to help with the current energy shortages in states like California.

- Establish more stringent nonproliferation and arms trade criteria.The Administration should insist that Russia limit its sales of arms, military, and dual-use (military-civilian) technology to China, cease such sales to rogue states, and severely limit them to countries in conflict, such as India and Pakistan. According to President Putin, Russia must speed up its integration into the Western community; if he is serious, Russia should not be involved in activities that undermine the security of the West. While striving to strengthen existing nonproliferation regimes, such as the MTCR, the United States should work with other countries to develop new export controls for the conventional and strategic arms trade.

- Convince Russia to halt nuclear and ballistic missile cooperation with Iran. The Administration should discuss with Moscow the potential effects of Russia's cooperation with Iran in weapons of mass destruction and convince it to stop, in exchange for a deal in a lucrative high-tech area such as satellite launches or for purchasing more highly enriched Russian uranium from dismantled nuclear weapons. In 1993, the United States signed a 20-year, $11 billion deal to purchase 500 tons of Russian weapons-grade uranium to use as fuel in civilian reactors. As compensation for Russia's verifiable cessation of nuclear and missile cooperation with Iran, Washington could also relax or suspend antidumping measures applied to such Russian imports as certain types of steel. A time frame should be established for the cessation of all proliferation and arms cooperation with Tehran.

- Seek cooperation in terminating Iraq's missile and weapons programs and Russian support for Saddam Hussein at the United Nations. The Russian Foreign Ministry and U.N. representatives have defended Saddam and his rogue regime and sought to protect Iraq from further U.N. sanctions. Since kicking U.N. weapons inspectors out of Iraq in 1998, Saddam has succeeded in rebuilding Iraq's conventional military capabilities and, it is feared, has restarted its ballistic missile and nuclear weapons programs. Moscow should work with the other Security Council members to see that U.N. weapons inspectors return to Iraq. The Kremlin should cease calling for the lifting of the sanctions. Moscow should use its influence with Iraq to insist that its resistance to inspections and violations of the U.N. sanctions stop. In exchange for intelligence-sharing about Saddam's WMD programs, the Bush Administration should offer Moscow incentives, such as preferential economic treatment in Iraq after Saddam is deposed. The United States should also increase pressure on Moscow to ensure that arms sold by Russia to other countries do not wind up in Iraq.

If Russia refuses, the Administration should ensure that the sanctions embodied in U.S. law are imposed. This includes Russian oil companies violating the U.N. sanctions by selling Iraqi oil or investing in Iraq. Congress should examine the application of sanctions against such companies as they seek U.S. financing through initial public offerings and American Depository Rights (ADRs) in U.S. capital markets. These are efficient steps that would punish companies that are boosting Saddam's arsenals and replenishing his treasury to their own gain. Such sanctions would not, however, affect America's ability to export food to Iran or Iraq or limit non-military trade relations.

- Seek limits on Russia's cooperation with China. China is not only aggressively remodernizing its military, but also has been proliferating weapons and technology to rogue regimes that threaten security in Eurasia and worldwide. The Russian military-industrial complex allowed China almost unlimited access to Soviet-era and post-Soviet arsenals. Recent reports of a forthcoming Treaty of Friendship and Cooperation between Moscow and Beijing deeply concern many American policymakers. However, Russian politicians and experts increasingly are recognizing the potential threat to Russia from a rising militaristic China. The United States and Russia should open discussions to highlight potential threats from China to both countries.

- Express support for Russia's accession to the WTO. Russia is taking a slow approach to WTO accession. However, President Putin has proclaimed Russia's integration into international economic flows and liberalization of the Russian economy as paramount goals. Minister of Economic Development German Gref announced that Russia wants first to join the WTO and then to hold talks on economic liberalization. Such an approach is a negotiating tactic that will slow the process of trade liberalization and delay accession to the WTO. The Bush Administration should offer Moscow technical support both in developing policy measures, laws, and regulations that meet WTO standards and in developing a specific strategy to achieve WTO accession.

The Bush Administration must firmly defend America's national security interests, but it should also send a signal to Russia's elites that it seeks better relations and a growing dialogue with the people of Russia about freedom, economic opportunity, and prosperity. To facilitate this dialogue, the Administration should encourage Congress and non-government organizations to expand exchange programs with the Russians and the countries in Eurasia, similar to a program for Russian political elites hosted by the Library of Congress (though the selection of participants in that program could be improved). Academic exchanges, especially in the fields of economics, public administration, law, and business, should be expanded. Students from Russia who study in the United States become its best ambassadors when they return to their homeland. The United States should also consider military-to-military and civilian expert exchanges where issues of doctrine, strategy, and peacekeeping can be discussed.

Conclusion

The new U.S. Administration faces a more determined, disciplined, and organized Russian government led by an energetic president: a former Soviet intelligence officer and a tough Kremlin insider who is intent on maximizing Russia's international prestige. The Bush Administration must do its homework on Russia and then offer to host a summit with President Vladimir Putin to develop important policies, especially on missile defense, proliferation, regional security, Russia's foreign debt, and other economic issues. Most important, Washington should stand firm on matters of national security and national interest.

Anatol Lieven

 **NO**

Against Russophobia

Ever since the Cold War ended, Western officials and commentators have been telling the Russians how they need to grow out of their Cold War attitudes toward the West and Western institutions, and learn to see things in a "modern" and "normal" way. And there is a good deal of truth in this. At the same time, it would have been good if we had subjected our own inherited attitudes toward Russia to a more rigorous scrutiny. For like any other inherited hatred, blind, dogmatic hostility toward Russia leads to bad policies, bad journalism, and the corruption of honest debate—and there is all too much of this hatred in Western portrayals of and comments on Russia.

From this point of view, an analysis of Russophobia has implications that go far beyond Russia. Much of the U.S. foreign policy debate, especially on the Republican side, is structured around the belief that American policy should be rooted in a robust defense of national interest—and this is probably also the belief of most ordinary Americans. However, this straightforward view coexists with another, equally widespread, view that dominates the media. It is, in Secretary of State Madeleine Albright's words, that "the United States stands taller than other nations, and therefore sees further." The unspoken assumption here is that America is not only wise but also objective, at least in its perceptions: that U.S. policy is influenced by values, but never by national prejudices. The assumption behind much American (and Western) reporting of foreign conflicts is that the writer is morally engaged but ethnically uncommitted and able to turn a benign, all-seeing eye from above on the squabbles of humanity.

It is impossible to exaggerate how irritating this attitude is elsewhere in the world, or how misleading and dangerous it is for Western audiences who believe it. Not only does it contribute to mistaken policies, but it renders both policymakers and ordinary citizens incapable of understanding the opposition of other nations to those policies. Concerning the Middle East, it seems likely that most Americans genuinely believe that the United States is a neutral and objective broker in relations between Israelis and Palestinians—which can only appear to an Arab as an almost fantastically bad joke. This belief makes it much more difficult for Americans to comprehend the reasons for Palestinian and Arab fury at both the United States and Israel. It encourages a Western interpretation of this anger as the manipulation of sheep-like masses by elites. At worst, it can encourage a kind of racism, in which certain nations are classed as irrationally, irredeemably savage and wicked.

Concerning Russia, the main thrust of the official Western rhetoric with respect to the enlargement of NATO [North Atlantic Treaty Organization], and Russia's response, has been that the alliance is no longer a Cold War organization or a threat to Russia, that NATO enlargement has nothing to do with Russia, that Russia should welcome enlargement, and that Russian opposition is not merely groundless but foolish and irrational. It is of course true that Russian fears of NATO expansion have been exaggerated, and some of the rhetoric has been wild. Still, given the attitudes toward Russia reflected in much of the Western media (especially among the many supporters of NATO enlargement), a Russian would have to be a moron or a traitor to approve the expansion of NATO without demanding guarantees of Russian interests and security.

This is not to deny that there has been a great deal to condemn in many aspects of Russian behavior over the past decade, the war in Chechnya being the most ghastly example. But justifiable Western criticism has all too often been marred by attacks that have been hysterical and one-sided, and it has taken too little account of the genuine problems and threats with which Russians have had to struggle. This has been especially true of comment on the latest Chechen war, which began in the summer of 1999.

Outworn Stereotypes

Western Russophobia has various roots. One shoot is the continuing influence of what the political scientist Michael Mandelbaum has called "residual elites": groups and individuals who rose to prominence during the Cold War and have lacked the flexibility to adapt to a new reality. To these can be added others who have sought to carve out careers by advocating the expansion of U.S. influence into the lands of the former Soviet Union, in direct competition with Russia. Then there are various ethnic lobbies, whose members hate and distrust Russia for historical reasons and whose sole remaining raison d'être is to urge an anti-Russian geopolitical agenda. Finally, there are those individuals who need a great enemy, whether from some collective interest or out of personal psychological need.

Much of the intellectual basis for, and even the specific phraseology of, Russophobia was put forward in Britain in the nineteenth century, growing out of its rivalry with the Russian Empire. Given Britain's own record of imperial aggression and suppression of national revolt (in Ireland, let alone in India or Africa), the argument from the British side was a notable example of the kettle calling the pot black. Many contemporary Russophobe references to Russian expansionism are almost word-for-word repetitions of nineteenth-century British propaganda (though many pre-1917 Russians were almost as bad, weeping copious crocodile tears over Britain's defeat of the Boers shortly before Russia itself crushed Polish aspirations for the fourth time in a hundred years).

When it comes to Western images of other nations and races, there has been an effort in recent decades to move from hostile nineteenth-century stereotypes, especially when linked to "essentialist" historical and even quasi-racist stereotypes about the allegedly unchanging nature and irredeemable wickedness of certain peoples (though it seems that this enlightened attitude does not apply to widespread American attitudes toward Arabs).

If outworn stereotypes persist in the case of Russia, it is not only because of Cold War hostility toward the Soviet Union (identified crudely and unthinkingly with "Russia," although this was a gross oversimplification). It is also the legacy of Soviet and Russian studies within Western academe. Its practitioners were often deeply ideological (whether to the right or left) and closely linked to Western policy debates and to the Western intelligence and diplomatic communities. On the right, there was a tendency, exemplified by the Harvard historian Richard Pipes, to see Soviet communism as a uniquely Russian product, produced and prefigured by a millennium of Russian history. In a 1996 article, Professor Pipes wrote of an apparently fixed and unchanging "Russian political culture" leading both to the adoption of the Leninist form of Marxism in 1917 and to the problems of Russian democracy in 1996—as if this culture had not changed in the past 80 years, and as if the vote of ordinary Russians for the Communists in 1996 was motivated by the same passions that possessed Lenin's Red Guards. Even after the Soviet collapse, this tendency has persisted, and developments in post-Soviet Russia are seen as a seamless continuation of specifically Soviet and tsarist patterns—patterns which, it goes without saying, are also specifically and uniquely wicked.

To be sure, many of the crimes of communism in Russia and in the Soviet bloc *were* uniquely wicked. But the behavior of the tsarist empire and the dissolution of its Soviet version in the 1990s can only be validly judged in the context of European and North American imperialism, decolonization, and neo-colonialism. Pre-1917 imperial Russia's expansionism was contemporaneous with that of Spain, France, Holland, Belgium, Britain, and the United States. As far as the Soviet Union's disintegration is concerned, Russophobes cannot have it both ways. If the Soviet Union was to a considerable extent a Russian empire, then the legitimate context for the study of its disintegration is the retreat of other empires and their attempts to create post- or neo-colonial systems. In this context—particularly bearing in mind France's retreat from its Asian and African empire—the notion that the Soviet/Russian decolonization process has been uniquely savage becomes absurd. Such comparisons are essential in attempting to determine what has been specifically Soviet, or specifically Russian, about this process, and what reflects wider historical realities.

A Historicist Approach

These comparisons are rarely made. References to allegedly unique and unchanging historical patterns in Russian behavior are an ongoing trope of much of Western journalistic and academic comment. Take for example a recent statement by Henry Kissinger: "For four centuries, imperialism has been Russia's basic foreign policy as it has expanded from the region around Moscow to the shores of the Pacific, the gates of the Middle East and the center of Europe, relentlessly subjugating weaker neighbors and seeking to overawe those not under its direct control." This not only implies that expansionism was uniquely Russian but that it represents an unchangeable pattern. Yet for virtually this entire period, the same remark could have been made about the British, the French, or (within North and Central America at least) the United States. It is also extremely odd that in 1989–93, "Russia" conducted what was probably the greatest, and most bloodless imperial retreats in history and that this has simply vanished from Kissinger's account. At worst, such attitudes can approach a kind of racism, as in the conservative political commentator George Will's statement that "expansionism is in the Russians' DNA."

Another example of such thinking is former national security adviser Zbigniew Brzezinski's statement that "[the Russians] have denied many, many times now that they have committed atrocities [in Chechnya]. . . . In 1941, they killed 15,000 Polish prisoners, officers in Katyn, and they denied that for 50 years." In his account, "the Russians" as a collectivity are fully responsible for the crimes committed by the Soviet Union under the Communist dictatorship of Joseph Stalin—an ethnic Georgian who at the time of the massacre [of some 4,000 Polish officers in 1940] at Katyn was also responsible for murdering or imprisoning millions of ethnic Russians who were accused of hostility toward communism or toward Stalin himself. This Stalinist past is then made part of a seamless continuity of "Russian" behavior, running unchanged through the years since Stalin's death. The condemnation of Stalinism by Nikita Khrushchev, the reforms of Mikhail Gorbachev, the peaceful Soviet withdrawal from Poland, the Russian recognition of the independence of the other Soviet republics—all this is ignored.

As Brzezinski's statement illustrates, this essentialist attitude toward Russia has played a major part in the reporting of and commentary on, the latest Chechen war. Take, for example, a recent editorial in the *Los Angeles Times*: "Russians also fight brutally because that is part of the Russian military ethos, a tradition of total war fought with every means and without moral restraints." Unlike, of course, the exquisite care for civilian lives displayed by the French and American air forces during the wars in Indo-China, Korea, and Algeria, the strict adherence to legality in the treatment of prisoners, and so on. The editorial read as if the wars against guerrillas and partisans involving Western powers had been wiped from the record. . . .

This historicist approach toward Russia also reflects the decline of history as an area of study, an ignorance of history on the part of international relations scholars, and the unwillingness of too many historians themselves to step beyond their own narrow fields. The attitudes it reveals also spring from a widespread feeling that Russophobia is somehow legitimized by the past Western struggle against Communist totalitarianism, a struggle I strongly supported. This is deeply mistaken. With communism dead as a world ideology, dealing with Russia—or China for that matter—has become the much more familiar, historically commonplace question of dealing with nations and states, which we on occasion may have to oppose and condemn, but whose behavior is governed by the same interests and patterns that historically have influenced the behavior of our own countries. In fact, both the policy and the statements of Russian generals with respect to Chechnya not only recall those of French generals during the Algerian War of Independence (1954–62), but of Turkish generals during the recent war against the Kurdish PKK [Kurdish Workers Party]: the ruthless prosecution of the war (including in the Turkish case major attacks on PKK bases in Iraq); a refusal to negotiate with the enemy; no role whatsoever for international organizations. None of this is, or ever was, praiseworthy, but "communism" plays no role in it.

I might add that many old hard-line Cold Warriors-turned-Russophobes like Brzezinski and Kissinger have in any case rendered their pretensions to anticommunist morality dubious by the warmth with which they embrace the Chinese state, as well as their wooing of hard-line ex-Communist dictators in Central Asia and elsewhere.

Architectures of Hatred

Russophobia today is therefore rooted not in ideological differences but in national hatred of a kind that is sadly too common. In these architectures of hatred, selected or invented historical "facts" about the "enemy" nation, its culture, and its racial nature are taken out of context and slotted into prearranged intellectual structures to arraign the unchanging wickedness of the other side. Meanwhile, any counterarguments, or memories of the crimes of one's own are suppressed. This is no more legitimate when directed by Russophobes against Russia than when it is directed by Serb, Greek, or Armenian chauvinists against Turkey, Arabs against Jews, or Jews against Arabs.

The most worrying aspect of Western Russophobia is that it demonstrates the capacity of too many Western journalists and intellectuals to betray their own professed standards and behave like Victorian jingoists or Balkan nationalists when their own national loyalties and hatreds are involved. And these tendencies in turn serve wider needs. Overall, we are living in an exceptionally benign period in human history so far as our own interests are concerned. Yet one cannot live in Washington without becoming aware of the desperate need of certain members of Western elites for new enemies, or resuscitated old ones. This is certainly not the wish of most Americans—nor of any other Westerners —and it is dangerous. For of one thing we can be sure: a country that is seen to need enemies will sooner or later find them everywhere.

As an antidote, Western journalists and commentators writing on the Chechen wars might read Alistair Horne's *A Savage War of Peace* (about the French war in Algeria), Max Hastings's *Korean War* (especially the passages dealing with the capture of Seoul in 1950 and the U.S. air campaign), any serious book on the U.S. war in Vietnam or French policies in Africa, or more general works like V. G. Kiernan's *Colonial Empires and Armies.* With regard to Russian crimes in Chechnya, they could also read some of the remarks on the inherent cruelty of urban warfare by Western officers in journals like the *Marine Corps Gazette* and *Parameters.* Neither Horne nor Hastings (both patriotic conservatives) were "soft on communism"; nor are most military writers "soft on Russia." They are true professionals with a commitment to present the facts, however uncomfortable—and they have the moral courage to do so. Concerning the pre-1917 Russian Empire in the context of European imperial expansion in general, I could also recommend (by way of a family advertisement and to reveal my own intellectual influences) my brother Dominic Lieven's recent book, *Empire: The Russian Empire and Its Rivals.*

A familiar counterargument to this approach is that Western colonial and neo-colonial crimes are long past, and that we have atoned for them. To this there are a number of responses, the first of which is that some allowance has to be made for the fact that Russia only emerged from Communist isolation about ten years ago, whereas at the time of their crimes the Western colonial powers were democracies and longstanding members of the "free world." And while some have excused the crimes of other former communist states on the nature of the system they have abjured, such leniency has not been shown toward Russia.

Then there is geography. Western powers escaped involvement in ex-colonial conflicts by putting the sea between themselves and their former colonies. Britain, for example, was not directly affected by wars in any former colonies except Ireland, because they occurred at a distance. Russia thought it was making a similar break when it withdrew from Chechnya in 1996—but in its case of course there was no ocean in between. If France had had a land border with Algeria, the war there might well have gone on far longer than it did.

I believe that the Russian invasion of Chechnya in October 1999 was a terrible mistake, and that the government in Moscow ought to have done everything in its power to find other ways of dealing with the Chechen threat. At the same time, any honest account must recognize that forces based in Chechnya had carried out attacks on Russia that would have provoked most other states in the world—including the United States—to respond forcefully. How would France have reacted if the French withdrawal from Algeria had been immediately followed by Algerian raids into France?

And then there is the question of the brutal way in which the Russians conducted the war, especially the destruction of [the Chechen capital] Grozny. Since the early 1970s, it has been difficult to say whether the Western conduct of antipartisan wars or urban operations has improved because, as a result of Vietnam, Americans have taken enormous care to avoid involvement in such wars—and once again, geography has given the United States that option. But when American soldiers became involved in a lethal urban fight in Mogadishu [Somalia] in 1994, the indiscriminate way in which retaliatory firepower was used meant that Somali casualties (the great majority of them civilian) outnumbered U.S. casualties by between twenty-five and fifty to one. In other words, to some extent the degree of carnage in Chechnya reflects not inherent and historical Russian brutality, but the nature of urban warfare.

That the Russians have been extremely brutal in Chechnya is beyond question—but explanations for this should be sought less in Russian history than in the common roots that produced U.S. atrocities in Vietnam—a demoralized army under attack from hidden enemies operating from within the civilian population. I have no doubt that even in Chechnya, Western troops would have behaved much better than the Russians. But then again, the West's soldiers come from proud, well-paid services, and are honored and supported by their societies. If American, French, or British troops had undergone the treatment by their own state that Russian soldiers suffered in the 1990s (notably the catastrophic decline in spending on the armed forces, and especially on military pay), and were then thrown into a bloody partisan war, one would not like to answer for their behavior.

Moreover, especially with regard to the French and their sphere of influence in Africa, it is not true that Western crimes are necessarily long in the past. If one examines French "sphere-of-influence" policies toward Rwanda before and during the 1994 genocide (as analyzed by Gerard Prunier, Philip Gourevitch, and others), one finds a record uglier than anything Russia has done since 1991 beyond its own borders. Why should Russians listen to French lectures? In France, leading figures deeply implicated in the Algerian debacle— like former president François Mitterrand—continued to play leading roles until their deaths. In both Algeria and Vietnam (and in British campaigns such as that against the Mau Mau), the punishments meted out to Western officers accused of atrocities were either derisory or nonexistent. Is this of no relevance to present demands that Russia punish its soldiers for atrocities in Chechnya?

To draw these parallels in no way justifies Russian crimes in Chechnya or elsewhere—and I firmly believe that the Russian state should try to punish some of the officers directly responsible for crimes in Chechnya—both as a matter of justice and morality, and as a means of reimposing order on what too often resembles an armed rabble more than a modern organized force. I also believe, however, that Western pressure for this would be better phrased in the terms used by President Clinton during a visit to Turkey. When he criticized the Turkish government and military for their policies toward the Kurds, he made it clear that he was doing so not from a position of moral superiority but as the representative of a country which itself had been guilty of racism and ethnic suppression.

This I believe is a more honorable and effective way of making the point. In contrast, I would condemn the statements of certain German and Belgian politicians who oppose Turkish membership in the European Union—not for economic reasons or because of particular actions by contemporary Turkish governments, but because of supposedly innate, unchanging Turkish national features such as adherence to a negatively stereotyped Islam.

Rejecting Bigotry

Rejecting this sort of bigotry with regard to Russia, and insisting on proper balance and use of evidence, is what has led me to the extremely unwelcome position of appearing to defend some aspects of Russian policy in the Caucasus—not because I wish to defend Russian crimes (which have been legion) but because I cannot accept that Russia should be judged by utterly different standards than those applied to other countries.

The crimes of a General Massu against Algerian civilians in the 1950s do not justify the crimes of a General Kvashnin in Chechnya, any more than the crimes of a General Kitchener against South Africans during the Boer War jus-tified those of Massu. Nor do French sphere-of-influence policies in Africa in themselves justify similar Russian policies in its "Near Abroad." In fact, if the French (for example) who harangue Russia on its sins would make some refer-ence to their country's own past crimes, it would actually make their arguments stronger. Then, one could have a rational argument with a Russian about his-torical, ethnic, political, and geographical similarities *and* differences between, say, Algeria and Chechnya, and about what are Russian crimes, what is truly in Russia's interest, and how Russia should reasonably be expected to handle Chechnya.

Such a comparative approach would eliminate the essentialist, or chauvin-ist/historicist/racist element in critiques of Russia. It would allow an analysis based on common moral standards and, equally important, common standards of evidence and logic in the reporting and analysis of Chechnya and other is-sues involving Russia. This, in turn, would permit a policy toward Russia based on reason and Western interest, not on bigotry, hysteria, and nationalist lobbies.

An example of how blind hostility toward Russia—and the absence of any comparison to other postcolonial situations—can warp Western reporting may be seen in the following passage from the *Economist* of last September: "Russia may be using still dodgier tactics elsewhere. Uzbekistan, an autocratically run and independent-minded country in Central Asia, is facing a mysterious Islamic insurgency. Its president, Islam Karimov, said crossly this week that Russia was exaggerating the threat, and was trying to intimidate his country into accepting Russian bases." As Sen. Daniel Patrick Moynihan once said, "Everyone is enti-tled to his own opinion, but not his own facts." I do not know of a single shred of evidence or the testimony of a single reputable expert to support this insin-uation, which is in any case counterintuitive, given the Islamic Movement of Uzbekistan's links to Russia's most bitter enemies. It is a passage reminiscent of the baroque Russian conspiracy theories suggesting, among other things, that the CIA is actually behind the terrorist Osama bin Laden.

Instead, we would do better to listen to Owen Harries, editor of the *Na-tional Interest*, a conservative who was a tough anticommunist and is certainly no Russophile:

> During the Cold War, a struggle against what was truly an evil empire, there was some justification in maintaining that similar behavior by Washing-ton and Moscow should be judged differently, because the intrinsic moral character of the two actors was so different. But that was due less to the unique virtues of the United States than to the special vileness of the So-viet Union, and even then applying double standards was a tricky business, easily abused. In the more mundane world of today there is no justification for applying one standard to the rest of the world and another to America. Not only does insistence on double standards seem hypocritical to oth-ers, thereby diminishing American credibility and prestige, but even more seriously, it makes it impossible to think sensibly and coherently about in-ternational affairs. And that is a fatal drawback for an indispensable nation.

Hatred of Soviet communism helped take me to Afghanistan in 1988 as a journalist covering the war from the side of the anti-Soviet resistance, and then to the Baltic States and the Caucasus in 1990. In the 1970s and 1980s, I was prepared to justify nasty Western crimes as a regrettable part of the struggle against communism. But I never pretended these crimes did not occur, or that the reasons for them did not include a good measure of crude traditional national power politics.

The Cold War was a profoundly necessary struggle, but it was also one in which Western morality suffered and Western soldiers on occasion behaved badly. Westerners greeted their qualified but peaceful victory with overwhelming joy and relief. Ten years after the end of the Cold War, it is time to liberate ourselves from Cold War attitudes and to remember that whether as journalists or academics, our first duty is not to spread propaganda but to hold to the highest professional standards.

POSTSCRIPT

Is Russia Likely to Become an Antagonistic Power?

The debate over Russia's future is not a matter of idle speculation. There are two very real policy considerations. The first involves the fact that the direction Russia takes in the future is likely to have important consequences for the world. Both the right and left wings of Russian politics favor a much more aggressive foreign policy. Under President Yeltsin the Russian government sometimes strongly criticized such U.S.-favored actions as the expansion of the North Atlantic Treaty Organization's (NATO's) intervention in Kosovo, but many say that Moscow confined itself to rhetoric and did little or nothing to try to block U.S. preferences. For an analysis of Russia's conditions in the 1990s and U.S. policy, read Stephen F. Cohen, *Failed Crusade: America and the Tragedy of Post-Communist Russia* (W. W. Norton, 2000).

Many believe there is still little Russia can do, but its government has gotten somewhat more assertive. Russia strongly opposed the alliance's air raids on Yugoslavia during the Kosovo crisis in 1999, and Putin criticized the air war, saying that NATO "sometimes ignores international opinion and international agreements when it makes its decisions." Putin has also spoken out strongly against any further NATO expansion in the direction of Russia and against the plans of the administration of President George W. Bush to abrogate the Anti-Ballistic Missile Treaty and to build a national missile defense system. Putin has also moved to create better relations with potential partners. In particular, Moscow and Beijing have worked to settle border disputes and other outstanding differences and to forge new areas of cooperation, including the sale of Russian weapons systems to China.

There are also doubts about whether or not democracy can survive in a country that is in such poor condition and that has no democratic tradition. Also, the collapse of democracy in Russia might mean that tensions between it and the Western democracies might increase. On this matter, read Harry Eckstein et al., eds., *Can Democracy Take Root in Post-Soviet Russia? Explorations in State-Society Relations* (Rowman & Littlefield, 1998).

With regard to policy differences, the NATO expansion can be examined by reading Hall Gardner, *Dangerous Crossroads: Europe, Russia, and the Future of NATO* (Greenwood, 1997). The topic of missile defense and Russia's views are covered by Bruce Blair in "The Impact of National Missile Defense on Russia and Nuclear Security," on the Center for Defense Information Internet site at http://www.cdi.org/dm/2000/issue8/nmdrussia.html. For a pessimistic view on the future, see Eric Shiraev and V. M. Zubok, *Anti-Americanism in Russia: From Stalin to Putin* (St. Martin's Press, 2000).

ISSUE 6

Is China an Expansionist Power?

YES: Aaron L. Friedberg, from "The Struggle for Mastery in Asia," *Commentary* (November 2000)

NO: Nicholas Berry, from "Is China an Aggressive Power?" *The Defense Monitor* (vol. 29, no. 9, 2000)

ISSUE SUMMARY

YES: Professor of politics Aaron L. Friedberg depicts China as wanting to become the dominant power in Asia, replacing the United States as the preeminent power in the region.

NO: Nicholas Berry, a senior analyst at the Center for Defense Information in Washington, D.C., contends that China will not seek regional hegemony and that Americans who see China as the new imperialist power need to review the historical record.

China has a history as one of the oldest, most sophisticated, and most powerful countries (and empires) in the world. Four thousand years ago, under the semi-legendary Emperor Yu of the Hsia dynasty, the Chinese built irrigation channels, domesticated animals, engaged in cultivation, and established a written language. Through 14 Chinese dynasties—from the Hsia dynasty (1994–1523 B.C.) to the Manchu dynasty (1644–1911)—China built a civilization marked by great culture, engineering feats, and other advances.

On the other side of the globe, Europe languished amid the Dark Ages. Then, as the world moved into the second Christian millennium, Europe began to revive. Even though the West and East still had scant contact, the balance of power between the two had begun to shift by the 1500s. In search of spices and other treasures, European traders increasingly sailed to Asia, and they were quickly followed by European soldiers.

By the 1800s outside powers came increasingly to dominate a decaying China. Over the next eight decades, China underwent what was to the Chinese a period of humiliation. Huge tracts of their territory were occupied by other countries. During the Boxer Rebellion (1898–1900), Chinese nationalists tried to expel the foreigners. The Chinese forces were defeated by an international coalition that included American troops. The moribund imperial dynasty fell in 1911 and was replaced by a republic headed by Sun Yat-sen.

Sun's government marked the beginning of China's change from decline to growth, but Sun died in 1916, and a struggle for power among various factions led to the establishment of a central government under Nationalist Chinese leader Chiang Kai-shek. Although Chiang's government proved corrupt and ineffective in many ways, it did largely consolidate power and moved to edge foreign influences out of China. That trend became even stronger in 1949 when Chiang's government fell to the Communists of Mao Zedong.

For two decades, many in the West were caught up in the psychology of the cold war and perceived China to be part of the communist threat. Whatever the U.S. ideological view, however, by the late 1960s China had gained enough strength and showed enough independence from the Soviet Union that even the coldest warrior had to see that China was a rising power in its own right. This led to important shifts in U.S. policy and a normalization of relations that began with President Richard Nixon's visit to China in 1972. Relations improved even more after Chairman Mao Zedong died in 1976. The waning of the cold war further persuaded both powers to seek better relations.

Other changes occurred within China. After some turmoil following the death of Mao, the Chinese government moved to moderate the impact of communist ideology on China's economic policy. Greater economic ties with the industrialized West were sought. China moved slowly to establish limited capitalism to improve economic performance. China's economy is now rapidly expanding and stands as one of the largest in the world. The view of Americans toward China steadily improved during the 1980s.

The world was shocked in May 1989 when Chinese troops opened fire on antigovernment demonstrators in the giant Tiananmen Square in Beijing. It became clear that the so-called liberalization of China extended to economic but not political matters.

During the 1990s American investment in and trade with China grew rapidly, and the two countries cooperated (or at least did not oppose one another) on numerous diplomatic fronts. Yet there were also many sore points. China's human rights record was one of them. On other fronts, the United States accused China of supplying nuclear weapons and missile technology to Pakistan and a number of other countries. Economic disputes led the United States to block China's admission to the World Trade Organization. Other disputes have regularly soured relations.

The rise and fall and rise of China's power and the ambiguity that the United States feels toward China set the stage for this debate. In the following selection, Aaron L. Friedberg argues that China has begun to contest the United States for hegemony in Asia and that U.S. willingness to support China's economic and technological development, particularly by supplying advanced technologies to China, is a major stategic blunder. In the second selection, Nicholas Berry disagrees. He takes the position that China is mostly a status-quo power that will not seek an empire.

Aaron L. Friedberg

The Struggle for Mastery in Asia

O ver the course of the next several decades there is a good chance that the United States will find itself engaged in an open and intense geopolitical rivalry with the People's Republic of China (PRC). Such an outcome is not inevitable; few things in international politics are. But there are strong reasons to believe that it is at the very least plausible, and even quite likely. Indeed, there are reasons to believe it is already under way.

In what follows, my aim is to consider what such a Sino-American rivalry might look like, and how it could unfold. In doing so, I make three basic assumptions. The first is that, as a nation-state, China will continue to hang together—that, however dramatically its economy and political system may change over the next several decades, they will not collapse. My second assumption is that, in the words of a recent U.S. Defense Department report, China "wants to become the preeminent Asian power," which necessarily means that it will seek ultimately to displace the United States as the preponderant power in the region. Third, I assume that the United States, while seeking to satisfy China's ambitions by at least to some degree acceding to its wishes, will not be willing to abandon its own present position of preponderance in Asia or to surrender pride of place to China. To permit a potentially hostile power to dominate East Asia would not only be out of line with current U.S. policy, it would also mark a deviation from the fundamental pattern of American grand strategy since at least the latter part of the 19th century.

The combination of growing Chinese power, China's effort to expand its influence, and the unwillingness of the United States entirely to give way before it are the necessary preconditions of a "struggle for mastery" in Asia (to adopt a phrase from the British historian A.J.P. Taylor). How, then, might that struggle arise?

The Sino-American relationship today contains a mix of cooperative and competitive elements. The two countries trade with each other, American businesses invest considerable sums in China, and many Chinese students come to study in the United States. Beijing and Washington engage in sporadic military-to-military dialogues and ongoing discussions of various regional and global issues, including the future of the Korean peninsula and the proliferation of ballistic missiles and weapons of mass destruction. At the same time, however, the U.S. and China have strong disagreements on a variety of matters, human rights and the Taiwan question being foremost among them. And in recent years the two sides have begun to regard each other as potential military rivals, although both are reluctant to acknowledge this openly.

It is precisely this mix of cooperative and competitive elements that may shift sharply in the competitive direction. In the new configuration of things, China and the United States would most likely continue some form of economic relationship, they would not be openly at war with one another, and they would maintain diplomatic ties. But flows of trade and investment would increasingly be distorted by strategic considerations, the two powers would be engaged in a much more open military competition—designing, deploying, and training their forces with an eye toward possible conflict—and this military rivalry would be accompanied by a political contest waged throughout the Asia-Pacific region and perhaps beyond.

Any number of pathways could lead from the present to this imagined future. Thus, a single catalytic event, such as a showdown over Taiwan, especially if it entailed a significant loss of life on either side, could transform the U.S.-China relationship virtually overnight. Whichever side prevailed, the loser would look for ways to exact revenge, and each power would likely redouble its efforts to strengthen its military and diplomatic postures in Asia and undermine those of its rival. Or there could be a gradual deterioration in relations, an accumulation of lesser disputes and failed efforts to resolve them that would lead the United States and China to become increasingly suspicious and hostile. Or there might be some combination of these trends—say, a period of gradual deterioration punctuated by one or a series of crises (like the one that followed the accidental American bombing of the Chinese embassy in Yugoslavia in the spring of 1999), no one of which might seem in itself to be of overwhelming importance but which, taken together, could culminate in a much more contentious relationship.

Regardless of how it arose, an intensified Sino-American rivalry would likely manifest itself in different spheres and along different dimensions. Let me take these in order, beginning with the economic.

II

Ever since it began market reforms in the late1970's, the PRC has become heavily dependent for its continued well-being on the outside world, and, in particular, on the United States. Without heavy inflows of American capital and technology, and without access to the huge U.S. market, China would not have been able to progress as far and as fast as it has. Whether or not the United States could have used its position of relative economic advantage for strategic purposes during this period, the fact is that, for the most part, it did not try. Despite some efforts in the late 1980's and early 1990's to punish China for violations of human rights and arms proliferation, U.S. economic pressure was half-hearted and largely ineffectual. By the mid-1990's, the United States was lifting most sanctions, loosening or abandoning most controls on dual-use technology exports to China, and moving to grant it status as a normal trading partner.

It did so based largely on the belief that trade leads to peace. Mutual economic exchange is assumed to forge a shared interest in good relations, and a powerful disincentive to conflict. According to advocates of "engagement" with the PRC, international trade and investment will fuel economic growth, economic growth will speed democratization, and a democratic China will be far less likely to use force or threats against other democracies, including the United States.

It is certainly possible that, if it continues to grow richer, China will also become, from the American perspective, more benign. But it is also conceivable that this may not happen. If it does not, the United States will be faced with a challenge with which it has not had to cope in over a century: a strategic rival that is economically and technologically dynamic, deeply engaged in the world economy, and whose total output may come eventually to approach America's own.

Will an era of more openly competitive relations be marked by renewed U.S. efforts to exert economic leverage on China? The answer will depend a great deal on how such an era begins. A sudden, severe crisis could galvanize American domestic opinion, overwhelm the objections of business groups and others with a strong vested interest in continued commercial contacts, and lead to the imposition of near-total restrictions on imports, exports, and capital and technology flows. But if the deterioration is gradual, a sufficient political consensus may not exist in the United States to support even limited sanctions. To the contrary, it is precisely when relations falter that arguments for keeping trade on an even keel will be advanced most strenuously.

As time passes, China will probably become even less susceptible to American economic pressure than it is today. Chinese exports to the United States may be large, but even now they are greatly overshadowed by China's exports to its Asian neighbors. And as important as the U.S. is as a source of capital, it now comes in only third among the five largest providers of direct foreign investment to China; the other four (Hong Kong, which serves as a conduit for Taiwanese investment on the mainland, Japan, Singapore, and South Korea) are all Asian players. In the future, the Chinese government will have a strong strategic incentive to encourage and expand such diversification, above all in order to lessen excessive dependence on the United States.

In the long run, China will become relatively less reliant not only on the United States but on the outside world generally. Rising incomes will mean a growing pool of domestic savings and a declining reliance on foreign investment. In time, the technological advance of Chinese industry will be fueled more by indigenous developments and less by ideas, techniques, and machinery imported from abroad. The maturing of its vast domestic market will probably also mean that trade will diminish as a share of GNP [gross national product] and that China will become less dependent on exports and imports than it is today (though at least in the medium term it is likely to depend *more* heavily on certain critical imports, especially of food and fuel.

As China develops and becomes more deeply integrated into the global economy, it will not only be less susceptible to economic pressure from others but more capable of exerting economic pressure of its own. This pressure need not even be deliberate to be felt: as the experience of the United States in the Western hemisphere suggests, a big, dynamic economy can exert an almost gravitational pull on the smaller units that surround it. The analyst Ross Munro has noted in [the journal] *Orbis* that the rapid growth of China's economy has produced a significant expansion in its influence all along its interior land frontier, as its mostly poor neighbors in South, Southeast, and Central Asia have begun to look to it increasingly as a source of markets, aid, and business deals.

Beyond its immediate neighborhood, the sheer size of the potential Chinese market has also helped to create powerful business lobbies favoring good relations with the PRC. In the major industrial powers, these groups can be expected to pressure their own governments in favor of policies that happen also to be in Beijing's interest: easing restrictions on exports of capital and technology, avoiding sanctions, tariffs, or other market-closing measures that might provoke Chinese retaliation, and, in general, doing whatever is possible to maintain good bilateral relations and a "positive business climate."

The activities of pro-PRC lobbying groups may be perfectly legitimate and predictable; but in democratic societies they have nevertheless had the effect of dulling the reactions and limiting the strategic repertory of governments. These effects have been especially pronounced in the United States. Barring some truly severe crisis, trade with China will continue to exercise its muffling influence on American strategy.

Even if the United States should, at some point, adopt a more openly competitive stance, it would have great difficulty getting others to go along. This is not only because of genuine differences of perspective over how best to cope with China's increasing power and assertiveness, but also because each of the members of a potential coalition will be subject to its own domestic pressures. To get some sense of this, imagine, during the cold war, the debates on strategic policy that would have gone on within NATO if the members of the alliance had also been, to varying degrees, deeply engaged in economic exchange with the Soviet Union. As Andrew J. Nathan and Robert S. Ross conclude in their book *The Great Wall and the Empty Fortress* (1997), "It is almost unthinkable that the rest of the world would unite to isolate China as the West did in the era of containment."

In addition to what it gains passively, as it were, simply by engaging with the rest of the world, China has also been actively deploying its growing economic weight to shape the strategic behavior of others. First, and most obviously, Beijing uses access to the Chinese market as a means of rewarding or punishing foreign firms and, through them, influencing their home governments. Ross Munro and Richard Bernstein relate in *The Coming Conflict with China* (1997) that PRC officials promoted an unusual array of business deals with American companies in the spring of 1994, just as the Clinton administration was considering revoking China's most-favored-nation status over human-rights violations. Two years later, having headed off this threat, Prime Minister Li Peng announced that China would buy $1.5-billion-worth of aircraft from Airbus Industrie rather than Boeing because, in his words, the Europeans did not "attach political strings to cooperation with China, unlike the Americans who arbitrarily resort to the threat of sanctions or the use of sanctions."

China has been especially assertive in attempting to exert direct economic influence over Taiwan. Following the election of [President] Chen Shui-bian in the spring of 2000, the Beijing government began to warn Taiwanese companies with investments on the mainland that (according to a report in the *New York Times*) "they would be subject to unspecified sanctions if they advocated independence for Taiwan." To drive home the point, the PRC has evidently begun to make examples of companies whose chief executives are associated with the cause of independence. (In one case, a large petrochemical concern whose chairman supported Chen found its facilities on the mainland subjected to numerous inspections.) Even more visible is the case of Ah-mei, a Taiwanese singer popular on the mainland who performed the national anthem at Chen's inauguration. Her music and videos have since been banned from Chinese state-controlled media; in response to official pressure, Coca-Cola withdrew TV, radio, and billboard advertisements featuring her image.

$$IV$$

Beijing clearly hopes to use economic threats and inducements, then, to discourage the United States from ever pursuing a more confrontational policy toward it. The same economic instruments could also prove extremely important in efforts to affect American interests in Asia, discouraging Japan and Korea from participating in the development of theater missile-defense systems, for example, or persuading Singapore to abandon its present policy of permitting U.S. naval vessels to dock at its ports. The PRC could also do more than in the past to separate the U.S. from its European allies by shifting business from American firms to their EU competitors.

The PRC has begun to get into the financial-diplomacy game as well, if so far on a rather modest scale. In 1994, China stole a march on India by financing, building, and equipping a $200-million coal mine in Bangladesh. And during the summer of 1997, as the Asian financial crisis was reaching its depths, China joined the IMF and a group of much wealthier Asian countries in extending a financial bailout package to Thailand—the first time that it had ever participated in such an effort. Eighteen months later, at the beginning of 1999, Thailand surprised the United States, its nominal ally, by signing a "Plan of Action for the 21st Century" with China—an agreement described by one Thai observer as "a strategic move by China to seek an alliance to counter the influence of the United States." If the Thai example is any indication, economic assistance in various forms will probably become an increasingly significant means for China of winning friends and influencing people.

There are also other, more subtle financial instruments at its disposal. During the Asian crisis, China extracted the maximum diplomatic benefit from its (self-interested) decision not to devalue its currency despite sharp drops in the currencies of many of its smaller neighbors. It thereby earned plaudits as a responsible regional "citizen," an upholder of stability, and, in contrast to Japan, a country able to take tough economic decisions. But China's much-vaunted restraint may also have carried with it an implicit and more menacing message: the PRC is now, as one senior official of the People's Bank put it at the time, "a big player," and what it does or fails to do in the economic realm can have large and potentially devastating effects on the well-being of other, lesser players.

One final possibility: because China promotes exports while restricting imports, it has run substantial trade surpluses in recent years and accumulated large foreign-exchange reserves. In 1998, for example, the PRC's reserves stood at over $140 billion, second only to Japan's. If China continues to amass large reserves and if, as seems likely, the bulk of these are held in dollar-denominated assets, they could provide Beijing with an economic weapon against the United States. By dumping its reserves at the right moment, China might hope to trigger a run on the dollar, an increase in U.S interest rates, and perhaps a stock-market crash. It is true that such an attack, if it produced the intended immediate results, could also do serious damage to China's economy; the mutually destructive effects of attempts at currency manipulation and financial coercion have caused some analysts to compare them with nuclear weapons. But the prospect of mutual devastation does not necessarily provide an ironclad guarantee that a weapon will never be used.

The bottom line is simple: one way or another, China's economic growth will provide it with an increasing array of instruments with which to try to exert influence on other countries and, if it chooses, to carry forward a strategic competition with the United States.

V

The second dimension of a possible struggle for mastery in Asia will be military. From the early 1970's until (at the latest) the early 1990's, the United States and the PRC pursued what might be described as parallel rather than convergent military programs. While both countries were augmenting their capabilities and planning for future warfare, neither was explicitly or overtly focusing its activities on the other. Rather, for almost two decades, American and Chinese defense planners shared a common adversary: the Soviet Union. The weakening and subsequent collapse of the USSR removed the basis for this tacit Sino-American alliance, and also freed the two countries to devote more of their military resources to other potential rivals. Over the course of the 1990's, they came increasingly to regard each other in just this light.

Starting in 1985, China's armed forces, at the direction of their top political leaders, downgraded preparations for an "early, major, and nuclear war" with the Soviet Union and began to focus on the possibility of local, limited wars on China's periphery. This change had the general effect of directing the attention of the Chinese military outward—away from the need to absorb a massive enemy nuclear attack and subsequent invasion and toward the problem of projecting power at least some distance from China's frontiers. Then, the 1991

Gulf war heightened Chinese awareness of the military impact of new technologies and, partly as a result, caused Chinese planners to concentrate with new intensity on the possibility of a future conflict with the United States. According to Allen Whiting, writing in the *China Quarterly*, "war games played against the American 'enemy' have been standard since 1991."

For a variety of reasons, the United States has been slower to focus similar attention on China. During the early post-cold-war years, American armed forces were preoccupied first with fighting the Gulf war, then with managing reductions in their size and budget, and finally with carrying out a variety of operations, from peacekeeping missions of varying scale to a sizable air war in Kosovo. Throughout the 1990's and down to the present there was also a strong political inhibition against considering China a future military rival.

The turning point probably came in 1995–96, when China fired ballistic missiles in the Taiwan Strait. Since then, as the *Washington Post* correspondent Thomas Ricks has reported, U.S. military planners have been devoting greater energy to potential Asian contingencies and, however reluctantly, thinking about a possible confrontation with China. If present trends continue, over the next several years the United States and China will move toward an increasingly obvious military competition, with several facets.

Ⅵ

Offense vs. Defense

China has placed heavy emphasis on the development and deployment of missiles: short-, intermediate-, and long-range, nuclear and conventional, cruise and ballistic.

Since the mid-1990's, the PRC has added substantially to its arsenal of short-range conventional ballistic missiles (the DF-11's and DF-15's), and by 2005 it is expected to have roughly 600 of these weapons within range of Taiwan.[1] Older, liquid-fueled, intermediate-range missiles capable of striking targets throughout East and South Asia with nuclear weapons (DF-3A's) are being supplemented with newer, more accurate, solid-fueled missiles (DF-21A's). Finally, China's small force of fixed, liquid-fueled intercontinental-range rockets (DF-5's and DF-5A's) is expected to be upgraded over the course of the next decade to include two new types of land-based mobile missile (the DF-31 and DF-41, both of which may be capable of carrying multiple warheads) and one submarine-launched ballistic missile (the JL-2). If, as is widely assumed, some of these weapons are equipped with multiple warheads, the number of weapons deliverable against the United States will rise into the low hundreds. If the number of new launchers deployed is larger than expected, that total could grow to as many as 1,000.

China's interest in missiles may be due in part to the fact that, as opposed to manned long-range aircraft, submarines, or surface naval vessels, they are relatively cheap, comparatively simple, and potentially very effective. While the Chinese air force and navy continue to work at acquiring and improving more traditional kinds of military systems, missiles, as the analyst Mark Stokes observes, "are rapidly becoming the sole credible long-range firepower projection asset which the [military] has in its inventory, and this will remain likely true for the foreseeable future."

At the same time that China has been augmenting its missile forces, the United States has been developing and moving toward the deployment of both national and theater ballistic-missile defense systems. Our intensified interest in defense was not driven initially by concern over China, but rather by the threat from "rogue" states like North Korea and Iran. Nevertheless, at least since the 1995-96 Taiwan Strait crisis, the question of the possible utility of defenses against Chinese missiles has inevitably arisen. For their part, and whatever American decision-makers may say or believe, Chinese strategists probably *assume* that our missile-defense programs are directed in large measure at blunting their offensive forces.

For the moment, PRC planners have reason to hope that American defensive deployments will be delayed by some combination of technical problems, budgetary concerns, domestic political developments, and diplomatic pressure. But they are unlikely to be so imprudent as to ignore the possibility that, sooner or later, some kinds of defenses will be deployed. Even a limited national missile-defense system could well be capable of intercepting all of the PRC's present ICBM [intercontinental ballistic missile] force. If they cannot derail the U.S. National Missile Defense (NMD) program through diplomatic means, the Chinese will therefore want to be in a position to defeat it militarily, probably by deploying larger numbers of missiles, at least some of which will be capable of carrying either decoys or multiple warheads. (Another form of insurance might be submarines carrying long-range cruise missiles, or ballistic missiles that could be fired at depressed trajectories.)

Then there is the prospect that the United States may deploy *theater* missile defenses (TMD), either alone or in conjunction with its regional friends and allies. A working TMD system would decrease China's confidence in its ability to intimidate other Asian countries by threatening to attack them with nuclear weapons; it might also seriously complicate Chinese hopes of disrupting American military operations in the western Pacific by quickly disabling a handful of fixed bases and facilities. A Japan able to shelter behind a defensive shield might also feel freer to develop its own offensive capabilities, perhaps even including nuclear weapons. Last but not least, a TMD system deployed on or around Taiwan could blunt what is now China's most potent threat against the island, perhaps opening the way for moves toward formal independence.

China's options for responding to these possibilities are similar to those it has in dealing with NMD, although, because of the shorter distances involved, some countermeasures may be easier and less expensive to implement. Preventing deployment in the first place through diplomacy and intimidation would be an obvious first choice. Preparing to swamp a TMD system with ever-larger numbers of warheads would be another. Circumventing defenses by developing long-range cruise missiles or other means of attack would be a third. Finally, if the United States and its allies seemed to be developing defenses sufficiently capable to blunt a *conventional* missile attack, the Chinese might seek to up the ante by adding to their force of short- and intermediate-range missiles equipped with nuclear warheads. A defensive system able to shoot down 75 percent of the missiles fired against it might look very impressive against an all-conventional attack, but much less so against one that could contain a mix of more and less destructive warheads.

VII

Projecting Power

The United States is today able to project conventional air and naval power virtually unimpeded anywhere in the western Pacific, including all along China's eastern seaboard and, conceivably, hundreds of miles inland. American forces, brought to bear at long distances, and with the help of a handful of local friends and allies, pose the single greatest obstacle to any Chinese effort to establish itself as the dominant power in East Asia. Chinese planners must fear that, in a crisis or future conflict, the U.S. could close China's ports, unleash precision conventional attacks with cruise missiles and stealthy manned aircraft against targets on the Chinese mainland, and, by sinking Chinese submarines and surface ships, break an attempted blockade of Taiwan. If they are to displace the United States as East Asia's dominant military power, Chinese strategists must come up with ways of countering American forces.

I have already mentioned one such way: the possible use of missiles against U.S. regional bases. At present and for the foreseeable future, the ability of the United States to sustain air and naval operations in the western Pacific depends heavily on access to a small number of facilities in Japan and South Korea. If these (plus a handful of others in Singapore, Australia, and perhaps in the Philippines and Guam) can be destroyed or rendered unusable, America's ability to project power will fall precipitously.

Next in order of technical difficulty for China would be acquiring weapons with which to sink American surface ships, and especially the aircraft carriers on which the United States now relies so heavily. In most conflicts involving U.S. and Chinese forces, these vessels would have to operate at the far western edge of the Pacific and might therefore be especially vulnerable to attacks by cruise missiles, torpedoes, and intelligent mines. Such weapons could be unleashed in large numbers from swarms of relatively inexpensive platforms, including small submarines and surface ships, and remotely-piloted aerial vehicles. Anticarrier attacks by land-based ballistic missiles are another possibility.

More challenging than sinking carriers but of potentially even greater benefit would be the capacity to disable American intelligence, communications, and navigation satellites and to disrupt U.S. information systems, both in the region and beyond. In contrast to China, which in conflicts close to home would enjoy the benefits of interior lines of communication, the United States would have to control its forces at great distances from home and across a vast theater of operations. Even temporary disruptions could have devastating and potentially disastrous consequences. This is something that has not escaped the attention of Chinese observers. According to Mark Stokes, "Chinese strategists and engineers perceive U.S. reliance on communications, reconnaissance, and navigation satellites as a potential 'Achilles' heel,'" and they are looking for ways to attack it, including by means of ground-based lasers, jammers, and kinetic kill vehicles.

Defeating American power projection will also require defending Chinese territory against airborne attack. Toward this end China has apparently been devoting considerable resources to developing a nationwide air-defense system capable of locating, tracking, and intercepting aircraft and cruise missiles, including those with stealthy characteristics. Improved coastal defenses, perhaps including anti-submarine-warfare ships, attack submarines, and aircraft, could also force U.S. cruise-missile-launching submarines to operate at greater distances from China's shores, thereby reducing the array of targets they could cover.

In this regard, and more generally, the thrust of Chinese programs will be to push American forces back and, at the very least, seriously complicate their efforts to operate in the western Pacific.

Deterrence

For decades we have promised, explicitly or otherwise, to defend our Asian allies if they were attacked by China. Until very recently we have done so from a position of virtual immunity to direct Chinese attack on our own soil. The development of Chinese long-range strike capabilities and, in particular, a visible and substantial increase in China's ability to hit the continental United States with nuclear weapons could raise profound questions in Asia about the continuing utility of the American nuclear "umbrella."

Assuming for the moment that the United States does *not* go forward with a national missile-defense system, the deployment by China of a fairly limited number of sea- and land-based mobile missiles will effectively guarantee it a secure second-strike capability. As things now stand, the small Chinese ICBM force would take hours to make ready for launch, and it could conceivably be destroyed in a preemptive American attack, perhaps one involving only the use of precision conventional weapons. A larger, more diverse, and more mobile force of solid-fueled rockets will be far less vulnerable. Such a force could conceivably also be used to conduct limited attacks on U.S. military targets rather than simply lobbing a few large and inaccurate warheads at a handful of American cities.

In certain respects, the next ten to fifteen years may thus come to resemble the early stages of the cold war. In the late 1940's and well into the 1950's, the United States enjoyed a huge advantage in its nuclear competition with the Soviet Union. American forces operating from bases around the Eurasian periphery (and, with the introduction of the B-52 bomber, from American soil) were poised to deliver nuclear weapons virtually anywhere in the USSR; for a long time, the Soviets had no comparable capability. Yet even the *anticipated* Soviet development of intercontinental bombers and ballistic missiles triggered major worries within the Western alliance. American policy-makers were long preoccupied with convincing their NATO allies, the Soviets, and perhaps themselves that the United States would, indeed, intervene in a European war even if in doing so it risked nuclear attack on its own soil.

Much of what the United States did in Europe—maintaining and augmenting ground forces, deploying large numbers of tactical nuclear weapons, tolerating (and even encouraging) the acquisition of national nuclear forces by at least two key allies, and increasing the flexibility of American strategic nuclear forces—was motivated by the desire to strengthen deterrence in the face of increasing Soviet intercontinental-strike capabilities. Until nearly the final moments of the cold war, the Soviets, for their part, tried to raise doubts about American resolve as a way of weakening the Western alliance. There is already some evidence that China may try to use similar tactics to undermine the U.S. position in Asia.

In 1995, a high-ranking Chinese official was widely quoted as having told a visitor that the United States would not come to Taiwan's rescue because, in the end, Americans cared more about Los Angeles than Taipei. More recently, during the run-up to the March 2000 Taiwanese presidential election, China's official armed-forces newspaper warned that, unlike Iraq or Yugoslavia, China is "a country that has certain abilities of launching strategic counterattack and the capacity of launching a long-distance strike. . . . It is not a wise move to be at war with a country such as China, a point which the U.S. policy-makers know fairly well also."

These threats were evidently intended to give pause to anyone contemplating possible conventional strikes on Chinese forces or territory in the context of a fight over Taiwan. In the future, Chinese strategists may issue more generalized warnings, perhaps suggesting that the growth in their striking power means that the United States will have to contemplate sacrificing Washington to save Tokyo, or Seoul, or Sidney, or Manila, or Singapore. Such comments would be directed more at Asian than at American audiences, and their aim would be not so much to deter the United States as to raise questions about the ability of the United States to deter China. The ultimate aim would be to raise doubts in the minds of Asian observers as to the continuing value of American security commitments.

IV

Any intensified military rivalry between the United States and China will be accompanied by a stepped-up competition in the political or diplomatic realm, which is the third dimension of a possible future struggle in Asia. The central issue of this particular contest would be the making and breaking of alliances.

As in the military arena, the United States starts with a number of very considerable advantages: it enjoys good relations with most countries in East Asia and has alliance ties or other security connections with many of them, including most of the wealthiest and most powerful. China, on the other hand, has problematic relationships with a number of major players in both East and South Asia and its closest collaborators (North Korea, Myanmar, Pakistan, and Russia) suffer from profound domestic liabilities.

The United States also benefits from what is, for the moment at least, a major geopolitical advantage: the possible threat posed by the sheer magnitude of its material power is offset to a degree by its remoteness from the heart of

Asia. Because it is far away, the U.S. is less menacing than China, which is nearby and thus potentially overwhelming. Indeed, as China's capabilities grow, there may be a strong tendency on the part of the other Asian states to draw closer to one another, and to the United States, in order to counterbalance Chinese power and preserve their own independence.

If power-balancing were automatic and inevitable, the United States could afford to sit back and let nature take its course. But the societies of Northeast and Southeast Asia also have long historical experience with Chinese preponderance, and they could choose to live with it again in the future, especially if the only alternative appeared to be a period of protracted and dangerous rivalry between China and the United States. Moreover, if the United States appears weak and vacillating, or if its withdrawal from the region begins to seem inevitable, these countries may conclude that they have little choice but to cut the best deal they can.

The aim of Chinese diplomatic strategy, therefore, will be to turn America's geographical remoteness from an advantage to a disadvantage, weakening existing American relationships and preventing the formation of new ones, feeding doubts about U.S. resolve and staying power, and making China's rise seem both as inevitable, and as unthreatening, as possible.

How might this be done?

First, Chinese leaders could transform their country's longstanding but largely rhetorical opposition to bilateral military alliances into a central feature of their foreign policy. In the 1970's and 1980's, the Chinese were willing to accept that America's Asian alliances served the useful purpose of countering Soviet "hegemonism." During the 1990's, China preferred that Japan continue under American tutelage rather than being left free to expand its power and pursue its own objectives. But, as has already begun to happen, deteriorating U.S.-PRC relations and stepped-up efforts at U.S.-Japan security cooperation will cause Chinese strategists to reexamine their permissive position and ultimately to take a much tougher, anti-alliance stance.

Accompanying this shift could be the amplification of another persistent theme in Chinese diplomacy. As it works to displace the United States from Asia, China will intensify its campaign against "hegemony" by criticizing America's cultural and economic "imperialism" and attacking its arrogance and intrusiveness. China will seek friends among those in Asia (and beyond) who feel they have suffered at the hands of U.S. corporations, American-led international institutions, and/or American efforts to enforce conformity with U.S. views on political liberties and human rights. At the same time that it seeks to gain the benefits of greater integration into the world economy, China could also emerge as a leading critic of the ills of globalization and a leading proponent of various kinds of regional (as opposed to global and hence American-dominated) institutions. Chinese policy may even take on a racial aspect, perhaps appealing to those who share ethnic and cultural characteristics across East Asia or, more generally, making the case against "the West" and for "Asia for the Asians."

As it has done in recent years, China will no doubt become an even more enthusiastic participant in multilateral security dialogues and other forums in Asia, using them to convey the image of a good international citizen and an open, unthreatening power. Active Chinese participation will also ensure that multilateral mechanisms cannot be used against the PRC's interests. As relations with the United States degenerate, China may also begin to advocate *new* institutions that will exclude "non-Asian" powers and seek "local" solutions to regional economic, environmental, and security problems.

Its strictures against bilateral alliances notwithstanding, China will also attempt to develop its own "strategic partnerships," both in Asia and beyond. In some cases (as in its current dealings with Russia, Israel, and a number of European countries), China's goal will be to obtain military hardware and advanced technology. In others (as, most likely, with Pakistan) the PRC will be supporting the enemy of an enemy (India).

Next, in order to circumvent U.S. efforts to apply economic sanctions or technology controls, China may hope to cultivate a much closer relationship with a more independent and perhaps openly anti-American European Union. In the Persian Gulf region, it may align itself more openly with Iran as a way of deflecting American attention and scarce military resources from East Asia, and in order to ensure its own access to oil. In continental Southeast Asia (especially Myanmar and Thailand), it may use threats and inducements to gain access to facilities for its own military forces or to deny access to the forces of its rivals. In Central Asia, it may work to establish client regimes that will protect oil pipelines and control Islamist groups that might otherwise foment discontent among China's own non-Han minorities.

Finally, while China will probably continue to shun any pretension to global power, it may provide assistance to states or nonstate actors around the world that see themselves as being opposed to the United States. Like the Soviet Union before it, albeit more for geopolitical than for ideological reasons, China could become a low-key but important supporter of rebel movements, "rogue states," and terrorist groups throughout the Middle East, North Africa, and Central and Latin America.

But it is in East Asia, their main sphere of activity, that Chinese strategists will most want to focus attention. In order to do this, they will probably aim first to secure their continental "rear areas." Toward this end, China will work hard to maintain a good relationship with Russia and to avoid being drawn into debilitating conflicts in Central Asia. In South Asia, although China will probably opt to continue its present policy of supporting Pakistan to distract India, it could also try to take India out of the larger strategic equation by offering a spheres-of-influence arrangement that would leave India dominant on the subcontinent in exchange for its continued nonalignment.

In East Asia itself, China may seek to execute the diplomatic equivalent of a pincer movement, applying pressure from the north (the Korean peninsula) and the south (the South China Sea) in order to gain its primary objectives at the center: the acquisition of Taiwan and the neutralization of Japan. Following the success of an initial gambit this past spring, the Chinese will probably continue to press North Korea to negotiate with the South, while at the same time attempting to build themselves up as the indispensable intermediary. In return for its continued help in delivering North Korea, China may hope to gain some assurances from South Korea about the role of the United States on the peninsula. Even if Chinese strategists cannot extract much in the way of concrete promises, they may nevertheless come to believe that progress toward reunification will unleash popular forces in the South that will lead irresistibly to an American withdrawal. Continued improvement in North-South relations would also help to lull Japan and undermine U.S. efforts to build support for theater missile defenses.

While these events are unfolding, the PRC will use a variety of tactics to aid the further extension of its influence in Southeast Asia. Here, in contrast to its role as peacemaker in Korea, it may show a harder, tougher face. An increase in piracy (perhaps supported covertly by China) could provide the justification for an expansion of naval activities in the South China Sea, enabling the PRC to assert its territorial claims in the area. China may also seek to encourage the activities of ethnic and religious separatist movements in Indonesia and the Philippines in the hope that, if these countries become wracked by civil unrest, they will be much less capable of acting to oppose the growth in Chinese power. After years of tolerating Singapore's military cooperation with the United States, China may also begin to press that country to choose sides or, at the very least, abandon its tilt toward the U.S. And if Chinese leaders feel the need to flex their muscles, and perhaps also to demonstrate the limits of American power and commitment, they may pick a fight they think they can win, most likely by provoking and then pummeling Vietnam in what their military planners have called a quick "local war with high-tech characteristics."

The consolidation of China's position to its north and south will set the stage for the final resolution of the core strategic issues of Japan and Taiwan. With regard to the former, China's goal must be to detach it from the United States without at the same time stimulating a resurgence of Japanese assertiveness and militarism. Despite their oft-expressed fears, Chinese strategists may become less worried about Japan as that country's population ages, its political system continues to founder, and its economy fails to regain its former luster. A Korean settlement that results in a greatly reduced U.S. role on the peninsula could yield a corresponding increase in Japanese discomfort at being the last major remaining outpost of American military power in Asia. If so, the moment may have arrived for China to offer Japan some kind of "grand bargain," perhaps involving a mutual non-aggression pact and a pledge to maintain freedom of navigation in the South China Sea in exchange for a sharp curtailment or outright abrogation of the U.S.-Japan alliance. At this point, if not before, Taiwan would have little choice but to accept the PRC's terms for reunification.

V

These, then, are the main elements of the possible struggle to come in Asia. Of course, it is one thing for Chinese strategists to fantasize about easing the U.S. out of East Asia without firing a shot; actually doing so is another matter altogether. For one thing, if the PRC is impatient, if it underestimates the impact of its actions on its opponents, if it is excessively high-handed or overly brutal, it could well wind up stimulating precisely the kind of determined, unified response that could foil its plans and block its ambitions. For another thing, it is conceivable that China will mellow with the passage of time, or suffer from domestic weaknesses that will prevent it from pursuing its objectives in a consistent and effective way. And most important of all, the United States could either adjust its current policies so as to make an open Sino-American confrontation less likely or, if conflict cannot be avoided, prepare for its eventuality while simultaneously preserving America's own position in Asia.

If I have purposely refrained from dwelling on American strategic options in the coming decades, it is hardly because we are without them—whether economic, military, or political. Rather, it is because the first order of business is to see the situation plain—namely, that in several important respects a U.S.-PRC strategic competition is already under way, and there is a good chance that it is only going to become more intense and open. In recognizing these realities, the Chinese are well ahead of the United States.

Militarily, the PRC will continue to do what it is already doing: working to offset or neutralize current U.S. advantages, increasing its ability to target U.S. forces, facilities, and command-and-communications systems in, around, and over the western Pacific while improving its capacity to deter or defend against American attacks on its own forces and territory. These military activities will likely be accompanied by an effort to break up the American-led alliance system in Asia and ultimately to detach the United States from most of its present partners and to push it as far back across the Pacific as possible. To this end, the PRC will use every instrument at its disposal, including especially its growing economic clout.

In this respect, what one needs to bear in mind is that China will be a very different kind of strategic competitor from the Soviet Union. The PRC's size, dynamism, and relative openness confer a much greater ability to shape the behavior of other countries, thus helping to dissuade the United States from confrontation, diminishing the effectiveness of any unilateral American attempt to use economic instruments against it, driving a wedge between the U.S. and the other advanced industrial nations, and enhancing China's own capacity to exert influence over the countries in its region. The threat all this holds out to American interests can be countered, but first it must be acknowledged.

Note

1. In the aftermath of the Gulf war, the Chinese military also reportedly intensified its efforts to develop long-range land-attack cruise missiles.

NO ⬅

Nicholas Berry

Is China an Aggressive Power?

Is China an aggressive power? The answer to this question will largely determine the future size and shape of the U.S. military establishment.

The drafting of the Pentagon's 2001 Quadrennial Defense Review [QDR] is underway. With threats from Iraq and North Korea fading, the current scenario of simultaneously fighting two major theater wars becomes increasingly less credible. The emergence of a perceived Chinese threat, however, would demand that the U.S. military's force structure, troop deployments, weapons procurement, and research and development be primarily focused against China. Needless to say, it would also keep the Pentagon's budget moving up. Without a Chinese threat, force levels and deployments could be reduced and a national security strategy based on building multilateral regional stability could be adopted.

History tells us a good deal about the rise of aggressive powers. A review of Chinese history reveals that the Asian giant does not fit the mold, and thus the likelihood of Chinese aggression is close to zero.

Five factors appear to be crucial before a country uses military force to establish hegemonic control over foreigners—or at least attempts to do so. They tend to be sequential, each one feeding on the preceding ones: a large, unified state; a rising economy; an ideology of dominance; a superior (relatively) military capability; and (5) popular support for an aggressive foreign policy.

Large, Unified State

Logically, one may suspect that the other four factors precede this one—and to some extent they have. But a unified political unit of relatively significant size must first be established before it can embark on foreign domination. Athens, once a dusty little village, had to grow, incorporate surrounding land for agriculture, develop its port at Piraeus, and enlarge its population. It was then positioned to create an empire beyond its established polity. Rome followed the same pattern, most importantly subduing and replacing its Etruscan neighbor and competitor to establish a secure city-state on the Italian peninsula. Islam roared out of Arabia after Mohammed united all of the Arab-speaking

From Nicholas Berry, "Is China an Aggressive Power?" *The Defense Monitor*, vol. 29, no. 9 (2000). Copyright © 2000 by The Center for Defense Information. Reprinted by permission.

tribes. The Spanish in the 15th century had to unite under Ferdinand and Isabella, Elizabeth I had to consolidate control of the British Isles and ward off the Spanish Armada, and the Dutch in the 17th century had to expel their Spanish occupiers before any of them could contemplate empire.

The Russians under Ivan the Terrible [in the sixteenth century] warded off invasions from both east and west. The United States fought its war of independence and sought its "Manifest Destiny" to expand coast-to-coast. The Germans and Italians only achieved national unity in the 19th century in an era of rampant European nationalism. Japan was the next to the last modern state (before China) to consolidate central government control with the 1868 Meiji Restoration.

China united in 221 B.C. under the emperor Qinshihuangdi after the Warring States era, but was not pacified until conquered by the Mongols. In the 13th century under the Khans, China moved westward, conquering all. Although two attempted invasions of Japan failed because "divine winds" (*kamikaze*) scattered the Chinese amphibious force, China dominated the Asian land mass north of the Indian subcontinent. In the 15th century it seemed poised to become the world's greatest expansionist power. Its economy was bureaucratically integrated; it had developed printing, paper, and advanced metallurgy; it had gunpowder and rockets and was home to the world's leading mechanical engineers.

China built huge warships, some over 400 feet in length with eight, even nine, masts carrying hundreds of people. Its fleets—one totaled 317 vessels—plied the Indonesian islands and entered the Indian Ocean in the first half of the 15th century. But the enterprise collapsed. A combination of discomfort with dealing with non-Chinese people, the huge expense of the maritime enterprise, unprofitable trade, and an internal power struggle won by the isolationists ended China's overseas expansion. The new emperor called the fleet home and had it destroyed. In 1477, even the logs of the great voyages were burned. David S. Landes in his *The Wealth and Poverty of Nations* (W. W. Norton, 1998) concluded: "Isolationism became China. Round, complete, apparently serene, ineffably harmonious, the Celestial Empire purred along for hundreds of years more, impervious and imperturbable. But the world was passing it by."

China remained an isolated Middle Kingdom for the next 400 years. Internal power struggles were frequent. By the 19th century China was technologically backward. It lost the Opium War to Britain and a naval war to Japan (which took Taiwan as booty). Foreigners carved up China's coast into spheres of influence, and Christian missionaries arrived to convert the people.

Anti-foreign, anti-imperialist Chinese nationalism surged, first with the Boxer Rebellion in 1900 followed by the overthrow of the Qing (Manchu) dynasty in 1911. Under Sun Yat-sen and then Chiang Kai-shek, the Nationalists (Koumingtang or KMT) methodically defeated regional warlords but then faced two challenges. A KMT-Communist alliance broke down in 1927, with the KMT defeating the urban-based Communists. (Mao Zedong's rural-based wing of the Chinese Communist Party [CCP] survived.) Before the KMT could consolidate its power, the Japanese in 1931 seized Manchuria and began a full-scale invasion in 1937. That put the second round of the KMT-CCP struggle on hold until war's end in 1945. The CCP emerged victorious on October 1, 1949, and Chiang and his KMT fled to Formosa (Taiwan) where they came under the protection of the U.S. Seventh Fleet after China intervened in the Korean War. Nevertheless, except for Taiwan, the 20th century can be seen as China's search for national unity and sovereignty which culminated in its regaining Hong Kong in 1997 and Macao in 1999.

China's historic pattern of seeking territorial integrity is both old and new. The old unity, which spawned the fizzled 15th century attempt at overseas imperialism, left a strong distaste for imperialism that militates against military aggression. The possible exception is the uncompleted effort to re-incorporate Taiwan. Resolving this issue will be a major determinant for future Chinese foreign policy assertiveness. If Taiwan is reunited with the mainland by military force, China would aggressively seek to limit U.S. influence throughout East Asia to ward off a hostile United States. On the other hand, a peaceful reunification with Taiwan would tend to dampen Chinese assertiveness.

A Rising Economy

The struggle to consolidate state unity always creates a feeling of collective energy and an urge to use the state to promote greater production and create larger markets. Recent studies have shown that the economy—land, labor, capital, and trade—is the best predictor of national power, more so than military might. Athens excelled in agriculture, health measures, water management, crafts, and trade to build its economy. Rome added a safe land and water transit/trade infrastructure and introduced factories powered by waterwheels to increase production. For a time, science, technology, and trade flourished in the Islamic world.

Later, the Industrial Revolution [beginning in the mid-eighteenth century] shifted economic development to Europe where Great Britain became its first beneficiary. Few areas on the planet have been more hospitable to economic growth than North America with its climate, arable land, rivers and harbors, and natural resources. Add to this mix the pioneering spirit of immigrants and the first program of mass public education, and an economic takeoff became inevitable. The U.S. by 1900 was the world's leading economy. Economic growth rates in Russia, Germany, and Japan also soared before World War I.

The imperial thrust of all these states rested on expanding economies. A country's popular belief in a "place in the sun" is largely determined by its rate of economic growth compared to others. Superiority in what sustains and enriches life "naturally" suggests superiority in other areas. The notion of the political survival of the fittest existed long before Darwin. In fact, those with the economy to produce a strong military and the pride to inflame popular enthusiasm would not only survive but dominate.

China historically resisted labor-saving technology in favor of a labor-intensive economy, which encouraged rapid population growth. It resisted the comparative advantage of trade, stressing self-sufficiency. It resisted the diffusion of literacy, the growth of an urban middle class, and modern science and social science in favor of maintaining elitism and tradition. China entered the 20th century as "the sleeping giant."

World War II and the civil war hampered economic development. The consolidation of mainland China under CCP rule provided an opportunity to modernize the economy. For all the horrors of Mao Zedong's Great Leap Forward and Great Proletarian Cultural Revolution, his dictatorship destroyed feudal land relationships, instituted mass education (including for women), and began large-scale industrialization. However, by the time of Mao's death, the Chinese economy had stagnated.

It fell to Mao's successor to abandon the stale communist economy by introducing private enterprise, market pricing, foreign direct investment, and trade-promoting policies. From 1978, when he took power, Deng Xiaoping never wavered from his central idea that a growing economy would maintain Chinese unity, keep the CCP in power, facilitate the reunion of separated parts of China, prevent foreign military intimidation, and make China a major world player. He called for the "four modernizations"—economy, agriculture, education/technology, and military.

Data confirm the success of Deng's economic reforms. China's economy averaged over 9% in annual GDP growth. Since 1980 the GDP has quadrupled to $4.8 trillion, making it the world's fifth largest economy. Per capita income (purchasing power parity) is $3,600. Trade has zoomed to an annual (1998) $340 billion.

On the surface China has created the foundation for an expansionist foreign policy. However, substantial internal and external impediments remain. Internally, the western region of China has not prospered as have the coastal provinces, although major programs are underway to redress the imbalance. Attention is being paid to failing state enterprises where labor strikes, protests, and regional unemployment present immediate problems. Endemic corruption in the form of bribes, influence peddling, smuggling, and protection rackets —all enemies of entrepreneurship—are being addressed. Finally, environmental pollution has reached the point that health concerns in major cities, especially Beijing, indicate that expensive corrective measures cannot be put off.

But most inhibitors of Chinese aggression are external. At one time a nation's "place in the sun" referred to a rising state acquiring colonies. A place in the sun today is a seat at the policy-making table in powerful international organizations. China is a member of the World Bank, the International Monetary Fund [IMF], and is about to join the WTO [World Trade Organization]. It occupies one of the five permanent seats on the UN Security Council. It wields influence in ASEAN's Regional Forum (ARF) and the Asia-Pacific Economic Co-operation (APEC) forum.

Nowhere is China denied its rightful place in world affairs. Globalization decrees that what a state achieves is up to that state. Although this system does penalize those that have difficulty competing (and the World Bank and IMF are now considering debt relief and other ways to help the less advantaged), China has benefitted greatly from globalization. Its economy is highly integrated with the world via trade, foreign direct investment, education (China ranks first in the number of foreign students studying in America), and technology transfers. Why would it risk economic collapse and becoming an international pariah by embarking on imperialistic adventures?

As regimes in Iraq and Serbia have learned, aggression provokes isolation. More importantly, all China's major economic partners have close relations with the U.S., and Washington would insist that an aggressive China be quarantined. Furthermore, the U.S. economy is more capable than China's of sustaining the arms and ideology to promote international power. In short, Chinese leaders have no intention of taking on the U.S. and its allies in a quest for regional or world dominance. They prefer a multipolar world and have not formulated an ideology of dominance.

An Ideology of Dominance

The Greeks saw barbarians beyond their borders. The Romans saw uncivilized and unwashed tribes that needed to be under Rome's protection. Islam believed it had God on its side, as did the Spanish New World conquerors. The Dutch, French, and British believed that people in their "nonage" required enlightened European civilization, so they assumed the "white man's burden." Americans held to the myths of occupying the "city on the hill" and racial superiority; they took the Philippines, as President McKinley said, to guide "our little brown brothers." The Soviet Union believed its ideology was universal and inevitable. Nazi Germany saw racial superiority as fully supporting its military superiority. Japan saw itself as a superior civilization—one that had resisted European colonialism. It could simultaneously rid Asia of European colonialism and create its own empire, the "Greater East Asian Co-prosperity Sphere."

China may think it represents one of history's great civilizations, but it has no dogma on racial superiority. Quite the opposite. The Chinese have long argued that European and American notions of race were simply devices to justify imperialism, nothing more. Perhaps it once believed in the inevitability of communism, but Beijing has been running away from Marxist-Leninism at Olympic speed. Culturally, the Chinese have great difficulty integrating with non-Chinese. Their civilization is only for them, not for other peoples. Even in melting-pot America, many Chinese-Americans find security in Chinatowns. Other overseas Chinese act the same. Their ethnocentrism is not a prescription for dominating foreigners—their Uihgar and Tibetan minorities excepted. Without an ideology of dominance, China is missing a key ingredient for embracing imperialism. Its military forces, therefore, have other duties.

Superior Military Capability

Athens had its fleet and subservient allies. Rome had invincible legions. Islam had its cavalry and was the first to use cannons effectively. The Spanish, Dutch, and British employed advanced ships and firepower to establish empire. The

Soviets used the Red Army to create and dominate its East European empire. And Nazi Germany and imperial Japan believed their martial spirit and modern military strategies gave them superiority over the states they would attack.

The People's Liberation Army (PLA) is heavily skewed to land forces. Only recently has the emphasis shifted to ballistic missiles and air and sea capabilities. It has twenty or so antique DF-5 liquid-fueled ICBMs and its solid-fueled DF-41 is still four or five years away from deployment. It has no aircraft carriers. Of 3,500 jet fighters, only fifty or so are advanced—the Russian made SU-27. It has two modern Sovremenny-class destroyers with Sunburn anti-ship cruise missiles—also bought from Russia. Its amphibious and air assault capability is insufficient to conquer Taiwan, although 250 or so ballistic missiles across the Taiwan Strait target that island.

Put simply, the PLA seriously menaces none of its neighbors, all of whom have some relationship with the United States. This is not to say that there is no concern, but if China is planning to create an empire, it certainly is casual about developing the military means to do so.

The PLA does have an agenda. It serves to defend the homeland, although that mission is fading in the absence of threats. (Land forces are being reduced by the hundreds of thousands.) The PLA is an instrument of internal control, deterring and combating separatists in Xinjiang and Tibet, pro-democracy dissidents in the cities, and guarding against rural protests. Its conventional units back China's territorial claims in the South China Sea, while its nuclear forces deter any attempts at nuclear blackmail. (The ability for nuclear retaliation, the Chinese leadership believes, will prevent the U.S. from again using nuclear threats against China as it did in the 1950s over Quemoy and Matsu.) Finally, the PLA is gearing up to punish Taiwan if Taipei dares to declare independence.

The threat to Taiwan is real. PLA officers frequently say: "We have no intention of attacking anyone, but if called upon [to punish Taiwan] we will do so without question." Such a threat is highly credible regardless of the consequences. There is an arrogance in the PLA born of China's rise to prominence and all the attention paid to it—especially by Americans—as a nation on the move. There is no doubt that any U.S. attempt to foster and uphold Taiwan independence will result in armed conflict. Taiwan is considered an internal matter, and any outside intervention on the issue would affront Chinese "sovereignty and territorial integrity." It is not imperialism, Chinese officials insist, to regain a "renegade" province. A proud China on the verge of unity simply would not tolerate dismemberment.

At the same time, the maintenance of the "one China principle" will keep Beijing patient. The costs of developing an assault capability, of provoking international economic isolation, of killing fellow Chinese, and of risking military failure if the U.S. supports Taiwan will keep China focused on peaceful efforts to regain Taiwan.

Until recently, Chinese leaders have not fully grasped that Taiwan needs to be wooed, not bullied, into reunification. As long as the costs of reunification are perceived on Taiwan as unacceptable, the marriage will not occur. Eventually, the sentiment for Chinese unity may well push Beijing to adopt further, more rewarding approaches to woo Taipei.

Popular Support for an Aggressive Foreign Policy

Perhaps the only historical exception to this factor as a prerequisite for imperialistic adventures is Italy beginning in the 1930s. Mussolini had some enthusiastic public support for his attack on Ethiopia, but it soon faded with Italy's aggression against Albania, Greece, France, and the Soviet Union. The clear confirmation of this is the dismal combat record of Italian forces. An army and a people must believe that surrender would be cowardly. Most of all, they must believe that killing foreigners is morally acceptable—as seems to have been the attitude of Greeks, Romans, Arabs, Turks, Dutch, British, Russians, Germans, and Japanese.

Americans were bothered by the U.S.-Philippine War. An extensive anti-imperialist movement emerged led by people as disparate as Andrew Carnegie and Mark Twain. Many historians have suggested that America's own history as a colony of Great Britain has produced an ingrained streak of anti-imperialism in the American psyche.

The same anti-imperialism sentiments exist in China. China cannot continually protest its history of foreign exploitation and then adopt a cultural norm that its exploitation of foreigners is acceptable. The Chinese may accept that life is full of contradictions, but this one would exemplify cognitive dissonance in the extreme. Taiwan, of course, is not populated by foreigners.

Conclusions

Americans who see China as the new imperialist threat need to review the historical record. Unless history is meaningless as a predictor of events, China will not seek an empire. As long as China's periphery is secure—and no country is prepared to attack it—the PLA will carry out its internal and defensive tasks, including putting pressure on Taiwan not to leave the fold.

China will, however, use military force to secure its territory if its leaders believe such action is necessary. China did so in Korea, in border wars with India and Vietnam, in suppressing Tibetan separatists, and in a border skirmish with Soviet forces on Damansky Island. Taiwan remains under the Chinese gun.

Overall, globalization renders imperialism passe. Countries, especially the major powers that benefit most from globalization, are status quo powers usually willing to intervene to prevent regional hegemons from disrupting the system. Coalitions in a globalized world have proven relatively easy to organize against major threats, beginning with the UN operation in Cambodia through Desert Storm, Bosnia, Kosovo, and East Timor. The existence of globalization has not been challenged by any major power.

Therefore, the central task for U.S. foreign policy is to sustain globalization by striving to integrate all states into international organizations; assist weak states to the point that the system rewards them; work with other states to settle regional conflicts; promote trade, direct investment, and financial stability; and moderate weapons proliferation and arms races. China can be a partner in each area. There is no need for it to be a "strategic partner" because there is no common enemy; a "normal partnership" would do.

A realistic Pentagon assessment of the Chinese military threat for its QDR will conclude that a smaller U.S. military establishment focused on regional stability in Asia would be more than sufficient to provide for U.S. security.

POSTSCRIPT

Is China an Expansionist Power?

There can be no doubt that China's power continues to develop. It has the world's largest military and an array of nuclear weapons. It is one of the world's 10 largest economies in terms of overall gross domestic product (GDP) and exports. It is the third largest producer of steel, ranks second in the production and consumption of energy, and is fourth in the production of oil.

Yet from another perspective, China remains a poor and, in many ways, weak country. Dividing its impressive GDP, exports, and production figures by its more than 1 billion people leaves China one of the poorest countries in the world by most per capita measures. China's nuclear and advanced conventional weapons systems are less numerous and less sophisticated technologically than those of the United States. Thus, an important question in this debate is whether to consider China a great power rival of the United States or a country struggling to develop. Two recent studies that would be good to review are Solomon Karmel, *China and the People's Liberation Army: Great Power or Struggling Developing State?* (St. Martin's Press, 2000) and David Shambaugh, "China's Military Views the World: Ambivalent Security," *International Security* (Winter 2000). For a regularly updated review of China's military capabilities, go to the Project for Defense Alternative's Internet site at http://www.comw.org/cmp/.

There will likely be outstanding issues between the United States and China. During 2001, for example, the two countries experienced high tensions after a U.S. intelligence plane and a Chinese interceptor collided just off China's coast. The 24-person U.S. crew was detained by China after the crippled plane was forced to land on Hainan Island. Soon thereafter, China raised major objections to the sale of modern U.S. warships and other military equipment to Taiwan, which China considers to be one of its provinces.

Those who take a pessimistic view of China's current and future policies worry that through normal trade and other relations, Americans are not only whistling past the proverbial graveyard but helping to build it. From this point of view, China has its own interests; those interests are in some cases antithetical to those of the United States; China will become more aggressive as it becomes stronger; and U.S. strategic engagement with China hastens the day when China will be a full-fledged rival of the United States in Asia and perhaps elsewhere. Insight on how the Chinese perceive this issue is available in Michael Pillsbury, *China Debates the Future Security Environment* (National Defense University Press, 2000).

ISSUE 7

Should Israel Take a Hard Line With the Palestinians?

YES: Daniel Pipes, from "Israel's Moment of Truth," *Commentary* (February 2000)

NO: Herbert C. Kelman, from "Building a Sustainable Peace: The Limits of Pragmatism in the Israeli-Palestinian Negotiations," *Journal of Palestine Studies* (Autumn 1998)

ISSUE SUMMARY

YES: Daniel Pipes, director of the Middle East Forum, a policy analysis center in Philadelphia, Pennsylvania, contends that Israel should not give up any of its existing advantages in the face of Arab intransigence and outside pressure.

NO: Herbert C. Kelman, director of the Program on International Conflict Analysis and Resolution at Harvard University, contends that to move the Middle East peace process forward, Israel and the Palestinians have to commit to a solution that includes, among other things, the creation of a Palestinian state.

The history of Israel/Palestine dates to biblical times when there were both Hebrew and Arab (Canaanite) kingdoms in the area. In later centuries, the area was conquered by many others; from 640 to 1917 it was almost continually controlled by Muslim rulers. In 1917 the British captured the area, Palestine, from Turkey.

Concurrently, a Zionist movement for a Jewish homeland arose. In 1917 the Balfour Declaration promised increased Jewish immigration to Palestine. The Jewish population in the region began to increase slowly, then it expanded dramatically because of refugees from the Holocaust. Soon after World War II, the Jewish population in Palestine stood at 650,000; the Arab population was 1,350,000. Zionists increasingly agitated for an independent Jewish state. When the British withdrew in 1947, war immediately broke out between Jewish forces and the region's Arabs. The Jews won, establishing Israel in 1948 and doubling their territory. Most Palestinian Arabs fled (or were driven) from Israel to refugee camps in Gaza and the West Bank (of the Jordan River), two areas that had been part of Palestine but were captured in the war by Egypt and Jordan, respectively. As a result of the 1967 Six Day War between Israel and Egypt, Jordan, and Syria, the Israelis again expanded their territory by capturing several areas, including the Sinai Peninsula, Gaza, the Golan Heights, and the West Bank. Also in this period the Palestine Liberation Organization (PLO) became the major representative of Palestinian Arabs. True peace was not possible because the PLO and the Arab states would not recognize Israel's legitimacy and because Israel refused to give up some of the captured territory.

Since then, however, continuing violence, including another war in 1973, has persuaded many war-exhausted Arabs and Israelis that there has to be mutual compromise to achieve peace. Perhaps the most serious remaining sore point between the Arabs and Israelis is the fate of the Palestinians, who live primarily in the West Bank and Gaza.

That issue has been frustrating, with the past dozen or so years a time of fitful progress toward, and then seeming retreat from, the goal of peace. In 1991 Israelis and Palestinians met in Spain and held public talks for the first time. Israeli elections brought Prime Minister Yitzhak Rabin's liberal coalition to power in 1992. This coalition was more willing to compromise with the Arabs than had been its more conservative predecessor. Secret peace talks occurred between the Israelis and Palestinians in Norway and led to the Oslo Agreement in 1993. Palestinians gained limited control over Gaza and parts of the West Bank and established a quasi-government, the Palestinian authority led by Yasser Arafat.

The peace process was halted, perhaps even reversed, when in 1995 Prime Minister Rabin was assassinated by a Jewish fanatic opposed to Rabin's policy of trying to compromise with the Palestinians and even to meet their demand for a homeland.

Soon thereafter, the conservative coalition headed by Prime Minister Benjamin Netanyahu came to power. He dismissed any possibility of an independent Palestine, made tougher demands on the PLO, and moved to expand Jewish settlements in the West Bank. With some 200,000 Jews already in the West Bank and East Jerusalem, this compounded the difficult issue of the fate of those people in a potentially Palestinian-controlled area.

Pressure from a number of quarters, including the United States, kept the Israelis and Palestinians talking. Meeting in 1997 at the Wye River Plantation in Maryland under the watchful eye of President Bill Clinton, Israel agreed to give the Palestinians control over additional areas of the West Bank, and the Palestinians agreed to work to protect Israel from Arab terrorist attacks and to remove language in the PLO charter that called for the destruction of the Jewish state. The immediate impact of the Wye River Agreement was negligible.

Writing less than two years later, but with a new, liberal coalition under Prime Minister Ehud Barak in power in Israel, Daniel Pipes holds in the following selection that given Arab hostility, compromising with the Palestinians and the Arab states that support them could lead Israel into a time of extreme peril that might lead to war. In the second selection, Herbert C. Kelman, writing shortly after the Wye River Agreement, expresses his belief that a true Palestinian state offers the path to peace.

Daniel Pipes  **YES**

Israel's Moment of Truth

It might appear that things have never been going better for Israel, or worse for those who wish it ill.

Consider: the Jewish state has signed peace treaties with Egypt and Jordan, and five agreements with the Palestinian Authority (PA), its "partner for peace." With Syria, high-level negotiations now under way appear so promising that both sides have publicly predicted they could be wrapped up within a few months. Other diplomatic ties are stronger than ever: Israel has a powerful regional ally in Turkey, enjoys growing links to such giants as India and China, and is generally shedding the near-pariah status that hobbled it in the recent past. The connection to the United States is warm, deep, personal, and reciprocal.

Should diplomacy fail for any reason, moreover, Israel can fall back on its military strength. As the only country in the Middle East participating in the much-bruited "revolution in military affairs"—essentially, the application of high-tech to armaments—it has built so great a lead in conventional arms, including planes and tanks, that several Arab states have basically conceded they cannot compete with it on that level. Instead, they have directed their attention higher (to weapons of mass destruction) and lower (to terrorism). But even in those arenas, Israel is far from helpless: it has a missile-defense system, the Arrow, in the works and, for retaliatory purposes, weapons of mass destruction of its own, as well as formidable anti-terrorist capabilities.

Security matters hardly exhaust the list of Israel's advantages. Economically, it enjoys today a per-capita income of $18,000, placing it a bit ahead of Spain and a bit behind Canada—in other words, in the big leagues. Better yet, it has shown a very impressive annual growth rate since 1990. Thanks to its "Silicon Wadi," Israel is a high-tech giant, with a computer and Internet sector larger *in absolute terms* than that of any other country in the world outside the United States. Demographically, the birth rate of 2.6 children per woman among Israeli Jews is one of the highest in the West, and the country also remains a magnet for immigration; with 5 million Jews, it is quickly gaining on the United States as the place with the largest Jewish population in the world.

Finally, there is the political scene. Unlike its neighbors and rivals, Israel benefits from a lively and robust civic culture in which everyone has his say, party lines are (notoriously) fluid, and no one defers to politicians. And yet, however colorful and argumentative the public forum, when it comes to key security issues the major parties find much common ground. In [recent] elections, for example, the two candidates for the post of prime minister differed on the tone and pace but hardly at all on the substance of the peace process: yes, they concurred, the Palestinians should do more to live up to their promises, but no, their failings in this area were not reason enough to cut off negotiations.

చ0్ర

By contrast, Arabs—and Iran, too—seem to be faring less well. Arab countries are, in the words of a UN official, "particularly exceptional in being the highest spenders in the world on military purposes": they devote 8.8 percent of their GDP [gross domestic product] to the military, versus 2.4 percent for the world as a whole. Nevertheless, despite all this spending, Arab conventional forces are in decline. To be sure, a few states (like Egypt) have access to advanced American arms, but their lack of technical proficiency means that they are nearly always consumers and not producers of military hardware, paying for completed goods that others have to teach them how to operate.

Allies? The Soviet Union is gone, and no one has come close to replacing it. The Arab states darkly suspect the United States of engaging in conspiracies against them, and these suspicions—as, most recently, in the case of the Egypt Air crash off Massachusetts—impede closer relations with the world's only superpower. Arabs also lack an effective counterpunch to the pro-Israel lobby in Washington, and have failed to respond to the growing cooperation between Turkey and Israel in a way that would advance their own interests.

Outside Israel, the Middle East boasts—if that is the right word—the world's highest quotient of autocratic regimes, not to mention an inordinate number of rogue states, including Iran, Iraq, Syria, Sudan, and Libya. A culture of deference and intimidation remains dominant everywhere; movements for democracy and human rights are feeble. Arab states are particularly vulnerable to Islamism, a totalitarian ideology in the tradition of fascism and Marxism-Leninism. While Islamists have suffered reverses in recent years, they are still the major opposition force in countries like Algeria, Egypt, and Saudi Arabia, threatening the stability of government after government.

Nor are Arab economies doing well. The recent jump in oil prices, however welcome to producers, cannot obscure some dismal realities, principally a per-capita annual income among Arabic-speaking peoples that does not rise to one-tenth of Israel's. Yes, Kuwait weighs in (just like Israel) at $18,000; but in Yemen the annual per-capita income is $270; more to the point, Egypt, Jordan, and Syria all hover in the neighborhood of $1,000. A paltry one percent of world equity flowing to emerging markets these days ends up in Arabic-speaking countries. When it comes to high technology, the Middle East is a black hole, with few sales and even less innovation. As the historian R. Stephen Humphreys has noted, "with the partial exception of Turkey and of course Israel ... there is not one Middle Eastern manufactured item that can be sold competitively on world markets."

Demographically, the Arabs and Iran have *too* much of a good thing: a birth rate so high that schools cannot maintain standards, and economies cannot manufacture enough jobs. The demographer Onn Winckler has named population growth as the Middle East's "most critical socioeconomic problem."

Taken together, all these factors seem to suggest that Israel has at long last achieved a definitive edge over its historic enemies. Such, indeed, appears to be the view of Israeli leaders themselves. Thanks to Israel's position of strength, Prime Minister Ehud Barak now speaks confidently of an "end to wars" and of his country's being finally accepted as a permanent presence by its neighbors. These sentiments are widely echoed both in Israel and in Washington.

And yet—two trends suggest otherwise. The first has to do with Arab strengths, the second with Israeli weaknesses. In both cases, the phenomena I will be discussing are only partly material in nature, lying more in the realm of such elusive and intangible qualities as internal spirit and morale. But these are precisely the qualities that in the end can decide the fates of nations and peoples.

⋅✦⋅

Some improvements in the Arab position, whether actual or imminent, have long been recognized: greater control over a huge portion of the world's oil and gas reserves, steady acquisition of weapons of mass destruction, movement toward economic modernization (notably in Egypt). Progress in any or all of these areas can seriously threaten Israel's qualitative edge and its security in the medium term—unless Arab enmity toward the Jewish state has dissipated in the interim. But just here is where the greatest reason for concern resides.

Historically, Arab "rejectionism"—that is, the refusal to accept the permanent existence of a sovereign Jewish state in its historic homeland—has been based on one or another local variant (pan-Arab, pan-Syrian, Palestinian, or the like) of nationalism, a European import into the Middle East. It has suffered from two disabilities: limited reach and factionalism. But in recent years, as the rejection of Israel has taken on a less secular and more Islamic complexion, it has also gained a deeper resonance among ordinary Arabs, with Israel's existence now cast as an affront to God's will, and has also benefited operationally from a somewhat greater degree of unity (Islamists are surprisingly good at working together). The net effect has been not to moderate but, on the contrary, to solidify and to sharpen Arab antagonism to Israel—vocal rejectionist elements now include pious Muslims and Islamists, Arab nationalists, despots, and intellectuals—and to give fresh impetus to the dream of destroying it.

The point cannot be made often or strongly enough that, in their great majority, Arabic speakers do continue to repudiate the idea of peace with Israel. Despite having lost six rounds of war, they seem nothing loath to try again. In one of the most recent in-depth surveys of Arab opinion, conducted by the political scientist Hilal Khashan of the American University of Beirut, 1,600 respondents, divided equally among Jordanians, Lebanese, Palestinians, and Syrians, stated by a ratio of 69 to 28 percent that they personally did not want peace with Israel. By 79 to 18 percent, they rejected the idea of doing business with Israelis even after a total peace. By 80 to 19 percent, they rejected learning about Israel. By 87 to 13 percent, they supported attacks by Islamic groups against Israel.

This is the view of Israel that dominates political debate in the Arab world and that is conveyed to the public in every arena from scholarly discourse to the popular media to nursery-school jingles. True, some Arabs think otherwise. The late King Hussein of Jordan spoke eloquently of the need to put aside the conflict with Israel and to get on with things; his son and successor appears to be of like mind. Some Arab army officers would undoubtedly prefer not to confront Israel's military forces any time soon. Kuwaitis and Lebanese Christians, sobered by occupation, now mostly wish to leave Israel alone. And there are business leaders who believe, as one Arab banker succinctly put it, that "the whole purpose of peace is business." But these elements, overall, represent but a minority of the Arab population, and have not shifted the underlying hostility. . . .

Twenty years of relations between Egypt and Israel since the treaty of 1979 testify bitterly to the same state of affairs. Formally there is peace, but Cairo permits, even sponsors, a vicious propaganda campaign against Israel that includes the crudest forms of anti-Semitism, and it is rapidly building up offensive military forces that could be deployed against the Jewish state. In effect, what Egyptian authorities are telling their people is this: for all sorts of reasons we have to be in contact with Israelis and sign certain pieces of paper, but we still hate them, and you should, too. In Jordan, where the government does not play this double game, things are in some ways worse: the best efforts of two kings have failed to induce in the Jordanian populace a more peaceable and friendly outlook toward Israel.

⋅◈⋅

Fueling the dream of Arab rejectionists is the immensely important fact that within Israel itself (that is, within the old 1967 borders), the Jewish proportion of the population has fallen from a one-time high of 87 percent to 79 percent today, and is inexorably trailing downward. In 1998, of Israel's total population growth of 133,000, only 80,000 were Jews, with Arabs making up the bulk of the remainder. From such statistics, some demographers predict a non-Jewish majority in Israel by the middle of the 21st century.

But the Jewish nature of the "Jewish state" will shift in the Arabs' favor long before they reach majority status there. At present, were Israeli Arabs to be represented in the Knesset in proportion to their numbers, they would already hold 24 out of its 120 seats. Even with the seven seats they now occupy, as the analyst Eric Rozenman has noted,

> the Arab electorate and Arab Knesset members . . . have helped override Jewish majorities on such vital matters as the creation of Prime Minister Yitzhak Rabin's coalition in 1992 and approval of the Oslo and Oslo II accords in 1993 and 1995 respectively. All seven Israeli Arab members voted for both

agreements; the former passed 61 to 50, with nine abstentions, the latter passed 61 to 59.

These trends will undoubtedly persist, Rozenman writes, especially as Israeli Arabs become "energized by a new Palestinian state next door (and perhaps also by an increasingly Palestinian Jordan)." By the time the numbers of Arabs approach or even exceed parity with the Jews, "the state might still be democratic, but the civic atmosphere, the public culture, would not likely be Jewish in the tacit, general sense it is today."

The growing power and enfranchisement of Muslims in the United States provide further grounds for Arab optimism. Not only is the American Muslim community approaching the Jewish community in absolute size, it is also making strides in education, economic well-being, and political savvy. If the old pro-Arab lobby was hampered by its dependence on oil money, retired American diplomats, and left-wing Christian Arabs, dynamic new organizations like the American Muslim Council and the Council on American-Islamic Relations are another matter altogether. Although foreign policy is hardly their only cause, "Palestine" remains the single most mobilizing issue for American Muslims, and the position articulated by Muslim organizations on this issue is almost uniformly extremist—against negotiations with Israel or accommodation with it in almost any form.

Not only are these extremist Muslim organizations intent on making themselves heard, but the Clinton administration, at least, . . . openly welcomed them at the highest levels. At a dinner she hosted to break the fast of Ramadan [in] December [1999], Secretary of State Madeleine K. Albright told her guests: "I want to be sure that the legitimate concerns of Muslim-Americans are taken into account when shaping the programs, activities, and reports of this Department." Seated before her was a Who's Who of American Muslim radicals.

Is it any wonder that many Arabs, knowing such facts, or hearing such heady words from the lips of the American Secretary of State, should become newly imbued with a sense of confidence about the future? And that sense can only be bolstered by what they see happening on the other side, within Israel itself.

~◈~

Once renowned for its self-confidence, bravery, and purpose, Israel today is a changed society. Whatever the undoubted strength of its military machine, few in a position to know the heart and soul of the country try to hide the fact of a widespread demoralization, even within that military machine itself. As a retired colonel summed it up neatly, "the Israeli public is really tired of war."

Fatigue takes many forms in contemporary Israel. The pervasive feeling that they have fought long enough, and that the time has come to settle, leads many to express openly their annoyance with the need for military preparedness and the huge expense of maintaining a modern armed force. They weary of the constant loss of life, they want escape from the fear that terrorism imparts, they yearn to close down an atavistic tribal war—and peace treaties promise a quick way out. (As one Israeli put it to me, "My grandfather, father, myself, and my son have all fought the Arabs; I want to make sure my grandson does not also have to.") Among young people, draft evasion, hitherto all but unknown, has become a serious problem, and within the army itself, morale is hardly what it once was, as the IDF's [Israel Defense Forces's] decidedly unheroic recent record in Lebanon has revealed to all, including the Hezbollah enemy.

At the same time, Israel's soaring economy has given many citizens a taste for the good life that cannot be easily reconciled with the need for patience and fortitude—and, especially, sacrifice—in confronting a seemingly unchanging enemy. Middle-aged Israeli men are increasingly unwilling to go off and "play soldier" on reserve duty for several weeks a year when they could be at the office increasing their net worth or enjoying what that net worth makes possible. For those with an active social conscience, a number of long-deferred domestic problems—persistent poverty, a faulty educational system, worsening relations between secular and religious—seem much more deserving of attention, and of state expenditure, than does grappling endlessly with Israel's opponents.

Finally, Israelis are tired of the moral opprobrium their country has long suffered—at the United Nations, in Western academic circles, and in editorial boardrooms. Indeed, in an extreme reaction to this ongoing moral ostracism, some of the country's foremost intellectuals have, as it were, defected: they have accommodated sizable chunks of the Arab side's version of the Arab-Israeli conflict, promulgating them as important new truths. Thus, to cite an especially influential expression of this line of thinking, the school of "new historians" in Israel argues that the Jewish state is guilty of an "original sin"—the alleged dispossession of Palestine's native inhabitants—and can therefore be considered to some extent illegitimate. Others, known as "post-Zionists," have characterized Jewish nationalism—Zionism—as, if not racist, then at best an outdated and parochial ideology, and one which should no longer form the basis of Israel's public life.

Such ideas, first incubated on the far Left and in the prestige universities, then spread to students, artists, and journalists, and are now the stuff of television documentaries and educational textbooks. As of the current Israeli school year, ninth graders no longer learn that Israel's war of independence in 1948–49 was a battle of the few against the many but, to the contrary, that the Jews enjoyed military superiority over the Arabs. They also learn that many Palestinians fled the country in those war years not to clear the way for invading Arab armies thought to be on their march to victory, but out of well-founded fears of Jewish brutality and terror.

In a front-page report on the introduction of these books into the schools, the *New York Times* rightly characterized them as marking a "quiet revolution." That revolution has by now reached the consciousness of politicians, business leaders, and even military officers; its impact can hardly be exaggerated. Thanks to the inroads of post-Zionism, as Meyrav Wurmser has observed in the *Middle East Quarterly,* Israeli society "is now facing a crisis of identity and values that strikes at the basic components and elements of [its] identity: Judaism and nationalism." Without those two components, clearly, little remains of the Zionist project.

What are the implications, for politics and diplomacy, of Israeli fatigue, and of the intense self-absorption that is its corollary? What strikes one above all is how little attention Israelis are paying these days to their Arab neighbors. Sick of fighting, bent on building an Internet economy, they seem to have decided that Arabs feel the same way, and want the same things, they do. (In psychology, the term for this is projection.) According to a survey conducted by the Jaffee Center at Tel Aviv University, fully two-thirds of Israelis now agree with the following dubious assertions: that most Palestinians want peace; that signing agreements will end the Arab-Israeli conflict; and that if forced to choose between negotiations and increased military strength, Israel should opt for the former. Prime Minister Ehud Barak perfectly sums up this outlook in his repeated invocation of a peace that will "work for everyone," the unspoken assumption being that Arabs no less than Israelis seek to resolve their century-old conflict on harmonious terms.

Of course, at some level Israelis know full well about continued Arab rejectionism: the signs are too conspicuous for even the most ostrich-like to be truly clueless. But they have clearly chosen to de-emphasize or even ignore the phenomenon. How else to explain the absence of a single full-time Israeli journalist reporting from an Arab capital, or the fact that Hilal Khashan's meticulous survey of Arab opinion, with its thoroughly dismaying news, received no attention whatsoever in the Israeli press when it appeared [recently]? "These are only words. Let them talk," is how Shimon Peres [former Israeli prime minister], speaking for many of his countrymen, has airily dismissed the undeniable evidence of Arab feelings and attitudes.

Peres's disdainful remark encapsulates a delusional but widespread Israeli assumption: that peace in the Middle East is Israel's for the making, and that if Israelis want to end the long-drawn-out struggle, they can do so on their own. They can "solve" the Palestinian problem by acceding to the creation of a state in the West Bank and Gaza; they can eliminate anti-Zionism by helping to funnel money to the Arabs, who will use their newfound affluence to become good neighbors (and never to amass more powerful arsenals); or—in the post-Zionist scenario—they can win Arab hearts by dismantling the Jewish attributes of the Jewish state.

Whatever the preferred tactic, the underlying premise is the same: that the key decisions of war and peace in the Arab-Israeli conflict are made in Jerusalem and Tel Aviv rather than—what is in fact the case—in Cairo, Gaza, Amman, and Damascus. Under the spell of this fantasy, Israelis now seem prepared to execute what will amount to a unilateral transfer of hard-won territory—to Syria in the north, to the Palestinian Authority in the center of the country—in the hope that their troubles will thereby disappear. Indeed, they sometimes appear prepared to go to extreme lengths to induce their Arab interlocutors to accept the gifts they mean to confer on them.

Listening to the Israeli prime minister and the foreign minister of Syria as they inaugurated a new round of talks in December 1999, for example, one might have thought that Israel was the party that had instigated—and then lost

—the Six-Day War of 1967, and was now desperately suing Damascus for terms. Barak spoke pleadingly of the need "to put behind us the horrors of war and to step forward toward peace," and of creating, "together with our Syrian partners, . . . a different Middle East where nations are living side by side in peaceful relationship and in mutual respect and good-neighborliness." By contrast, the Syrian foreign minister blustered like a conqueror, insisting that Israel had "provoked" the 1967 clash and demanding the unconditional return of "all its occupied land." The very fact that a prime minister had agreed to meet with a mere foreign minister, breaching a cardinal protocol of diplomacy, was signal enough; that the foreign minister of Syria lacks any decision-making power whatsoever further confirmed who in this encounter was the wooer, who the wooed.

When it comes to Lebanon, Israelis appear to have convinced themselves that the unilateral withdrawal of troops from their "security zone" in the south will cause their main Lebanese opponent, Hezbollah, to leave them alone, despite repeated and overt statements by Hezbollah leadership that it intends to continue fighting until it reaches Jerusalem and that it "will never recognize the existence of a state called Israel even if all the Arabs do so." More, Israelis seem persuaded that the prospect of their withdrawal from Lebanon is one of the things that have the Syrians worried, quite as if the best way to scare your enemy were to threaten a retreat.

On the Palestinian track, the ostensibly more muscular party—Israel—has pointedly refrained from requiring that the ostensibly more vulnerable party fulfill the many obligations it has undertaken since 1993, with the result that the PA has neither turned over criminals and terrorists, nor ceased its unrelenting incitements to violence, nor restricted the size of its armed forces.[1] The PA's logo brazenly shows a map of a future Palestine stretching from the Jordan River to the Mediterranean Sea—a Palestine, that is, not alongside Israel but instead of it. To all this, the Israeli body politic appears to pay no heed.

The newspaper *Ha'aretz* reports that Israeli negotiators have already conceded in principle to the Palestinian Authority day-to-day control of parts of Jerusalem. At the very end of 1999, when Prime Minister Barak took the unprecedented step of releasing two Palestinian prisoners who had killed Israelis, his action was met, predictably, not with Arab gratitude but with noisy demonstrations chanting aggressive slogans—"Barak, you coward. Our prisoners will not be humiliated"—and by the demand that Israel now let go all of the estimated 1,650 jailed Palestinians. No doubt, the demonstrators will eventually get their way. Israelis are on their own road to peace, and no "partners," however hostile, will deflect them from it.

❧

Today's Israel, in sum, is hugely different from the Israel of old. For four decades and more, the country made steady progress vis-à-vis its enemies through the application of patience and will, backed when necessary by military courage and might. From a fledgling state in 1948 invaded by five Arab armies, it established itself as a powerful force, overcoming oil boycotts, terrorism, and the enmity of a superpower. But by the time of the Oslo accord of August 1993, the signs of exhaustion were becoming increasingly manifest; by now they are unmistakable.

As recently as the 1996 national elections, a lively debate took place in Israel over Palestinian noncompliance and over the wisdom of handing the Golan Heights back to Syria. By the time of the 1999 elections, with very little having changed on the ground, those issues had disappeared. Perhaps 10 to 15 percent of the population still adheres to the old Likud view that Israel should keep control of the territories until the Arabs have shown a true change of heart. Today, the debate is over timing and tone, not over substance. Symbolic of the new consensus is the fact that the Third Way, a party that was exclusively focused on retaining the Golan Heights under Israeli control and that took four Knesset seats in 1996, vaporized in 1999, winning not a single seat. Even former Prime Minister Benjamin Netanyahu, the reputed arch-hard-liner, signed two empty agreements with Arafat and, on the Syrian track, was ready to concede virtually everything Hafez al-Assad demanded. As Ehud Barak has correctly noted, "there are only microscopic differences between the things Netanyahu was willing to discuss and those discussed by [Shimon] Peres and [Yitzhak] Rabin."

Many who bemoan the weakness of current Israeli policy are tempted to place the onus on Washington. But (to put it symbolically) how can one become exercised over Hillary Clinton's advocacy of a Palestinian state when, only weeks earlier, Shimon Peres had already specified a date for such a state's inception? Israelis are perfectly capable of choosing leaders prepared to resist American pressure, and they have done so in the past. The collapse of a meaningful opposition party in 1999—Menachem Begin won two elections as prime minister in 1997 and 1981, but [in 1999] his son and political heir had to withdraw from the race because his support was so trivial—rebuts the notion that weak politicians are doing the bidding of Washington; rather, they are doing the bidding of their electorate. No, it is inward to the Israeli spirit that one must look for the roots of the present disposition to ignore repeated Palestinian flouting of solemnly signed agreements, to turn the Golan Heights over to a still-fanged Syria, to withdraw unilaterally from Lebanon, and to acquiesce in huge American sales of military equipment to an unfriendly and potentially threatening Egypt.

Israel today has money and weapons, the Arabs have will. Israelis want a resolution to conflict, Arabs want victory. Israel has high capabilities and low morale, the Arabs have low capabilities and high morale. Again and again, the record of world history shows, victory goes not to the side with greater firepower, but to the side with greater determination.

Among democracies, few precedents exist for the malaise now on display in Israel. Imperfect analogies include the atmosphere of pacifism and appeasement that pervaded significant sectors of opinion in England and France in the 1930's, the United States during the Vietnam period, and Western Europe in the early 1980's. But none of these situations quite matches Israel's in the extent of the debilitation. Even more critically, none of those countries lived with so narrow a margin of safety. France succumbed to the Nazis, but was able to recover. England nearly succumbed, but had time to rally with American help. The United States lost a long, bloody war in Vietnam, but the nation as a whole was hardly at risk. In Israel the stakes are far higher, the room for error correspondingly minute.

This is not to say that the Jewish state is in immediate danger; it continues to have a strong military and a relatively healthy body politic, and democracies have demonstrated the capacity to right their mistakes at five minutes to midnight. But one shudders to think of what calamity Israel must experience before its people wake up and assume, once again, the grim but inescapable task of facing the implacable enemies around them.

Note

1. The threat to Israel's security already posed by the PA's military is the subject of Yuval Steinitz's "When the Palestinian Army Invades the Heart of Israel," COMMENTARY, December 1999.

Herbert C. Kelman

 **NO**

Building a Sustainable Peace

The prospects for Israeli-Palestinian peace are probably dimmer now than they have been at any time since the beginning of negotiations at the Madrid Conference in 1991. The Oslo agreement represented a major breakthrough in the conflict, which was made possible by the consummate pragmatism of the leaders on both sides; indeed, Oslo could stand as a virtual monument to pragmatism. Both Israeli prime minister Yitzhak Rabin and PLO [Palestine Liberation Organization] Chairman Yasir Arafat were persuaded of the political necessity of an early peace agreement and recognized that they needed each other to reach that agreement. They were not deterred by ideological dogma from making the necessary compromises as long as their fundamental interests—Israeli security and ultimate Palestinian statehood, respectively— were safeguarded. Out of these pragmatic commitments, Rabin and Arafat were able to develop a partnership that, in due course, probably would have achieved a mutually satisfactory agreement.

With the current Israeli government, that partnership has broken down. Prime Minister Benjamin Netanyahu and his coalition are not prepared to make the compromises required for achieving an agreement. Under the circumstances, it is highly unlikely that the strictly pragmatic, step-by-step process of exchanging concessions and confidence-building measures in the hope that this will eventually lead to some kind of agreement can succeed. Without the understanding that the two sides have to work together to shape a mutually acceptable agreement addressing the central concerns of both parties, the step-by-step approach will either collapse without an agreement or, if there is sufficient outside pressure, produce an agreement that is not workable and not conducive to a sustainable peace.

To save the peace process today, it is necessary to go beyond a pragmatic peace to a principled peace, opening the way to resolution of the conflict and to reconciliation. I am arguing, paradoxically, that at this low point in the peace process it is necessary to aim higher than the Oslo Accord—that, at this stage, there can be no peace without reconciliation. I am not speaking of reconciliation as a precondition for negotiation or as an instant outcome, but rather as a process. There is no way to sidestep the essential political give-and-take of negotiating an agreement, but the process and outcome of negotiations must be

From Herbert C. Kelman, "Building a Sustainable Peace: The Limits of Pragmatism in the Israeli-Palestinian Negotiations," *Journal of Palestine Studies*, vol. 28, no. 1 (Autumn 1998). Copyright © 1998 by The Institute for Palestine Studies. Reprinted by permission of University of California Press, Journals Division. Notes omitted.

consistent with the requirements for ultimate reconciliation. Stated succinctly, this means that the negotiations must be anchored in the mutual acceptance of the other's nationhood and humanity.

The Oslo Accord

To understand the significance of the Oslo Accord, it helps to note that there were in effect two processes going on at Oslo simultaneously and that the agreement reflects the effect of both: a process of distributive bargaining between two parties with unequal power and an initial, rudimentary stage of a process of reconciliation. At the risk of oversimplification, one might describe the Declaration of Principles (DOP) as primarily a product of distributive bargaining and the letters of mutual recognition exchanged between Arafat and Rabin as a product of a rudimentary process of reconciliation.

The DOP reflected—both in what it included and in what it omitted—the power differential between the parties. To be sure, some of the DOP's features created a clear opening for a Palestinian state, which indeed made it possible for the PLO to sign the agreement: It established a territorial base for the Palestinian Authority (PA) in Gaza and the West Bank and provided for the early empowerment of the PA. But it did not *guarantee* an independent Palestinian state; it did not explicitly prohibit the expansion of settlements (although it did rule out changes on the ground that would preempt the final status negotiations); it did not address the question of refugees except to defer it to the final status negotiations. The items that did make it into the DOP—the terms of agreement—reflect the difference in power by favoring the stronger party. Moreover, the ambiguities that were purposely left in the DOP in order to make an agreement possible also work in favor of the stronger party, which is better positioned to resolve them in its own favor. It was this advantage, resulting from power-based, distributive bargaining, that led some Palestinian critics of Oslo to describe it as a Palestinian surrender and defeat. Interestingly, in characteristic mirror-image fashion, some Israeli and Jewish writers have criticized Oslo as a surrender by Israel. Thus, one writer described Oslo as "Zionist surrender that was driven by the palpable yearning of Israelis for normal life in a very dangerous neighborhood."

What these critics miss is that there was a second process going on alongside the distributive bargaining process, captured best by the letters of recognition. Although those letters also reflect the power differential in that Rabin's response to Arafat was much briefer and less specific in its commitment, the essence of this exchange of letters (and, by implication, of the DOP itself) is an act of mutual recognition. It is this exchange, more than the DOP, that states the underlying principle of the Oslo agreement. It provides the basis for a just solution—at least in the sense of pragmatic justice—that goes beyond the balance of power.

The breakthrough character of the Oslo agreement, from the Palestinian perspective, was Israel's recognition of the PLO as its negotiating partner. Because the PLO has, since the late 1960s, stood for the concept of an independent Palestinian state, recognition of the PLO clearly conferred legitimacy on that concept. It was tantamount to recognition of Palestinian peoplehood with the implication that, at the end of the day, a Palestinian state would be established. From the Israeli perspective, the breakthrough character of the Oslo agreement was Palestinian recognition of Israel's legitimacy, thus opening the door to recognition in the Arab world. Indeed, the Oslo Accord led, in short order, to an agreement between Israel and Jordan, to diplomatic relations between Israel and several Arab states, and to Israel's increasing economic integration in the region—gains that are now at risk because of the policies of the current government. In short, the mutual recognition of the Oslo agreement "represented a fundamental shift in the relationship between the two peoples. Acknowledging each other's legitimacy was a significant affirmation of the other's national existence, which the two sides had systematically denied to each other throughout the history of their conflict.... This conceptual breakthrough ... is irreversible, even if the current peace process were to collapse."

The logic of the Oslo Accord was to move toward a final political outcome through a series of interim stages. There was no commitment on Israel's part that the final outcome would take the form of an independent Palestinian state, but the recognition of the PLO and some of the terms of the DOP clearly pointed in that direction. This was well understood by Palestinians, by Israelis, and by the rest of the world. In this sense, the Oslo agreement represented a move toward a principled solution of the conflict—toward a historic compromise, opening the way to reconciliation.

A Political Partnership

In signing the Oslo agreement, with its far-reaching implications and limited commitments, both Rabin and Arafat took significant risks. Rabin took the risk that even if the experience of the interim period did not reassure Israel that a Palestinian state would be consistent with its own security requirements, the logic of the process might inexorably lead to a state anyway. He felt able to take that risk because the agreement contained no explicit commitment to a Palestinian state; thus the option of saying "no" in the end, though politically costly, remained available. Arafat took an even greater risk by signing an agreement that unambiguously recognized Israel—giving away what he used to call his last card—without an explicit promise of an independent state. He took the risk because his options were severely limited and because he had reason to believe that the process he was entering offered a high probability of a Palestinian state at the end of the day. Ultimately, the two leaders took these risks because their assessment of the political realities in relation to their interests led them to conclude that the time had come for a historic compromise based on mutual recognition.

Because both men also recognized that they needed each other to succeed in the peacemaking process, they entered into a political partnership despite serious reservations and initial distrust of each other. The evolving partnership between Rabin and Arafat, and the subsequent partnership between Peres and Arafat, were clearly limited. Each side tried to gain advantages for the interim negotiations and for the final status negotiations that lay ahead. Neither side observed the letter and the spirit of the Oslo agreement in all respects. The continuing settlement process during the Rabin and Peres era represented the most serious violation of the spirit of the agreement. Rabin, while often disdainful of the settlers, was clearly worried about the political costs of blocking settlement expansion; he missed an opportunity to dislodge the Hebron settlers after the Hebron massacre, when there was support for such a move in his cabinet. The PA, on its part, did not always adhere to the precise terms of the agreement with respect to such issues as establishment of PA offices in Jerusalem or the size of the security forces.

Despite its flaws, the partnership took hold in a way that partly transcended the balance of power. Each side was cognizant of the concerns and constraints of the other and refrained from creating situations that would be embarrassing or politically sensitive for the other side. They consciously tried to be responsive to each other and to avoid actions that might undermine their counterparts' political standing in their own community. They closed their eyes to occasional violations, with a degree of understanding of the political necessities that prompted them. Thus, the partnership developed during those years into a relationship characterized by significant elements of working trust and responsiveness at the leadership level.

One of the regrettable consequences of Rabin's and Arafat's consummate pragmatism is that they did not draw their publics into this evolving partnership. They preferred to see and present themselves as pragmatists yielding to necessity rather than as visionaries preparing for a process of long-term reconciliation. It seems that they did not trust their publics sufficiently to be able to share with them what I believe was their own readiness for a historic compromise. As a result, they did not educate their publics with respect to both the realities and the underlying principles that led them to Oslo and the subsequent partnership.

Rabin and Peres did not tell the Israeli public that the peace process was expected, ultimately, to lead to a Palestinian state. The evidence from public opinion data and informal observations suggests that the Israeli public would not have been surprised to hear that. It was generally understood, by both supporters and opponents of Oslo, that this was what the agreement meant. Instead of downplaying that fact, public education could have stressed that the successful unfolding of the process would probably lead to a Palestinian state and that such an outcome would be both just and in Israel's long-term interest. Such a message would have confirmed the Israeli public's expectations about the likely outcome and, at the same time, increased the perceived legitimacy of this outcome and the public's commitment to it as a goal that was necessary and right from the Israeli point of view.

Similarly, Arafat did not tell the Palestinian public that the Oslo agreement, although clearly pointing in the direction of a Palestinian state, did not guarantee this outcome. Nor did he explain to his public why he concluded that this was the best agreement he could achieve at this time, why he had strong reason to expect that it would ultimately lead to an independent state, and why the current process and its anticipated outcome were necessary and right, given the realities and the ultimate hopes of the Palestinian people. Just as Rabin underplayed the degree to which the Oslo agreement implied a Palestinian state, Arafat overplayed the degree to which a commitment to such a state had already been achieved. Neither leader told his public that there were risks, but that they were worth taking, or that there would inevitably be setbacks, but that they could be overcome.

Although the publics were not fully brought into the process, the partnership at the leadership level was sufficiently solid to allow Arafat and his Israeli counterparts to pursue the peace process in a pragmatic mode and wait until they had clear evidence of success before strengthening the public consensus in favor of a two-state solution as a fair and just historic compromise. Had Labor stayed in power, chances are good that the parties would eventually have achieved an agreement in the form of a two-state solution. But this pragmatic process could not survive the change in Israeli leadership that brought to power a coalition that was not committed to the political partnership that Arafat and the Labor party leaders had developed.

Netanyahu's Approach to the Peace Process

The approach to the peace process of the present Israeli government is qualitatively different from that of the previous government. Netanyahu has not made the strategic decision to end the conflict with a historic compromise based on mutual recognition. He has not accepted the Oslo agreement's implication that Israel will yield territory and control to an independent Palestinian state at the end of successful negotiations. He has shown no willingness to continue the political partnership with the PA that his predecessors established. He gives no consideration to what the Palestinians would need if a solution to the conflict is to be feasible from their point of view and politically acceptable to them. Indeed, he takes systematic steps that destroy the possibility of such solutions—for example, by unilaterally changing the status and demography of Jerusalem, expanding settlements, confiscating Palestinian lands, and blowing up Palestinian houses.

To be sure, Netanyahu has accepted certain political realities. A Palestinian self-governing authority is in place in Gaza and most of the West Bank cities, and it is universally recognized. Netanyahu does not intend to reoccupy these areas or to expel the Palestinians. He has thus found himself in a situation in which he has to deal with the PA as a territorially based political entity. His much-publicized handshake with Arafat visibly broke his long-standing taboo against negotiating with the PLO. In January 1997, he signed the Hebron agreement calling for partial redeployment of Israeli troops from Hebron and other West Bank areas. In June of that year, he presented a final status map to his inner cabinet, showing the areas of the West Bank (some 40 percent) that he might be prepared to turn over to the PA in a final agreement. By negotiating with the PA about redeployment and territory, Netanyahu demonstrated that he —along with a significant part of the Israeli Right—has recognized that the consequences of the Oslo agreement are not entirely reversible and is entertaining the concept of territorial compromise and some kind of partition of Greater Israel. Indeed, many settlers and right-wing ideologues, including members of his own party, are accusing him of selling out the cause by showing willingness to give up even a small part of the land.

Accusations from the more extreme elements of his coalition and constituency do constrain his ability to maneuver. But he has also given no indication that, in the absence of these constraints, he would vigorously pursue a peace process. While he accepts some of the new realities and responds to outside pressures when they become sufficiently persistent, it has become increasingly clear that he is not prepared to pay the price for peace. He remains committed to keeping as much of the land and as much control as possible. He has given no indication that he is prepared to allow the Palestinians to establish anything resembling a contiguous, viable, independent state on the pieces of land they may in the end be offered.

Netanyahu and much of the Zionist Right have now embraced the Oslo agreement and present themselves to the Israeli public and the American mediators as ready to pursue the peace process. However, as Ian Lustick points out in his detailed analysis, they use the Oslo agreement as a legal document rather than as the opening to a political partnership that it was intended to be. Netanyahu does not deal with the Palestinians as partners who are responsive to each other's concerns and constraints, but wields the terms of the agreement as a weapon against them, demanding that they honor certain specified terms before Israel will take the next step. These demands have been one-sided, have not considered the constraints of the Palestinian leadership, and have denied Israel's own failures to live up to its obligations under the accord.

Netanyahu has used the term "reciprocity" to frame his demands on the Palestinians. But reciprocity is a norm governing a relationship between equals, in which each party has both rights and obligations. In a relationship based on this norm, each party is expected to consider the needs, aspirations, and constraints of the other and to give the other what it asks for itself: reassurances regarding security, acknowledgment of identity, respect for dignity, understanding of sensitivities. A relationship can flourish only if both sides adhere to the norm of reciprocity. In Netanyahu's vocabulary, however, the word "reciprocity" is used as an ultimatum. For example, the Israeli government has refused to carry out the next (previously agreed-upon) stage of redeployment unless the PA takes certain "reciprocal" steps in curbing terrorism, such as arresting or extraditing a specified list of suspects. Yet security itself is best addressed in the context of a partnership, within a framework of reciprocal rights and duties, in which the parties jointly work out cooperative arrangements that are technically and politically feasible and consistent with the welfare and dignity of each. In this regard, the partnership between the Rabin/Peres government and the PA was actually quite successful in developing cooperative security arrangements that seemed to work, but that with the collapse of the partnership have been eroding.

Netanyahu's embrace of Oslo and demand for reciprocity seem designed to delay any further redeployment as long as possible and to set conditions that the Palestinians are likely to reject. The resultant breakdown of the negotiations could then be blamed on the Palestinians, setting the stage for Israel's unilateral imposition of a solution. It remains quite possible, however, that a combination of external and internal pressures may yet bring about a further Israeli redeployment and a return to the negotiating table. It is even possible that this government (though not without a great deal of internal opposition) will in the end agree to the establishment of some entity that could be called a Palestinian state. This possibility has been bruited by some of Netanyahu's associates. Their idea seems to be to turn over to the Palestinians whatever disconnected pieces of land they are prepared to offer and to tell the Palestinians that, if they wish, they can call it a state.

With or without negotiations, however, it is quite clear—from Netanyahu's map, his actions, and his pronouncements—that what he is prepared to offer the Palestinians, whether or not it is called a state, comes nowhere near to what Palestinians would minimally expect. It is, essentially, a limited autonomy in Gaza and several West Bank enclaves, excluded from Jerusalem, and heavily dependent on Israel. Even if this entity were to be called a state, it would lack the geographical contiguity, control over its population and resources, and all of the attributes of sovereignty, viability, and security that an independent state requires. Moreover, such a state would not solve the central problem of the Palestinian people, which is their lack of citizenship—a fundamental human right in the modern world. It would in effect be a set of Bantustans offering only the pretense of citizenship, without the capacity to protect the population or meet its needs. Even if the Palestinians accepted such an arrangement, it could not form the basis for a stable, sustainable peace.

The very fact that a Palestinian state is now being talked about by elements on the Israeli Right underlines the inevitability and growing legitimacy of a two-state solution based on territorial compromise. It is a solution that is now almost universally viewed as a fair historic compromise, widely accepted by Palestinians, and increasingly by Israelis. But ironically, the Right's adoption of the concept of a Palestinian state poses a danger of distorting and trivializing that concept as a key element of a just solution to the conflict. If the Palestinian state envisaged in a two-state solution is to take the form that Netanyahu and his associates are prepared to accept, it will have lost its meaning as a way to terminate the conflict and establish a basis for long-term peace and cooperation.

It is no longer enough, therefore, to engage in a peace process that envisages a two-state solution without specifying what *kind* of two-state solution it is to be. One must be clear about the nature of the Palestinian state that will emerge from the final negotiations and its precise relationship to Israel.

The Need for a Principled Peace

To revive the peace process now, the parties need to recreate the working trust and reestablish the political partnership that have broken down. This can no longer be achieved by the step-by-step approach of distributive bargaining that seemed to be working when the Labor party was in power. The parties must now go beyond the pragmatism of the Oslo process and commit themselves to a *principled* outcome of the negotiations that not only serves the interests of both parties, as it must, but that is also fair and just. Thus, to restore Palestinian trust in the peace process, Israel must commit itself, on a principled basis, to a two-state solution as the end point of negotiations and negotiate the remaining issues on the premise of a Palestinian state. Such an Israeli commitment will allow the Palestinians, in return, to commit themselves to a principled two-state solution and thus help revive the political partnership. . . .

Elements of a Principled Peace

To move the peace process in the direction of a principled peace and ultimate reconciliation, there are four key ideas that need to be understood, promulgated, and acted upon in the coming negotiations. . . .

Prior Commitment to a Two-State Solution

The Oslo agreement left the question of Palestinian statehood open until the end of the negotiations. With the total erosion of working trust, that option is no longer available. For the process to fulfill itself under the present circumstances, it must be clear at the outset that there will be a two-state solution and that only the modalities are the subject of negotiation. Such commitment can restore the trust necessary for productive negotiations to proceed.

Moreover, both sides' commitment to a two-state solution as the end point of the negotiations must be a *principled* commitment, comparable to the commitment of the South African parties to majority rule as the end point of their negotiations. The two-state solution must be adopted on the grounds that it is right—that it is perceived by the parties, and indeed by the rest of the world, as a just and fair historic compromise to the long and bitter conflict. Although this solution may not give each side all it wants and feels it deserves, it can at least address each side's basic needs for identity, security, well-being, and self-determination, and it can serve both sides' long-term interests. Only a commitment to this kind of principled outcome can lead to a sustainable peace—to a stable, cooperative, and mutually enhancing relationship between the two states for the long term.

A Genuinely Independent Palestinian State

In a principled two-state solution, the Palestinian state, like Israel, must be sovereign, viable, and secure. If the state is to meet these criteria, it must have contiguous territory in the West Bank and a secure link between the West Bank and Gaza; it must be free of foreign troops and extraterritorial settlements; it must be able to exercise control over its land, resources, and population; and it must be able to secure the rights of its citizens.

In the debate about a two-state solution, it has to be made very clear that what Netanyahu and his government now envisage as the Palestinian entity is very different from a genuine Palestinian state, even if in the end they are willing to call it a state. What they seem prepared to offer would in effect continue the occupation, while allowing the Palestinians to establish a limited, nonsovereign autonomy, which could be called a state only in the sense that the South African Bantustans were called states. It is important to forestall the co-optation of the concept of a Palestinian state by the Israeli Right and its redefinition as another version of a Bantustan. In advocating and committing to a two-state solution, it is now essential to specify that what is being called for is a genuine Palestinian state possessing the essential attributes of an independent polity.

Meaningful Citizenship for the Palestinian People

The necessity of an independent Palestinian state at this historical juncture can perhaps be framed most persuasively in terms of the issue of citizenship. Citizenship is a central human right in the modern world, since it is a condition for assuring many other basic rights both at home and abroad. To lack citizenship is to lack protection, access to resources, and even personhood. One of the political and moral imperatives of an Israeli-Palestinian peace agreement is that it must provide meaningful citizenship to the Palestinian population of the West Bank and Gaza, as well as to the refugee population.

The only feasible and mutually acceptable vehicle for providing meaningful citizenship to the Palestinian people is a two-state solution that establishes a genuinely independent Palestinian state. The limited autonomy that the Netanyahu government envisages could offer the Palestinians under its jurisdiction passports and other trappings of citizenship. But even if it were called a state, it would be heavily controlled by Israel and would not have the capacity to offer the population most of the benefits and protection that citizenship normally entails. In effect, this arrangement would offer Palestinians the pretense of citizenship while denying them citizenship rights in the polity that controls their lives....

Mutual Recognition of the Other's Nationhood and Humanity

Over the decades, the parties have engaged in systematic denial of each other's national identity, with the aim of delegitimizing the other's national movement and political aspirations. Clearly, if the parties are to conclude a principled agreement, conducive to sustainable peace and reconciliation, they will have not only to reverse this pattern, but also to take active steps to acknowledge the other's nationhood and humanity in word and deed....

On the Israeli side, commitment to a genuinely independent Palestinian state, which would be able to offer full citizenship to its population, would represent the most concrete form of acknowledging Palestinian nationhood.... [In addition, there is need for official Israeli acknowledgment] that the Palestinians, as a nation, have rights in the land in which they have lived for generations; ... an injustice has been done to them; and ... an independent state providing Palestinian citizenship is designed to rectify the historical injustice by establishing their national rights.

[It is also necessary to reverse] the policies and practices of the Israeli government [that] seem designed to squeeze Palestinians out of large portions of the remaining land. In the densely populated and impoverished Gaza Strip, several thousand Israeli settlers occupy some 20 percent of the land and use a disproportionate amount of the water. In the West Bank, Israeli settlements are expanding, Palestinian land is being confiscated, Palestinians are denied building permits and houses built without permits are demolished, and water is in short supply for Palestinians—though not for their settler neighbors. In Jerusalem, there are deliberate attempts to reduce the number of Palestinian residents—for example, by denying building permits or by canceling the ID cards required for residency—while houses for Jewish occupants are being built or bought in the Palestinian parts of the city. The effect of these policies and practices is to leave the Palestinians very little space on which to establish a national presence in the country, to make it difficult for them to claim ownership of any part of Jerusalem, and to deprive them of the opportunity to lead normal lives.

... [O]nce Israel—perhaps the next Israeli government—takes the initiative in acknowledging Palestinian nationhood and humanity, it is essential that the Palestinian leadership be prepared to reciprocate. Notwithstanding Israel's power advantage, the Israeli public, if it is to support a principled peace and reconciliation, needs the reassurance that can only come from Palestinians' acknowledgment of Israelis' humanity and nationhood. At the human level, the core issue is Palestinian attitudes toward violence against Israelis. There must be no ambiguity about Palestinian renunciation of violence. Violence cannot be used as a bargaining chip or as a negotiating tactic that can be turned on and off as the situation requires. There can be no glorification of suicide bombers or rhetoric hinting that violence remains a political option. Violence must be renounced as a matter of principle, not only because it undermines the peace process, but because it kills and harms human beings. Palestinians will have to declare and demonstrate that they attach value to the lives and welfare of their Israeli neighbors. Clearly, Palestinians can offer this acknowledgment only in the context of genuine reciprocity.

As for acknowledging nationhood, Palestinians have come a long way in recognizing Israel's legitimacy—both in Arafat's letter to Rabin accompanying the Oslo agreement and in prior and subsequent actions of the Palestine National Council. Ultimately, however, they will need to take one further step required for a principled peace conducive to reconciliation: the acknowledgment that the Jewish people have authentic links to the land—that they are not just European colonial settlers engaged in an imperialist project, but a people that has returned to its ancestral homeland. Such an acknowledgment is extremely difficult and painful for Palestinians because it threatens the basic tenets of their national narrative. It can be made only in a context of genuine reciprocity. But a sustainable peace, conducive to reconciliation, ultimately requires each side to acknowledge that the other belongs in the land and has rights there. This acknowledgment of the other's nationhood began with the Oslo agreement but has been kept at a level of pragmatic accommodation. It now must be pushed to the level of principle.

Conclusion

Sustainable peace is not possible if the long-term relationship between the two peoples will be based on perpetuating Israeli power and Palestinian grievance: on Israel's continuing belief that it must maintain control over the lives of

Palestinians, and on the Palestinians' continuing belief that Israel's existence is illegitimate. It is essential now to work toward a principled peace, based on the four components that I have described. It may seem utopian to advocate a more demanding process at a time when a less demanding, more pragmatic process is on the verge of collapse. But I believe that, with the right leadership, the two peoples are ready for such a principled approach. I would argue that it is the most realistic option under the present circumstances, with the capacity of setting a new dynamic into motion.

POSTSCRIPT

Should Israel Take a Hard Line With the Palestinians?

T he Middle East's torment is one of the most intractable problems facing the world. In addition to the ancient territorial claims of Jews and Palestinian Arabs, complexities include long-standing rivalries among various religious and ethnic groups and countries in the region. To learn more about the history of the current conflict, consult Thomas A. Baylis, *How Israel Was Won: A Concise History of the Arab-Israeli Conflict* (Lexington Books, 1999) and Walter Laqueur and Barry Rubin, eds., *The Israel-Arab Reader: A Documentary History of the Middle East Conflict* (Viking Penguin, 2001).

Complicating matters for Israel is the fact that the country is divided—many analysts think increasingly so—between relatively secular Jews, who tend to be moderate in their attitudes toward the Palestinians, and orthodox Jews, who regard the areas in dispute as land given by God to the Jewish nation and who regard as sacrilege giving up the West Bank and, especially, any part of Jerusalem. Furthermore, there are at least 150,000 Israelis living in the West Bank, and removing them will be traumatic for Israel.

Although Israeli elections turn on more than the "security question," it is a major factor, and it has played an important role in determining who governs Israel and what the policy on the Palestinian question is. On this matter, Israelis have swung back and forth. For more on Israel's political system, read Alan Dowty, *The Jewish State: A Century Later* (University of California Press, 2001).

In May 1999 a new prime minister, Ehud Barak, garnered 56 percent of the vote to defeat Benjamin Netanyahu. Those who believed that Netanyahu had been an impediment to peace and that Barak would be more accommodating rejoiced. Barak took a number of steps that seemed to give greater hope for peace. But he was unable to come to a comprehensive agreement despite cooperative efforts by many, including a summit between Barak and Arafat in the United States hosted by President Bill Clinton.

Then, in February 2001, Barak lost in a landslide election and was replaced by the very conservative Ariel Sharon. If Barak's attitudes somewhat correspond to those of Kelman, then Sharon's views can be equated to those of Pipes. Soon after Sharon came to office, violence flared anew to alarming heights, with the Israelis and Palestinians blaming each other for the plunge in relations. For a view that is sympathetic to the Palestinians, see Edward W. Said and Christopher Hitchens, eds., *Blaming the Victims: Spurious Scholarship and the Palestinian Question* (W. W. Norton, 2001). The opposite perspective is available in Netanyahu's *Durable Peace: Israel and Its Place Among the Nations* (Warner Books, 1999).

ISSUE 8

Should Sanctions Against Iraq Be Continued?

YES: Walter B. Slocombe, from Statement Before the Committee on Armed Services, U.S. Senate (September 19, 2000)

NO: Sophie Boukhari, from "Embargo Against Iraq: Crime and Punishment," *UNESCO Courier* (July/August 2000)

ISSUE SUMMARY

YES: Walter B. Slocombe, who was undersecretary of defense for policy at the time of his statement before the Committee on Armed Services, argues that the complete unwillingness of Iraq to comply with UN inspections means that sanctions should continue.

NO: Sophie Boukhari, a journalist for the *UNESCO Courier*, maintains that the sanctions are causing unconscionable suffering among the Iraqi people and should be ended.

On August 2, 1990, Iraq launched a massive invasion of Kuwait and quickly conquered the tiny emirate. There was an immediate and strong reaction by many countries, particularly the United States, to the aggression by Saddam Hussein's Iraq. Within days, President George Bush announced Operation Desert Shield, whereby the United States sent approximately 250,000 troops to Saudi Arabia to protect that country from a possible further move by Iraq. Working with its allies, especially the British, and through the United Nations, the United States also undertook a diplomatic effort to build a coalition to apply economic, then military, pressure on Iraq to withdraw from Kuwait. The United Nations passed a series of resolutions denouncing Iraq's actions and taking economic and other measures against Iraq. These moves culminated on November 29, 1990, with the passage of Resolution 678 by the UN Security Council. Resolution 678 demanded that Iraq comply with all earlier UN resolutions (the core of which was withdrawal from Kuwait), established a deadline date for Iraqi compliance of January 15, 1991, and authorized all UN members to use "all necessary means" after that date to compel Iraqi adherence to the UN's demands.

Iraq refused to comply, and on January 17, 1991, a coalition of more than a dozen countries, with a vast preponderance of American forces, launched Operation Desert Storm. The coalition action utilized air power for approximately six weeks to pound Iraqi military positions in Kuwait and southeast Iraq and to attack Iraqi command and communications facilities, air bases, Scud missile positions, weapons manufacturing plants, and other targets throughout Iraq. Then over a half million coalition troops moved forward and overwhelmed the already devastated and dispirited Iraqi forces in a matter of days.

The terms of the peace for Iraq were embodied in Resolution 687, passed by the UN Security Council on April 3, 1991. The most important stipulations of the resolution were that Iraq was required to give up all of its remaining weapons of mass destruction (WMDs), both chemical and biological, and was barred from producing any more such weapons, including nuclear. The UN inspectors were to be granted unhindered access anywhere in the country to ensure that Iraq was disarming, and a trade embargo was to remain in place until Iraq was found to be in full compliance with the weapons of mass destruction and inspection clauses of Resolution 687.

In the years that have followed, Iraq has claimed to be implementing the clauses but has progressively refused to allow UN inspectors unimpeded access to suspect weapons sites and plants. The atmosphere has been generally a cat-and-mouse game, with bombing attacks, especially by U.S. and British forces, and mutual recriminations.

Analyses of the impact of the sanctions conducted by the UN, Harvard University's School of Public Health, and others have consistently found that the sanctions have caused abnormal levels of ill health and death among Iraqi children. Currently, 125 of every 1,000 Iraqi children die before they reach age five. That mortality rate is approximately eight times higher than in neighboring countries, such as Jordan, Iran, and Syria.

Such findings led the UN Security Council in April 1995 to pass Resolution 986, which allows Iraq to sell up to $1 billion of oil every 90 days and to use the proceeds, under UN supervision, for humanitarian supplies to the country.

There in essence rests the state of affairs that forms the backdrop to this debate. Iraq has generally resisted allowing UN inspectors free access throughout the country and has occasionally expelled them altogether. The Iraqi people still suffer mightily. A key question is why.

One view is that Saddam Hussein is at fault. From this perspective, he is a brutal dictator who would rather let his people suffer than comply with the legitimate disarmament and inspection requirements imposed by the United Nations. Those who take this view also contend that while the Iraqi government may be using the "oil for food and medicine" for its stated purpose, that flow of funds allows Iraq to spend other money (that it might otherwise have to use for food and medicine) to rebuild its military might. Walter B. Slocombe takes this position in the following selection.

The alternative view is that the sanctions are the problem. In the second selection, Sophie Boukhari condemns the sanctions as political and moral failures because they are devastating everyday Iraqis while having little or no effect on government leaders, the Iraqi military, or Iraqi policy.

Defense Aspects of United States Policy Toward Iraq

Nearly ten years after the defeat of Iraq's invasion of Kuwait, Saddam Hussein remains a threat to the region and to our interests. Iraq's recent statements against both Kuwait and Saudi Arabia remind us (and them) of the continuing threat Saddam Hussein poses to his neighbors. Similarly, his pre-emptive refusal to cooperate with the new UN inspection regime or to permit independent UN-sponsored assessment of humanitarian needs re-confirms his complete unwillingness to comply with the requirements imposed by the UN. His efforts to provoke a military confrontation on his terms demonstrate his continuing recklessness and aggressive potential. His efforts to maintain a capability to develop and produce long-range missiles and terror weapons for them to carry make clear that he is a danger to the whole region and indeed the world, not just the immediate neighbors. And, of course, his continued tyranny over the people of Iraq and his exploitation of their needs for propaganda advantage show on a continuing basis, his unfitness to govern.

As a result, the US has, since 1991, joined with our friends and allies to pursue a policy, fully consistent with the relevant UN resolutions, that has as its objective to contain Iraq and prevent renewed aggression, pending the time when a different regime in Iraq is prepared to take the actions necessary for Iraq no longer to be a threat [to] its neighbors and international security generally. This is a policy that is not without risks and it certainly carries substantial costs; but compared with ignoring the problem and seeking simplistic quick fixes it is both cheap and safe.

The key elements of our efforts to this end are familiar—and they call on the full range of instruments of international policy, political, economic, diplomatic, intelligence, "informational," and military. They include:

- maintenance of the system of UN-imposed sanctions,
- our forward military presence in the region,
- our capacity to reinforce that presence rapidly if need be,
- the no-fly zone (NFZ) enforcement operations,

From U.S. Senate. Armed Services Committee. *Defense Aspects of United States Policy Toward Iraq.* Hearing, September 19, 2000. Washington, D.C.: Government Printing Office, 2000.

- monitoring Iraq's actions to detect preparations for renewed aggression and reconstitution of Saddam's programs to acquire weapons of mass destruction (WMD),
- diplomatic efforts and close consultations with friends in the region, other coalition members, and at the UN,
- efforts to counter smuggling in violation of the sanctions regime,
- information efforts, through the full range of available channels, to tell the truth about Saddam and his actions,
- support for meeting the humanitarian needs of the Iraqi people,
- support for resuming effective UN inspections of potential WMD programs and other steps to bring Iraq into compliance with UN resolutions, and
- steps to advance the day when Iraq will have a government consistent with stability in the region and justice for its people.

Managing the Iraq problem is not a short-term effort. It requires patience, vigilance, perseverance—and a sensitivity to the realities in Iraq, in the region, and at the UN. In particular, it requires work with other nations, who, with very few exceptions, share our basic reasons for resisting Saddam's ambitions, but have their own perspectives, interests, and approaches.

So far as our fundamental military policy, we have been clear:

- If Iraq reconstitutes its weapons of mass destruction program,
- threatens its neighbors or US forces,
- or moves against the Kurds,

we maintain a credible force in the region and are prepared to act in an appropriate time and place of our choosing. This warning, the so called "red-lines," serves as a clear signal of our resolve that aggression will not be tolerated. At the same time, we need to recognize that there are no military solutions to many of the problems in dealing with Iraq and that military over-reaction would disserve our interests and needlessly endanger our personnel....

Iraq's United Nations Obligations

Over the course of almost ten years the United Nations has set a clear and unambiguous set of conditions that would allow Iraq to rejoin the world community of nations in good standing. Instead, Saddam has chosen to ignore and defy these multilateral conditions. UNSCR [United Nations Security Council Resolution] 678, passed in November 1990, was the basis for the use of military force to free Kuwait. In April 1991, UNSCR 687, the cease fire resolution, clearly defined Iraq's post-conflict obligations, especially as they apply to the elimination of WMD programs and continuation of sanctions until compliance is achieved. UNSCR 688, passed two days later, insisted Iraq end its repression of its own citizens and allow humanitarian access to all parts of the country. This resolution, with others, serves as the basis for the no-fly zones and their enforcement. UNSCR 949, passed in 1994, condemned Iraq's military deployments to the south, demanded Iraq withdraw its forces, not threaten its neighbors, and ordered that Iraq take no action to enhance its military capability in the south. That resolution is buttressed by our declaration, supported by key coalition members, that we will take action to stop any such enhancement before it could represent a significant threat.

Deterrence

A key part of our military operations in the region is, of course, our maintenance of substantial forces in the region. These forces not only enable us to conduct on-going operations, notably the NFZs and oil embargo enforcement, but also to respond immediately to Iraqi provocations and aggression. Our presence and continuous interaction with the militaries in the region reinforce the coalition's unity of purpose and resolve, and the capacity of local forces to contribute to the defense of the region. The in-place forces are backed up by our capacity and that of our allies to reinforce rapidly as needed, a capacity that depends on preparations, such as pre-positioning of equipment and maintenance of facilities, and on the readiness of regional powers to accept both the in-place units and, as needed, additional forces.

Weapons of Mass Destruction

That Saddam Hussein should be prevented from having a WMD capability is not just a critical interest for the US and our friends in the region; it is a requirement unambiguously approved by the United Nations Security Council.

Today, Iraq refuses to comply with this requirement, and specifically, to abide by UNSCR 1284, adopted in December 1999 to lay out a road map for Iraq's cooperation in meeting its key UN obligations, particularly as regards WMD and for a phased easing of sanctions in parallel with that cooperation. As explained in greater detail in Ambassador Walker's statement, Resolution 1284 created a new disarmament commission (UNMOVIC [UN monitoring, verification, and inspection]) to resume inspections and set up a mechanism for Iraqi actions to comply with its WMD obligations.

The essential element in implementing 1284 is for UNMOVIC to be able to operate to verify that Iraq has divested itself of all weapons of mass destruction and that the appropriate monitoring systems for their continued compliance are established. It is critical, of course, that any international monitoring be meaningful. A sham monitoring regime would be a great deal worse than none at all, because it would give a false sense of security and provide a basis for calls to dismantle sanctions without meaningful compliance. UNSCR 1284 provides for a monitoring system that would fully meet the standard. We are pleased that Hans Blix [head of the UN monitoring team] has quickly assembled and trained a professional team for UNMOVIC to begin its task in Iraq and we expect the Iraqi regime to comply with UNSCR 1284. We stand ready to support UNMOVIC when (and if) it is able to carry out its functions, just as we supported its predecessor, UNSCOM [UN Special Commission].

To date, however, Iraq has rejected the resolution and refused to cooperate with UNMOVIC. So long as inspectors are excluded, we continue to pay special attention to Iraq's potential for rebuilding its WMD program. We are willing, and have demonstrated in the past our ability, to use military force in response to Iraq's failure to meet its obligations regarding the elimination of weapons of mass destruction.

No-Fly Zones

As a result of attacks by the Iraqi regime on its own citizens in defiance of UN Security Council resolutions, no-fly zones have been established by the coalition in the north and south of Iraq. The United States leads operations Northern and Southern Watch to ensure the no-fly zones are maintained.

[In recent years following Iraqi violations], we have continued this effort, with more robust procedures. Operations Northern and Southern Watch have the authority to respond to violations of the NFZs and to threats to coalition aircraft.

[There are] important benefits, military and otherwise, that flow from enforcing the NFZs. In summary, the enforced zones prevent Saddam from using aircraft against Iraqi citizens in large segments of the country. The enforcement of the NFZs also reduces the capabilities of the Iraqi military and limits their ability to conduct training. It also provides significant information about Iraqi troop movements in the zones, particularly action to enhance military capability in the south, in violation of UNSCR 949.

Iraqi air defense forces continue to challenge coalition aircraft flying in both NFZs. As the Committee is aware, coalition forces respond to these challenges by strikes at Iraqi military targets, with broad flexibility for the commanders in the field to shape the response.... Response strikes are directed at military targets, and, if Iraq wishes to stop response strikes, all it need do is stop violating the NFZs and threatening the coalition aircraft that enforce them.

Anti-Smuggling Operations

In 1989, the last full year before the invasion of Kuwait, Iraq earned $15 billion from oil exports, and spent $13 billion on its military. [In 2000] Iraq [was] projected to earn nearly $20 billion from its oil exports authorized under the oil-for-food program. This income, however, must be devoted to purposes consistent with UN resolutions. As a result, Iraq cannot use these revenues for military purposes. To provide funds for the regime's priorities, Iraq seeks to circumvent the United Nations sanctions by smuggling.

The US leads a multinational Maritime Interception Force (MIF) in the Gulf to enforce the UN sanctions by intercepting smugglers carrying illicit oil, other illegal exports, and other contraband. These operations are conducted under UNSCR 665, which was passed in 1990 and authorizes the use of force to halt all maritime shipping in order to inspect cargo and destinations and ensure the strict implementation of sanctions. Some eighteen different nations have provided support to the MIF since its inception and today coalition partners Canada, the United Kingdom, Kuwait, and the United Arab Emirates are participating in MIF operations in the Persian Gulf. The patrols of the MIF are supplemented by extensive diplomatic efforts to disrupt complicity in Iraqi smuggling and secure cooperation with the sanctions and their enforcement.

While not a perfect system, the MIF and the associated diplomatic efforts have been highly successful in serving as a deterrent to large scale illegal export operations and thereby sharply limiting the ability of Iraq to gain hard currency for the regime's priorities, notably to rebuild its military. Iraq's illegal exports are only a tiny fraction of its total oil exports. Without the MIF, there would be little to prevent Saddam from vastly expanding the part of his oil revenues that are under his exclusive control.

Humanitarian Relief

We are all sympathetic to the suffering that the Iraqi people have endured and we have supported an increasingly effective oil-for-food program to reduce that suffering. Our quarrel is with the Iraqi regime, not its people. Saddam Hussein is deliberately contributing to the hardship of the Iraqi people in a cynical attempt to manipulate international sympathy and deflect the blame for Iraq's internal problems.

The government of Iraq has no direct access to revenue generated by the UN-monitored oil sales under the oil-for-food program. Funds from these oil sales are deposited directly into a UN escrow account, and purchases are approved by the UN sanctions committee. The Department of Defense [DoD] assists the State Department in screening contracts for possible dual-use and military applications.

The oil-for-food program allows Iraq to use the proceeds from its oil sales only on humanitarian and other approved items. To date, Iraq refuses to take full advantage of these humanitarian opportunities. Nonetheless, the oil-for-food program has improved the lives of the Iraqi people and will continue to do so. The increase in revenue under the program from $4 billion the first year to a projected $20 billion this year means a tremendous amount of money is available for humanitarian goods for the Iraqi people, even after part of the proceeds are set aside for the UN compensation commission to compensate victims of Iraq's aggression against Kuwait and for other UN-approved purposes.

The oil-for-food program has been a particular success in northern Iraq, where the UN implements the program and the overall health of the people, especially children, living there has improved. Even in southern and central Iraq, where the Iraqi government administers the program, there has been a substantial improvement in food supplies. To the degree child mortality and disease rates are higher in central and southern Iraq than in the north, it is due to corruption, smuggling, and the regime's apparent willingness to deliberately increase the suffering of the Iraqi people for propaganda purposes.

Critics of sanctions, who say that they are a hardship on the Iraqi people, should know it doesn't have to be that way. The UN Security Council resolutions have established Iraq's obligations, and it is clear what Iraq has to do to get sanctions suspended and then lifted. The UN Security Council resolutions also permit Iraq to use the assets sitting in its escrow account to provide nourishment and much needed medicine for its people.

Coalition Support

The key to our efforts in the region is the support of the coalition of nations who share our determination to contain Iraqi aggression, prevent acquisition of WMD capabilities, and to improve the lives of the Iraqi people—and ultimately see a different regime in Baghdad. From a military point of view, cooperation with regional friends is critical because we can conduct operations and remain forward deployed in the Gulf on the necessary scale only at the invitation of and with the willing support of, our coalition friends and partners. Equally, maintenance of sanctions and insistence on compliance with UN standards, notably those regarding WMD, depends on the political support of nations in the region and around the world.

We share with our friends in the Gulf and beyond a broad common interest. Our coalition partners know that Saddam Hussein is a threat to them and their nations and that he is responsible for the hardships and oppression of the Iraqi people. They know the effects of Saddam's aggression and they support both our continued military presence in the region and our overall strategy.

Maintaining the coalition requires constant effort and sensitivity. Without the dedicated work of our diplomats throughout the region and the recurring engagement of the thousands of men and women in uniform assigned to United States Central Command and European Command, we could not maintain the solidarity and support of our coalition partners. DoD plays a key role in sustaining the coalition by enforcing the NFZs, operating the MIF, and maintaining significant forward deployed troops.

DoD personnel, both military and civilian, also play a key role in the consultation that is essential to sustain the coalition. ...[We] will continue to reaffirm our strong security partnership with our allies. ...[W]e have just completed our annual Joint Planning Committee meetings with our Saudi Arabian counterparts and we will do the same in Kuwait.... Additionally, our continuing series of exercises throughout the region, including Operation Desert Spring, provide us an excellent opportunity to remain engaged with the region's militaries. We have had open and honest discussions with our coalition partners and we understand the regional pressures they face on a daily basis.

Sustaining the coalition is a demanding job, and sometimes requires that we adjust our actions to take account of our partners' concerns, which we do not entirely share. Working with a coalition requires constant effort and painstaking efforts to do what is necessary to secure coalition support for our policies.

This process can be frustrating, both for those who work on the problem directly and those who watch the process, hoping for quicker results or action more in line with strict American ideas. However, the coalition—and the compromises maintaining it requires—is essential. It is hard to build an Iraq policy based on a coalition, but without a coalition it would be simply impossible to carry out any effective Iraq policy.

And we have, overall, been remarkably successful in sustaining the effort for a decade. Sanctions remain in place. Our friends in the region accept unprecedented levels of US military presence, and have been willing to cooperate as needed to support US operations, both on-going and emergency. The UNSC continues to insist on effective implementation of resolutions as the price of sanctions relief.

Regime Change

The Department of Defense works closely with the State Department's Special Coordinator for Transition in Iraq with regard to regime change. The Department of Defense has a comprehensive program providing non-lethal aid, under the Iraq Liberation Act (ILA), aimed at improving the opposition's effectiveness as a political force. We are working with the Iraqi National Congress (INC), the main umbrella organization for the opposition, and have developed with the INC a comprehensive training plan based on its requirements. Training focuses across a wide spectrum of over 30 different courses of instruction, including public affairs, international law, health care skills, the management of humanitarian assistance, and the provision of basic services (power, water, etc.). To date, 31 students have received training and 13 are currently enrolled in courses. We have identified courses for the remaining candidates provided by the INC and training will continue through the end of 2001.

Of course, training the members of the INC will not alone bring about the regime change in Baghdad that we all desire. We will continue to work with people and groups both inside and outside Iraq that share our common interests —a peaceful Iraq that does not threaten its neighbors, is free of weapons of mass destruction; an Iraq that supports the basic human rights of all its citizens, and an Iraq that is prepared to rejoin the community of nations. We stand ready to assist such a new government. At the same time, our efforts in supporting the opposition to the Iraqi regime must be based on a clearheaded assessment of the situation and the need to avoid needlessly putting at risk the lives of those who share our goals.

Ending Military Operations

... [Let me] address the consequences of ending our military operations in the area.

Dealing with Saddam Hussein's Iraq is a long term problem. Saddam knows that the only way he can prevail and break out of the "box" in which he has put himself is by outlasting the US and undermining coalition and UN efforts. Our efforts are costly in dollars and in the burden it places on our personnel; the on-going military operations inevitably involve risks and the commitments we have made potentially involve very substantial ones. Nonetheless, if we let impatience or unwillingness to tolerate reasonable current costs and risks drive us to abandon our long term effort, Saddam will have won in the only way he can, and the costs to our interests would be immense.

Accordingly, our military contribution to the overall effort must continue on a long term basis. The operations are conducted as efficiently as we know how. We regularly review our operations and deployments to determine what is needed in the light of changing circumstances and adjust accordingly. We are careful not to be drawn into situations where military over-reaction exposes our personnel to unnecessary risks or compromises our broader strategic interests. But our operations and presence do involve real costs—in money, in burdens on personnel and equipment, in impact on competing priorities, and in risk of casualties.

However, the consequences of ending our military operations would be severe not only for the people of Iraq and for the region, but for critical US interests. If we reduced our military presence in the region below the levels assessed as needed in prevailing conditions, we would simultaneously encourage Iraqi aggression and cripple our ability to meet it. We would compromise our ability to respond rapidly to aggression or preparations for it. We would be less capable of responding to other violations of our redlines. We would also severely undermine regional confidence in our commitments, with accompanying loss of support, not only for our diplomatic efforts, but also for our arrangements to respond and to reinforce in times of crisis.

This general observation about the effect of withdrawing militarily would also apply were we to cease our NFZ and MIF operations. "If we stopped our active enforcement of the NFZs, Saddam would quickly take advantage to augment his forces in the zones, and would be able to use air power effectively in his internal suppression efforts." Ending NFZ operations would also cost us important intelligence, particularly about possible Iraqi preparations for aggression.

Without the MIF operations, Saddam would be free to shift increasing shares of his oil exports from UN-controlled oil-for-food channels into smuggling routes through the Persian Gulf, where he controls the proceeds. His ability to import contraband would be increased drastically. That would increase his resources to rebuild his military, develop WMD, and serve his other priorities.

Moreover, ending or sharply curtailing our deterrent presence, our NFZ enforcement, or our MIF operations would hand Saddam a huge political and strategic victory. That action would say to the regime and to the world that Saddam had been able to outlast the US and break out of key elements of the restraints under which he has been placed. Maintaining our non-military efforts—notably in the region and through the UN—would be vastly more difficult. Those who seek to replace Saddam's regime would be discouraged, and his ability to block their actions increased.

Conclusion

Our overall policy toward Iraq has been successful in containing Iraqi aggression. It is a policy that the Department of Defense, in cooperation with the

State Department and other agencies of government, executes on a daily basis. It is a policy that has required and will continue to require patience, tact, and perseverance. We have developed and are implementing this policy because if left to pursue its objectives unhindered by international sanctions and coalition forces, Iraq would pose an unacceptable threat to our national interests and the interests of our allies and friends in both the Middle East and around the world.

NO

Sophie Boukhari

Embargo Against Iraq:
Crime and Punishment

Should the economic embargo imposed on Iraq a decade ago be numbered among the crimes that have made the 20th century one of the darkest in history? Can the international community, led by the United States and Britain, keep on invoking the United Nations Charter to prolong indefinitely, and with impunity, the sufferings of a people? Why does the media make a fuss about some humanitarian disasters and not about the dozens of Iraqi children who die each day?

William Bourdon, secretary-general of the International Federation of Human Rights Leagues (FIDH), hints at an answer to the last question: "It would be easier to mobilise public opinion behind this worthy cause if the Iraqi dictatorship was not one of the world's worst," he says.

A... resolution of the UN Human Rights Commission, on 18 April 2000, "strongly condemns," inter alia, "the systematic, widespread and extremely grave violations of human rights" in Iraq, "resulting in an all-pervasive repression and oppression." It also condemns the "summary and arbitrary executions, including political killings," and "widespread, systematic torture."

The subject of the Iraqi embargo may be a trap, just as the Iraqi people are trapped. To talk about it might be to play into the hands of Iraqi President Saddam Hussein's regime. To keep quiet might be tantamount to failure to help a people in distress.

But the wall of silence is starting to crack after reports from UN bodies that the sanctions may have killed more than half a million children under five, and because of the despair of humanitarian organizations and the revolt of UN officials who have resigned from their jobs in Iraq. Even the U.S. State Department's website, long silent about reports of the plight of civilians, has posted remarks by Congressman Tony P. Hall, who returned from Iraq at the end of April 2000.

"I fear that no matter how quickly sanctions are lifted, the future of most of the people I met in Iraq will be bleak," he writes. "That is because its children are in bad shape, with a quarter of them underweight and one in ten wasting away because of hunger and disease. The leading cause of childhood death, diarrhoea, is 11 times more prevalent in Iraq than elsewhere—while polio has

From Sophie Boukhari, "Embargo Against Iraq: Crime and Punishment," *UNESCO Courier* (July/August 2000).

been wiped out throughout the Mideast, it has returned to plague Iraq's people. Schools and water systems—the infrastructure any nation's future depends upon—are decrepit and hospitals lack basic medicine and equipment. Ordinary civilians have exhausted their resources and their health trying to survive on $2 to $6 per month.... It will take Iraqi people a generation to recover from their present situation."

The toughest economic blockade in recent times, voted by the UN Security Council in August 1990, four days after Iraqi troops invaded Kuwait, originally aimed to prevent Iraq rearming and to neutralize its regime. Five years later, on 14 April 1995, the so-called "oil for food" resolution gave the Iraqi regime permission to sell a limited amount of the country's oil and to use 53 per cent of the proceeds[1] to buy food, medicine and basic necessities. But the sanctions committee, which has to approve the purchases, can block some items (ranging from lead pencils to chlorine to vaccines) if it thinks they could be used to make weapons of mass destruction. Meanwhile, a UN special commission, UNSCOM, was sent to Iraq to monitor the disarmament process.

When the commission was disbanded at the end of 1998, all of Iraq's nuclear, chemical and biological weapons programmes had been dismantled or destroyed and the threat from them reduced to "zero, none," said the American former chief of the UNSCOM inspection team, Scott Ritter, in a recent BBC [British Broadcasting Company] documentary which attacked those responsible for maintaining the embargo.

But the UN Security Council set up a new arms control commission in its resolution 1284 of 17 December 1999. "The aim is to check that nothing nuclear has been rebuilt and to see what the situation is concerning chemical and biological weapons," says the French foreign ministry. "After that we can move towards lifting sanctions if Iraq co-operates."

France, along with China and Russia, nevertheless abstained in the vote to approve resolution 1284, saying the wording did not describe "in completely good faith" the procedure for suspending the embargo. The Iraqi regime is refusing to co-operate.

So the people of Iraq are still hostages. "What was an acceptable situation in 1991 no longer is," says Germany's Hans von Sponeck, the latest UN humanitarian coordinator in Iraq to have resigned his post, in March 2000. The embargo, decided upon in full compliance with the UN Charter, is now "a clear violation of human rights," he says. Even worse, states former French foreign minister Claude Cheysson, it is a crime against humanity, "as defined by the UN itself" (see box).

In the United States some people agree, including former Attorney-General Ramsey Clark and Francis Boyle, professor of international law at the University of Illinois. Von Sponeck's predecessor, Irishman Denis Halliday, who resigned in September 1998, has also joined the opponents of the embargo. "I've been using the term 'genocide,' because this is a deliberate policy to destroy the people of Iraq," he recently stated. Some legal experts are sceptical about or even against using such terminology. "People who talk like that don't know anything about law," retorts Mario Bettati, who invented the notion of "the right of humanitarian intervention." "The embargo has certainly affected the Iraqi people badly, but that's not at all a crime against humanity or genocide."

FIDH secretary-general Bourdon says "one of the key elements of a crime against humanity and of genocide is intent. The embargo wasn't imposed because the United States and Britain wanted children to die. If you think so, you have to prove it."

Timeline

- 2 August 1990: Iraqi forces invade Kuwait.
- 6 August 1990: UN resolution 661 is adopted, imposing economic sanctions on Iraq.
- 16-17 January 1991: US-led coalition forces launch the Operation Desert Storm air attack, with the approval of the Security Council.
- 27 February 1991; Iraqi forces retreat from Kuwait.
- 30 June 1991: The newly-created UN Special Commission (UNSCOM), begins its first inspection.
- 15 August 1991: Iraq rejects resolution 706 authorising it to sell oil to finance the purchase of humanitarian supplies.
- 14 April 1995: An "oil-for-food" agreement between the UN and Iraq is reached.
- 16 December 1998: UNSCOM withdraws from Iraq. The U.S. and UK launch the Operation Desert Fox air campaign, without UN approval. Bombing takes place on a close to daily basis.
- 17 December 1999: The Security Council adopts resolution 1284 replacing UNSCOM by a new monitoring, verification and inspection commission known as UNMOVIC.

Definitions

- The Statute of the International Criminal Court defines "crimes against humanity" as acts "committed as part of a widespread or systematic attack directed against any civilian population, with knowledge of the attack," including "inhumane acts ... intentionally causing great suffering, or serious injury to body or to mental or physical health."
- Genocide includes acts "committed with intent to destroy, in whole or in part, a national, ethnical, racial or religious group," including "causing serious bodily or mental harm to members of the group" and "deliberately inflicting on the group conditions of life calculated to bring about its physical destruction in whole or in part."

But what about today, when the whole world knows Iraqi children are dying because of the sanctions?

"Leaving in place a measure which you know is killing people isn't the same as applying measures deliberately calculated and planned to cause the maximum number of people to die," he says.

Patrick Baudouin, FIDH's president, is less sure. He says he "hesitates" to call the embargo a crime against humanity. "As a lawyer, I'd say it wasn't. But its open-ended extension does raise serious questions." All these lawyers agree, however, that the embargo violates basic human rights, starting with the right to life.

There is also a lot of argument about who is responsible for the humanitarian disaster in Iraq. The U.S. State Department, which does not even accept UNICEF [United Nations Children's Fund] and WHO [World Health Organization] figures, puts the blame on Saddam Hussein. Samuel Berger, of the U.S. National Security Council, said in May 2000 that "by obstructing UN relief, refusing to order nutritional supplements, even selling food and medicine to build palaces, Mr. Saddam has aggravated his people's suffering and used the spectacle to seek the removal of sanctions."

Von Sponeck spends most of his time rebutting these arguments. "The UN publishes a monthly stock report that shows what has arrived in Iraq, what has been distributed, what is stored away and why. The picture that emerges for food is perfect. (...) Transport is a problem, but people are receiving their food baskets every month and warehouses are empty the day after distribution," he says.

When Washington accuses Baghdad of not distributing about a quarter of the medical supplies, he notes that "Who recommends that a country should have 25 per cent of its drugs in stock to prepare and be prepared for an epidemic. Iraq said it could not afford this, but keeps 15 per cent in stock. The drugs all undergo quality control tests, which 5.8 per cent of them have failed. Then you have medical components that are unusable because they can only be used in combination with others." Halliday points out that the sanctions committee "would deliberately approve nine [items] but block the tenth, knowing full well that without the tenth item, the other nine were of no use.... It's a deliberate ploy."

Reforming the UN Charter

Unease over the Iraqi embargo has reopened debate about the use of embargoes as a weapon. Article 41 of the UN Charter says the Security Council can enforce its decisions by applying measures that include "the complete or partial interruption of economic relations and of ... means of communication."

This trend has increased in recent years. Since 1990, the United Nations has imposed sanctions on Yugoslavia, Somalia, Sierra Leone, Libya, Liberia, Haiti, Angola's Unita rebels and Iraq.

Supporters of sanctions say it is often the only way to punish countries that threaten peace. They cost little at a time when Western public opinion frowns on the huge expense and loss of human life involved in military interventions. The opponents of sanctions stress the serious effects on the civilian population while the targeted regimes become more entrenched and manage to smuggle in supplies regardless.

The Iraqi example confirms their argument. The people have been bled dry. There is abundant proof that the ruling clique is becoming wealthier and that oil is being smuggled out. At the end of January 2000, the British House of Commons issued a report admitting the embargo had failed and expressing the hope that no other country would ever be submitted to such an ordeal.

"Nearly all embargoes penalize civilians and boost the power of the political leaders they aim to bring down," says Bourdon, who nevertheless adds that "one can perhaps say that developments in South Africa were the result of international sanctions against apartheid."

Along with others, he points to the excessive weight of the United States, backed by its British ally, in Security Council decisions. He thinks the UN Charter should be amended and UN decision-making procedures changed. In particular, victims of human rights violations should be represented by a consultative committee attached to the Security Council. "It's unacceptable that the future of a whole people should be in the hands of two states," he says. "We can no longer allow states to pursue cynically their regional or international interests, as is the case in Iraq."

Many analysts, including Halliday and von Sponeck, think the embargo is being prolonged so as to maintain the status quo in the Middle East. According to them, its protagonists are in favour of a weak Iraq, without necessarily getting rid of a regime that prevents the country splitting apart. These analysts say the break-up of Iraq, with a Kurdish government in the north and a Shiite authority in the south, could destabilize a region that provides the bulk of the oil needed by the major world powers and would threaten key U.S. allies such as Turkey, Saudi Arabia and Israel. Furthermore, says Halliday, maintaining tension in the region has enabled U.S. arms manufacturers to sell about $100 billion worth of weaponry to Baghdad's enemies.

But with the Western media increasingly outraged at the embargo and three members of the UN Security Council (France, Russia and China) openly against continuing it, von Sponeck sees a glimmer of hope. "I don't think the sanctions will be extended far into 2001," he says, "but think of all the children who'll die in the meantime."

Note

1. The rest was to go to victims of the war with Kuwait (30 per cent), to the Kurdish lands in northern Iraq not under Baghdad's control (13 per cent) and to fund the operation of the embargo, including the cost of maintaining UN troops.

POSTSCRIPT

Should Sanctions Against Iraq Be Continued?

Soon after President George W. Bush took office in January 2001, his administration instituted two policy initiatives with regard to Iraq. One was not surprising to many observers; the other was. Given Bush's campaign rhetoric about being tougher on Saddam Hussein than he claimed the Clinton administration had been, it was not surprising that less than a month after taking office, Bush ordered an especially strong series of air attacks on Iraq. The raids were in response to the Iraqis' firing on patrolling U.S. warplanes. That had happened before, though, and there had been counterattacks, but not on the level that Bush ordered.

The second policy initiative—and the one that was a surprise—was launched by Secretary of State Colin Powell in February. He indicated that the United States was seriously considering shifting its policy to one of support for ending all nonmilitary UN sanctions against Iraq. Many say that the proposed change did not reflect any moderation of the U.S. government's views on Hussein's government or its willingness to disarm. Rather, it reflected a reaction to world opinion. Arab countries have become increasingly critical of the sanctions, and some commentators have suggested that the willingness to let Iraqi children and other citizens suffer sickness and death reflects a level of racism in U.S. policy. Even some North Atlantic Treaty Organization (NATO) allies, such as France, have come to oppose continuing the sanctions.

Another issue was mounting evidence that Iraqi oil was being transshipped in violation of the sanctions through surrounding countries, including Iraqi's erstwhile enemy, Iran. Indeed, President Bush at one point compared the sanctions to Swiss cheese: full of holes.

What Powell proposed was increasing the vigilance against the construction or importation of weapons in Iraq. "I have every reason to believe we are able to keep the box as tightly closed as we have the last 10 years, without receiving the baggage that goes with it," Powell commented.

Part of the U.S. plan would require the reintroduction of UN inspectors, a move that Iraq has steadfastly refused to accept. Thus, it is not clear whether or not Iraq has or is building WMDs. In the words of Hans Blix, who heads the United Nations Monitoring, Verification and Inspection Commission on Iraq, "It would be inappropriate for me to assume [the Iraqis] still have weapons of mass destruction, but at the same time, it would be naive to exclude that possibility." There are numerous studies and commentaries on the sanctions on Iraq and the U.S. role in maintaining them. Three examples are John Mueller and Karl Mueller, "Sanctions of Mass Destruction," *Foreign Affairs* (May 1999);

Daniel L. Byman and Matthew C. Waxman, *Confronting Iraq: U.S. Policy and the Use of Force Since the Gulf War* (Rand, 2000); and Sarah Graham-Brown, *Sanctioning Saddam: The Politics of Intervention in Iraq* (St. Martin's Press, 1999).

Enforcing UN resolutions and, in general, putting pressure on "outlaw" countries to comply with the norms of the system are proving difficult. As with most sanctions, those on Iraq are difficult to enforce and are not proving to be very effective tools to achieve UN goals. But, one might ask, what else should be done in lieu of sanctions: simply let Iraq rearm? Increase military action against Iraq? For more on sanctions and their impact, see Jean-Marc F. Blanchard, Edward D. Mansfield, and Norrin M. Ripsman, eds., *Power and the Purse: Economic Statecraft, Interdependence, and National Security* (Frank Cass, 2000) and Steve Chan and A. Cooper Drury, *Sanctions as Economic Statecraft: Theory and Practice* (St. Martin's Press, 2000).

International Development Exchange (IDEX)

This is the Web site of the International Development Exchange (IDEX), an organization that works to build partnerships to overcome economic and social injustice. The IDEX helps people gain greater control over their resources, political structures, and the economic processes that affect their lives.

http://www.idex.org

United Nations Development Programme (UNDP)

This United Nations Development Programme (UNDP) site offers publications and current information on world poverty, the UNDP's mission statement, information on the UN Development Fund for Women, and more.

http://www.undp.org

Office of the U.S. Trade Representative

The Office of the U.S. Trade Representative (USTR) develops and coordinates U.S. international trade, commodity, and direct investment policy and leads or directs negotiations with other countries on such matters.

http://www.ustr.gov

The U.S. Agency for International Development (USAID)

This is the home page of the U.S. Agency for International Development (USAID), which is the independent government agency that provides economic development and humanitarian assistance to advance U.S. economic and political interests overseas.

http://www.info.usaid.gov

World Trade Organization (WTO)

The World Trade Organization (WTO) is the only international organization dealing with the global rules of trade between nations. Its main function is to ensure that trade flows as smoothly, predictably, and freely as possible. This site provides extensive information about the organization and international trade today.

http://www.wto.org

International Monetary Fund (IMF)

This Web site of the International Monetary Fund (IMF) offers a highly detailed description of the organization and its activities.

http://www.imf.org

PART 3

Economic Issues

*I*nternational economic and trade issues have an immediate and personal effect on individuals in ways that few other international issues do. They influence the jobs we hold and the prices of the products we buy—in short, our lifestyles. In the worldwide competition for resources and markets, tensions arise between allies and adversaries alike. This section examines some of the prevailing economic tensions.

- Is the Capitalist Model for Third World Development Destructive?

- Does the International Monetary Fund Do More Harm Than Good?

ISSUE 9

Is the Capitalist Model for Third World Development Destructive?

YES: Vandana Shiva, from "Is 'Development' Good for the Third World?" *The Ecologist* (April 2000)

NO: Bill Emmott, from "Is 'Development' Good for the Third World?" *The Ecologist* (April 2000)

ISSUE SUMMARY

YES: Vandana Shiva, director of the Research Foundation for Science, Technology and Ecology in New Delhi, India, asserts that development that follows the capitalist model more often than not destroys the environment, the livelihoods, and the cultures of Third World communities.

NO: Bill Emmott, editor of *The Economist,* contends that places in the Third World that have followed capitalist principles to guide their development have prospered much more than those that have followed socialism and other models.

Despite their many differences, Vandana Shiva and Bill Emmott would certainly be able to agree on one fact: We live in a divided world. There is an economic gulf of disparity between the relative wealth of the small percentage of humanity who live in a few countries and the relative and even absolute poverty of the majority of the world's people who live in most countries. Enjoying relative advantage are the economically developed countries (EDCs), also referred to as the North and as the industrialized countries. Suffering great disadvantage in most cases are the less developed countries (LDCs), also called the South and the Third World.

As with most economic and political situations, the North-South divide is not absolute. There are a few Third World countries that have industrialized significantly and whose standards of living have risen rapidly. Moreover, there are some wealthy people in LDCs and numerous poor people in EDCs.

The lack of absolutes in the economic division of the world does not, however, take away from the reality that there is a vast gap between the North and the South. The per capita gross national product (GNP) in 1998 of the North was $25,510, an amount more than 20 times greater than the $1,250 per capita GNP of the South. This wide gap in wealth has devastating consequences for the poor. Their children, for instance, suffer a mortality rate almost 7 times greater than the infant mortality rate in the wealthiest countries. Adults in the South are 3 times more likely to be illiterate than adults in the North. The average person in the North will live 20 percent longer (13 years) then their contemporaries in the South. More such data would only serve to reinforce the fact that by economic, health, and educational measures, the people of the North and those of the South live in virtually different worlds.

Why should the North be interested in the economic development of the South? There are several reasons. First, there is simple humanitarianism. Second, and more pragmatically, an economically sound South will increase prosperity for the North. People in the LDCs will be able to buy more of the goods and services produced by the EDCs, and history demonstrates that increased production and competition bring more, better, and cheaper products, which increase the standard of living for all. Third, prosperous countries tend to be more stable and democratic and less prone to violence. Turmoil in the South can negatively affect the North in many ways.

The next question is how to proceed with Third World development. That is the subject of this debate. The views of Shiva in the first reading are close to the economic structuralist perspective. Structuralism is associated with such terms as *dependency theory, Marxism,* and *radical economic theory.* Scholars and others who take this view believe that capitalism inherently leads to the exploitation of workers, to unacceptable economic divisions within societies, to the sacrifice of the environment to profits, to monopolistic tendencies, and to other damaging practices. Structuralists also believe that vast changes in the economic-political system are necessary. They advocate reforms that emphasize the common good over what they contend is the self-interested national, corporate, and individual greed that drives capitalism.

The views of Emmott in the second reading generally coincide with a school of thought called "economic liberalism." This approach is associated with such terms as *capitalism, laissez-faire, economic internationalism,* and *free trade.* Economic liberals contend that the best way to create prosperity is by freeing domestic and international economic interchange from political restrictions. This view is at the root of capitalism.

With specific reference to the development of the Third World, economic liberals believe that the major impediments to the South's development are its weakness in acquiring capital, its shortage of skilled labor, and some of its domestic economic policies, such as centralized planning and protectionism. These difficulties, the liberals believe, can be overcome through free trade and foreign investment, outside assistance, and reduced government interference in the economy. Such policies, economic internationalists argue, will allow unimpeded international economic exchange within and among states, which will eventually create prosperity for all.

Vandana Shiva  **YES**

Is "Development" Good for the Third World?

O ver the years, magazines like *The Economist* have promoted the idea that financial growth is 'development' and that this 'development' is good for the Third World. However, this sort of growth is not 'development'—it is more often than not destruction of the environment, the livelihoods and the cultures of Third World communities.

What is referred to today as 'development' is actually 'maldevelopment'. It is designed and driven by external forces for the profits and control of external agents and actors. The World Bank generates $3 of business for western companies for every dollar it lends to the Third World for 'development'. 'Development' allows $500 billion to flow out from the Third World to the rich West in interest and debt payments and low prices for Third World products, while $50 billion goes in the opposite direction as development aid.

'Development' is a trick played on the people of the Third World, especially rural communities, to rob them of their resources and wealth, and leave them dispossessed and in debt. While the people of the Third World are supposed to be 'developed' by this process, they are instead uprooted and displaced. Their resources are snatched from them, converting them into 'development' refugees. Two hundred million people have been forcibly removed from their homes, ecosystems and cultures in the name of development. The [tribes] in India's Narmada Valley, the indigenous peoples of the Amazon and Papua New Guinea, and the coastal communities along India's 7,000 km coastline do not view the giant dams, superhighways, mines, ports and industrial aquaculture that uproot them as 'development'. For them, these activities spell disaster, which is why they are resisting.

One of the most ominous commercial developments of the past decade has been the merger of chemical, pharmaceutical, biotechnology and seed companies to create what are called 'Life Sciences' corporations. A more accurate name would be 'Death Sciences', because these are the bodies that produce genetically engineered, herbicide-tolerant seeds which lock farmers into dependence on chemical inputs, destroy biodiversity and render agriculture more vulnerable. For farmers, the shift from open-pollinated plant varieties to hybrids, genetically engineered crops and sterile 'terminator' seeds, is not a symbol of 'development' but of debt, dependency and destitution. For seed corporations, forcing farmers to buy seed every year implies bigger markets and faster growth. But this increase in corporate profits is based on the destruction of nature and her processes of renewal and abundance, as well as a destruction of local economies.

This destruction of nature's economy and peoples' economics is never taken into account by modern economics, and hence processes that lead to ecological destruction and poverty and deprivation for millions are presented as 'growth' in national accounts and the global economy. However, it is not growth when assessed in terms of the health of ecosystems and societies. This contrived pseudo-growth camouflages the destruction it unleashes on the lives of Third World communities.

A good example of such pseudo-growth is in Third World agriculture. The shift from a 'food first' to an 'export first' agricultural policy in India is justified on grounds of food security, because export earnings are supposed to pay for food imports. In fact, export-oriented agriculture has reduced food security by encouraging a shift from small-scale, sustainable local production to large-scale, non-sustainable industrial production. It also brings changes in ownership over natural resources and means of production, from small autonomous producer/ owners to large corporate interests. Peasants are displaced from farming, while commercial interests take over land for production of export commodities. These enterprises often have negative environmental impacts, creating further hardship for local communities.

Meat, vegetable, shrimp and flower exports, for example, have costs that often far exceed the earnings generated. Large-scale meat exports have an external 'shadow' cost that is 10 times higher than export earnings. This is due to the former ecological contribution of livestock in small-scale agriculture, now on the wane.

Particularly in developing countries, livestock is not just meat on legs. Livestock in India helps produce $17 million-worth of milk and $1.5 billion-worth of food grain; they also provide $17 million-worth of energy. If the animals are slaughtered, all these benefits are lost. In the case of one export-oriented slaughterhouse alone, meat exports earned $45 million, whereas the estimated contribution of the slaughtered animals to the economy if they had been allowed to live was $230 million.

Multidimensional, multifunctional economies based on mutuality are being systematically destroyed by a development model which is unable to take diversity, reciprocity, complexity and sustainability into account. It is time to ask the basic questions: growth of what? Development for whom? It is time to move beyond the fictions and illusions of economic growth which siphons wealth from the poor to the rich, and take into account the reality of ecological catastrophes and social disintegration that have been unleashed by 'development' processes and which leave the poor poorer.

Hoping that the new millennium will bring new economic thinking based on principles of inclusion rather than exclusion.

... It is interesting how rapidly [this] debate on development, the global economy and the environment has moved on to assumptions about 'human nature'.

[Mr. Emmott's] basic assumption is that greed is the predominant human trait, and that 'profits are the prime incentives for human behaviour and allocation of resources'. [He has] universalised [his] values and imposed them on all of humanity, even though most of us do not live our lives guided by profits. We could not care for our children and future generations, we could not live in communities, we could not protect our forests and rivers if profits were the only calculus and competition our only logic.

Ignoring ecological limits, globalisation and free trade have elevated greed and the profit motive to the organising principle of society, eclipsing our human values and marginalising diverse cultures which organise themselves on other lines.

The profit motive and logic of 'competition' on which [Mr. Emmott's] 'development model' is based is creating gigantism and monopolistic control which dwarfs the projects of Mao, Stalin and Nehru. The superhighways, ports, thermal power plants and chemical factories being built by global corporations in post-Nehruvian India are displacing more people and destroying more fragile ecosystems than all the destructive development of the past fifty years.

The mergers of America Online and Time Warner, Glaxo Wellcome and SmithKline Beecham, Cargill and Continental, Monsanto and Upjohn, for example, are creating giant monopolies. The limitless profits made by these monopolies cannot be equated morally and socially with the small and limited incomes of peasants, tribal peoples, craftspeople and other autonomous producers. Peasants I work with return organic fertility to the soil and replenish biodiversity through mutual exchange. Corporations, on the other hand, relate to nature and the 'Third World' as a one-way flow of resource extraction for unlimited profits.

Peasants and small producers are real people with multiple identities, multiple roles, multiple rights and duties. Corporations are legal fictions with only one function: profit maximisation. [Mr. Emmott's] argument seems to suggest that people everywhere measure worth primarily or exclusively in terms of monetary value. But the problem with monetary value is that it reflects all the gender, race, class and ecological biases of the world's dominant (Western) culture—it is not a neutral, universal measure.

We cannot have global laws (such as those being drawn up in the WTO) to protect freedom of commerce, but only local systems to protect nature and people, as [Mr. Emmott] suggest[s]. It is this asymmetry between the rights of corporations and the rights of citizens under globalisation which mobilised thousands of protesters in Seattle last December [1999].

Like me, the thousands of women, young people, farmers, workers and environmentalists who gathered in Seattle [to protest during the World Trade Organization ministerial meeting in 1999] believe in co-operation rather than competition, compassion rather than greed, diversity rather than monoculture, economic democracy rather than corporate monopoly, and decentralisation rather than gigantism.

I would like to hear [Mr. Emmott's] reflections on corporate gigantism and corporate rule today, and the threat this poses to democracy and sustainability. . . .

Since [Mr. Emmott] seem[s] so fixed on the opinion of a 70-year-old Bengali, I asked an audience in Calcutta when I was in the city recently if they would have preferred to go the Korean way rather than the Indian. I am afraid not one person in the 2,000-strong audience voted in support of [his] assumption.

By the way, the chosen ideology of Bengal is not Nehruvian Socialism but Marxism. For the past 30 years, Bengalis have voted Marxists into power, and have prospered through equity, especially in land reform. For the Bengali peasant, secure in land ownership, the government has created an open society. In Karnataka, where land reform has been undone by removing limits on land ownership, and peasants are losing their land to large corporations for growing export crops, trade liberalisation is closing off their future. What is an open society and what is a closed society depends on where one is located in it. Societies free for corporations are becoming unfree for people.

[Mr. Emmott is] misplaced to equate traditional producers with modern corporations. The moral, cultural, ecological and economic worlds they inhabit are utterly different. The world of the traditional farmer is governed by human relations; relations with ancestors and future generations, with the common, the sacred, the right and the wrong, the good and the bad. The world of the latter is governed by the dollar.

We need to move beyond both the State and the global market, to create economic democracies in which people and nature are at the centre of economic organisation. Democracy cannot be reduced to competition law, nor equated with freedom for capital. Democracy is freedom for people.

Bill Emmott

Is "Development" Good for the Third World?

[I] thank [Ms. Shiva] for starting such a stimulating and important debate. Let us first see what, on the evidence of your [argument], we agree upon.

We are both against 'tied aid', namely aid or lending which, sometimes by accident but often intentionally, primarily gives business to rich-country firms. I am, incidentally, pretty sceptical of all aid except when it is given to relieve a specific humanitarian crisis (such as famine, natural disaster or war) because it is so often tied, and because it tends to make the recipients less self-sufficient. 'Give a man a fish and you feed him for a day; teach him to fish and you feed him for life,' runs the old Chinese cliché, and it is a very valuable point.

We are both against the forced removal of people from their homes. I oppose this on every ground, whether it is development, national security, national cultural or environmental policy, or whatever. Furthermore, you seem to equate 'nature's economy' and 'peoples' economies', while my observation suggests that these quite often are not identical, even at a local level.

We are both against the capital-intensive 'gigantism' of many dams, superhighways and so on. These generally (though not always) are based on the idea, pioneered by Stalin and Mao and often copied by Nehru and his successors, that poor countries must leap into a capital-intensive, industrial economy. From such centrally planned policies, people rarely benefit and nor does the economy.

Finally, we are also both against monopolies that can force customers (in your example, farmers) to buy goods they would not buy if given a free choice (in your example, seeds that require undue amounts of herbicide and that are designed not to reproduce). This does not, however, make me against all genetic engineering: seeds that allow farmers to use fewer pesticides, for example, or less fertiliser, strike me as likely to be useful. The choice, though, must remain with the farmer, and the role of national and local government should be to ensure that farmers retain that choice.

So where do we disagree? Judging by [Ms. Shiva's argument], we seem to face three fundamental disagreements.

First, on the nature of the starting point. [She says] that 'multidimensional, multifunctional economies based on mutuality' are being destroyed.

I find it hard to accept this as a good description of, for instance, the India either of today or of recent decades. To me, [her] phrase would be a good description of Britain, as long as [she] were to agree that the free exchanges, of jobs and spending and ideas and family development, enjoyed by 55 million Britons, can be called 'mutuality'. That is certainly what we have thought of it as, ever since Adam Smith's two great 18th-century works, *The Theory of Moral Sentiments* and *The Wealth of Nations*. But in India, my observation is that Nehruvian Socialism brought widespread damage to the multidimensional, multifunctional nature of a country already badly damaged by the British Empire (of which, by the way, I am ashamed), bringing in more monopolies, gigantism, rigid state enterprises, rigid state regulation and pollution from unaccountable big businesses, while simultaneously failing to improve literacy, health or other welfare measures at anything like the pace achieved since 1950 by other similarly endowed Asian countries.

Second, on the role of profit. Please accept my apologies if I am mistaken, but [Ms. Shiva] seem[s] to believe that the incomes of 'corporations' and of 'commercial interests' are of a different nature, and of a different moral or social value, from the incomes of farmers, small 'producer/owners' and 'peasants'. To me, they are the same. Neither is better nor worse than the other. Profits are, like it or not, the prime incentives for human behaviour and allocation of resources. And both big business and small farmers are prone to fail to take account of real costs that are not being given, in our societies, a monetary value: namely, environmental and other social costs.

Which brings in the third point of probable disagreement, on how to think about and deal with environmental costs. It certainly is not easy, and many economists (though not, I would claim, *The Economist*) are too reluctant to accept that ways need to be found to take such costs into account. I feel that the only way to do this in a sustainable and equitable way is to use market mechanisms themselves, by imposing taxes or offering subsidies in such a way as to lead, for example, farmers to make their choices about products and processes in a way that takes in (democratically determined) 'shadow' costs. I always distrust government, since it so often, in all countries, leads to corruption and to arrogance. I would want these measures to be used at as local a level as possible, so that the imposers were close to local conditions and subject to local accountability.

That, I would suggest, is the way forward for any country, whether Third World or First World. The 'development model' I favour stresses freedom, competition and the profit motive, within the accountability framework of the rule of law and local democracy. South Korea, I would acknowledge, has followed only some of these points. But if I were, for example, a 70-year-old Bengali, I might well feel that I would rather my region had, during my lifetime, done more of the things that South Korea did, from a similar starting point in 1950 or 1960. I suspect [Ms. Shiva] disagree[s].

I find it interesting, and a pity, that [Ms. Shiva] thinks that the word 'profit' and the word 'greed' are the same thing. I certainly do not believe so, and I do not assume that greed is the predominant human trait. If it was, then life would be miserable indeed. I would not want to live in such a world.

Let me substitute the word 'benefit' for 'profit'. Farmers, big or small, plant the crops and keep the livestock that they think will bring them the most benefit, either directly by meeting their families' needs for food, or indirectly by providing them with produce to exchange with others for other produce and services they need. By their own sense of benefit, honed through generations of experience, they plant what they think are the best crops for their own interests, and to give their families and associates the best chance of survival and happiness.

This self-interest is not the only value by which people operate, nor is it blind to the virtues of cooperation and compassion. But it would be wrong, I believe, to pretend that people the world over, and since the beginning of time, have not directed their activities according to their views of their own benefit, sometimes narrowly defined, more often (and better) broadly defined.

And what of companies? They are not 'legal fictions'. They are groups of people, real people like you and me, or the staff of *The Ecologist,* who work together in voluntary cooperation. Modern companies are owned by the pension funds held by millions of ordinary people. They are groups of co-operating individuals in which there is no longer a sensible distinction between 'bosses' and 'workers'. I see no reason why 50,000 people working in a group called 'a company' should be given a moral and social value lower than (or, indeed, higher than) 50,000 people working as small farmers or craftspeople.

Like other groups, these corporate groups are capable of either good or evil, of operating well or badly. I neither laud the individual as especially morally worthy nor the group. Communities of all kinds in all countries have been shown to be capable of religious-led slaughter, genocide, environmental degradation, exploitation of others, and many other evils. Sometimes these groups have been corporations, sometimes tribes, sometimes armies, sometimes smaller, local groups.

In all cases what is essential is the rule of law, and the balance provided by competition from, and scrutiny by, other groups, all of which is only possible in an open society. Such a balance is the means by which large companies— which is what all the merged firms [Ms. Shiva] name[s] are, since none is a monopoly—can be and should be kept in check. My belief is that the World Trade Organisation is part of that process of establishing the rule of law and keeping a check on such groups. It is not sufficient to achieve this on its own, but it is necessary. It is necessary if people wish to trade across borders, and do so equitably.

Our mutual concern is with people.... I [have] suggested that a 70-year-old Bengali might well, looking back, believe that he would rather his country or province had, during his lifetime, acted like fairly open trading South Korea rather than the closed, state-led, Nehruvian system that India has followed until recently, for Korea has 'developed' more successfully, and to greater benefit for its people, than has India. . . .

My contention is that in those parts of the Third World where, during the past half century, development has been permitted to take place, people have benefited hugely: in their welfare, health, lifespan, range of choices and, though I know this is a dirty word for [Ms. Shiva], income. These places are predominantly in East Asia, such as South Korea, Thailand, Malaysia, Singapore and Taiwan. They were as poor, or sometimes poorer, than India (and indeed Bengal) in the 1950s. The process has been far from perfect, and it has been riddled with abuses. Plenty needs to be done to make it better. But it has been far, far better than the alternative (little or no development).

What I am 'fixed on', as [Ms. Shiva] put it, is people: the 1.2 billion who live in extreme poverty; the billions more who have stunted lives, with poor diets, a lack of access to health and education, a lack of opportunity to make a difference for themselves and for their children. The point of development is, or should be, those people: to give them opportunities and freedoms to change and improve their lives, if that is what they want.

This is never going to be possible without capitalism, though capitalism alone is insufficient. That is what Jyoti Basu and his 'Marxist' colleagues in Bengal have now realised, as they told me when I visited Calcutta [recently].

The small farmer is also a capitalist, and needs to be given the opportunities to arrange his business for his own benefit. If that includes selling his land to a corporation, or growing crops for export, those choices should be available to him. The biggest obstacle to that is rich-country protectionists who seek to keep out Third World farm products. Another is people who seek to stop farmers having that freedom of choice. Democracy is freedom for people, as [Ms. Shiva says]; but it is people who own capital; and [her] model seeks to deny them, big or small, from using their capital as they see fit. That is no democracy. Nor will it help improve the lives of the billions of the poor.

POSTSCRIPT

Is the Capitalist Model for Third World Development Destructive?

Scholar Robert Isaak, in *Managing World Economic Change: International Political Economy* (Prentice Hall, 2000), presents an insightful analysis of the debate over the best path to development. He begins by asking two questions. First, "How much capitalism is necessary for modernization?" Second, "How much modernization is possible without undermining cultural integrity?" For another recent analysis of the issue surrounding development, see Yujiro Hayami, *Development Economics: From the Poverty to the Wealth of Nations* (Oxford University Press, 2001)

Isaak asserts that the evidence since World War II indicates that capitalism as an economic model is becoming ever more rooted across the world. Taiwan, South Korea, Singapore, and a handful of other newly industrializing countries have adopted this approach and have prospered well beyond what most Third World countries have been able to achieve. Communism fell in the Soviet Union, Eastern Europe, and most everywhere else. These countries are now referred to as "transitional economies," in that they are moving from their former socialist to a new capitalist orientation. Even China, which is still governed by its Communist Party, now has stock exchanges, private enterprise, and many of the other trappings of capitalism. The changes have helped to fuel rapid economic growth in China, although one has to wonder what Mao Zedong would have thought.

At least part of this progress, Isaak reasons, is because "economic growth depends on the effective collection of motivation of human activity" and "economic motives necessarily address the self-interest of individuals." From this perspective, he is agreeing with Adam Smith's belief that what are ultimately selfish motives (profit, wealth accumulation) drive personal and national economic development. For more on this eighteenth-century Scottish philosopher and economist and those who adhere to his vision, go to the Web site of the Adam Smith Institute at http://www.adamsmith.org.uk/.

It is also the case that there are social costs to following the capitalist model. As Isaak puts it, "Every recipe has its opportunity costs." One is winners and losers. Perhaps it is possible to create win-win situations, but the very logic of the self-interested pursuit of maximizing profit and wealth accumulation embedded in capitalism drive employers to try to keep down wages, to resist taxes, to shun expensive technologies and processes that will prevent environmental destruction, and to take many steps that are arguably socially responsible but that would also cut profits and limit wealth accumulation. Capitalism can also undermine aspects of many cultures. In the United States, for example, the

Sunday afternoon dinner and other aspects of togetherness for families have succumbed to the capitalist urge to maximize profits by keeping stores open seven days a week, sometimes 24 hours a day. In Mexico, the siesta, the traditional nap taken during the heat of the midafternoon sun, has given way to the necessity of making business more efficient by putting it on a "9-to-5" basis. A classic study that address these issues is Daniel Bell, *The Cultural Contradictions of Capitalism* (Basic Books, 1976). For a general view from the structuralist perspective, read Ron P. Baiman, Dawn Saunders, and Heather Boushey, eds., *Political Economy and Contemporary Capitalism: Radical Perspectives on Economic Theory and Policy* (M. E. Sharpe, 2000).

There are those who talk about putting a "human face on capitalism," of regulating it so that its worst abuses are constrained. Most domestic economies have done that through minimum wages, mandatory health insurance, child labor laws and other statutes, and regulations. Yet no country is anywhere near a win-win situation internally. In the United States, the wealthiest 20 percent of the people command 46 percent of the country's total income; the poorest 20 percent make just 5 percent of the total income. Some countries, such as those in Western Europe, have put too many restraints on capitalism in an effort to lessen income gaps and other social costs. As a result, they have lost some of their ability to be competitive in the world market, have suffered ecnomically, and have retreated from some of their social problems.

183

ISSUE 10

Does the International Monetary Fund Do More Harm Than Good?

YES: John Cavanagh, Carol Welch, and Simon Retallack, from "The IMF Formula: Generating Poverty," *The Ecologist Report* (September 2000)

NO: Michel Camdessus, from "A Talk With Michel Camdessus About God, Globalization, and His Years Running the IMF," *Foreign Policy* (September/October 2000)

ISSUE SUMMARY

YES: John Cavanagh, director of the Institute for Policy Studies in Washington, D.C.; Carol Welch, an international policy analyst at Friends of the Earth USA; and Simon Retallack, managing editor of *The Ecologist,* charge that the International Monetary Fund (IMF) has consistently elevated the need for financial and monetary stability above any other concerns.

NO: Michel Camdessus, managing director of the IMF (1987–2000), in an interview conducted by Moisés Naím, editor of *Foreign Policy,* contends that there is extraordinary confusion behind the criticism of the IMF.

The International Monetary Fund (IMF) is one of the key players in Third World development and in the larger realm of international political economy. The formation of the IMF stemmed in part from the belief of many analysts that the Great Depression of the 1930s and World War II were partly caused by inflation, lack of convertibility between currencies, and other monetary problems that characterized the years between 1919 and 1939. To address this problem, the anti-Axis allies met in 1944 at Bretton Woods, New Hampshire, to establish a new monetary order. The delegates established the IMF and several other institutions to help promote and regulate the world economy as part of the U.S.-led drive to increase international economic interchange.

The IMF, which began operations in 1947 with 44 member countries, has expanded steadily, and now virtually all countries hold IMF membership. The IMF's primary function is to help maintain exchange rate stability by making short-term loans to countries with international balance-of-payment problems caused by trade deficits, heavy loan payments, or other factors. The IMF receives its usable funds from hard currency reserves ($114 billion in 2000) placed at its disposal by wealthier member-countries and from earnings that it derives from interest on loans made to countries that draw on those reserves.

During 2000 the IMF had $69 billion in outstanding loans and credit lines to 96 countries, all of which were either economically less developed countries (LDCs) or countries in transition (CITs) to a free-market economy, such as Russia and other formerly communist countries. What the IMF usually does is loan money to a country in a situation when overspending or other problems are harming faith in the currency. This lack of faith in the currency causes monetary instability because people abroad and even in the country are less willing to accept the country's money. To counter this instability, the IMF typically loans a country money to support its currency or to stabilize its financial situation by refinancing the country's debt.

Although the IMF has played an important role in preserving or restoring monetary stability and has many supporters, it also has its detractors. Indeed, in recent years the IMF has been one focus of struggle between the North and the South. It is possible to divide the controversies with regard to the IMF into two categories: voting and structural adjustment policies.

The first issue centers on the vote distribution of the IMF's board of directors. Voting is based on the level of each member's contribution to the fund's resources. Under this formula, the United States has 18 percent of the votes, the countries of the European Union (EU) combine for 31 percent of the votes, and Canada has 3 percent. This gives control to a handful of countries, which constitute less than 10 percent of the IMF's total membership. The same formula leaves the LDCs with little or no power in the organization's decision making.

The second criticism of the IMF is that it imposes unfair and unwise economic conditions on countries that use its financial resources. These conditions require recipients to make structural adjustments. That means, among other things, moving toward a capitalist economy by privatizing state-run enterprises, reducing barriers to trade and the flow of capital (thus promoting foreign ownership of domestic businesses), reducing domestic social programs to trim budget deficits, and devaluing currencies. Although such "strings" attached to IMF assistance may seem reasonable on the surface, they evoke sharp criticism by some analysts. This view is taken by John Cavanagh, Carol Welch, and Simon Retallack in the following selection. These authors charge that such conditions violate a recipient country's sovereignty. They also criticize structural adjustment demands on the grounds that the IMF's requirements force recipient LDC governments to harm the quality of life of their citizens by reducing economic growth and by cutting social services in order to maintain a balanced budget.

The reply to these charges is voiced by Michel Camdessus in the second selection. He argues that it is only sensible to require financial reforms when the existing policies of a country caused the monetary instability that the IMF is being asked to help remedy. Reforms, Camdessus asserts, are necessary to ensure that IMF assistance helps address underlying problems.

John Cavanagh, Carol Welch,
and Simon Retallack

The IMF Formula: Generating Poverty

When the [International Monetary] Fund [IMF] and the [World] Bank announced at their 1999 annual meeting that poverty reduction would henceforth be their overarching goal, this sudden 'conversion' provoked justifiable scepticism. The history of the IMF shows that it has consistently elevated the need for financial and monetary 'stability' above any other concern. Through its notorious structural adjustment programmes (SAPs), it has imposed harsh economic reforms in over 100 countries in the developing and former communist worlds, throwing hundreds of millions of people deeper into poverty.

The IMF came to hold virtual neo-colonial control over developing countries as a result of the Third World 'debt crisis' of the 1980s. In the 1970s, commercial banks made large loans to developing countries that were mostly wasted by dictators and military regimes. When oil prices shot up in 1979 and US interest rates were raised sharply in the early 1980s, heavily indebted countries suddenly found themselves unable to make soaring interest payments. Default to the banks could only be avoided with continual refinancing. That is where the IMF stepped in.

Unless the IMF certified that an economy was being 'restructured' and 'maintained soundly', the world's public and private lenders would refuse to extend loans. The IMF decided that this meant adherence to the policy package of structural adjustment, which essentially integrates national economies into the global market, enabling multinational corporations to access cheaper labour markets and natural resources, and increase exports. Sold as means to increase domestic growth and living standards, measures have to be introduced to remove restrictions on trade and investment, promote exports, devalue national currencies, raise interest rates, privatise state companies and services, balance national budgets by slashing public expenditure, and deregulate labour markets.

Caught in the trap of having to repay massive debts, most developing country governments—representing four billion people or 80 per cent of the world's population—have felt they have had little choice but to agree to implement these reforms in exchange for IMF assistance. The results, however, have brought ruin to national economies, cut-backs in schools and hospitals, increased poverty and hunger, and environmental harm.

The Impact on Employment

The IMF has ardently promoted so-called 'labour market flexibility' through changes in labour laws and wage policies designed to make countries more competitive and attractive to foreign investment, and to remove 'disincentives' for employers to hire more workers. According to the 1995 United Nations Trade and Development Report, however, employers are using extra 'flexibility' in labour laws to shed jobs and downsize rather than add to productive capacity and create work, as reforms are introduced to make it easier to fire workers and undermine the ability of unions to defend them.

In Spring 2000, for example, Argentinian legislators passed the harsher of two labour law reforms after IMF officials spoke out strongly in support of it, even though tens of thousands of Argentinians carried out general strikes against the reform.

Also contributing to unemployment is the IMF requirement that countries privatise public companies and services and fire public sector workers. In many developing countries, the public sector has provided a great deal of employment. As the IMF forces countries to downsize government agencies, the ranks of the unemployed grow faster than the private sector can absorb them. Removing barriers to foreign investment and trade, meanwhile, makes it much harder for private local producers to compete against better-equipped and richer foreign suppliers, and so also often leads to the closure of businesses and layoffs.

Reorienting the economy towards production for export can have similar results. With most developing countries under structural adjustment, nearly all of them are trying to export similar, often identical, agricultural products and mineral resources to the industrialised nations. The result is a glut, the collapse of staple export prices and the further loss of livelihoods.

Similarly, the IMF policy of devaluing national currencies in less developed countries, makes imports—which usually include energy resources and machinery—more expensive, squeezing import-reliant domestic industries which are forced to lay off more workers. Likewise, the IMF policy of raising interest rates prevents small businesses from getting the capital needed to expand or stay afloat, often leading them to shut down, leaving yet more workers unemployed.

The IMF's purely market-based approach has contributed to the fact that at least one billion adults—more than 30 per cent of the global workforce—are unemployed or seriously underemployed today. In Senegal, touted by the IMF as a success story because of increased growth rates, unemployment increased from 25 per cent in 1991 to 44 per cent in 1996. In South Korea, a US $58 billion structural adjustment loan in 1998 contributed to an average of 8,000 people a day losing their jobs. Compounding this harsh reality is the lack of existing social safety nets that can support people out of work.

Even those in work suffer, as the IMF frequently encourages countries to keep wages low in order to attract foreign investment. This often translates into the lowering of minimum wages and the weakening of collective-bargaining laws. In Haiti, for example, the government has been pressured to freeze wages and rewrite the labour code to eliminate a statute mandating increases in the minimum wage when annual inflation exceeds ten per cent. By the end of 1997, Haiti's minimum wage was only $2.40 a day, worth just 19.5 per cent of the minimum wage in 1971. Currency devaluations also depress wages. According to Professor Michel Chossudovsky, in sub-Saharan Africa, the devaluation of the CFA [African Financial Community] franc imposed by the IMF and the French Treasury in early 1994, abruptly "compressed the real value of wages and government expenditure by 50 per cent". Such outcomes are widespread. Costa Rica, the first Central American country to implement a SAP, saw real wages decline by 16.9 per cent between 1980 and 1991, while during the first four years of Hungary's SAP, the value of wages fell by 24 per cent.

The Impact on Health Care

Even though rich country governments commonly engage in deficit spending, the IMF and World Bank have made this a taboo for poor countries. Faced with tough choices, governments must often cut social spending since this doesn't generate income for the federal budget. Consequently, in the 1980s alone, expenditures on health in IMF–World Bank programmed countries in Africa declined by 50 per cent, according to the UN Economic Commission for Africa. Meanwhile, to reduce budget deficits, fees for medical services are often increased, leading to less treatment, more suffering and needless deaths.

In Zimbabwe, spending per head on healthcare has fallen by a third since 1990 when a structural adjustment programme was introduced. UNICEF reported in 1993 that the quality of health services had declined by 30 per cent since then; twice as many women were dying in childbirth in Harare hospital compared to 1990; and fewer people were visiting clinics and hospitals because they could not afford user fees.

In the Philippines, an IMF programme has caused allocations to preventative health care budgets for malaria and tuberculosis to fall by 27 per cent and 36 per cent respectively, and immunisation programmes to fall by 26 per cent.

In Kenya, the introduction of fees for patients of Nairobi's Special Treatment Clinic for Sexually Transmitted Diseases (vital for decreasing the likelihood of transmission of HIV/AIDS) resulted in a decrease in attendance of 40 per cent for men and 65 per cent for women over a nine month period.

Throughout much of Africa, cuts in government health spending arising from structural adjustment programmes have caused a shortage of funds to be allocated to medical supplies (including disposable syringes). This, in combination with IMF-ordered price hikes in electricity, water and fuel (required to sterilise needles), has increased the incidence of infection (including HIV transmission). As Michel Chossudovsky points out, "even the World Bank concedes that the communicable disease control programmes of developing countries for diarrhoea, malaria and acute respiratory infections have deteriorated". Yet the proposed 'solutions' still consist of the effective privatisation of public health and the massive lay-off of doctors and health workers.

The Impact on Education

The same policies have had an equally devastating effect on the provision of education in developing countries. Under the mandate of reducing the size of the state, the IMF has encouraged the privatisation of schools. When this was undertaken in Haiti, an IMF report indicates extreme deterioration in school quality and attendance that will hamper the country's human capacity for many years to come. For example, only eight per cent of teachers in private schools (now 89 per cent of all schools) have professional qualifications, compared to 47 per cent in public schools. Secondary school enrolment dropped from 28 to 15 per cent between 1985 and 1997. Nevertheless, the report ends with recommendations for Haiti to pursue further privatisation initiatives.

Cuts dictated to balance government budgets have meant that in the 1980s alone, spending on education in African countries undergoing structural adjustment declined by 25 per cent, according to the UN Economic Commission for Africa. Meanwhile, to make up shortfalls, school fees are often introduced, forcing parents to pull children—usually girls—from school, so that literacy rates and skills decline.

In Ghana, the Living Standards Survey for 1992–93 found that 77 per cent of street children in the capital city Accra dropped out of school because of an inability to pay fees. In Zambia, the government has been forced to slash its spending on education from £40 per primary school pupil in 1991 to £10. Enrolment, consequently, has fallen from 96 per cent in the mid 1980s to 77 per cent [in 2000].

In sub-Saharan Africa, as explicit conditions of adjustment, education budgets are curtailed, the number of graduates in the teacher training colleges frozen, the number of contact-hours spent by children in school cut, and a 'double shift system' installed so that one teacher now does the work of two. The remaining teachers are laid off and the resulting savings to the Treasury are funnelled towards interest payments on debt.

The Impact on Food Security

Because of structural adjustment, food security has declined dramatically in many developing countries. The shift from domestic to export-oriented agricultural production has undermined people's ability to provide for their families by reducing the amount of food cultivated for household consumption. The increased dependence on food imports that it creates places countries in an extremely vulnerable position, because they lack the foreign exchange to import enough food, given falls in export prices and the need to repay debt. It should come as no surprise therefore that 80 per cent of all malnourished children in the developing world live in countries where farmers have been forced to shift from food production for local consumption to the production of crops for export to the industrialised world. Furthermore, as Davison Budhoo, a former IMF economist, notes, export orientation "has led to the devastation of traditional agriculture and the emergence of hordes of landless farmers in nearly every country in which the Fund operates".

Hunger and farmer bankruptcy is also a product of budget cutting under IMF programmes, which often leads to the removal of price supports for essential items, including food and farm inputs such as fertiliser, whose prices then rise dramatically (a problem that is compounded by IMF-inspired currency devaluations which make imports of food and inputs more expensive). This often leads to large-scale riots. In Caracas in 1989, for example, following a 200 per cent increase in the price of bread, riots ensued in which the army responded by firing upon and killing 1,000 people. Higher interest rates, meanwhile, often prevent small farmers from getting the capital needed to stay afloat, forcing them to sell their land, work as tenants, or move to the slums of large cities.

The Impact on the Environment

The natural environment is another major casualty of structural adjustment. IMF-dictated government spending cutbacks have inevitably targeted environmental ministries, including in Brazil (which slashed funding for environmental enforcement by over 50 per cent), Russia, and Indonesia—countries that are renowned for their great biodiversity. In all but one of nine countries the World Wide Fund for Nature studied to gauge the impacts of structural adjustment, staffs of natural resource departments were reduced, budgets were cut and mandates were scaled back. The result is a downward spiral of environmental management and protection.

The premium placed by IMF programmes on attracting foreign investment and hence increasing competitiveness also encourages countries to lower environmental standards. In Guyana, for example, under IMF guidance, a new investment code was drawn up in 1988 that contained almost no environmental restrictions on foreign corporations. The IMF's focus on export-led growth has also led countries to extract natural resources at unsustainable rates. In Guyana, large-scale mining permits (largely owned by foreign companies) now cover ten per cent of the country's surface area, and timber concessions span the majority of the country's forests, transforming local ecosystems, polluting waterways, destroying forests and ruining soil.

Failure on Their Own Terms

Although the Fund and the Bank have promoted SAPs as a virtual religion for nearly 20 years, they cannot even claim that they have achieved their own narrow objectives. IMF internal studies reveal that many SAPs have failed to enhance economic growth, reduce fiscal and balance of payments deficits, lower inflation and reduce external debt. In fact, between 1980 and 1997, the debt of low income countries grew by 544 per cent and that of middle income countries by 481 per cent. Poor countries have thus gone through all the pain of structural adjustment only to continue to engage in a net transfer of wealth to the industrialised world.

A decade and a half ago, we likened the Bretton Woods institutions to medieval doctors. No matter what the ailment, they applied leeches to the patient and bled them. At the onset of the new millennium, the doctors' cruel ministrations have been exposed in dozens of studies and in increasingly vocal street protests. Yet thus far, the Fund and the Bank's response has been largely cosmetic. New leeches are applied, dressed up by public relations experts. However, the growing public outcry in North and South alike indicates rough sailing for these institutions in the years to come.

Michel Camdessus

 **NO**

A Talk With Michel Camdessus About God, Globalization, and His Years Running the IMF

M ichel Camdessus does not often make the shortlist of individuals who have shaped our time. Margaret Thatcher and Ronald Reagan, Mikhail Gorbachev and Nelson Mandela, Bill Gates and perhaps even Alan Greenspan—all loom in our imagination as the figures who defined the final years of the 20th century. Yet, as the managing director of the International Monetary Fund (IMF) for 13 years, Camdessus enjoyed a global influence that rivaled the power of the most exalted world leaders....

In November 1999, when Camdessus announced his intention to resign from the IMF, he stated that serving his full third term would be "inappropriate in a world in permanent need of renewal of its institutions." During his years at the fund, renewal and dramatic change were permanent features of the global landscape. International trade and cross-border capital flows soared, poor countries became "emerging markets," and the Internet changed everything. Such revolutionary transformations—and their accompanying economic turmoil—vaulted the IMF to the forefront of global policymaking. For every currency that tumbled in Mexico, Asia, Russia, or Brazil, the IMF's influence only grew—and with it, the power of Michel Camdessus.

... It is no small irony that in a period of frenzied technological breakthroughs and economic globalization, an unassuming French civil servant—a career bureaucrat—could still become one of the most controversial figures of his day. To a remarkable extent, Camdessus's actions and omissions, values and prejudices, and visions and blind spots have shaped today's world.

Michel Camdessus recently sat down for several hours with *FP* [Foreign Policy] Editor Moisés Naím for a wide-ranging conversation. What follows is an edited and abbreviated version of that dialogue, which took place in Paris, France, in early June 2000.

From Michel Camdessus, "A Talk With Michel Camdessus About God, Globalization, and His Years Running the IMF," *Foreign Policy*, vol. 120 (September/October 2000). Copyright © 2000 by The Carnegie Endowment for International Peace. Reprinted by permission of *Foreign Policy*.

One World, Under God

... Moisés Naím: Almost every interviewer has stressed two things about you. First is the enormous power you wielded as managing director of the IMF. But then there was always a comment about your sense of humor and how lightly you carried that power.

Michel Camdessus: [Laughing] You cannot do such a job if you take yourself too seriously!

MN: In recent years, however, interviewers have begun to note how religious you are, your deeply felt Christian values. I have traced your early interviews and that aspect was not evident at the beginning. Are you now becoming more ostentatious with your religiosity?

MC: [Laughing] Here you have a scoop! You are the first to pose that question, and I must reassure you I am not born-again recently. But it's true that journalists start knowing you more and go deeper in trying to analyze the individual behind the position. And this is why they pushed me to reveal things that are part of my inner life. Here we are back to your first question about humor. I must tell you that humor is a gift of God that makes your life more pleasant. It is also a kind of discipline, if you want to be an acceptable fellow to those living with you, if you want to accept criticism and not only live with it but benefit from it. So humor is very, very important and I thank God and my family, where a sense of humor has always been cultivated, as music or art.

MN: I want to link your faith to a statement you have made repeatedly. You have often said that globalization is the best way to improve the human condition throughout the world.

MC: Yes, I have said that. . . .

MN: [D]o you believe that globalization is human destiny?

MC: Globalization is not human destiny, but human destiny develops itself, I believe, in this long-lasting trend of unification of the world. Globalization is only an acceleration of it. This is not an article of my religious faith; it is a historical observation that leads you to take very seriously the phenomenon— with its opportunity and its risk. But not to see in globalization formidable opportunities for bringing the human race closer, working together for common prosperity, is just boxing with one hand behind your back. You will do the job, but you will do it without a guiding perspective.

MN: Yet, many scathing denunciations of globalization come from religious groups. A few years ago there was a meeting of the Jesuit Provincial Superiors in Mexico. They signed a document stating that neoliberalism, structural adjustment, and all these things that you feel are important and good and benefit humankind are not only anti-Christian but antihuman. How do you reconcile that sort of denunciation with your own perspectives?

MC: The way in which you put that shows the extraordinary confusion of concepts behind this denunciation. You put in the same bag neoliberalism, globalization, and structural adjustment as if they were from the same origin. But we must be very careful with this mixture. Structural adjustment is adaptation to a new world. You cannot denounce structural adjustment and be—as the Christians are—against the structures of sin, to take the words of the Holy Father. If you are against the structures of sin that plague our world —corruption, nepotism, collusion, protectionism, rigidities of that kind—you must go for structural adjustment, like it or not. If you want to fight poverty, you must go for structural adjustment, like it or not.

Neoliberalism is not my religion. Neoliberalism only sees the invisible hand of the market. My conception of the economy includes the invisible hand of the market, but also the hand of solidarity and what we call in French *la main de justice* [the hand of justice], which is the symbol of the state as regulator, providing a market framework that maximizes society's potential for prosperity and good.

So with due respect to the Jesuits, I would invite them to exert in this domain the sense of discernment that is one of their key virtues in other fields.

MN: But the Jesuits are not alone. A wide variety of individuals, groups, governments, and writers around the world disagree sharply with you. How did you become the most criticized man in the world?

MC: Are you sure of that? If so, I would tell you a Hungarian saying I like and meditate upon frequently. It goes, "What great favor did I do to you for you to hate me so much?" I have observed that there is a direct proportionality between the volume of criticism and the success of our actions. The more we do, the more we are criticized. The IMF is seen as the financial power of the world and as a very anonymous institution, and the managing director is the face of this institution. So it's normal that the criticism has concentrated on me.

This was a risk I had to take. We could have been much more low-key, tried to engage less those who are so critical of us. But I prefer to take risks in meeting with people and entering the debates, hoping and believing—possibly this is too much optimism—that eventually people will understand that you cannot change the world for the better without going through painful processes.

MN: In order to get this message across, you tried very hard to make the IMF more transparent, more open, and more engaged. You tried to deal with the communications problem.

MC: Yes, but I tried with very limited means. I was very tough in not spending, because I consider that the money of the IMF is the money of the poor. My bottom line was that we shouldn't spend any money in image building but only in providing information and then people will reach the right conclusions. This was possibly naiveté. It was not a good strategy because it didn't consider that we were in an uphill battle. The more we were moving toward structural adjustment and the more we attacked vested interests, the more we should have been prepared to deal with negative and vicious campaigns. To counter them we should have accepted the need to spend money. We didn't do that, except recently when we concluded that not to be more proactive was self-defeating for the fund, its policies, and its members.

MN: But at the same time you had second thoughts about how effective a more aggressive communications strategy could be, because the IMF serves as a scapegoat. Governments that adopt tough adjustment policies often say that it is not their fault, that the IMF is forcing them to do it.

MC: No doubt. The IMF is the scapegoat of first resort.

MN: Did governments frequently support certain policies in the IMF's board of directors and then distance themselves from the IMF's actions in public?

MC: Yes, it occurred from time to time.

MN: You once said that the fund could never be popular because it stands for economic rationality, and that economic rationality goes against the grain of human societies. What did you mean by that?

MC: [Laughing] I don't remember saying that, but I remember thinking it. There is a very strong human tendency to believe that the government must improve the plight of people, that governments are there, as the Roman Empire, to provide bread and circus to people right away. And the expectation is often that the IMF must provide economic stability and growth right away, and that the United Nations must make peace right away. Governments tend to be complacent about this perception and do not educate their citizens about the painful reforms and time needed to achieve such goals. Also, as donors, governments very frequently prove slow in financing the social safety nets necessary to shelter the poor or the most vulnerable during adjustment processes. Then, of course, the IMF appears indifferent to the plight of the poorest and only concerned with long-term improvements. But this was not true and was very harmful for our image and for the acceptance of our actions.

Tackling the Critics . . .

MN: Your point about the origins of the criticisms is twofold. First, the criticisms come because you tried to impose economic rationality and that goes against the grain of comforts and habits. And then the other source of criticisms is the vested interests—the people, organizations, and corporations that are going to see their privileges, power, and resources diminished by your recommendations.

MC: Let me briefly elaborate on the second aspect. You can observe, for instance, that the response to the Asian crisis has been an outstanding success, not of mine but of the countries themselves and of all those who supported them, including the IMF people working on these countries. We succeeded not only in [South] Korea and Thailand but also in Indonesia, despite the formidable political problems in that country. These successes resulted from our strong focus on structural adjustment and reform as well as our efforts at dismantling the conglomerates, the *chaebols*, in Korea, the family monopolies in Indonesia, and nepotism, collusion, and corruption everywhere.

MN: So, those are the vested interests that attack IMF policies?

MC: Yes, among many others. It is no wonder that vested interests reacted by fighting and paying for campaigns against us.

MN: Your tenure at the IMF coincided with a global explosion in the number, scope, and influence of nongovernmental organizations (NGOs). You have noted and praised this trend. However, there is a growing apprehension that many of these organizations also represent only narrow, single interests.

MC: [Laughing] And often only themselves! But certainly, it is good for civil society to express its concerns, to complement the more traditional—and indeed, more respectable—constitutional means of representation. I value the work of NGOs, particularly their role in raising awareness about crucial issues. I have been helped by many of them to perceive better the cruel reality of poverty. I could tell you about the work NGOs do with the children in Romania, the women in Nigeria, the *favelas* [squatter slums] in Rio.

MN: But is there a downside to the emergence of these new actors? Did you encounter any examples of irresponsible NGO behavior?

MC: [Laughing] Please don't ask me to repeat... the accusations of how the World Bank ruins the African economy and how IMF programs kill children! Such preposterous charges always ignore that, if anything, our programs reduce poverty and create opportunities for the poorest. I deplore when NGOs try to make themselves stronger by misrepresenting the work of multilateral institutions. But this is not a reason not to pursue dialogue with them.

MN: There is an additional form of criticism against the IMF; we can call it "technocratic" criticism. For instance, during the Asian crisis, former MIT [Massachusetts Institute of Technology] economist Paul Krugman vehemently argued that IMF policies would result in total failure and would only exacerbate Asia's economic struggles.

MC: I'm sure he does not think so today.

MN: Harvard economist Jeffrey Sachs also denounced the IMF policies in Asia and also said they would fail.

MC: I am somewhat puzzled when people with reputable academic credentials speak with such lightness on such dramatic issues. I would be surprised to learn that Mr. Sachs continues to say that IMF policies have failed in Asia.

MN: Of course, the other very interesting critic is Joseph Stiglitz, the former chief economist at the World Bank. And there, for example, and I quote—... that in many countries the leaders are "brighter or better educated than IMF staff, which frequently consists of third-rank students from first-rate universities".

MC: For that, please consider the response of another eminent academic, Rudi Dornbusch of MIT. He has provided the appropriate answer to Stiglitz.

MN: Yes, Dornbusch answered that the best students may be too theoretical for the hands-on work of policymaking. But Dornbusch, in February 1999, also wrote, "If emerging markets have become a speculative casino, surely the managing director, Monsieur Camdessus, is the chief croupier."

MC: Yes, but he seems to have changed his mind, possibly because he observed that the "chief croupier" was working hard to provide emerging markets with the appropriate rules of the game. Now he says that what the IMF did in Asia was outstanding.

MN: Stiglitz says that, in theory, the fund supports democratic institutions in the nations it assists, but that in practice it undermines democracy by imposing economic policies.

MC: Did we undermine the democratic process in Indonesia? I'd be surprised to hear that. Did we undermine democratic processes in Korea or Thailand? I'd be surprised to hear that, too.

MN: Are you saying that the IMF's economic policies actually strengthened democracy in these countries?

MC: No doubt at all! And I suggest that you interview Mr. Mark Malloch Brown [United Nations Development Programme administrator], who, despite being at times a critic of the fund, has said, I think, that no institution has contributed more to democracy in Asia in recent years than the IMF. But you are making me sound negative about criticism!

MN: I'm just reading to you what people have said.

MC: I am negative only about criticisms that are not motivated by real analytic concern. Many of the critics you have quoted are clearly motivated by ideology or personal agendas. The staff of the IMF will tell you that I wanted to see all the critics' writings because when they were not motivated by ideology but by facts, then you could always learn something to improve your approach. I was always open to and interested in what the objective IMF critics had to say.

MN: Let me quote to you another critic of the IMF—yourself: "International agencies, including the IMF, had failed to pay sufficient regard to the short-term human costs involved during adjustment or transition to a market economy. The social component of interventions was sporadic, financially inadequate, late and disorganized." That was Michel Camdessus analyzing the situation in 1992.
    Are you prepared to say that today, in 2000, the social component of IMF interventions is no longer sporadic, financially inadequate, or disorganized?

MC: What is still lacking, as in 1992, is enough bilateral financial support from the richer countries to complement IMF action. But social policy is now at the heart of our strategies. Look at our last programs in Africa, look at our poverty reduction and growth facility, look at IMF programs in Indonesia, Korea, and other countries. Look at the fight we had with Asian governments to convince them to add social elements to their programs.

MN: Look at Russia.

MC: Russia is a good case in point. My last battle with Russia was to convince them to increase tax payments by Gazprom—the gas monopoly—in order to finance the social safety net and pay the arrears on pensions and salaries. This social concern reached the point where the economy minister of Russia said, "I have at last found someone who is more communist than myself."

MN: That would not be the first time you have suffered such an accusation. U.S. Senator Trent Lott [Republican, Mississippi] called you a "socialist from France."

MC: A French socialist. It means a socialist of the worst kind, in the same way I am seen here in France as a neoliberal of the worst kind, namely an Anglo-Saxon neoliberal.

MN: Another Anglo-Saxon neoliberal, George W. Bush, stated in February 2000 that he would not support more IMF loans to Russia.

MC: Well, Dad had a different view when we started working in Russia.

MN: His father, former President Bush, you mean?

MC: Yes [laughing], and this is a political statement that you must take with a grain of salt. Mr. George W. Bush sees U.S. relations with Russia as an important part of the activities of Mr. Gore during several years, and so he needs to see everything that was done with Russia as bad, and indeed, he implies he will do better with Russia.... This is electoral politics and we should take it that way. As long as an alternative strategy is not defined, this is simply more public relations.

Playing Politics With the Poor

MN: You have noted with pride that poverty reduction and social issues are now at the center of IMF strategies. However, the new IMF Managing Director Mr. Horst Köhler appears to be moving away from your emphasis on poverty issues. He has stated that the core responsibility of the IMF is in the financial field: monetary issues, exchange rate issues, and everything else linked to fiscal policy and the financial sector. He has argued for dividing responsibility more clearly between the work of the World Bank and the fund. What do you think of this?

MC: There is no difference between us here. Mr. Köhler has stated that poverty reduction is a vitally important issue and that our policy must include higher goals for the benefit of the poor. This will be a great contribution toward long-term poverty reduction and global political stability.

MN: What do you consider the IMF's core competence?

MC: Monetary and macroeconomic analysis.

MN: Given this expertise, how do you justify the IMF's incursion into these new arenas? Your critics refer to this as "mission creep," meaning that the IMF appears to be expanding its mandate into areas that should be under the purview of the World Bank or other organizations. Are the IMF's macroeconomists really equipped to deal with the microlevel issues associated with poverty alleviation and social policy?

MC: No, of course they are not. But those who see "mission creep" in what I was doing have not listened seriously to what I was saying. Read all my speeches of the last year. I have said that poverty reduction, although central to IMF programs, should be designed, elaborated, and financed by the World Bank. But IMF programs must allow room for poverty reduction, not as a cherry on the cake, but really at the heart of the programs and with an economically solid connection to exchange-rate policy, budgetary policy, and even monetary policy. This adds to the complexity of the design of the program, but not to the mission of the IMF.

MN: Is there a tension between this new emphasis on poverty and the IMF's role as lender of last resort? A lender of last resort makes funds available to a country when all other sources of financing are reluctant to lend or invest, but in exchange requires the adoption of stringent economic policies that help restore investor confidence. How can you ask for fiscal austerity and at the same time request that governments spend more on helping the poor?

MC: I don't see it that way. My conviction is that poverty reduction comes with stronger monetary and budgetary discipline. The key social policy element is a good, strong monetary policy that defeats inflation. It's a budget that cuts unproductive spending to allow for well-targeted support to the poorest. All of that is perfectly compatible with the policies of a lender of last resort.

MN: Of course, the proliferation of financial crises during the last decade forced the fund to act as a lender of last resort quite often—in Mexico, Asia, and Russia, etc. But some argue that the very reason we are experiencing such frequent financial turmoil is that IMF policies demanding the free movement of money across borders—what is called capital account liberalization—often leave developing countries vulnerable to the sudden swings in financial markets. In other words, the IMF creates the problem and then rushes in to fix it. In fact, the editorial page of the *Wall Street Journal* has often criticized the IMF and you personally, saying that you do not put out fires in the global economy but rather that you fuel the flames of crisis—

MC: [Laughing]

MN: —because you and the IMF have forced countries to liberalize their financial—

MC: We have never forced a country to liberalize its capital account. Never! It is true that countries have liberalized on their own and at times in the wrong way, liberalizing first their short-term, volatile, and dangerous flows while restricting more stable flows like long-term, direct investment. Basically, we want orderly liberalization with strong macroeconomic balances and improved banking supervision, both of which are needed for liberalization to be safe and fruitful....

The Ugly Americans

MN: The United States accounts for about 18 percent of the IMF share quotas. Is the U.S. influence in the fund roughly proportional to that percentage?

MC: It is difficult to compare quantitative and qualitative factors. It is true that the United States has an important influence in the fund, but it's due to several factors. First, European nations would have a bigger share than the United States, but they are divided and generally less keen than the United States to involve themselves in the global picture. And you have the influence of the country where the institution is located. IMF staff live in Washington, D.C., read the newspapers there, go to cocktail parties there. They are exposed predominantly to U.S. culture.

I would add another factor. If you look at American international economic policy over the last 50 years, you will see that its purposes and objectives often have coincided with the basic thrust of the IMF's purposes: freedom of trade and a market economy. So, we have been very frequently in the same court as the United States.

MN: Former U.S. Trade Representative Mickey Kantor once referred to the IMF as a "battering ram" for U.S. interests.

MC: I totally disagree. We have not been a battering ram; at times we have disagreed with the United States because its policies were not in line with its own basic principles. At times our views and efforts coincided—particularly in promoting trade openness....

Last Regrets

MN: Will we have a global, systemic financial crisis in the next five years?

MC: We might have one in the next five years. Fortunately, we are doing well in fighting the weaknesses that led to the last crisis. But our success has fostered complacency; the urgency to implement reforms is less present than it should be. A crisis is by nature unexpected, and the next crisis will probably develop in a different way than the last. It could also develop in a similar way if we do not recognize that we should deal with the offshore centers, the speculative hedge funds, etc.

MN: What key reforms are needed in the global financial system? What should be the pillar of a better system?

MC: The pillar is transparency.

MN: How would you go about it?

MC: We have already gone a long way, but more is needed in terms of opening up government and central-bank accounts to more scrutiny, improving our knowledge of private capital flows—

MN: But when you think of reforming the global financial architecture, you really don't think about a major institutional redesign?

MC: I have made many proposals about changing the IMF.... But this comes second. What matters now is the private sector, their flows, the knowledge we have of their flows, and the proper framework for surveillance.

MN: You mean the regulation of the private sector at the global level?

MC: But we must take care that overregulation not provide us with a false security. Regulations are needed when and where seriously unethical behavior must be prevented. But as much as possible we must rely on well-defined, voluntary codes of good conduct and effective surveillance by the IMF.

MN: Now let's imagine a world without the IMF. Describe how the world would look if the fund did not exist.

MC: Well, you would have immediately a high-level commission... with a few key economists proposing a new global monetary fund.

MN: So if it did not exist, the IMF would have to be invented.

MC: Of course. And what would be the situation in the meantime? We would still be in the Asian crisis, and probably the world would be, if not in recession, in a very turbulent situation. Protectionism would have developed, tensions would have mounted and—

MN: Wars?

MC: Well, we have enough of that already. I'm not sure we would have that, but certainly protectionism and global financial instability....

MN: What would you like to be remembered for?

MC: [Long pause] For having served the world to the best of my ability....

MN: What are your biggest regrets about your tenure as managing director?

MC: I regret not being able to do more for Africa. I regret not having convinced world leaders to draw more active conclusions from the Mexican [1994–1995 financial] crisis. If we had been able to share deeply with them what we saw in Mexico, we possibly could have avoided the Asian [1997–1998 financial] crisis and particularly the crisis in Korea. But we could not. Perhaps the world, fascinated by the so-called Asian miracle, was not ready for such warnings.

Now is the blame with the IMF alone? Or is it also broadly shared by governments? I believe so.

POSTSCRIPT

Does the International Monetary Fund Do More Harm Than Good?

A recurrent theme in economic debates today is the rising resistance to globalization, especially among poorer people and countries, many of whom worry that they are not receiving the benefits of globalization or may even be suffering harm from it. Additional information is available about the IMF's role in this controversy in Devesh Kapur, "The IMF: A Cure or a Curse?" *Foreign Policy* (Summer 1998).

Control is also an issue. Opponents of globalization worry that their political control, including sovereignty for countries, is weakening. As one critic from Nepal put it, "Interference in the internal affairs of a sovereign country ... is now admissible in international social and political conduct, ... and multilateral financial establishments [like the IMF] are now increasingly treading on more complex and sensitive areas of domestic governance in the recipient countries." A related topic in the case of the IMF involves what some analysts see as a racial imbalance, intended or not. They say that the cause is the IMF voting formula, which gives majority power to a small group of countries whose people are predominantly of European-white heritage while effectively disenfranchising the much larger groups of countries peopled largely by Asians, Africans, Latinos, and other people of color. For more on the issue of control in an era of globalization, read Thomas L. Friedman, *The Lexus and the Olive Tree: Understanding Globalization* (Farrar, Straus & Giroux, 2000) and Strom C. Thacker, "The High Politics of IMF Lending," *World Politics* (October 1999).

The IMF's demand that recipient countries make structural adjustments has also faced a rising tide of criticism. None of this particularly persuaded Camdessus during his 13 years as head of the IMF to relent on this requirement. "The stronger the program [of capitalist reform], the stronger the financing will be," he asserted at one point. In the end, that position may have cost Camdessus his job. He was appointed to serve a third five-year term as managing director, beginning January 16, 1997. Then, after only serving a bit more than three years, Camdessus retired from the IMF on February 14, 2000. As is evident in his selection, he makes no apologies for the policies he followed as head of the IMF.

It was symbolic that as Camdessus arrived to deliver his last speech as IMF managing director, he was hit in the face by a cream pie thrown by Robert Reuel Naiman of Washington, D.C. Naiman told reporters that he wanted to give the IMF head "a friendly reminder of what we think of his policies and to give a warning to his successor that we expect different policies." Camdessus laughed off the attack with the comment, "I like pastry," but it must have been a troubling end to his career.

Horst Köhler, a German and former president of the European Bank for Reconstruction and Development who succeeded Camdessus in May 2000, will find it challenging to steer the IMF between the demands for social justice from one set of critics and the demands for financial prudence from another set of critics. Setting the tone, Köhler told bankers at one of his first speeches as managing director that the IMF must "work patiently but persistently to convince developing and emerging-market countries not to interpret these standards primarily as a 'dictate' by the industrialized countries but rather to see them as useful guideposts in their own efforts to strengthen institutions and gain greater access to international investment capital." Whether that represents a less stern approach or a "velvet glove" around iron demands for structural adjustment remains to be seen. For more on a conservative critique of the IMF, see Lawrence J. McQuillan, *The Case Against the International Monetary Fund* (Hoover Institution Press, 1999).

On the Internet . . .

The Center for Security Policy

The Web site of this Washington, D.C.–centered "think tank" provides a wide range of links to sites dealing with national and intenational security issues.

http://www.security-policy.org/links.html

Selected Papers on National Security

A supportive view of the military can be found at this Heritage Foundation site.

http://www.nationalsecurity.org/spons.html

Office of the Coordinator for Counterterrorism

This worthwhile site explores the range of terrorist threats and activities, albeit from the U.S. point of view, and is maintained by the U.S. State Department's Office of Counterterrorism.

http://www.state.gov/www/global/terrorism/

Centre for the Study of Terrorism and Political Violence

The primary aims of the Centre for the Study of Terrorism and Political Violence are to investigate the roots of political violence; to develop a body of theory spanning the various and disparate elements of terrorism; and to recommend policy and organizational initiatives that governments and private sectors might adopt to better predict, detect, and respond to terrorism and terrorist threats.

http://www.st-and.ac.uk/academic/intrel/research/cstpv/

PART 4

Military Security and
Intervention Issues

*W*hatever we may wish, war, terrorism, and other forms of physical coercion are still important elements of international politics. Countries calculate both how to use the instruments of force and how to implement national security. There can be little doubt, however, that significant changes are under way in this realm as part of the changing world system. Strong pressures exist to expand the mission and strengthen the security capabilities of international organizations and to gauge the threat of terrorism. This section examines how countries in the international system are addressing these issues.

- Should U.S. Military Spending Be Increased?

- Is There a Great Danger From Chemical or Biological Terrorism?

ISSUE 11

Should U.S. Military Spending Be Increased?

YES: Henry H. Shelton, from "Force, Forces, and Forecasting: Preparing America's Armed Forces for an Uncertain Future," Remarks Made to the National Press Club, Washington, D.C. (December 14, 2000)

NO: Carl Conetta, from "Toward a Smaller, More Efficient, and More Relevant US Military," Project on Defense Alternatives Briefing Paper (October 2000)

ISSUE SUMMARY

YES: Henry H. Shelton, a general in the U.S. Army and chairman of the Joint Chiefs of Staff, argues that the United States, its citizens, and its interests are threatened in many places in the world and across a wide range of issues. He contends that while the dangers may not seem as menacing as they did during the cold war, it is prudent to invest in force modernization in the near term to ensure razor-sharp forces for the long haul.

NO: Carl Conetta, director of the Project on Defense Alternatives at the Commonwealth Institute in Cambridge, Massachusetts, contends that U.S. military overspending derives from a lack of realism in threat assessment, an unnecessarily ambitious post–cold war military strategy, and failure to adapt to the specific challenges of the new era.

P rior to World War II, the United States participated in world politics only fitfully. In part, this stemmed from a feeling of security based on the fact that the country is guarded by three vast bodies of water and has only two relatively weak neighbors, Canada and Mexico. Much of this sense of security was shattered by World War II and its aftermath. During the war, aircraft carriers, submarines, long-range bombers, and other weapons systems were developed or improved to the point that the possibility of an enemy attacking the United States seemed quite real.

Soon, however, danger from these weapons systems was far exceeded by the extraordinary killing power of atomic weapons. The Soviet Union rapidly developed atomic and hydrogen bombs. In the late 1950s, the Soviets seemed to eclipse U.S. missile technology when they launched the first satellite, then put the first person in space.

After World War II the United States demobilized most of its military forces and slashed its military spending. The number of military personnel shrank from about 12 million in 1945 to under 1 million in 1947. The onset of the cold war reversed this trend, and threats by the Soviet Union led to an immense build-up of American military power and the expenditure of a huge proportion of the U.S. budget for defense.

The military establishment again increased during the Vietnam War era. Defense spending rose 24 percent between 1965 and 1970. The number of people in uniform also increased, peaking at just over 3 million in 1970. After the Vietnam War ended, military spending and personnel both plunged, only to rise again during the years roughly equivalent to the presidency of Ronald Reagan. Then the waning of the cold war in the late 1980s again reversed the trend.

The final episode in the cold war roller-coaster ride of defense personnel and spending came when the Soviet Union collapsed and was replaced by Russia and a number of other, smaller former Soviet republics. What had been a declining sense of threat in the United States dissipated even more rapidly. Changes in China, the other great communist power, further accelerated Americans' growing sense of security. China began to welcome foreign businesses and visitors and to reform its economy to parallel the capitalist model. China seemed less a potential nuclear enemy and more like a potential business opportunity. By 1992 the world looked safer to Americans than it had in many decades.

U.S. defense spending during the cold war exceeded $5 trillion, and it seemed time for a change of focus. The budgets and defense projections presented by President Bill Clinton during his first term reflected the sense of security and the urge to cut defense spending. At $268 billion, Clinton's 1994 defense budget represented a 35–40 percent reduction from what the defense budget had been less than a decade earlier.

Safety is relative, however, and the degree to which threats ended is debatable. The Russian nuclear arsenal remains massive, and the Chinese nuclear arsenal is growing. India and Pakistan joined the nuclear weapons club in 1998. Worries about terrorism have been increased by the fear that terrorists might be able to obtain and use nuclear, chemical, or biological weapons.

After a continuing decline in real-dollar defense spending during most of the 1990s, the debate on the level of spending has once again come to the fore. The basic issue is whether or not serious threats exist and whether or not U.S. defense spending is enough to provide reasonable security against those threats and others that could reasonably occur. In the following selections, Henry H. Shelton contends that there are serious threats to U.S. national security and that U.S. forces must be well funded now to meet the danger when it arises later. Carl Conetta disagrees, arguing that it is possible to provide adequate defense and to cut defense spending significantly.

 **YES**

Force, Forces, and Forecasting

Remarks at the National Press Club, Washington, D.C. Dec. 14, 2000

... Over the years, the press and the military have had their ups and downs characterized at one extreme by Admiral Ernie King, who, when asked to state the Navy's public affairs policy in 1942 said, "Don't tell them anything. When it's over, tell them who won." Contrast that with then-General Dwight Eisenhower's view during the same war. He maintained that the commander in the field must understand the mission of the press and assist the press corps in carrying out that mission. As much as some of us in uniform may admire Admiral King's style we know the right approach lies with President Eisenhower, who also wrote, "I found that correspondents habitually responded to candor, frankness, and understanding." I would echo President Eisenhower's comments. I believe that's a good lesson for all of us and also a good beginning for my discussion....

Today, I think most of you know that the defense budget is about $300 billion. And to many $300 billion is viewed as an excessive amount to spend on defense. "Defense from what?" they ask. "Why so much?... The Cold War is over." "Where's the peace dividend?" Well, in 1985, we were spending 6.5% of our Gross Domestic Product [GDP] on defense. And today, as you know, we spend just over 3% of GDP. At the 1985 rate, our budget this year in DoD [Department of Defense] would be double what it is today. That... is quite a peace dividend!

Maybe we need to look at what we spend on defense in a different light. Although we are the Department of Defense, what we're really about is national security—not just defense. Our national security—in a broader context than defense—provides for our economic prosperity, our role as a world leader, and also the assistance programs we provide for friends, partners, and allies around the globe. Our national security is enhanced by a strong defense industry making world-class equipment that becomes the envy of all and ultimately it contributes to strong overseas sales which also enhances our security, increases our military interoperability, binds us closer to friends and partners, and promotes our Nation's economic prosperity. So, the peace dividend has been significant, and the contributions defense dollars make to our

From Henry H. Shelton, "Force, Forces, and Forecasting: Preparing America's Armed Forces for an Uncertain Future," Remarks Made to the National Press Club, Washington, D.C. (December 14, 2000).

national security allow our great citizens to enjoy freedom, economic prosperity, and the opportunity to live in the greatest Nation on the face of the earth.

We live in interesting times, as the old Chinese saying goes. Interesting not only because of the security challenges that exist in this new millennium, but interesting also because next year we undertake the next Quadrennial Defense Review (QDR). This QDR gives us a great opportunity to correct what I view as a "strategy to force structure imbalance." Executing the current strategy —as right as it may be—and as we have done since the 1997 QDR, places an unsustainable burden on parts of our force structure. Today, we face the dilemma of plenty of strategy, not enough forces. How we got into this situation, I think, is instructive. Today's smaller force structure was built from the framework of the last (1997) QDR, and parts of it are under considerable strain.

In many ways, it's a reflection of our success! Flush from historic victories in the Cold War, Desert Storm, and most recently in Kosovo, the extraordinary capabilities of our Armed Forces are in great demand. We were just unable to anticipate how high that demand would be! The results are that our men and women in uniform are busier than ever before. And the wear and tear on their equipment is significant, leading to what has been termed "the fraying of the force." Allocating the lion's share of finite resources—including those intended for modernization of the force—on near-term readiness in order to keep today's force, particularly our first-to-the-fight forces, razor sharp, is not a sustainable approach for the long haul.

When I spoke to the graduating class at Annapolis [at the U.S. Naval Academy] last May, it struck me that these young men and women and their peers across America would be among our senior leaders of the force of 2020. In the meantime, we will be counting on them to be the junior leaders of today's force. For them to do what we ask of them—to be the best force in the world —we must give them the best tools! This means ensuring that they have the resources necessary to remain trained and ready today, it means recapitalizing our weapons systems that we place in their hands as well as the infrastructure that we ask them to work and live in, and it means properly compensating them throughout.

We simply cannot afford to support near-term readiness at the expense of future readiness and modernization. It's not an "either-or" proposition. We must do both. The essential question, of course, is HOW? Let me explore that just a bit. We should take the National Security and National Military Strategies, figure out what is necessary to support the objectives of those strategies, and then develop the force structure to support them. In other words, we should figure out what to do before we decide how we are going to do it. The resourcing piece then comes after these two steps. This ... is the critical part! We have to get this right and we must do it in the right order! Strategy first, then force structure. We should not establish a budget ceiling absent strategy and then build a force structure that's constrained by the top line. Force structure cannot be "reverse-engineered." To do this would cost us more in the long term—in terms of dollars, in terms of readiness, and, potentially, in lives.

That means, of course, that we need a "feed-back" mechanism to revisit force structure when the strategic environment changes or the strategy itself changes. We must, therefore, understand the changing nature of the international security environment. Because it holds the key to what our strategic imperatives will be, and thus what our military capabilities MUST be. Let me spend a few minutes or so on how I see the security environment changing over the next few years.

For starters, events over the past decade in such places as Southwest Asia, the Balkans, Haiti, Africa, Indonesia, the Kashmir, and elsewhere provide a window into the future strategic landscape. It's murky, it's frustrating, and it's increasingly dangerous. And while, today, North Korea and Iraq may pose the most serious challenges to America's interests, I do not believe these near-term threats will determine the shape of the world through the first decades of this new century. It's clear to me that the future of Asia will not be decided in Pyongyang [the capital of North Korea], but rather on the high frontiers of the Kashmir, on the floor of the Tokyo stock exchange, and in the special economic zones of Shanghai and Hong Kong.

Now, let me specifically address the challenge of an emerging China, a country that I had the opportunity to visit just last month. I'm firmly convinced that we need to focus all elements of US power and diplomacy on ensuring that China does not become the 21st century version of the Soviet bear. It's clearly in America's interests to remain engaged with China across the full spectrum of activities and to convince them that a peaceful resolution of the Taiwan issue is the only way ahead. But let's not underestimate the challenges we face. China takes a distrustful view of US intentions as articulated in their recent defense white paper. They are aggressively modernizing their military forces— both conventional as well as nuclear. At the same time they hope to maintain control of an expanding capitalist-like economy under a communist hierarchy that embraces centralized planning and centralized control. This situation is a contradiction that could threaten China's internal power and, consequently, threaten stability throughout the region.

Turning to the Middle East, although Iraq is still troublesome and threatens our pilots daily, Baghdad is only one of the serious long-term concerns in the region. Iraq is a damaged regime, internally insecure, and with its armed forces a shadow of their former strength. Rather, it's the instability throughout the Middle East that presents the greatest challenges to American interests for the long haul. The focal points are the Israel-Palestine issue and the tensions between modernism and fundamentalism in a region that is already a tinderbox of economic, political, and religious conflicts.

In much the same way . . . the Balkans remain a serious concern in Europe, but the situation there pales in comparison with events in Russia. The future of Europe will not swing on the status of Kosovo or the establishment of a new Serbia. No, the future of Europe swings on the path that Russian nationalism takes and whether Russia can continue its peaceful evolution into a fully democratic nation with a stable economy that abides by the rule of law. As I discussed with my counterpart, Russian Chief of Staff [Anatoly] Kvashnin, . . . one of the most potentially destabilizing factors in the region is the thousands of nuclear and chemical weapons, stored in facilities throughout Russia. And as we all know, there are still thousands of nuclear warheads in the Russian arsenal. They present a very profound danger to our security should they fall into the wrong hands, and there are many "wrong hands" out there trying to get them.

... Although we have reason to be somewhat encouraged by the recent signs of at least "rhetorical" moderation in Tehran [the capital of Iran], in Pyongyang, and, to a lesser degree, in Beijing it would be premature to let our guard down. In order to shape tomorrow we must deal effectively with the Bosnias, the Koreas, the Kosovos, and the East Timors today. However, we cannot allow them to distract us from the truly vital issues that loom before us. Developments in Asia, the Middle East, and Russia have the potential to dramatically affect America's economic, political, and security interests. This demands our greatest investment in time, in energy, and in diplomacy.

The United States' global leadership role with our inherent worldwide interests continues to demand a broad range of military activities from engagement to warfighting. It's clear that the military has and will continue to become involved in areas other than just those that affect our vital national interests. The strategic environment will undoubtedly cause us to deploy forces to achieve limited military objectives. However, we must be mindful that long-term commitments to achieve nation building, and the like, place our readiness at risk.

Obviously, the decision to use force is the most important decision that our Nation's leaders make. In arriving at decisions of such consequence, we would all do well to remember that there's no cookie cutter solution that can be applied to the complex array of contingencies—both great and small—which confront America in this new Century. There are, ... however, at least four clear parameters that should inform decisions about employing force:

- First, any intervention, unless linked to a discernible national interest, is, in all probability, not sustainable.
- Second, the further removed from our vital national interests that an intervention is, the more challenging it becomes to sustain support over time.
- Third, sustaining our involvement in military operations abroad requires the support of the American people as reflected by the Congress.
- And, finally, we must be willing to ask ourselves two very tough questions: the first, "Do we dare to use force when force is needed?" And, second, just as important for the world's sole superpower, "Do we dare admit that force cannot solve every problem?"

As I look to the future and consider the possible scenarios that could result in a decision to use force, there are some general trends that become apparent, such as:

- The strategic "Flash to Bang" time is getting shorter. I don't need to tell this audience about instantaneous communications that compresses the time between finding out about events and the demand to "do something."

- As the diversity of threats and non-state actors increase, so, too, will the complexity of military tasks. Future adversaries may try to stay below the threshold of clear aggression, further complicating appropriate response options.

- We can expect more failed states, as people struggle for independence, for political legitimacy, and economic and resource advantage in climates of violence, repression, and deprivation.

- The range and types of conflict will expand. We can expect non-state actors, asymmetric attacks, anti-access strategies, retreat to the lower ends of the spectrum of conflict, and information warfare. When you combine these with the very real potential for high-intensity regional conflict or even threats to our homeland, you can see the enormous challenges that our future Joint Force Commanders will face.

The world remains a dangerous place, indeed, and America's superiority generates envy in many and outright hatred in others. As I've said before, I'm not in the business of playing "Chicken Little." I fully recognize that, today, America has no peer competitor. However, we must remain alert to the possibility of peer competition in the future. And there is also the potential for the emergence of a single conventional power or a combination of forces that could mount a focused campaign against US interests. In our business, we need to keep in mind that this environment could develop a lot sooner than any of us might think.

Well, we've been discussing the "what" and the "how" of our national security challenges, the next question is "How much?" The last QDR set a goal for procurement, for example, at $60 billion, which we were able to achieve in the fiscal year '01 budget. Based on the best projections available at the time, we thought this would be adequate to maintain an acceptable level of modernization. Reality has dictated otherwise! In the last three years alone, the demanding pace of operations demonstrated how inadequate that level was. $60 billion might have been adequate to sustain modernization had not the increased operational tempo and unknown aging factors driven us to consume it at increasing rates.

Many have worked hard at figuring out what procurement figure would be appropriate. Deputy Secretary of Defense John Hamre left office [in March 2000] arguing for $100 billion. The Congressional Budget Office pegged it at about $90 billion. While those figures are probably closer to the mark, I cannot today give you a precise dollar amount. One of the challenges of the QDR will be to determine what is an acceptable, sustainable rate. But I think we need to keep a larger perspective in mind. That calls for understanding what, in the larger sense, we're here for. I've mentioned it fairly frequently throughout my tenure as Chairman. It must be the fundamental focus of our efforts in the QDR and in the larger military planning system.

Despite the changing security environment in which we find ourselves, the Armed Forces exist to fight... and win... America's wars. The global interests, responsibilities, and the obligations we have as a Nation will endure. And there is no indication that the threats to those interests, and responsibilities, or obligations to our allies will disappear. This is the one place where there is clarity about the future and that is undeniable. Given this emerging security environment—and our broad interests—the force must have the capability to dominate across the full spectrum of military operations all at once. Not only able to dominate in one place, at one moment in time, but be flexible and responsive enough to undertake multiple tasks in multiple locations simultaneously. That's what our friends, allies, and our partners expect of a global power. That's what is required for a Nation with worldwide interests.

... I had the opportunity to speak at the Army's Fletcher Conference. I said that our biggest challenge was not to prepare the Army for the future, but, rather, to create a truly joint Total Force in which the Army is an integral part. The core military competency of our future capabilities will NOT be merely our great Army, or our great Navy/Marine Corps Team, or our great Air Force. The core competency will be a seamless joint task force—this is Joint Vision 2020. The individual Service transformation efforts in progress are right and proper only if they mesh fully with joint transformation. To do or think otherwise is pure folly. Let me assure you that this is not an academic discussion, a "sand-table" of jointness, if you will. And, we are not waiting for pundits and critics to take the lead. The Joint Chiefs and CINCs [commander in chiefs] have been aggressively stepped out on four primary fronts.

First, we are investing in people. We've made great strides in pay, retirement, and healthcare reform thanks to the Congress and the Administration. A quality force is what gives America a decisive edge.

Second, we continue to demand greater jointness among the Services. While there is great value in preserving the individual Service cultures, when it comes to warfighting, the Joint Task Force must become our new core competency. To this end, we have established Joint Forces Command out of what was previously US Atlantic Command (USACOM) in Norfolk. Its charter is nothing less than developing operational concepts to advance the tenets of joint warfighting.

Third, we are taking a hard look at technologies to enhance interoperability. We've established interoperability as a key performance parameter for all of our major high dollar acquisitions. Let me be perfectly clear, this parameter is not waiverable, it is non-negotiable. And to institutionalize the importance of interoperability:

- We made significant changes to the Joint Requirements Oversight Council and our Joint Warfighting Capability Assessment process.
- We are transforming our logistics systems to take advantage of improvements in information technologies.

- And we are exploring ways to transform our acquisition process to rapidly take advantage of the results of joint experimentation.

Finally, America must be strong at home to be strong abroad. Therefore, we created a number of organizations to address specific emerging threats:

- We stood up Joint Task Force–Civil Support to assist Federal, state, and local agencies responding to disasters caused by domestic acts of terrorism. And I stress the word "support" because other Federal Agencies, such as FEMA [Federal Emergency Management Agency], or the Justice Department, will take the lead, and will remain in the lead.
- We established Joint Task Force Computer Network Defense at Space Command to lead the Department of Defense effort to protect our vital networks.
- And we expanded Space Command's responsibilities to include Computer Network Attack, which, when directed by the National Command Authority, will allow offensive operations against an adversary's systems.

But all these initiatives will be for naught if we fail to recruit and retain a quality force. The progress we've made in pay, retirement, and health care reform must be sustained. We must come to grip with the facts that today's military is a better-educated married military, often juggling two careers. Therefore, to attract and retain today's quality Armed Forces we need an innovative approach to how we pay, assign, promote, and otherwise reward our people. To complete the equation in attracting and retaining a quality force, we must also replace the aging equipment and infrastructure as a priority. Finally, we must continue to review how we use our military. As a tool of national policy, it's capable of many things and preeminent in one: warfighting.

... America is a very prosperous Nation and America can afford whatever defense it wants. But without a strong defense, the prosperity that makes America the envy of the world is threatened. And let's remember—what we spend on our "Defense" budget must be viewed in the context of what America spends for our National Security—something that affects every American.

Let me close with one final thought. Just as it is your sacred trust to keep the American people informed, it is our sacred trust to defend America and American interests. As I testified [recently], your military is ready today to meet any threat. But part of our great military are showing strain and are starting to fray and so we must take clear, concrete, and bold steps to keep it well prepared in this new century. As President-Elect Bush said in his [recent] address—"A military that is equal to any challenge and superior to any adversary."

NO ↵

Carl Conetta

Toward a Smaller, More Efficient, and More Relevant US Military

Introduction

While visiting Texas in March 2000 Secretary of Defense William Cohen pronounced the peace dividend over. "What we have to do now," said Secretary Cohen, "is build up our forces, our capability." Although mistaken, this proposition is probably the closest we have come in recent years to a bipartisan view on defense issues. President Clinton started the ball rolling in late 1998 with the addition of $112 billion to the Pentagon's five year budget. Thus, the nation entered the 21st century spending $285 billion on defense—almost 80 percent as much as the average for the 1980s, the peak decade for peacetime Cold War defense spending.

President Clinton's largess did not, however, mollify its intended audience: the Joint Chiefs of Staff. In response to the President's initiative they have been lobbying assiduously and with remarkable independence since late 1998 to add as much as another $30 billion a year to the Pentagon budget. Regardless of who occupies the White House in 2001, it is virtually certain that the Defense Department budget will soon after exceed $300 billion annually in FY 2000 dollars.

The recent bipartisan willingness to contemplate major increases in defense spending has several origins. Political realities play a part, beginning with the 1998–1999 presidential impeachment crisis and continuing into the 2000 election season. Also key are the genuine difficulties faced by our armed forces as they wrestle with the unique requirements of the post–Cold War era. Finally, the remarkable performance of the US economy in recent years has been an important driver of the new fiscal liberalism regarding defense.

This policy memo will address only in passing the question, Can we afford to spend more on defense? Its central focus is whether we truly *need* to spend more from the vantage point of military security. In addressing this issue the memo not only aims to clarify the sources of our armed forces' recent difficulties but also to ventilate options for moving toward a smaller, more efficient, and more effective military.

From Carl Conetta, "Toward a Smaller, More Efficient, and More Relevant US Military," Project on Defense Alternatives Briefing Paper (October 2000). Copyright © 2000 by The Commonwealth Institute. Reprinted by permission of The Project on Defense Alternatives and the author. Notes omitted.

1. Can We Afford to Spend More on Defense?

... Today we devote about 3 percent of our GDP [gross domestic product] to defense—the smallest share since 1940; throughout the 1980s we had averaged close to 6 percent. Such comparisons have become central to the arguments for increased spending. Put simply, the contention is that because the United States devoted a much greater share of its wealth to defense during the Cold War than it does today, we can afford to raise the defense budget—and perhaps significantly so.

It is a peculiar myopia, however, that compares today's US defense investment rate with that of the Cold War era while ignoring current comparisons between the United States and its competitors. Regarding military competitors: some spend a greater percentage of national wealth than does the United States, but their absolute level of spending is much lower than that of the United States and NATO [North Atlantic Treaty Organization].... Russia and China together spend less than 38 percent as much as the United States and approximately 20 percent as much as the group of all NATO states plus Japan. This compares to Cold War ratios (circa 1985) of 109 percent for the Warsaw Pact and China against the United States and 66 percent for the same against all NATO plus Japan. Adding smaller potential competitors and rogues—North Korea, Cuba, Iran, Iraq, Syria, Libya—only further accentuates the West's post–Cold War edge in military spending.

More relevant to the issue of *affordability*, however, is a comparison between the percentage of GDP devoted to defense by the United States and its potential economic rivals. Here we find that presently the United States invests a greater percentage of national wealth in defense than does its NATO allies, significantly more than the world average, and much more than its chief economic competitors. This comparison pertains to the economic aspect of strategic competition. Economic competitiveness is partly determined by such things as national debt reduction, national savings rates, infrastructure investment, and spending on market-oriented technology research—all of which vie with national defense for scarce resources.

... [Cost is] only part of the strategic equation, of course—and not the part with the greatest immediacy. The other part involves military security imperatives, narrowly defined. These provide the only positive rationale for spending any portion at all of a nation's wealth on military preparedness. In this sphere the calculation of requirements involves (i) a nation's interests and goals in the world, (ii) the nature and magnitude of the challenges to those interests and goals, (iii) the specific ways a nation plans to achieve its goals and protect its interests, and (iv) the effectiveness and efficiency of a nation's military in serving these ends. While economic imperatives compel us (especially today) to spend as little on defense as we safely can, the variables on the military side of the equation tell us whether it is indeed possible to spend less or, conversely, necessary to spend more.

2. Can We Safely Spend Less on Defense?

Is it possible to spend significantly less on defense without relinquishing important security interests? This question is related to another: How have we come to spend as much as we do on defense despite the Cold War's end? Several aspects of post–Cold War defense policy, pertaining to threat assessment, military strategy, and force development, are germane to answering both questions. Looking at each of these in turn:

- During the past decade our calculation of military requirements has become detached from a careful empirical assessment of threats, current or rising;
- Key aspects of our present military strategy (as codified in the 1997 QDR [Quadrennial Defense Review]) are unnecessarily ambitious, probably unworkable, and possibly even counter-productive; and, finally
- Our armed forces are not yet adapted very well to the challenges and opportunities of the present era—and this breeds inefficiency. Indeed, even the basic task of infrastructure reform remains unfinished. . . .

3. Rethinking US Military Strategy

The 1997 Quadrennial Defense Review set out three broad tasks for our military: (i) respond to current crises, (ii) shape the strategic environment, and (iii) prepare now for an uncertain future. Of course, our military has always performed these functions to some extent. The QDR distinguished itself, however, by increasing the relative emphasis on the second and third tasks. The result has been a significant expansion in the foreign policy role of our armed forces and a widening of their focus beyond the traditional concern with "real and present" dangers. Moreover, under the rubric of "crisis response," force planning and development has focused on the goal of being able to fight multiple, major regional wars at an accelerated pace. Paradoxically, the actual operational activity of our armed forces during the past nine years has focused on smaller-scale contingencies, including so-called "stability operations."

There is a tension between our military's preparations for major war and its actual activity in frequent smaller conflicts. This has contributed substantially to readiness problems in recent years. These problems were supposed to have reached crisis proportion in mid-1997—despite the Clinton administrations' having spent on readiness 30 percent more per person than the average for the 1980s. The first step toward a less expensive, more cost-effective military would be to focus military preparations on those forms of crisis response that our armed forces are actually undertaking and likely to undertake during the next 10–15 years. This means a greater emphasis on the requirements associated with smaller-scale contingencies. Also, our strategy should be adjusted to (i) de-emphasize the Pentagon's "environment shaping" activities and (ii) alter the way our military prepares for an uncertain future.

The next two sections of this memo address the issues of environment shaping and hedging against future possible threats. Subsequent sections address our crisis response strategy and priorities, how they should change, and the implications of change for force composition and cost.

3.1 Environment Shaping

Environment shaping encompasses not only traditional deterrence, which focuses on mature threats, but also more diffuse efforts to use military power to channel strategic change down paths favorable to US interests. Of course, almost any use of our military power can be said to "shape the strategic environment." But some activities, such as so-called "military diplomacy," bear only a distal relationship to core military missions. Such activities are consuming a greater part of our military resources than ever before and they represent the extension of Pentagon prerogatives into functional areas once reserved more exclusively for the State Department.

Today, our military engages in more than 170 multinational exercises a year. Military assistance programs and other forms of military-to-military contacts involve our armed forces in over 100 countries. Compared to the Cold War period, a greater percentage of these are occurring outside formal alliance relationships or outside cooperative arrangements with a clear, immediate, and assured security payoff. Many are supposed to serve a non-specific confidence-building function—a type of "getting to know each other" exercise. In these, information flows in both directions. The flow of expertise and technology, however, is more unidirectional—from us to our partners of the moment.

The environment shaping activity that is most consumptive of resources is "global military presence." During the Cold War our near-global presence was a byproduct of missions having to do with countering the power, activity, and influence of the Soviet Union and its allies. Now it has gained the status of a mission in its own right—and it is the closest we come in practice to embracing a "global cop" role. . . .

The problem with many "environment shaping" activities is that the supposed link between our actions and the desired effect is tenuous at best. The history of the practice suggests that unintended, unpredictable, and unreliable outcomes abound. Our considerable efforts to shape Iran, Iraq, Pakistan, and Afghanistan testify to this. Far from discouraging military competition, some forms of environment shaping may actually help provoke it.

Generally speaking, we should transfer many of our hopes and expectations for environment shaping back to where they belong: the State Department. This implies curtailing the practice of "military diplomacy" and rolling back some of our multinational exercises and military assistance programs. The Pentagon's role in environment shaping should focus more narrowly on traditional deterrence. And we should discard non-specific "global military presence" as a mission in its own right. Instead, America's military presence abroad should become more closely associated with specific confrontations and areas of concern.

3.2 Preparing for an Uncertain Future

The United States needs to rethink how best to prepare for threats that do not exist today and that may or may not exist 15, 20, or more years in the future. Two ways that the present strategy hedges against future uncertainty is (i) by maintaining an overly large active-component force structure and (ii) by proceeding with massive buys of advanced weapon platforms originally designed to counter Cold War adversaries. But these measures cannot assure us that we will have the type and quality of armed forces we actually might need in the future, if new and more capable foes arise. Instead, they merely preserve 20th century force structure, modernizing it along the most expensive lines available with turn-of-the-century technology. The only real assurance this provides is that we will spend hundreds of billions of dollars more than we might otherwise.

The QDR rationalizes maintaining an overly large active force as a hedge against the re-emergence of a peer competitor—an eventuality it says is unlikely before 2015. This time line is overly conservative. It is like saying that a child is unlikely to grow six feet tall before his sixth birthday. The proposition, although true, is trivial. In fact, there is no realistic prospect that we and our allies will face a military peer even on a regional basis before 2018. For Russia or China—the leading candidates for peer status—to do better than this, they would first have to surpass the Japanese economic development "miracle" of 1960–1990 and then surpass the German military development feat of the 1930s. This, of course, also assumes that Russia can achieve and that China can sustain domestic stability....

Meeting the challenge of a peer rival, should one begin to gestate, would involve a race between its emergence and the ability of the United States to reconstitute sufficient additional military power to ensure that, at minimum, the military balance does not slip below effective parity. Given America's incomparable military-industrial base, it would enjoy a unique advantage in any such competition. Today's huge gap between the United States and any potential rival defines America's strategic reaction time—its margin of safety.

Turning to the Pentagon's present modernization plans: if we believe that a dramatic revolution in military affairs (RMA) lies somewhere in the not-too-distant future, we should avoid buying into the most expensive interim technology today.... Should an RMA eventuate and spread, [this technology] may prove obsolete on arrival. And buying [it] beggars our ability to pursue and field twenty-first century technology in a timely way. The bottom-line question is, Should we be buying piloted combat aircraft that cost $180 million per unit when their capabilities far exceed today's needs, but may fall short against new types of foes that arise half-way through their service life?...

The Pentagon's present modernization programs are squeezed between a present characterized by much reduced threat and a longer-term future in which the nature of threats is uncertain. What should be clear today, however, is that the West is not currently in a modernization race with anyone, much less an RMA race. This can be substantiated by a variety of comparative measures: relative modernization programs, procurement and R&D [research and development] spending, growth and quality of research and military industrial base, or arms import and export activity. By all these measures, the West and its regional allies not only predominate, but are gaining on their potential competitors (including China.)

A less costly and more flexible way to hedge against future uncertainty would emphasize preparations for force reconstitution and the maintenance of a robust R&D establishment, military production base, and reserve military. We should economize on modernization for the next 10–12 years, emphasizing upgraded models of current generation platforms, while laying the economic and technological basis for re-capitalizing along revolutionary lines thereafter —if need be.

4. Key Determinants of Force Size and Readiness Requirements

Smaller-scale contingencies and peace operations have attracted a great deal of criticism as the source of our military's recent readiness woes. But the ire is misplaced. Far more consumptive of our time, energy, and resources are our preparations for large-scale regional wars and our maintenance of a global military presence. In key respects these two broad areas of activity substantially exceed our real needs.

4.1 Regional War Plans . . .

Present War Plans Exaggerate the Power of Regional Foes

Our current war plans focus on "regional rogue" states whose armed forces have been in steep decline for a decade. Stripped of superpower patronage, these states have lost the capacity to equip, train, sustain, or employ forces like those of the 1980s. Correspondingly, we should adjust our force packages for regional war downward by about 30 percent—a larger cut for the Navy and Marine Corps, a smaller cut for the Air Force.

In fact, rather than getting smaller and more manageable, our planned force packages for regional war have been growing in size. Since 1996, the Army's stated requirements for fighting a two war scenario have grown by 70,000 troops. Turning to the Navy: its Surface Combatant Force Level Study also foresees major regional conflicts requiring more surface combatants than had deployed for the 1990–1991 Gulf War. Looking forward to 2005 it sees 69 surface combatants needed for a Persian Gulf conflict and 76 for a conflict in the northwest Pacific. During the Gulf War the USN [U.S. Navy] rotated approximately 55 surface combatants through the region with no more than 45 directly engaged at any one time.

Present War Plans Seek to Substantially Accelerate the Pace of Conflict
Our regional war plans also incorporate the goal of winning major wars within 100–150 days (depending on region)—which is much less time than it took to complete the Gulf War. This accelerated schedule is supposed to dramatically reduce risks, but the case is not compelling. USAF [U.S. Air Force] Major General Charles Link has correctly criticized plans to greatly accelerate the deployment of ground troops as "a strategy for putting the largest possible number of Americans within range of enemy fire as quickly as we can." We can afford to relax the warfighting schedule for regional wars and, instead, retain the Gulf War practice of fighting in distinct defensive and offensive phases.

Present War Plans Are Based on Highly Unlikely Scenarios
Finally, our strategy for handling multiple wars is overly ambitious. It prescribes conducting two overlapping counter-offensives in wars that begin about 45 days apart. This puts tremendous pressure on swing assets, lift, and active-component forces generally. But the demands and costs of this approach are not commensurate with the very low probability of the scenario. It is unlikely to occur even given a 40- or 50-year time period. We should move further down the path of the "win-hold-win" alternative, which delays the second counteroffensive. And we should plan to rely more on reserve forces in our preparations for multiple wars.

Taken together these adjustments would substantially relieve force structure and, thus, modernization requirements. They would also impact significantly on readiness goals because these are pegged to executing the two war plan, as noted above. There would be a price to pay, of course, but the currency would be measured primarily in time, not casualties.

There is nothing in our recent experience of fighting regional conflicts to suggest that a headlong rush into large-scale offensive operations will ensure fewer casualties. This might be true in wars with opponents far more capable than the Iraqis (circa 1990) at persisting in offensive action against US-style defenses. At any rate, the potential enemy capabilities that most worry US planners today are ballistic missiles—and these are likely to be expended early in a shooting war, as Iraq demonstrated in the Gulf War. Massive rapid deployment of ground troops does nothing to undermine this threat; indeed, it only serves to enable it.

4.2 Global Military Presence

In recent years the United States has had between 40,000 and 60,000 personnel on average deployed in smaller-scale operations at any one time. It also has maintained a presence of less than 200,000 troops at permanent bases on foreign soil and 30,000 sailors and marines afloat in foreign waters. "Presence" refers to the latter two categories of overseas service personnel and not those temporarily deployed in operations.

When "presence" is associated with specific regions and confrontations that concern us, it facilitates rapid crisis response and serves deterrence. Units forward deployed on land constitute an immediate bulwark against aggression.

They embody an unmistakable statement of US interest, commitment, and intent—and, thus, constitute a strong deterrent. Strong deterrence is difficult to maintain against an adversary's tendency to misperceive or underestimate our interests and commitment. Thus, it is important to make clear who and what precisely is being deterred. The success of deterrence often hinges on the fact that land-based forces are deployed in a way that underscores a rather specific "line in the sand."

Today, only in Korea and the Persian Gulf do land-based deployments correlate closely with a major threat of aggression. Deployments in Europe, by contrast, have come to serve more of a political-military function, reassuring our allies of our continued commitment to NATO. Our bases in Europe also are supposed to serve more than before as jumping-off points for deployments further east or south—although our attempts to use European land forces in this way (for operations in Bosnia and Kosova) have proved less than satisfactory.

The Navy and Marine Corps' rotational deployments afloat, involving carrier battle groups and Marine Expeditionary Units (MEUs), reinforce the land-based deployments and facilitate power projection to areas where no or relatively few US personnel are permanently stationed. These rotational deployments are also supposed to have a more general or nonspecific deterrent effect—suppressing the proclivity to aggression wherever they visit or pass. But this secondary effect can only be regarded as weak. Naval and Marine Corps rotational deployments lack the ingredients for strong deterrence—except in those places where US interests are otherwise strongly substantiated.

There are several steps we can take to maximize the utility of our military presence abroad:

- First, we should re-associate naval presence with those specific, critical areas of instability that concern us and that cannot be adequately covered by land-based forces. This means returning to a two-ocean standard focusing on the Pacific and Indian oceans. Marine Corps MEUs and smaller Navy flotillas might also occasionally respond as needed to temporary crises in the Atlantic and Mediterranean.
- Second, Army and Air Force units stationed in western Europe should be configured for more rapid and efficient deployment elsewhere—further east or south. Recent deployments of these forces to Bosnia and Kosova were too slow....
- Third, forward stationed forces in Northeast Asia should also be used more flexibly "out of area," as conditions in their "home" regions permit. The tendency to firmly anchor those assets based on the Korean peninsula should be adjusted as the confrontation there abates.

A return to a two-ocean standard, as suggested above, implies a substantial reduction in the requirement for naval forces.... [W]e should plan to deploy only two (or, briefly, three) reinforced carrier battle groups, one Marine Expeditionary Brigade, and one or two MEUs for each of two regional wars (presumably in the Persian Gulf and Northeast Asia).

5. A Smaller, Less Expensive Military

In line with a more realistic appraisal of threats as well as the adjustments in military strategy and roles suggested above, US active-component force structure could be safely reduced by about 18 percent.

Corresponding reductions in personnel might be limited to only 16–17 percent in order to ensure higher levels of readiness. Thus, the active-component military would comprise about 1.15 million personnel.....

Although smaller than today's US military, this force of 1.15 million active-component personnel would still be one-third larger than the combined forces of the United Kingdom, Germany, and France. And it would be 50 percent larger than the Russian armed forces currently planned by President [Vladimir] Putin. China's military would certainly remain larger—perhaps twice as large, even after reform. Nonetheless, the hypothesized future US military would remain the best trained, best equipped, most ready, and most technologically advanced in the world—by a substantial margin.

5.1 Budget

By 2005 this military would cost the nation approximately $248 billion (2000 USD) in outlays. This budget level is equivalent to the present defense budgets of the UK, France, Germany, Russia, China, and Japan combined.....

5.2 Operations

The hypothesized military of 1.15 million active-duty personnel could send 500,000 active troops to war with another 150,000 held in strategic reserve. In addition, 200,000 reservists might be made available for deployment in the case of major regional wars. Within this total number of deployable personnel there is a substantial capacity to fight two regional conflicts *against real world foes*— although it would take longer to win than we currently plan.

The real daily test of a smaller military, however, would be its ability to handle frequent and varied smaller-scale contingencies. A reasonable goal would be a capacity to routinely have as many as 55,000 troops deployed in such operations with another 170,000 troops stationed in foreign lands or at sea in foreign waters. (Of course, much less routine activity would be possible during those years in which major regional wars occur.)

Unit for unit, this would be asking more of a future military than we ask of our military today. But our current difficulty in dealing with the pace and nature of operational deployments has less to do with quantitative factors than qualitative ones. Put simply: there is presently a mismatch between the Pentagon's tool kit and today's missions—and this manifests itself in reduced efficiency and reduced effectiveness. At issue is not only the contents of the Pentagon's tool box—its mix of assets and units—but also the way in which they are used.

6. Toward a More Efficient, Effective, and Relevant Military

... Generally speaking, there are three impediments to the US armed forces' ability to manage today's contingency demands:

- First, the US military remains doctrinally fixated on high-intensity, decisive battles and ideal or "textbook" wars as the Prussian military philosopher Karl von Clausewitz theorized them 170 years ago. These are the 7-alarm blazes of history. But today's wars are more like brush fires, chemical fires, and multiple fires burning in the middle of urban riots—messy, complex affairs.
- Second, reviewing our military's menu of capabilities in light of today's threat environment reveals that we are remarkably well-equipped to fight the wrong types of wars: strategic nuclear war, conventional naval war, and big air-land wars involving heavy mechanized armies and powerful air forces on both sides. This doesn't correspond closely with today's distribution of threats.
- Finally, our armed services remain best suited to fighting very large conflicts, but infrequently. Our current military posture remains geared toward the rare, big push—rather than the smaller, varied, and more frequent contingencies that prevail today. This is reflected not only in our military's base and logistics infrastructure but also in its training and personnel management systems. It is evident even at the level of tactical organization.

Taken together these issues point to the danger of our armed forces becoming strategically irrelevant. This problem is sometimes recognized, but in an oblique way. We externalize it as a threat: asymmetric warfare. However, many of the asymmetries we face today—for instance in Kosova—do not indicate the emergence of new, resourceful foes who are rapidly adapting themselves to exploit our weaknesses. Instead, they indict our own failure to adequately adapt our armed forces to new circumstances and missions. Of course, America's military may be able to prevail eventually in most circumstances by bringing its vast and growing material advantages to bear. But this is not an elegant solution; it is like using a hammer to drive a screw. It merely transforms the problem of strategic irrelevance into problems of inefficiency and imprecise results....

7. Convergence

In one sense, the last thing the US military needs today is more money—because it would be a disincentive to what is truly required: transformation. Rather than pressing for fundamental change, successive administrations and the congress throughout the 1990s have merely salved the maladaptation of our armed forces with emergency budget increases and supplemental funding. Political leaders have failed as well to encourage a realistic portrayal of threats. Rather than fitting our armed forces to the much improved security environment, US military strategy—beginning with the Bush administration and continuing through President Clinton's tenure—has elevated our military objectives and prescribed an expanded foreign policy role for the Pentagon. Implicit in this is a fundamental misreading of the nature of strategic competition and instability in the new era.

The failures of the 1990s define a reform program for the next president. Today, the prerequisites of a smaller, less expensive military converge with those of a more efficient, effective, and relevant military:

- We need to think realistically about threats,
- Trim some of our strategic ambitions,
- Adapt our military to the tasks at hand, and, whatever else we do,
- Shed excess infrastructure.

POSTSCRIPT

Should U.S. Military Spending Be Increased?

Defense planning is said to be one of the toughest of all policy-making areas because (to paraphrase President John F. Kennedy) if you make a mistake in domestic policy it can hurt you; if you make an error in defense policy it can kill you. For a general discussion of the relationship between military development and capability and world politics, see Barry Buzan and Eric Herring, *The Arms Dynamic in World Politics* (Lynne Rienner, 1998). To put U.S. spending in a global context, see the Military Balance Project report of the Center for Strategic and International Studies (CSIS) at http://www.csis.org/military/index.html. Details on the current defense budget can be found at the Department of Defense Internet site at http://www.dtic.mil/comptroller/.

One factor that makes defense planning difficult is arriving at a threat estimate, not only for the present but for the future. It is also difficult to devise a strategy to counter threats. Are there dangers? If so, what are they? How many soldiers and how many and what types of weapons are needed to provide for the common defense? Yes, the cold war is over. And yes, Russia represents little threat for now. Yet it is also the case that a new, peaceful world order has not arrived. Perils persist and may proliferate in the future. Shelton and Conetta debate the level and reality of these threats. To better understand U.S. defense policy, consult Amos A. Jordan, William J. Taylor, Jr., and Michael J. Mazarr, eds., *American National Security,* 5th ed. (Johns Hopkins University Press, 1999).

Some analysts contend that Americans should not let down their guard because doing so will necessitate "crash spending" when the next crisis breaks out. This view is found in Daniel Goure and Jeffrey Ranney, *Averting the Defense Train Wreck in the New Millennium* (CSIS Press, 1999). For the moment, the thinking in the White House has shifted in this direction and away from further cutting defense spending and toward limited increases.

During the presidential election in 2000, both Vice President Al Gore and Governor George W. Bush advocated higher military spending, with Gore's projected expenditures somewhat higher than those of Bush. Those views were perhaps driven by public opinion. An October 2000 national CBS News/*New York Times* poll found 45 percent of Americans in favor of increasing defense spending, 42 percent wishing to keep spending at the same level, and just 8 percent for reducing spending.

Once in office President Bush recommended a Pentagon budget of $310.5 billion for fiscal year (FY) 2002. That included a 4.8 percent, or $14 billion, increase over the FY2001 budget, figures that adhered fairly closely to what the Clinton administration projected for military spending.

President Bush seems particularly interested in investing in more high-tech weaponry. During his presidential campaign he promised to create a "new architecture of American defense" and advocated $20 billion more to be spent on futuristic weapons research and on building a national missile defense system. Bush accused the Clinton administration of failing to use America's technical advantage to create a more lethal and mobile military. "The [Clinton years] have been wasted in inertia and idle talk," Bush charged. He also called for increased military funding to provide pay raises for troops and to increase the quality of their housing and other support.

ISSUE 12

Is There a Great Danger From Chemical or Biological Terrorism?

YES: James K. Campbell, from Testimony Before the Subcommittee on Technology, Terrorism, and Government Information, Committee on Intelligence, U.S. Senate (April 22, 1998)

NO: Jonathan B. Tucker, from "Chemical and Biological Terrorism: How Real a Threat?" *Current History* (April 2000)

ISSUE SUMMARY

YES: James K. Campbell, a terrorism expert and a commander in the United States Navy assigned to the Defense Intelligence Agency, testifies before the U.S. Congress that terrorists can acquire and use lethal chemical, biological, and radiological weapons.

NO: Jonathan B. Tucker, a visiting fellow of the Hoover Institution at Stamford University, argues that the threat of chemical and biological terrorism is not great enough to warrant a massive effort to prepare for and defend against an attack.

T errorism is a form of covert attack directed at targets that extend beyond a certain range of clearly military targets. The line between military action and terrorism is not precise, with some people arguing that actions conducted by uniformed military forces can sometimes fall into the category of terrorism.

Whatever the truth of that controversy, what this debate is about is the threat of chemical and biological terrorism and, by extension, radiological (nuclear) terrorism. As such this issue focuses on the potential threat of these weapons being used as part of a covert attack launched by individuals or groups rather than by military forces as part of an overt military campaign.

While the use of terrorism extends far back into history, recent decades have seen a rise in the practice for several reasons. One reason is the increase in civil strife within countries. A second cause of increased terrorism is the overwhelming advantage in weapons that governments usually have over dissident groups. With many governments armed with aircraft and other high-tech weapons unavailable to opposition forces, it has often become nearly suicidal for armed dissidents to use conventional tactics. Third, terrorist targets are now more readily available than in the past. People are more concentrated in urban areas and in large buildings; there are countless airline flights; and more and more people travel abroad. Additionally, with people becoming increasingly dependent on centralized sources of power and water, those providers become tempting targets. Fourth, the advent of the mass availability of instant visual news through television and satellite communications has made it easier for terrorists to gain an audience. This is important because terrorism is not usually directed as such at its victims but rather is intended to frighten others. Fifth, technology has created increasingly lethal weapons, which terrorists can use to kill and injure large numbers of people. The biological, chemical, and radiological weapons discussed by James K. Campbell in the following selection are among such "technological advances."

Terrorist attacks are a relatively regular event. For example, in 1999 there were 397 international terrorist attacks—those carried out across national borders—and many other incidents of domestic terrorism. These attacks have mostly involved conventional bombs and other terrorist weapons, but worries are increasing about the threat of terrorists' acquiring and using weapons of mass destruction (WMDs).

The concern over the possibility of terrorists' acquiring a nuclear weapon or radiological material that could be used for such purposes as poisoning water supplies has increased, especially given that security forces in the Czech Republic, Germany, and elsewhere have seized several small shipments (up to 12 ounces) of plutonium and several larger quantities (up to 6 pounds) of uranium 235.

The potential for chemical or biological attacks is also greater than it once was. Terrorism using chemical weapons is more likely than a biological attack because chemicals are not difficult to obtain and combine into lethal mixtures. A Japanese cult calling itself Aum Shinrikyo (Supreme Truth) used nerve gas in an attack in 1995 on a Tokyo subway station. Twelve commuters were killed, and 5,000 were injured. During the subsequent investigation, police found that Aum Shinrikyo was also trying to manufacture toxic biological agents.

The possibility of a terrorist attack using biological agents exists, with smallpox, anthrax, Ebola, and plague being just some of the infectious viruses that could be used. Spreading these viruses, some of which have no effective cures, in even small amounts could be devastating.

It would be naive to pretend that attack by WMDs is not a threat. The question is more to what degree an attack is a threat. Is the threat so serious—and the effects potentially so devastating—as to warrant a vast and intense effort to counter this threat? In the following selections, Campbell warns Congress that a sufficient threat exists to warrant the rapid development of effective intelligence, assessment, and warning procedures and an emergency response plan to ward off and, if necessary, deal with the aftermath of terrorist attacks using WMDs. Jonathan B. Tucker does not dismiss the possibility of the WMD attack but argues that the possibility of such an attack and the probable consequences do not justify security efforts on the massive scale suggested by some analysts in the government and elsewhere.

Chemical and Biological Weapons Threats to America: Are We Prepared?

Introduction: The Threat

"Terrorist groups are those who are impatient with democracy, undisci-plined, corrupt in their attitude toward life and unable to free themselves from the domination of murder and hatred."

— [Former Prime Minister] Shimon Perez of Israel

A review of terrorist activities in the 20th century clearly reveals that terrorists can acquire and use lethal chemical, biological, and radiological agents—if they wish to do so. On balance, such attacks have rarely produced significant casualties. In the last four decades, only a handful of cases have occurred where terrorist groups have threatened to use such lethal agents and materials (collectively referred to as Weapons of Mass Destruction or WMD) in a mass casualty causing act of super-violence. Nevertheless, the potential for even one successful terrorist related WMD attack portends such consequences that we cannot easily shrug off this threat, even in light of statistics which suggest bombings, kidnappings, and assassination will continue to be the terrorist's tactics of choice.

Though it has been three years since a terrorist group engaged in the use of WMD specifically to cause mass casualties (the Japanese terrorist group Aum Shinrikyo released a crude version of Sarin nerve agent in the Tokyo subway March 20, 1995), federal, state, and local authorities still "shudder" at the thought of such an event occurring in a US city. The Aum's WMD attack literally propelled the international order into the era of what might be called "post-modern terrorism," an era in which some terrorist groups appear to want both world attention and a large "body count." This transformation has left many fearful, wondering when and where the next terrorist related WMD strike will occur.

What truly is the percentage possibility that terrorists will engage in the use of WMD to cause mass casualties? Indeed, national vulnerabilities to terrorist attacks do exist. The bombing of both the World Trade Center and Oklahoma

From U.S. Senate. Committee on Intelligence. Subcommittee on Technology, Terrorism, and Government Information. *Chemical and Biological Weapons Threats to America: Are We Prepared?* Hearing, April 22, 1998. Washington, D.C.: Government Printing Office, 1998.

City Federal buildings are surely a testament to this axiom. However, the threat data concerning terrorist intentions is rarely sufficient to provide specific answers regarding the potential for such events to occur, WMD or otherwise. Terrorists are strategic criminals who operate outside the rule of law. These strategic criminals conduct their activities in a highly covert fashion in order to evade the authorities. As such, the motivations and capabilities of terrorists are difficult to investigate and analyze. Despite these difficulties, I undertook (in my book *Weapons of Mass Destruction Terrorism*) to:

- Explain why terrorists would want to venture into the politically "risky" realm of WMD use for the purpose of causing mass casualties
- Identify the type of terrorist group most likely to use Weapons of Mass Destruction in a mass casualty causing act
- Provide an analytic model useful for identifying a terrorist group's potential to threaten use of WMD

Why WMD Terrorism?

To date, many scholars continue to believe that terrorists will neither seek to develop nor threaten to use weapons of mass destruction to cause mass casualties. Arguments supporting this vein, are in my view, flawed and rest on outdated assumptions. Such assumptions indicate that:

> First, terrorist groups are nothing more than a collection of frustrated, political actors bent on correcting a perceived flaw in the socio-political order of the state. The cause to take up terrorism evolves as a function of their collective failure or inability to influence the political, economic and/or social conditions with their "homeland."

> Second, that these frustrated actors adopt terrorism as a means to force their political agenda through the use of directed and carefully modulated violence. This violence is designed primarily to communicate a complex message, which gains the terrorist group immediate public recognition for their cause. Unmitigated destruction is not the goal as "terrorists want a lot of people watching, not a lot of people dead."

> Third, that terrorists are "rational actors" who certainly understand the risks of exceeding a certain violence threshold (public and/or government tolerance for casualties). Indeed, killing many may result in global condemnation and a multilateral eradication effort focused at the terrorist group responsible.

> Finally it has been assumed that the technology and associated costs involved with the development and production of chemical and biological agents or even nuclear and radiological weapons are beyond the reach of most terrorist groups.

For these reasons the image of the classical terrorist of the twentieth century has not included the use of WMD.

However, these traditional arguments are breaking down in the face of evidence which suggests the nature of terrorism is changing. This change is being driven by what might be called the "supply side" and "demand side" of the terrorism. On the supply side:

- The availability of materials and technical requirements to produce an elementary WMD capability are well within the reach of contemporary terrorist groups.
- Many terrorist groups have the financial capacity to fund such programs.
- Individuals knowledgeable of WMD technologies are involved with terrorist groups that might desire to develop and use WMD in an act of mass casualty causing super-violence.

On the demand side, there are changing notions about the ownership and the use of WMD as a negotiating tool of great status and power. Notably, a terrorist group which achieves a WMD capability ascends to a higher position of relative power and prestige. Further, the absence of territorial boundaries in the case of trans-national terrorist groups serves to make retaliation more difficult as the terrorist becomes hard to target. Indeed, this alone may serve to "vitiate the retaliatory threats of the state." Of particular concern is the proliferation of religiously oriented terrorist groups and what this portends.

Terrorists which embrace a religious ideology affiliated with apocalyptic millennialism, redemptive fanaticism or racist/ethnic hate may be particularly attracted to WMD. Indeed, the terrorist that possesses radical, religious beliefs seems "primed" to commit acts of unconstrained violence. Statistics suggest that terrorism motivated by religion oftentimes results in mass killings done in such a horrific manner as to elicit total revulsion and anger from those who witness or become aware of the act. Where modern or "secular-political" terrorists typically operate within certain violence thresholds, such as the Provisional Irish Republican Army [PIRA], those groups or individuals which embrace a radicalized, religious belief are probably not subject to the same constraints as they conduct their violent acts to satisfy (in their belief) a higher authority, God. These groups may be attracted to the power ownership [that] WMD affords precisely because WMD use can result in mass casualties and mass disruption against an "enemy" defined by their religious belief.

The Ultra-Violent "Post-Modern" Terrorist

Recent studies suggest that terrorists are becoming increasingly more lethal and violent. The divergence from "traditional means to ends" in terrorist acts is evident from a review of events such as:

- The bombing of two wide-body commercial jet aircraft in the 1980's (Pan Am 103 and the Air India flight that crashed off the Irish coast).

- Terrorism in Algeria, where members of the "Armed Islamic Group" and the "Islamic Salvation Army" have slaughtered in excess of 60,000 people since 1992.
- The 1993 bombing of the World Trade Center complex in which six were killed but over a thousand injured.
- The 1995 bombing of the Oklahoma Federal building which resulted in one hundred and sixty seven killed.
- The 1995 nerve agent release in a crowded Tokyo subway resulting in 12 deaths though the intent was to kill hundreds or thousands—notably, 5,000 were injured.

Indeed, these attacks have created a new fear of what 21st century terrorist violence might portend. The availability of more lethal weapons and related technologies are enabling the terrorist group to threaten large scale death and destruction if they so desire.

The ultra-violent act followed by silence is increasingly frequent. Many times in recent years terrorist acts have been committed without a group stepping forward to claim credit for the event. The bombing of Pan Am and the Air India flights; the 1996 bombing of US personnel at Khobar Towers in Dhahran, Saudi Arabia; and the bombing of the Olympic Park Pavilion in Atlanta, Georgia, are prime examples of this phenomenon. This non-verbalization suggests a shift in terms of the message the terrorist act is supposed to send. Where traditional "secular-political" terrorists use the event to gain access to a "bullypulpit" to air their grievances, these "silent terrorists" desire to send a message that creates a superordinary sense of overwhelming fear, and vulnerability amongst their "enemies." Additionally, religious terrorists arguably have no great need for media assistance to articulate their cause as the intended audience is their own closed cell-constituency and God.

This change in the characterization of terrorism may be indicative of a new era, one in which the traditional, "constrained" terrorist of the twentieth century is supplanted by the ultra-violent "post-modern terrorist" of the twenty-first century. These terrorists are post-modern because of the manner in which they employ advanced technology, and anonymity, to conduct ultra-violent acts viewed as disproportionate to those conducted by the "modern terrorists" they are gradually supplanting.

Genesis of the Post-Modern Terrorist

The emergence of the post-modern terrorist appears to have two causes. One may be religious revivalism. Religion has played a part in legitimizing ultra-violent acts throughout history, acts which have generally been constrained when perpetrated by the "modern" secular terrorists. Ultra-violent terrorist acts rooted in religious imperatives can be seen in Ireland, where Catholics and Protestants have played a "tit-for-tat" game of murder and destruction that has spanned this century; in Sri Lanka, where Tamil Hindus are waging a bloody terrorist campaign against the Sinhalese Buddhists; and in Israel where both radical Palestinian and Israeli movements have caused great injury and death in the name of God. The success of Khomeini's 1979 Islamic Revolution and his calls to propagate Islam through the use of "holy-terror" have also been viewed as enhancing extremes of radical religiously motivated violence in many locations. History also takes note of the violence conducted by various revisionist Christian movements. Indeed, unscrupulous terrorist leaders with nefarious ideals have oftentimes used religious "veneers" to exploit the faith of the "true believer," manipulating this faith into a weapon of extreme violence that they might perpetuate their own violent agendas. This type of masterful-manipulation was evident in Shoko Asahara, leader of the Aum Shinrikyo cult; and the Reverend Jim Jones, leader of "The Peoples Temple." In 1978, 900 members of Jones's "Peoples Temple" committed mass suicide at the cult's facilities in Jonestown, Guyana.

The second cause is arguably related to the removal of constraints imposed by the Cold War, and the subsequent disintegration of a bipolar world order. As a result, disorder has emerged in which the legitimacy of many states is being challenged by increasing calls from subnational groups for self-determination. Samuel Huntington affirms this trend in a recent essay whereby he argues that the cause of future conflict will be rooted in a clash of non-state, transnational cultures. He suggests that ethnic and religious underpinnings will play key roles in supplanting traditional political ideologies with cultural ones. Where these movements cross each other, catastrophic, violent events can erupt. Prime examples of this phenomenon can already be seen in Somalia, Egypt, Sudan, Rwanda, Chechnya, the Balkans, and Indonesia.

Unfortunately, these religiously oriented movements often prey on the insecurities of the population, offering to fill psychological, sociological, political, or religious security needs of those who would join them. Examples of such groups include the Bgwan Shree Rajneesh cult (Oregon, California 1984); the Japanese terror cult Aum Shinrikyo; the Christian Identity movement in the U.S.; and radical Islamic revivalist movements that exist in many countries. These groups appear to share a common ideological thread whereby members become indoctrinated to believe that the rule of law, established by the secular government of the state [democratic or otherwise], is in direct conflict with the desires and plans of the Almighty. At the moment this "epiphany" occurs, members of such groups literally "de-legitimize" their government, totally rejecting existing societal and legal structures, demanding instead a structural revision of the world in a manner they believe to be in accordance with the desires of their "god." Capitalizing on the highly cultivated fear WMD use engenders may convince the leaders and hard core cadre of such groups that they possess a power great enough to compel the state to concede to their demands. To this end, the threat of actual use of WMD may be the method by which the religiously oriented terrorist group believes it can attack the state and achieve their objectives. If the state is not prepared to effectively respond to multiple WMD crises and manage the consequence of such attacks, terrorists equipped with WMD may believe that such use will allow them to circumvent the need to engage in a protracted, "modern" terrorist campaign.

Terrorist Use of WMD

Documented reports published by both State Department and the Center for National Security Studies in Washington DC indicate that terrorist incidents (in quantitative terms) seems to be on the decline, while the lethality of the incidents has risen. This note on the "qualitative rise" in terms of the casualties and damage produced by terrorist attacks provides an indication that terrorists may very well engage in more spectacular and sophisticated events that include the use of WMD. The bombing of Pan Am flight 103 over Lockerbie, Scotland, the World Trade Center Bombing, and the gas attack in Tokyo may be leading indicators that terrorist groups may consider adapting WMD as a primary weapon of choice. Indeed, Bruce Hoffman [director of the Centre for the Study of Terrorism and Political Violence] cites the occurrence of fifty-two incidents involving terrorist threats or actual uses of WMD between 1968 and 1994.

Notably, the Aum incident clearly demonstrated that use of WMD by terrorists poses a very different threat than conventional terrorism. For most western countries individual acts of "modern" terrorism do not generally constitute a serious threat to national survival. Even places such as Israel, India, Pakistan and Algeria, countries that experience terrorism on almost a daily basis, are not truly threatened with annihilation by conventional terrorism. Modern terrorism, with its ideology grounded in instrumental purpose, has been the tool of the weak employed against the strong; a poor man's coercive diplomacy. As discussed earlier, WMD significantly alters that context. Nuclear, chemical and biological weapons give terrorist organizations a strength that they could never hope to achieve through conventional means, allowing them to seriously threaten the security of a national population with a single blow. It is therefore more important than ever to explore those dynamics that may constrain or motivate terrorists to use WMD. Consequently, the following two fundamental questions are addressed:

- What constraints inhibit the use of WMD?
- What factors may weaken or remove these constraints?

Constraints Against Using WMD

Let me first address constraints. The use of WMD is nominally constrained by several factors.

The first constraint involves the technical complexities associated with developing and weaponizing chemical or biological agents. For years the intelligence and academic community have assessed that the technology and resources to construct a nuclear device has been well outside the practical reach of terrorist groups. Yet, while not as difficult to manufacture or expensive as attempting to develop nuclear or radiological weapons, the development and use of even chemical and biological weapons has been eschewed by terrorists. Why? Generally because conventional tactics have continued to provide the terrorist with the ability to command the desired attention or reaction from target audiences.

Perhaps a much more compelling constraint to terrorist employment of WMD is the concept of "backlash". Backlash manifests itself in two distinct forms e.g., government reaction and public reaction. Backlash occurs when an "act" of terrorism exceeds the acceptable violence threshold of the public. The result of this is twofold: as first, a loss of constituency (popular support and legitimacy) for the terrorist group may occur; and second, the targeted regime or government may adopt extraordinary efforts to eliminate the terrorist group. Backlash therefore represents a significant constraint to the use of WMD. Backlash is also applicable to state-sponsored terrorism. Indeed, the state-sponsor of a WMD attack would risk a response of massive retaliation from the United States following such an event. In both cases, WMD use can be convincingly self-defeating.

As mentioned, the continued utility of conventional tactics may deter terrorists from venturing into the politically risky world of WMD. While there has been a trend towards increased violence and more spectacular events over the past decade, such acts as "conventional" bombings and hijackings still receive substantial worldwide attention. As long as terrorists can use such incidents to achieve the response they desire (from media, public, and government) they may feel little need, especially in the face of backlash, to use WMD.

Constraints Are Weakening

[There are] constraints against the employment of WMD thus far, but they are, however, weakening. The psychological dynamics of "Group Think," combined with terrorism based on religious ideologies, are gradually easing the "taboos" that have constrained the use of uncontrolled or disproportionate violence. This, plus the availability of "dual use" materials, may portend an increase in terrorist use of WMD.

Factors Increase the Potential for Terrorist Use of WMD

As described above, terrorist attacks have become more spectacular and sophisticated over time. The tendency for a few spectacular events to capture world headlines and elicit dramatic government responses has set in motion a potential escalation spiral that may lead terrorists to employ WMD. If conventional methods of assassination and bombing become routine and accepted, it is much more difficult to capture the type of worldwide attention and government response that terrorists desire. In order to capture the level of media and government attention they need, terrorists may be compelled to use WMD.

Moreover, a global population desensitized to violence further weakens the constraints on WMD use. Violent acts that seemed excessive ten years ago may now be considered acceptable. This rise in tolerance may eventually allow terrorists to use WMD without that use being perceived as illegitimate. The advent of global communications network and a population desensitized to "run of the mill bombings and assassinations" provide encouragement for the use of WMD. In this regard, terrorist groups might escalate the level of violence in one of two ways:

"(1) they can escalate the level of violence to kill unprecedented numbers of people. Or (2) they can escalate symbolically, by employing new, more horrifying techniques—without necessarily killing more people ... (which alone inspires) a deep sense of dread ... (deeper than that caused by conventional terrorist attacks involving assassination, or bombings.).."

Intense urbanization increases the number and accessibility of targets. Terrorists using a chemical or biological agent can easily cause mass casualties or infrastructure disruption. Indeed, the multitude of potential targets vulnerable to a WMD attack permits the terrorist to selectively destroy a critical piece of urban infrastructure or kill a significant number of people if they so choose.

Concern for individual rights in Western democracies provides an environment where terrorist groups can emerge and develop their WMD potential. Today many countries guarantee individuals a range of personal freedoms and protection from state intrusiveness in areas of religion, speech, press, assemblage, and protection against unreasonable search and seizures. However, these cherished rights also permit sub and transnational terrorist groups to establish networks which: (1) allow them to develop financial resources; (2) facilitate military or paramilitary training for members; (3) provide advanced education opportunities for members; (4) facilitate the procurement of weapons, material, and WMD related technologies. Steven Emerson addresses this particular issue at length as he describes how several Islamic organizations here in the United States support terrorist groups operating in other countries. Notably, there are other terrorist groups known to maintain support networks in the United States as well.

Diffusion of WMD-related technologies and production information is occurring at an extremely rapid rate. Local bookstores, libraries, and the Internet provide the reasonably educated individual enough information to construct a "low-tech" chemical weapon. From certain web sites, one can draw the necessary reference material needed to manufacture an assortment of lethal chemical agents and dispersal systems. A book entitled *Assorted Nasties,* is available through several vendors. Within its pages are detailed recipes describing how to synthesize various toxins and the like. This type of publication demonstrates that the technical data needed to minimally assemble a crude WMD is available to the public.

The economic situation in the former Soviet Union which has led to the underemployment of many former top WMD scientists has created a potential "arms and minds" market, making it much easier for terrorist groups to obtain parts of the WMD related materials and expertise. While the extent of the problem is not well understood, media reports indicate that former Soviet Union scientists are providing consulting services to Iranian and Pakistani WMD related programs via modem, and others are leaving the country to work for North Korea. As one such physicist stated:

> "... If I had not agreed, they would have just found someone else. You think this (the decision) is hard? Look how many defense specialists are begging... So my conscience does not bother me at all."

Finally as I've discussed, a resurgence of terrorism motivated by certain religious ideologies, ethnic traditions, and race coupled with the growing sophistication of established, more "professional" groups is likely to lead to higher levels of lethality and destruction. Religion and prejudice certainly provide the moral justification and moral disengagement necessary to convince terrorists and supporters alike that using WMD is legitimate, particularly within groups that believe their crusade is sanctioned or demanded by God. For these groups WMD use can virtually create the "prophesied event," or annihilate God's enemies with a combination of simultaneous operations aimed at population centers and critical infrastructure. Some suggest, for example, that this was the rationale behind Aum's attack in Tokyo.

Type of Terrorist Group Most Likely to Use Weapons of Mass Destruction in Order to Cause Mass Casualties

Is there a specific type of terrorist group that possesses a "ripeness" to employ WMD in order to cause mass casualties? My research conclusions suggest that the type of terrorist group most likely to employ WMD is one which follows a radical, religiously oriented ideology. This disposition is heightened when the group incorporates racist or ethnic hate as part of their belief structure. Religiously oriented terrorists are searching for far more than the ability to change perceived flaws in the socio-political order of the state. Their aim: the total destruction of the existing order, supplanting it with a new one of their own design. Cases examined for my study included the Tokyo nerve agent attack committed by members of the terrorist cult, Aum Shinrikyo; the bombing of the World Trade Center conducted by a group of ad-hoc, transnational Islamic radicals; and a case involving a group of violent white supremacists living in the United States. These cases were analyzed and balanced against an assessment of the Provisional Irish Republican Army (PIRA). While PIRA is similar in many respects to the other three, I believe it unlikely that this group would engage in the use of WMD to cause mass casualties.

My research identified eleven key variables that, when present, provide the necessary and sufficient conditions for a terrorist group to threaten use of WMD to cause mass casualties. A brief description of each variable noted as key follows.

Ideologies That Support Extremist Violence Is a Key Indicator

An ideology is a comprehensive system of concepts and beliefs held by an individual or group. It is an organization of opinions, attitudes, and values that determine how we think about society and ourselves.

The ideologies of terrorist groups which manifest a ripeness for WMD use follow radical religious beliefs, affiliated with apocalyptic millennialism, radicalized redemption, or racist/ethnic hate. Destruction is part of the logic of religion. Every religious tradition carries with it images of chaos and terror. Some forms of religion seem to propel the faithful to militant confrontations. In an essay on "The Logic of Religious Violence," Mark Juergensmeyer identifies several key points that elucidate why religiously oriented ideologies can be dangerous to the extreme.

- Religion domesticates violence. Most histories of religion focus on the struggle between good and evil. Through the ages this struggle has been associated with horrific slaughters conducted against, or on the behalf of, the faithful. Religious stories, myths, and symbols (swords, crosses, and the like) make religiously oriented killing palatable, even if those acts are ultra-violent.
- Violence sanctioned by religion breaks the state monopoly on morally sanctioned killing and provides the perpetrators with a sense of political independence. It places them on the moral high ground above the state because God's judgment is giving them the "green light" to kill in his name.

Religious beliefs of an apocalyptic, radical redemptive, or racist/ethnic hate orientation often advocate the use of ultra-violence as a means to gain a desired end. The greatest danger occurs when they appeal to the most primitive and irrational wishes and fears e.g., the collective emotional needs of the terrorist group. When this happens, ultra-violent acts causing mass casualties or disruption are likely to follow.

Ideology Based in Apocalyptic Millennialism

The ideology of apocalyptic millennialism is rooted in a belief that the present age of the world is irredeemably evil ruled by a satanic figure personifying evil. This ideology professes a belief that the evil age will soon be ended, destroyed by God (or God's servant), who is good. The subsequent age to follow this event is lauded as one of utopia, where everything is perfect and only those who were formerly oppressed or those who are "true believers" will survive to enjoy it.

Norman Cohen writes that historical records documenting apocalyptic millennial cults show a variance in attitude from the most violent aggressiveness to the mildest pacifism, and from the most ethereal spirituality to the most earthbound materialism. The concern here is the cult that would engage in ultra-violence, viewing their acts as part of the prophesied apocalyptic event. In a report addressing technology and terrorism, [David] Ronfeldt and [William] Sater suggest that the potential users of such weapons (WMD) will most likely be apocalyptic millenarian cults or terrorists operating under a religious imperative.

Ideology Based in a Redemptive Religious Imperative

In Jewish history, from time immemorial, and in Jewish history today, that which will be is conditioned on one thing only: If you shall walk in My statutes, and if you shall disdain My statutes. . . . The former guarantees peace and tranquillity and bliss and redemption. The latter assures tragedy and catastrophe. There is no escape from this immutable law of creation. But if one does, indeed, walk in the footsteps of his Creator, then the Father of the Jewish people, the All Mighty, has obligated Himself to give to His children the promised reward. This is the answer; this is the key to the Gate of redemption. One who understands it shall enter it. One who does not is doomed to be scattered as the chaff in the wind and, God forbid, to take many of his brothers and sisters with him.

— Rabbi Meir Kahane

A redemptive religious imperative is based in a belief that God will reward his people only when certain prerequisites are fulfilled. The aforementioned quote taken from Rabbi Kahane's writings are cited to elucidate how his radical interpretation of religious scripture and Jewish theology is used to argue for the use of violence as a prerequisite to receiving God's promises and blessings. According to Rabbi Kahane, Israel and the Jewish people will never truly be "graced and protected" by the Lord until they return to orthodox Judaism and recover at least that part of "Eretz Yisrael" that encompasses the occupied territories (West Bank and the Gaza strip). To effect such gains, Rabbi Kahane engaged in alleged terrorist acts culminating with his 1980 arrest by Israeli authorities for planning to blow up the Dome of the Rock on the Temple Mount in Jerusalem. He was subsequently tried and incarcerated in the Ramla maximum-security prison for nine months. Rabbi Kahane saw this planned terrorist act as part of the redemptive process that would result in the Jewish people being favored and protected by the Lord.

Religious beliefs penetrate to the core of human existence for many people. Religion manipulated to provide legitimation for the use of violence by terrorists can thus unleash constraints that hold the use of ultra-violence in check. History has shown numerous occasions where this phenomenon is evident. The Sicarii Zealots who engaged in the wholesale slaughter of Romans occupying Palestine circa 66–73 AD is one example of how religion is used to justify horrific terrorist acts. Contemporary examples of extremely violent terrorist attacks motivated by religious belief can be found in the actions of groups such as Hizbullah, Hamas, and the Islamic Jihad. And we have learned in the aftermath of the World Trade Center bombing that the radical Islamic terrorist (Yamzi Yousef), who planned the attack, had hoped to release a chemical weapon. His intent was to cause the complete destruction of the World Trade Center's twin towers and the death of the thousands of people working in the building. This act was perpetrated as retribution for the corruption and decadence Western powers had introduced to the world in general and the Islamic states in particular. Luckily, Yousef reportedly ran out of money and time or he may have been able to assemble a chemical weapon.

Ideology Based in a Racist/Ethnic Hate Imperative

To the faithful, toil-burdened masses the victory was so complete that no further effort seemed required. Germany had fallen, and with her the world combination that had crushed her. Authority was dispersed; the world unshackled; the weak became the strong; the sheltered became the aggressive; the contrast between victors and vanquished tended continually to diminish. A vast fatigue dominated collective action. Though every subversive element endeavored to assert itself, revolutionary rage like every form of psychic energy burnt low. Through all its five acts the drama has run its course; the light of history is switched off, the world stage dims, the actors shrivel. The chorus sinks. The war of the giants has ended; the quarrels of the pygmies have begun.

— Winston Churchill, 1929

What is meant by a racist or ethnic hate imperative? The definition of the word "racist" in its basic form means to discriminate based on the belief that some races are by nature supreme. The same could be said for the concept of "ethnic hate." Winston Churchill's statement voices a concern that with the downfall of several dynastic regimes following the conclusion of World War I, the world would see an eruption of inter- and intra-state conflict based in ethnic prejudices. In its most radical state, race and ethnicity are used as a banner cry for prescriptions of terrorist violence and separatism. Witness the mass genocides in Rwanda and the Balkans in the early 1990's, and the Holocaust wherein six million Jews were executed by Hitler's Nazi apparatus. Here in the United States a growing movement of neo-Nazism and white supremacist groups operating under a loosely organized web of militia organizations and revisionist Christian movements may very well pose a threat that could result in the use of WMD. In 1985, members of a racist hate group known as The Covenant, Sword, Arm of the Lord (CSAL) were arrested on charges of sedition. The U.S. Justice Department raid on their compound resulted in the discovery of a cyanide producing laboratory and massive quantities of cyanide stockpiled for the express purpose of poisoning the water supply of an unnamed city.

Leadership Involving the "Mirror-Hungry Authoritarian-Sociopathic Personality" Is a Key Indicator

The terrorist group leader possessing the "Mirror-Hungry Authoritarian-Sociopathic Personality" is primed to commit (and direct) aggressive acts against "out-group others." In order to convince or manipulate group membership, such leaders frequently use emotionally charged ideas such as race or religion as a main component of their rhetoric. The leader with the "authoritarian personality" may also exhibit other attributes such as charisma, narcissism, and paranoia, which can further enhance the potential for the conduct of ultra-violence.

Extremist Use of Unmitigated Violence Is a Key Indicator

By examining ideology, rhetoric, and the results of terrorist incidents, it is possible to assess the potential for terrorist groups to cause a mass casualty act. A review of statements made by various leaders of terrorist groups that routinely employ terrorist attacks against the State of Israel indicate a desire and intent to destroy that Nation and all it stands for. Terrorist actions perpetrated by Islamic Jihad and Hamas demonstrate their willingness to commit disproportionate violence in the form of murder and injury. Statements made to the press by Ramadan Abdullah Shallah, the leader of Islamic Jihad (and former South Florida State University professor) exemplify the type of rhetoric that causes concern.

> ... so many Islamic Jihad youths wanted to be human bombs, (to attack Israel), that... bombers have been chosen by lot....

> ... Israel ... will pay a heavy price for the deaths of Shakaki (former leader of Islamic Jihad) and Yehi Ayyash (chief bomb-maker for Hamas)....

The leader of Aum Shinrikyo, Shoko Asahara, was known to suggest that a guru's order to murder meant that it was time for the victim to be elevated to a higher spiritual level. To this end he stated that:

> killing... may appear simply as murder in the objective view of the human world, but when a wise person views it, the person who has killed and the person who killed both benefited.

Operating under the rationale of such rhetoric and ideas, Aum followers committed a variety of terrorist acts, ranging from simple kidnappings, assassination of dissident membership, and the infamous Sarin attack against the Tokyo subway.

Often the concept of revenge is frequently seen as a rhetorical motive for engaging in ultra-violent behavior. Revenge, legitimized, as an act of retaliation against others perceived as having wronged the group, provides a powerful motivational force to conduct acts of disproportionate violence.

The Closed Constituency and Group Cohesiveness Is a Key Indicator

"Modern secular-political" terrorist groups conduct their violent acts as part of a strategy to correct perceived flaws in the socio-political order of the state. As their goals are typically grounded in a belief that their actions will bring beneficial change to the masses they insist they represent, their violent acts will be tempered and focused at state symbols. This is done largely because a terrorist group's survival is contingent on membership appeal. If their violent acts become too distasteful, recruitment suffers, defections occur, and the group loses strength, or worse, internal power struggles cause the same effect.

However, with the "post-modern" terrorists operating under a radical religious orientation, the concern is not with benefiting the masses, but with benefiting the group and pleasing God. This point is notable because the group that concerns itself with immediate members or an ambiguous constituency may tend to ultra-violence more easily than a group that claims to represent the "ignorant masses." In the closed cell group, close cohesion or bonds amongst members is very important. In some cases members may be required to pass an initiation ritual to demonstrate their commitment to the group. This initiation ritual may include murder. Group members' dedication to their cause is an important part of maintaining cohesion. Members who are willing to commit suicide or be killed for their beliefs arguably support a means to ends philosophy that enables the use of disproportionate violence.

Lack of Concern Over Public or Government Backlash Is a Key Indicator

For the terrorist group operating under a radical religious imperative, backlash possesses little deterrent value as death holds its own reward for the martyred, while perpetuating the struggle for the living by giving them heroes to avenge and emulate. In fact, backlash may reinforce the resolve of these groups to use WMD, viewing themselves as a closed cell surrounded by forces of evil who ultimately desire to destroy them. Violence to these terrorists is seen as an end in itself whereby the corrupt system of "out-group others" must be totally destroyed or substantially damaged so as to allow, minimally, a negotiated settlement favorable to the group. This to occur even at the risk of the terrorist group being reduced to an ineffective force in the process. As a result, WMD use becomes a rational choice for the closed cell terrorist group. This indicator is closely associated with the following one, though the two are arguably unique enough to require separate explanation.

A Willingness to Take Risks

What logic and rationale compels the terrorist group to engage in activities that risk the very existence of the group? The answer lies in the perceived pay-off. Extraordinary risks are taken in anticipation that actions will result in some type of "special reward." For the group operating under the apocalyptic imperative the reward is the "new life" following Armageddon; for the redemptive religious fanatic the reward is the blessing of the Almighty; for the racist/ethnic hate monger the reward is the destruction of the offending population. When the perceived pay-off is viewed as worth taking the risk, the group will do so. Of special note for the religious radical, when he or she dies in an act of terrorism, he/she becomes a martyr and goes to paradise, forever memorialized by those still fighting for the cause. If the terrorist survives the attack, he/she walks away knowing that the Almighty is pleased with the "contribution" to the cause. In any event the perceived high pay-off overrides concerns of risks involved.

Group Exhibits Sophisticated Use of Weapons or Tactics Is a Key Indicator

Terrorist groups that take slow incremental improvements in their use of technology to enhance their weapons potential and circumvent the authorities are arguably prime candidates to pursue development of a WMD capability.

Membership That Includes Personnel Knowledgeable of WMD Technical Requirement Is a Key Indicator

Various reports in recent years have concluded that clandestine (non-state) production of crude chemical and biological weapons requires no greater technical expertise than does the production of narcotics or heroin. While it is true that manufacturing a radiological weapon or high quality "bugs and gas" is a difficult proposition, and that manufacturing a delivery or dispersal system is equally difficult, terrorist group membership can include individuals possessing degrees in such disciplines as electrical engineering or nuclear physics. These individuals are more than capable of developing crude WMD given access to the appropriate materials. A key variable of concern is the terrorist group that recruits members from science and engineering fields.

Financial Resources to Fund a WMD Capability Is a Key Indicator

The ability of a terrorist group to develop a WMD capability is also contingent upon the financial resources they possess. While it is readily acknowledged that the production of a crude nuclear explosive device would be quite costly for a terrorist group operating without state sponsorship, on the order of millions of dollars, the financial resources needed to develop a chemical or biological weapon is relatively small. On balance, many terrorist groups certainly possess significant financial resources to pursue the development of a WMD capability, their coffers filled by cash generated from enterprises that include such things as legitimate businesses, bank heists, contract assassination, drug dealing, counterfeiting, covert weapons trade, extortion, and soliciting contributions from sympathetic supporters. The investigation into the Japanese cult Aum Shinrikyo uncovered assets exceeding $1.4 billion dollars.

Availability of Materials and Access to Technology Is a Key Indicator

Terrorist groups operating in a country where WMD related material sources and information is available is a key indicator. This also holds true for a terrorist group which is able to establish an international procurement network by which WMD required materials may be purchased.

Summary

To recap, a terrorist group possesses a ripeness or disposition to threaten use of WMD when certain key indicators are present in the group. These indicators consist of those related to desires for power, ideology, leadership, behavior, constituency, backlash, and risk combined with those related to sophistication of terrorist group weapons/tactics, knowledgeable membership, financial resources, and availability of necessary materials.

Using this analytic framework, my research conclusions indicate that terrorist groups embracing radical, religious based ideologies are surely the most likely "type" of group to use WMD in a mass casualty causing event.

Conclusion and Recommendations

Stopping the proliferation of WMD is indeed a difficult problem, particularly since some twenty-five countries (half of them located in the Middle East and South Asia) are known to have or are developing biological or chemical WMD programs. Since many of the technologies associated with chemical and biological agent production have legitimate civilian use totally unrelated to WMD production, controlling proliferation of this technology becomes a difficult proposition. Trade in dual use equipment can certainly not be banned. In nations where the necessary materials and equipment are present, terrorist groups desiring to acquire this capability are quite capable of attempting to do so.

Scholars and analysts concerned with the threat of WMD terrorism tend to agree that attacks involving the use of chemical or biological agents will probably be of a low-tech nature, though one should not discount the abilities or resourcefulness of terrorists to accomplish the unexpected. Indeed, even low-tech events which don't lead to high numbers of fatalities may lead to tremendous numbers of sick or injured. Low-tech should not be taken as synonymous with amateurism e.g., if the attack results in tens or hundreds of casualties and a tremendous amount of collateral disruption, does it really matter how "technically" competent the terrorist was? The key to resolving the fear we may feel in response to the threat posed by WMD terrorism lies in the development of effective intelligence assessment and warning, and emergency response plans. Minimizing our vulnerability to such attacks requires the use of a complex, fully integrated strategy. This effort involves the development of sound intelligence and physical security protocols and procedures and robust counter-terrorist crisis response-consequence management capabilities. This is the obvious answer though difficult to accomplish. However, the key to marginalizing the possibility-effects of terrorist attacks in general, and WMD terrorist attacks in particular, does indeed reside in the development and implementation of such a strategy.

Counter-terrorist measures include building and maintaining all-source intelligence gathering networks that fuse data effectively enough to permit the flagging and disrupting of potential terrorist activities (inclusive of WMD development efforts) before they can culminate in an attack. As mentioned, terrorist groups are underground organizations (strategic-criminal organizations) which do not lend themselves to easy analysis or observation. Where the development of intelligence concerning an adversarial nation's intentions may be accomplished via the use of robust technical methods, assessments regarding a terrorist group's capabilities, motivations, and intentions are heavily dependent on human intelligence gathering—no easy task as terrorist group security cells are often times engaged in counter-counter terrorist efforts to preclude compromise. Thus, improved coordination of efforts and sharing of information between national intelligence agencies, law enforcement, and our international allies is critical.

Part of the problem constraining better integration of interagency efforts lies with the conflicting objectives that exist between the various agencies and organizations involved in combating terrorism. This is evident upon examination of the relationship between the Federal Bureau of Investigation [FBI] and the Department of Defense [DoD]. Each of these agencies is responsible for combating terrorism. However, the focus of the FBI is towards prosecuting terrorists (those strategic criminals who have attacked or conspire to attack US citizens or property—whether at home or abroad), while the DoD is primarily concerned with protecting personnel, and infrastructure of the Department of Defense. The objectives of both agencies are extremely important. Unfortunately at times, these objectives are not necessarily compatible, particularly with regard to information sharing.

The bottom line for those chartered to combat terrorism: the ability to reduce threats posed by terrorist groups will only be realized if new ideas are encouraged and cooperative efforts are enjoined by those agencies that play a role in "combating terrorism" particularly in areas related to intelligence sharing.

As we move towards better integrating the efforts of those organizations and agencies chartered to combat terrorism, particularly in the area of intelligence sharing, we minimize our "having to exchange business cards" in the aftermath of a terrorist WMD attack. Indeed, this esteemed body may be able to assist in ensuring that the fusion of counterterrorism assets occurs in an integrated, force multiplying manner.

NO ↵

Jonathan B. Tucker

Chemical and Biological Terrorism: How Real a Threat?

The Clinton administration contends that terrorists armed with chemical and biological weapons pose a new strategic threat to the United States. In January 1999, President Bill Clinton said it was "highly likely" that a terrorist group would launch or threaten a chemical or biological attack against a civilian target within the next few years, and that this possibility kept him "awake at night." Defense Secretary William Cohen warned in July 1999 that "a plague more monstrous than anything we have experienced could spread with all the irrevocability of ink on tissue paper." And in October, ABC's "Nightline" aired a weeklong docudrama in which a hypothetical attack with anthrax bacteria on the subway system of a major American city results in more than 50,000 deaths.

This drumbeat of frightening official pronouncements and sensational media reports has helped to build political support in Congress for a major increase in spending on programs to counter the threat of chemical and biological terrorism—up to $1.4 billion in the fiscal year 2000 budget. Yet how likely is the threat that terrorists will resort to toxic weapons? Government concerns about chemical and biological terrorism have been driven largely by the vulnerability of large urban centers and the growing availability of knowledge and production equipment that have peaceful applications but could be turned to military ends. Such considerations alone, however, do not provide a solid basis for decision making about the measures needed to meet the terrorism challenge. Only a realistic threat assessment based on an analysis of terrorist motivations, patterns of behavior, and likely targets will make it possible to develop tailored and cost-effective strategies for prevention and response.

Toxic Agents as Terrorist Weapons

Despite all the hype, it would be wrong to conclude that the threat of chemical or biological terrorism is merely a figment of President Clinton's imagination. The current wave of official concern began in March 1995, when members of the Japanese religious cult Aum Shinrikyo released the nerve agent sarin in the Tokyo subway, killing 12 people and injuring more than a thousand. Although many analysts feared that this attack by Aum Shinrikyo (which recently

From Jonathan B. Tucker, "Chemical and Biological Terrorism: How Real a Threat?" *Current History* (April 2000). Copyright © 2000 by Current History, Inc. Reprinted by permission of *Current History* magazine.

changed its name to Aleph, the first letter of the Hebrew alphabet) was the harbinger of a new and more deadly form of terrorism, five years have passed and a copycat attack has yet to materialize.

The Aum Shinrikyo incident did demonstrate that at least some terrorists are motivated to acquire and use chemical or biological agents, and that the shock value of an attack could capture media attention and deeply frighten the general public. Nevertheless, the common tendency to classify chemical and biological agents as weapons of mass destruction is highly misleading. In fact, the ability of these materials to inflict mass casualties is not an inherent property but is highly dependent on the type and quantity of agent released and the means of delivery.

Chemical warfare agents are synthetic, super-toxic poisons that are inhaled or absorbed through the skin. Odorless, tasteless, and invisible, nerve agents such as sarin cause seizures and loss of voluntary control, and can kill in minutes by respiratory paralysis. Persistent nerve agents, such as vx, can contaminate buildings and people, sowing disruption and chaos in the affected area. Yet chemical weapons have major drawbacks for terrorist use. Large quantities of nerve agent—about a metric ton of sarin per square kilometer—must be dispersed to inflict mass casualties. Dispersal is difficult in open areas and thus unpredictable in its effects, and nerve agents can be countered with timely medical intervention such as the administration of antidotes.

Biological warfare agents are microbes that cause illness or death in people, livestock, or crops; this category also includes naturally occurring poisons such as botulinum toxin (produced by a bacterium) and ricin (extracted from the seeds of the castor bean plant). Most microbial agents developed for biological warfare, such as the bacteria that cause anthrax and tularemia, are infectious but not contagious. Because only people directly exposed to the agent would become sick, the effects of a terrorist attack would be self-limiting. Two exceptions are plague bacteria and smallpox virus, both of which are contagious and could spawn serious epidemics. But plague bacteria are fragile and difficult to weaponize, and the smallpox virus was eradicated from nature in 1977 by a global vaccination campaign and now exists officially in only two laboratories, making it difficult for terrorists to acquire.

Because microbial pathogens are living and reproduce inside the host to cause disease, they are theoretically far more potent than chemical weapons per unit weight: inflicting a 50 percent fatality rate over a square kilometer would require about a metric ton of sarin, but only a few kilograms of anthrax spores. Nevertheless, to be effective, anthrax spores would have to be dispersed as an aerosol cloud of microscopic particles small enough to be inhaled and retained in the lungs. The casualty-producing effects of a bioterrorist attack would therefore depend on several factors, including the type of agent used, the delivery system, the quantity of agent dispersed, the physical form of the agent (for example, wet slurry or dry powder), the efficiency of aerosolization, and the prevailing atmospheric and weather conditions at the time of release.

Biological weapons also have operational liabilities. Whereas chemical nerve agents such as sarin act in minutes, microbial pathogens induce illness only after an incubation period of up to several days, and their effects can vary depending on the immunological competence of the host. Because of the delay between infection and disease, an outbreak resulting from an act of bioterrorism might not be recognized for weeks, diluting its impact as an instrument of terror or coercion.

Assessing the Threat

In an effort to assess the threat of toxic terrorism, the Monterey Institute's Center for Nonproliferation Studies in Monterey, California, has compiled a worldwide database of documented incidents involving the terrorist use of chemical or biological agents from 1900 to the end of 1999, as well as a much larger collection of criminally motivated incidents, unsuccessful plots, and hoaxes. The Monterey database contains 101 cases of terrorist use, two-thirds of which took place outside the United States. Altogether, they produced a total of 103 fatalities and 5,554 injuries.

What does this historical record tell us about the most likely patterns of chemical and biological terrorism? Contrary to conventional wisdom, the documented attacks in which these weapons were used were small in scale and generally produced fewer casualties than conventional explosives. The sole United States fatality occurred in 1973, when the Symbionese Liberation Army used cyanide-tainted bullets to assassinate Marcus Foster, the Oakland, California, school superintendent. (Since the victim was shot eight times with a .38-caliber handgun, he would have died in any case.) In another incident in 1984, members of the Oregon-based Rajneeshee cult contaminated restaurant salad bars in the town of The Dalles with salmonella bacteria, temporarily sickening 751 people with a diarrheal illness. The purpose of this covert attack was not to kill but rather to keep voters at home, with the aim of throwing the outcome of a local election in the cult's favor.

Although it is clear that urban society is vulnerable to chemical and biological terrorism, the probability of future mass-casualty incidents is harder to assess. Those groups capable of carrying out a catastrophic attack would have three characteristics: a motivation to kill large numbers of people indiscriminately; an organizational structure that would enable them to avoid premature detection and arrest; and the technical expertise and financial resources needed to produce and deliver chemical or biological agents effectively. Fortunately, terrorist groups rarely possess this combination of characteristics.

Motivations

In 1989, Jeffrey Simon, a terrorism expert from RAND, published a hypothetical profile of a terrorist group most likely to resort to biological weapons.[1] In his view, such a group would lack a defined constituency and hence be unconcerned about political backlash; would have a track record of incidents that caused high casualties; would demonstrate a certain degree of technical sophistication and innovation in weaponry or tactics; and would have shown a willingness to take risks.

Simon's profile suggests that the types of terrorists most likely to resort to toxic weapons include religious or millenarian sects who believe that large-scale violence is a fulfillment of apocalyptic prophecy, brutalized ethnic minorities seeking revenge, and small terrorist cells driven by extremist ideologies or conspiracy theories. This "new breed" of terrorists is not motivated by a defined political agenda but by amorphous religious, radical, or antigovernment belief systems. They are potentially more prone to indiscriminate attacks because they have fluid objectives, perceive fewer political or moral constraints on the scope of their actions, may be interested in violence for its own sake, and are less easily deterred by threats of punishment. Disgruntled loners like Theodore Kaczynski (also known as the Unabomber, who is serving a life sentence for sending 16 mail bombs that killed 3 people and wounded 29 others) may also be motivated to employ toxic weapons, but technical and resource limitations would probably make them incapable of a mass-casualty attack.

In contrast, politically motivated terrorists generally operate at the level of violence sufficient to achieve their ends, while avoiding excessive or indiscriminate bloodshed that could alienate their supporters and provoke the full repressive power of government authorities. Traditional terrorist organizations also tend to be conservative and risk-averse with respect to their choice of weapons and tactics, relying on guns and explosives and innovating only when necessary.

These theoretical speculations are consistent with historical trends observed in the Monterey database. Most of the groups implicated in chemical or biological terrorism over the past century were not traditional, politically motivated terrorist organizations. Of the 101 documented attacks, 25 were perpetrated by religiously motivated groups, 17 by national-separatist groups, 8 by single-issue groups such as anti-abortion or animal-rights activists, 5 by lone actors, 3 by left-wing groups, and 2 by right-wing groups. (In the remaining 41 cases the perpetrators were unknown.)

In the volume *Toxic Terror*, detailed case studies of nine terrorist groups or individuals who acquired or used chemical or biological agents between 1946 and 1998 further suggest that "toxic terrorists" share a number of characteristics not seen in politically motivated terrorists.[2] The groups that acquired chemical or biological agents typically escalated their attacks over time, had, as Jeffrey Simon noted, no clearly defined base of political support, and believed they were fulfilling a divine command or prophecy that legitimated murder. These groups were motivated by a variety of perceived goals: destroying a corrupt social structure, fighting a tyrannical government, fulfilling an apocalyptic prophecy, punishing evil-doers or oppressors, or waging "defensive aggression" against outsiders seeking the destruction of the group.

In a few rare cases, a group's deep frustration or despair over the failure to achieve its objectives by conventional means, or the prospect of imminent arrest or extinction, has precipitated a resort to toxic weapons. In 1946, a group of Jewish Holocaust survivors calling themselves DIN (the Hebrew word for "justice" and also a Hebrew acronym for "Avenging Israel's Blood") sought retribution for the attempted Nazi extermination of the Jews by planning to poison the water supplies of major German cities. When this ambitious plan proved unworkable, members of the group secretly applied arsenic to the bread supply of a prisoner-of-war camp near Nuremberg that housed former ss officers, sickening a few thousand inmates.

The hothouse atmosphere present in a closed religious group led by a charismatic but authoritarian leader may also create psychological conditions conducive to extreme violence. Aum Shinrikyo, for example, sought to inflict mass casualties by releasing aerosols of anthrax bacteria or botulinum toxin in central Tokyo at least 10 times between 1990 and 1995 (fortunately, technical problems prevented the attacks from causing any known casualties). Cult leader Shoko Asahara's goal was to trigger social chaos, enabling the group to seize control of the Japanese government and impose a theocratic state. Aum even established a "shadow government" with a full set of ministries that were preparing to take power.

Despite these examples, the vast majority of chemical or biological terrorist incidents in the historical record do not involve attempts to inflict mass casualties but rather the tactical use of toxic weapons to kill or punish specific individuals. In 1991, for example, the Minnesota Patriots Council, a right-wing tax-resistance group based in Alexandria, Minnesota, extracted ricin from castor beans purchased by mail order and conspired to use the poison to assassinate local police officers and federal officials. (The group's four leading members were arrested before they could carry out an attack.) Aum Shinrikyo operatives also employed nerve agents in several assassination attempts—some of which were successful—against individual defectors and critics. In a June 1994 incident in the central Japanese city of Matsumoto, cult members released a cloud of sarin gas near a dormitory housing three judges who were about to issue a legal judgment against the cult in a real estate case. The judges were injured in the attack, which killed 7 people and led to the hospitalization of about 200. In the case of the March 1995 Tokyo subway attack, the immediate target was the national police agency, with the aim of disrupting an imminent police raid on the cult's headquarters.

Finally, terrorists seeking to incapacitate many people without killing them might select a nonlethal chemical or biological agent but employ it indiscriminantly, as in the Rajneeshee food-poisoning case. Thus, terrorist attacks with toxic weapons are potentially of four types: lethal/discriminate, lethal/indiscriminate, nonlethal/discriminate, and nonlethal/indiscriminate, with only a tiny minority of incidents likely to be in the much-feared lethal/indiscriminate category.

Structure

From an organizational perspective, a terrorist group capable of carrying out a large-scale chemical or biological attack would probably require most or all of the following characteristics: a charismatic leader who inspires total devotion and obedience; a set of technically skilled individuals who subscribe to the group's goals and ideology; a system of internal social controls that severely punish deviation or defection; and an organizational structure that resists penetration by police or intelligence agencies.

Most of the terrorist organizations in the United States that have sought to acquire chemical or biological agents have been stopped by local or federal law enforcement agencies before they could stage an effective attack. In 1972, for instance, an ecoterrorist group called RISE, which was led by two students at a community college in Chicago, plotted to wipe out the entire human race with eight different microbial pathogens and then repopulate the world with their own genes. They eventually scaled down their plans to contaminating urban water supplies in the Midwest. Before they could act, however, concerned group members told the FBI about the plot and the two ringleaders fled to Cuba.

Similarly, in 1986, a white-supremacist Christian Identity group known as the Covenant, the Sword, and the Arm of the Lord acquired 30 gallons of potassium cyanide to poison urban water supplies in an apparent attempt to hasten the coming of the apocalypse. Group members believed that God would direct the poison to kill only the targeted populations—nonbelievers, Jews, and blacks living in major cities. Before they could strike, the FBI penetrated the group and arrested its leaders.

In response to such setbacks, several right-wing terrorist groups in the United States have adopted a new organizational structure designed to resist infiltration or early detection by law enforcement agents. According to this strategy, known as "leaderless resistance," antigovernment militants operate in independent cells and receive their orders from underground publications and Internet web sites. This decentralized structure serves to immunize the movement's leaders from prosecution while allowing each cell greater operational flexibility and making it harder for federal and local law enforcement agencies to identify and track them. Nevertheless, small cells are unlikely to have the resources to carry out a major chemical or biological attack.

Finally, what about the threat of state-sponsored terrorism? Some analysts have warned that a "rogue" state with an advanced chemical or biological weapons program might supply terrorist proxies with military-grade chemical agents, seed cultures of contagious pathogens, sophisticated delivery systems, and financial support. To date, no such incidents have been reported, probably because of the danger that the state-sponsor would lose control over the terrorist group and the high probability of severe retaliation against the sponsoring government if its involvement were to become known. Even an aggressive tyrant like Iraqi President Saddam Hussein would probably not take the risk of delegating the use of chemical or biological agents to terrorists. According to Larry C. Johnson, former deputy director of the State Department's Counter-Terrorism Center, some governments that have long sponsored terrorism appear to be getting out of the game because the political costs outweigh the benefits. In October 1998, Syria expelled Abdullah Ocalan, the head of the Kurdistan Workers' Party who was wanted for terrorism in Turkey, and in May 1999, Libya turned over two suspects in the December 1988 bombing of Pan Am Flight 103 over Lockerbie, Scotland that killed 259 people on board and 11 on the ground.

The Technical Hurdles

Although some terrorist groups may be motivated by the desire to inflict mass casualties and a subset may be capable of avoiding premature arrest, the technical challenges associated with the production and efficient dissemination of chemical or biological agents make catastrophic attacks unlikely. Acquiring such a capability would require terrorists to overcome a series of major hurdles: hiring technically trained personnel with the relevant expertise, gaining access to specialized chemical weapon ingredients or virulent microbial strains, obtaining equipment suitable for the mass-production of chemical or biological agents, and developing wide-area delivery system. Toxic weapons also entail hazards and operational uncertainties much greater than those associated with firearms and explosives.

THE ANTHRAX SCARE

The news media have tended to echo and sensationalize the government's warnings about chemical and biological terrorism. In February 1998, for example, the FBI arrested Larry Wayne Harris, a self-promoting eccentric with white-supremacist sympathies, after he threatened to release "military grade" anthrax bacteria in Las Vegas. Newspapers around the country played up the story—even after Harris's "anthrax" was found to be a veterinary vaccine that was not hazardous to human health. Since then, more than 200 anthrax hoaxes have occurred in the United States, most involving envelopes containing harmless powders. This rash of hoaxes appears to have been inspired by the sensational reporting of the Harris incident, which had the unintended effect of making "anthrax" attractive to pranksters. Although the hoaxes have been disruptive and costly by forcing emergency responses from local police and fire departments, they pose more of a nuisance than a serious danger.

Some terrorist groups may be able to obtain small amounts of chemical or biological agents, but few are likely to have the technology and expertise needed to carry out an attack that inflicts thousands of casualties. Contamination of urban water supplies, for example, is beyond the ability of most terrorists because a huge volume of the harmful agent would be needed to overcome the effects of dilution, chlorination, and filtration. Open-air dispersal of a biological agent as a high-concentration aerosol over a large area would be even more technically challenging. To disseminate anthrax spores from a crop duster, an often-mentioned scenario, terrorists would need specialized spray nozzles capable of dispensing particles between one and five microns (millionths of a meter) in diameter, which is the particle size required for bacterial spores to lodge in the victims' lungs and cause infection. Most microbial and toxin agents are highly sensitive to temperature, sunlight, and drying, causing them to degrade rapidly after being released into the atmosphere, and the spread of the aerosol cloud would be affected by the prevailing wind and weather conditions. Although the dissemination of biological agents would be easier in an enclosed space such as a subway station, it would also be more apparent, increasing the risk of discovery and arrest.

The technical hurdles associated with the large-scale delivery of biological agents are suggested by the case of Aum Shinrikyo. Despite ample finances and scientific expertise, including 20 university-trained microbiologists working in well-equipped laboratories, the cult failed in at least 10 attempts to inflict mass casualties with anthrax or botulinum toxin. The terrorists switched to chemical nerve agents, which are easier to deliver, for their attacks in Matsumoto and on the Tokyo subway. In the latter incident, cult members entered subway cars carrying plastic bags filled with a dilute solution of sarin and wrapped in newspaper. At the prearranged time, they placed the packages on the floor and punctured the bags with sharpened umbrella tips, releasing toxic puddles that exposed nearby commuters by evaporation.

Of the nine cases of chemical or biological terrorism analyzed in *Toxic Terror,* only three groups—Avenging Israel's Blood, the Rajneeshees, and Aum Shinrikyo—staged successful attacks with chemical or biological agents. Tellingly, all three groups employed low-tech delivery systems. In the first two incidents, food was contaminated with arsenic or salmonella bacteria; in the third, a volatile chemical agent was released by evaporation in an enclosed space. These crude delivery methods are potentially capable of inflicting between tens and hundreds of fatalities—within the destructive range of high-explosive bombs, but not the mass death predicted by the most alarmist scenarios. Thus, although preventing and responding to catastrophic attacks calls for study and preparation, the historical record suggests that the most likely incidents of toxic terrorism will be tactical and relatively small-scale.

Some analysts worry that wealthy terrorist groups might try to overcome the technical hurdles to acquiring a chemical or biological warfare capability by recruiting weapons scientists and engineers formerly employed by countries with major offensive programs, such as the former Soviet Union, Iraq, and South Africa. Concerns about the "brain drain" of weapons scientists are warranted because of evidence that countries seeking chemical and biological weapons, such as Iran and Libya, have actively recruited foreign specialists. Yet with the possible exception of Aum Shinrikyo, which allegedly used a Russian military recipe for producing sarin, no available reports indicate that former weapons scientists have transferred sophisticated know-how or materials to terrorist organizations.

How to Respond?

The previous discussion suggests that the most likely scenarios for chemical or biological terrorism involve low-tech delivery methods that could inflict a level of casualties comparable to those caused by a conventional bomb. Because of the public fear surrounding chemical and biological terrorism, however, any terrorist use of these weapons, even if small-scale, would probably elicit a disproportionate level of disruption and terror. Indeed, by exaggerating the threat of a mass-casualty attack, United States policymakers and the news media have unwittingly played into the hands of terrorists and hoaxers by oversensitizing the American public.

The potential threat of chemical and biological terrorism is sufficient to warrant an ongoing investment in improved intelligence collection and civil defense as a prudent insurance policy, but not on the massive scale advocated by some publicists and federal officials. Given finite resources, it is essential to prioritize investments. The main emphasis should be on improving intelligence collection in an effort to prevent terrorist attacks before they occur. Reasonable preventive measures include developing early-warning indicators of terrorist interest in toxic agents, training intelligence and police officers in monitoring and interdiction techniques, and expanding intelligence-sharing arrangements with friendly countries.

Another form of prevention is to counter the "brain drain" of former Soviet weapons scientists. To this end, the United States and other like-minded governments should provide more funds for peaceful scientific research in Russia so that former chemical and biological warfare specialists can live in dignity and feed their families without being tempted to sell their dangerous knowledge to terrorists and proliferators. Effective but underfunded programs for this purpose already exist in Russia, such as the International Science and Technology Center in Moscow.

In the event prevention fails, a well-coordinated system for emergency medical response and decontamination will be needed to mitigate the consequences of a chemical or biological terrorist attack. Drawing on realistic threat assessments, investments in civil defense should be based on most likely rather than worst-case scenarios. Protective measures should focus on the targets of highest risk, namely government buildings and enclosed public spaces such as airports, subways, and sports arenas.

Still, a limited amount of planning and preparation for worst-case threats is necessary. In particular, although smallpox was eradicated worldwide in 1977, some countries may retain undeclared samples of the virus as a biological weapon. Because civilians have not been vaccinated against smallpox in more than 20 years, most of the world's population is now vulnerable to this deadly and contagious disease. It would therefore be prudent to produce and stockpile enough vaccine to contain the epidemic spread of smallpox in the unlikely event it is ever used as a biological weapon. Smallpox vaccine, derived from a related but harmless virus, can be stored almost indefinitely at low temperature. At the same time, the rationale for civilian stockpiles of vaccines against noncontagious biological agents, such as the bacteria that cause anthrax and tularemia, is much less compelling.

To build a streamlined and effective civil-defense capability, the president and other senior officials should rein in the natural tendency of government agencies to expand their budgets and turf. This bureaucratic hypertrophy has already resulted in the wasteful proliferation of redundant programs and "response teams" designed to mitigate the consequences of a chemical or biological attack. To give but one example, the National Guard is currently planning to establish 27 regional "Weapons of Mass Destruction Civilian Support Teams," even though two specialized military response teams—the Army Technical Escort Unit and the Marine Corps Chemical-Biological Incident Response Force—are already in place.

Government programs for responding to chemical or biological terrorism should also be designed to be multipurpose rather than highly specialized, allowing them to offer social benefits regardless of how seriously one assesses the terrorist threat. For example, instead of developing specialized training courses for first responders, existing hazardous-materials (Hazmat) programs that train firefighters to clean up spills of toxic industrial chemicals should be expanded to cover deliberate releases of chemical warfare agents. Similarly, upgrading the ability of state and local public health departments to detect and contain outbreaks of infectious disease would greatly improve the nation's security, whether the cause of a given outbreak is natural or deliberate. By leveraging civil-defense programs in this manner, it should be possible to sustain public and congressional support for such efforts over the long run.

Notes

1. Jeffrey D. Simon, *Terrorists and the Potential Use of Biological Weapons: A Discussion of Possibilities* (Santa Monica, Calif.: RAND, December 1989), p. 17.
2. Jonathan B. Tucker, ed., *Toxic Terror: Assessing Terrorist Use of Chemical and Biological Weapons* (Cambridge: MIT Press, 2000).

POSTSCRIPT

Is There a Great Danger From Chemical or Biological Terrorism?

One way to begin further exploration of this issue is to examine the extended writings of the authors of the selections. See Tucker's edited book *Toxic Terror: Assessing Terrorist Use of Chemical and Biological Weapons* (MIT Press, 2000) and Campbell's *Weapons of Mass Destruction Terrorism* (Interpact Press, 1997). Another important study is Nadine Gurr and Benjamin Cole, *The New Face of Terrorism: Threats From Weapons of Mass Destruction* (St. Martin's Press, 2000)

Concern about the potential of terrorist attacks began to come to the fore in the mid-1990s. The end of the cold war seemed to set off an increasing flow of radiological elements across borders, possibly because impoverished former Soviet scientists and military officers were willing to sell such material. The massive number of chemical and biological weapons found in Iraq after it was defeated is another illustration of the increasing availability of such weapons, as was the chemical attack in Tokyo in 1995.

Such incidents have caused a spate of reports and simulated exercises in the United States and elsewhere to judge the possibility of such terrorist attacks, assess the readiness to head them off and respond to them, and estimate the potential impacts. For example, a report by the U.S. Office of Technology Assessment (OTA) concluded that on a calm night, a light plane flying over Washington, D.C., and releasing just 220 pounds of anthrax spores, using a common crop sprayer, could deliver a fatal dose to 3 million people.

For these reasons and more, President Bill Clinton in 1995 issued Presidential Decision Directive 39 (PDD-39), defining responsibilities to detect, defeat, prevent, and manage the consequences of WMD terrorism. That was followed in 1998 by PDD-62, which established the Office of the National Coordinator for Security, Infrastructure Protection and Counter-Terrorism, which reports to the president's national security adviser.

Much of what the U.S. government is doing about potential terrorist attacks understandably remains secret, but there is evidence of increasing preparedness. During 2000, for example, the government ordered 40 million doses of a vaccine against smallpox, a disease supposedly eradicated in the late 1970s. For more on the efforts of the U.S. government and others to combat and prepare for terrorism, visit the Internet site of the Terrorism Research Center at http://www.terrorism.com/terrorism/links.shtml.

United Nations Department of Peacekeeping Operations

This UN site provides access to descriptions of current and past peacekeeping operations, maps, lists of contributing countries, and other data related to UN military, police, and observer missions.

http://www.un.org/Depts/dpko/

Just War Theory

For more on just war theory, consult this article from the Internet Encyclopedia of Philosophy.

http://www.utm.edu/research/iep/j/justwar.htm

The International Law Association

The International Law Association, which is currently headquartered in London, was founded in Brussels in 1873. Its objectives, under its constitution, include the "study, elucidation and advancement of international law, public and private, the study of comparative law, the making of proposals for the solution of conflicts of law and for the unification of law, and the furthering of international understanding and goodwill."

http://www.ila-hq.org

The United Nations Treaty Collection

The United Nations Treaty Collection is a collection of 30,000 treaties, addenda, and other items related to treaties and international agreements that have been filed with the UN Secretariat since 1946. The collection includes the texts of treaties in their original language(s) and English and French translations.

http://untreaty.un.org

Public International Law

The faculties of Economics and Commerce, Education and Law at the University of Western Australia maintain this Web site, which has extensive links to a range of international law topics, ranging from institutions, such as the International Court of Justice, to topical links on crime, human rights, and other issues.

http://www.law.ecel.uwa.edu.au/intlaw/

PART 5

International Law and Organization Issues

*P*art of the process of globalization is the increase in scope and importance of both international law and international organizations. The issues in this section represent some of the controversies involved with the expansion of international law and organizations into the realm of military security. Issues here relate to increasing international organizations' responsibility for security, the law of war, and the proposal to authorize international courts to judge those who are accused of war crimes.

- Should the United Nations Be Given Stronger Peacekeeping Capabilities?

- Did the NATO Military Action Against Yugoslavia Violate Just War Theory?

- Should the United States Ratify the International Criminal Court Treaty?

Should the United Nations Be Given Stronger Peacekeeping Capabilities?

YES: Lionel Rosenblatt and Larry Thompson, from "The Door of Opportunity: Creating a Permanent Peacekeeping Force," *World Policy Journal* (Spring 1998)

NO: John Hillen, from Statement Before the Subcommittee on International Operations, Committee on Foreign Relations, U.S. Senate (April 5, 2000)

ISSUE SUMMARY

YES: Lionel Rosenblatt and Larry Thompson, president and senior asssociate, respectively, of Refugees International in Washington, D.C., advocate the creation of a permanent UN peacekeeping force on the grounds that the present system of peacekeeping is too slow, too cumbersome, too inefficient, and too prone to failure.

NO: John Hillen, a policy analyst for defense and national security issues at the Heritage Foundation in Washington, D.C., contends that the United Nations was never intended to have, nor should it be augmented to have, the authority and capability to handle significant military operations in dangerous environments.

The United Nations seeks to maintain and restore peace through a variety of methods. These include creating norms against violence, providing a forum to debate questions as an alternative to war, making efforts to prevent the proliferation of weapons, diplomatic intervention (such as mediation), and the placing of diplomatic and economic sanctions. Additionally, and at the heart of the issue here, the UN can dispatch troops under its banner or authorize member countries to use their forces to carry out UN mandates.

UN forces involving a substantial number of personnel have been used more than two dozen times in the organization's nearly 50-year history and have involved troops and police from more than 75 countries. There is, therefore, a significant history of UN forces. Nevertheless, recent events and attitude changes have engendered renewed debate over the military role of the UN.

The increased number of UN operations is one factor contributing to the debate. Of all UN operations throughout history, about half are currently active. Furthermore, several of the recent missions have included large numbers of troops and, thus, have been very costly.

A second factor that has sparked controversy about UN forces is the successes and failures of their missions. Often UN forces have played an important part in the peace process; other times they have been unsuccessful. The limited mandate (role, instructions) and strength (personnel, armaments) of UN forces has frequently left them as helpless bystanders.

A third shift that has raised concerns about UN forces is the change in the international system. With the cold war ended, some people are trying to promote a new world order. This new world order would require countries to live up to the mandate of the UN charter that they only use force unilaterally for immediate self-defense or unless they are authorized to use force by the UN or a regional organization (such as the Organization of American States). This means that collective action under UN auspices is becoming more normal.

Two potential changes in the operation of UN forces apply to the issue here. The first is to increase the scope of the mission of UN forces. To date, UN forces have operated according to two concepts: *collective security* and *peacekeeping*. Collective security is the idea that aggression against anyone is a threat to everyone. Therefore, the collective body should cooperate to prevent and, if necessary, defeat aggression. The second, long-standing UN role of peacekeeping usually involves acting as a buffer between two sides to provide an atmosphere that will allow them to settle their differences, or at least to not fight. Neither collective security nor peacekeeping, however, precisely apply to situations such as domestic civil wars, in which there is no international aggressor or clearly identifiable aggressor. Some people consider this a gap in what the UN does to prevent the scourge of war and, therefore, would augment the UN's role to include *peacemaking*.

The second potential change for UN forces relates to proposals to create, at maximum, a standing UN army or, at least, a ready reserve of troops. These troops would remain with the forces of their home countries but would train for UN operations and be instantly available to the UN.

The immediate background to the issue debated here began with a January 1992 summit meeting of the leaders of the 15 countries with seats on the Security Council. The leaders called on the UN secretary-general Boutros Boutros-Ghali (1991–1996) to report on ways to enhance UN ability "for preventative diplomacy, for peacemaking, and for peacekeeping." In response, the secretary-general issued a report entitled *An Agenda for Peace,* in which he recommended a number of strategies to enhance UN peacekeeping.

That report set off a debate that continues today. In the following selections, Lionel Rosenblatt and Larry Thompson conclude that a permanent, rapid-reaction peacekeeping force should be created to respond at the beginnings of crises before they get out of control. John Hillen disagrees, arguing that if the UN is given difficult missions that it is not and cannot be ready to handle, then the result will be failure and damage to the UN.

**Lionel Rosenblatt and
Larry Thompson**

 **YES**

The Door of Opportunity: Creating a Permanent Peacekeeping Force

S omerset Maugham wrote a short story, "The Door of Opportunity," about a British colonial official who was dismissed in disgrace because he lacked the courage to face down a murderous crowd of rioters in some lonely, unimportant corner of the empire. "The utility of a government official depends very largely on his prestige," says the governor to the offender, "and I'm afraid his prestige is likely to be inconsiderable when he lies under the stigma of cowardice."

On the American scene, in John Ford's cavalry classic, *She Wore a Yellow Ribbon*, John Wayne and Ben Johnson, Jr. ride into a hostile Cheyenne village and avert an Indian uprising with a cultural sensitivity that would please a Berkeley don.

Are these two examples of fictional peacekeeping pure myth from a vanished time? Are the people in the age of the AK-47 [assault rifle] inherently more dangerous and less amenable to peaceful resolution of conflict than in the black powder era? Or is there some basis to believe that a few good men and women acting with "promptness and firmness" (Maugham's words) can avert some of the uncivil wars and ethnic slaughter that characterize our post–Cold War world?

Rwanda, 1994

Let us look at a contemporary example of a peacekeeping failure: Rwanda, April to August 1994.

On April 6, 1994, an airplane carrying Juvénal Habyarimana, the president of Rwanda, was shot down under mysterious circumstances, setting off a struggle for control of the country between the majority Hutu and minority Tutsi peoples, and the most horrific genocide of this decade. Some 800,000 people— mostly Tutsi and moderate Hutus—were killed by Hutu extremists in the space of three months.

Civil war and ethnic violence had been the norm in Rwanda for many years. A lightly armed U.N. peacekeeping force of 2,500 was stationed in the country on a "low-intensity" peacekeeping mission to monitor compliance with a prior agreement between Hutu and Tutsi, a "cakewalk" as one U.N. official said. In the spring of 1994, the flavor of the cake turned out [to] be devil's food. "They [Hutu extremists] were chopping off the breasts of women," said Gen. Romeo Dallaire, the Canadian commander of the U.N. peacekeepers. "They were slitting people open from their genitals right up to their sternum. They were chopping up the arms of two-year-old children just as if it [*sic*] was salami."

Among early victims were ten Belgian peacekeepers who were killed on April 7 by Hutu militia. With their deaths, the heart went out of the political masters of the peacekeeping mission in New York and other world capitals, especially Washington.

General Dallaire had minimal resources at his disposal to contend with the eruption of violence. According to the *Joint Evaluation of Emergency Assistance to Rwanda*, published in 1996, he had only "one working armored personnel carrier, a demoralized Belgian battalion, and an under-equipped, below-strength unit from Bangladesh." Moreover, the peacekeepers had no mandate from the U.N. Security Council to intervene to prevent the mass murders taking place before their eyes. But, in a sign of what might have been had the U.N. force been instructed to protect civilians, 12 "blue helmets" [U.N. soldiers who traditionally wear blue helmets with the U.N. emblem on them] at the Amahoro Stadium, armed only with bluff, hand weapons, and barbed wire, saved the lives of several thousand persons.

The response of Boutros Boutros-Ghali, the U.N. secretary general, and the Security Council to the events in Rwanda was to decide that there was no peace to keep, and on April 21, Boutros-Ghali ordered the withdrawal of most of the peacekeepers. A traumatized Belgium prompted the flight of the United Nations, but a jittery United States, which had recently lost 18 of its own army rangers in Somalia, backed the Belgians. (When the Belgian peacekeepers got back to Brussels, several of them shredded their U.N. blue berets for the television cameras.)

Later, as conscience crept back into the United Nations, Boutros-Ghali proposed a more forceful U.N. role, and the Security Council, including a reluctant and foot-dragging United States, finally approved sending a new peacekeeping force of 5,400 personnel to Rwanda. It was now May 17—six weeks and several hundred thousand lives into the genocide.

The U.N. Security Council, however, only mandates on paper. Several African countries came forward with offers of troops, but matching ill-equipped African troops with essential Western equipment (to be provided by the United States and other countries) proved to be too much of a bureaucratic obstacle to overcome quickly, given the lack of political will in Western capitals. On July 25, 1994, Boutros-Ghali reported sadly that only 500 of the 5,400 peacekeepers the Security Council had authorized were on the ground in Rwanda and that they were barely operational.

Disgracefully, the first American armored personnel carriers so vital to the success of a U.N. peacekeeping force arrived only on July 30. It was much too little, much too late. The civil war was over. The genocide was over. The United Nations and its members had fiddled for four months while Rwanda burned. The toll in a country of 8 million was astonishing: up to 800,000 people were dead, two million were refugees in neighboring Zaire and Tanzania, and three million were displaced within the country itself. The Rwandan conflict and genocide had a profound impact on Burundi, Uganda, Tanzania, and, especially, Zaire —now the Democratic Republic of Congo—the third largest country of Africa. President Laurent Kabila's rise to power in Congo began with the refugee flight from Rwanda and the spread of the Hutu-Tutsi conflict to eastern Zaire. Perhaps the least important of the consequences was that the international community would be saddled with a tab of half a billion dollars per year to feed the refugees and clean up the mess.

Fear and Loathing of the United Nations

The political commentator Michael Lind thinks the United Nations and its philosophy of collective security have been "finally and completely discredited" and the organization itself should be allowed to "wither away into irrelevance." Lind argues for a return to nineteenth-century statecraft, in which an ill-defined "great power concert" would run the world. But what, we would ask, will happen if the so-called great powers do not want to run the world? The abdication of responsibility by the great powers in the 1920s and 1930s led to the militaristic rise of Japan, Germany, and Italy. The great powers of the 1990s do not seem to have any more stomach for managing chaos than did France, Britain, or the United States back then.

The scholar David Rieff displays a spirit complementary to Lind's. Rieff discounts the ability of the world to have a positive effect on civil wars and ethnic conflicts. "I would go so far as to suggest that some of these conflicts are inevitable; that they have a certain political logic and also a certain political function; and that in the long run we're actually doing no one any favor by trying to intervene and prevent them."

A synthesis of the writings of the anti–United Nations, anti-intervention theorists might be that "the United Nations is no damn good but even if it were it would have no business sticking its nose into small wars in faraway places to save lives."

We beg to differ. It is precisely in these small wars in faraway places that the United Nations can make a difference. The United Nations is not going to be able to handle a conflict as big as the 1991 Gulf War for the foreseeable future. Even a Bosnia may be too big for the organization to handle. But the United Nations should be equipped to deal with the Liberias, Rwandas, and Macedonias of the world—with the chaos, ethnic conflicts, or threats of strife in countries that do not engage the urgent political concerns of the big powers: a few hundred thousand dead people here, a few hundred thousand there, add up.

It seems to us not too much to ask that the international community regard the preservation of lives as an important factor when it deliberates about intervention in crisis situations. We should be hardheaded; but we should not be coldhearted.

The Failure of a Peacekeeping Mission

International peacekeeping failed in Rwanda for several reasons. First, the U.N. peacekeeping force at the outbreak of the genocide was a mixed bag of soldiers from several countries, indifferently equipped and trained, inadequately financed, and barely coordinated because each national military unit ultimately looked to its own chain of command for orders rather than to the nominal commander, General Dallaire.

Second, the terms of reference for the peacekeeping force were all wrong. It was, to quote the *Joint Evaluation*, "a classic, minimalist peacekeeping operation," with no authority to protect innocent lives if the uneasy peace between Tutsi and Hutu it was supervising broke down. In fact, there was no option for action at all in case of trouble except withdrawal. With no peace to keep, the Security Council withdrew the peacekeepers.

Third, national considerations took precedence over the needs of the U.N. peacekeeping mission and the people of Rwanda. When the Belgian peacekeepers were brutally killed, the Belgian government decided immediately to withdraw its forces. The United States seconded Brussels, partially because of a penny-pinching attitude about peacekeeping worthy of Ebenezer Scrooge. (The U.N. peacekeeping mission to Rwanda cost the United States about $5 million per month; the failure of the peacekeeping mission would ultimately cost U.S. taxpayers $125 million in less than a month for an emergency military airlift to feed Rwandan refugees.) The French intervened unilaterally in southwestern Rwanda (Operation Turquoise). Although the French intervention undoubtedly saved some lives, it also reflected mixed political and humanitarian motives and helped the Hutu army and militia, the primary perpetrators of the bloodbath, remain intact.

Suppose a well-trained, well-equipped U.N. peacekeeping force had been in Rwanda when war broke out in April 1994. And suppose that it had had a mandate to protect civilian lives. Could such a force have stemmed the ensuing genocide and its many tragic aftershocks? Dallaire thinks so. "Had we been able to deploy the troops and equipment with a mandate to prevent a situation of crimes against humanity and to be more offensive in nature, I believe we could have curtailed a significant portion of it."

Dallaire goes on to pinpoint the U.N.'s number-one problem in its peacekeeping operations. "The United Nations is not a sovereign state with the resources of a sovereign state. It can take decisions but it has to go outside to get resources, particularly troops and equipment. When I left at the end of August 1994, I had barely 3,000 of the [promised] 5,500 troops."

Dallaire's words lead us to a proposal that is gaining currency in international circles: to create a standing, permanent, international rapid response force to deal with situations like the one in Rwanda.

A Rapid Reaction Force

The secretary general's "Supplement to an Agenda for Peace" in January 1995 called on the United Nations [to] consider the idea of a "rapid deployment force." Denmark and Belgium, mindful of the tragedy in Rwanda, are behind the idea; Canada lends support; and even the United States—reluctant though it may be—has come up with a variation on the theme: an African Crisis Response Initiative of 5,000–10,000 African troops, internationally trained and financed, to respond to crises on the continent.

The present system of international peacekeeping is too slow, too cumbersome, too inefficient, too prone to failure, too ad hoc to meet the necessities of the confusing, nameless era that has followed in the wake of the Cold War. Former U.N. under secretary general Brian Urquhart says the United Nations is at the "sheriff's posse" stage. "There are a lot of people who don't really agree with each other very much most of the time who suddenly are shocked by some horrendous human event into putting together some ad hoc and improvised posse to do something about it after the fact. It is better than doing nothing, of course. But we've got to move on from this stage." For one thing, the world body is too slow and unprofessional to create and mobilize a "sheriff's posse" whenever the need arises.

Stung by its failure in Rwanda, the United Nations has taken some steps toward improving its peacekeeping capabilities. U.N. headquarters in New York now has a 24-hour watch center to monitor crises around the world. A rapidly deployable headquarters team is being formed to assess crises early on, before peacekeeping forces are sent out. The Standby Arrangement System maintains a register of personnel and equipment volunteered by member states that can be utilized for peacekeeping missions. Planning, intelligence, and early warning functions have been enhanced.

All this may be superfluous if, when the necessity for deployment of peacekeepers arises, as it does suddenly, the need for troops and matériel cannot be met. "Unconditional commitments" of aid from member states have a way of evaporating when the United Nations calls in the chits. Domestic politics tends to govern the response of member states to an urgent demand for peacekeeping. National pride, particularly that of the French and the Americans, complicates command and control. The French do not work well with anybody, and the Americans will not work at all unless they are in charge.

Time is a critical factor. Opportunities to defuse a situation are lost in the time between a Security Council decision and the actual deployment of troops on the ground. Dallaire needed reinforcements in Rwanda in April [1998]—not in August.

The best solution to these problems would seem to be the creation of a standing, permanent international military and police force made up of volunteers and under the direct command of the U.N. Security Council: what has variously been called a rapid reaction force, a rapid deployment brigade, a U.N. foreign legion.

Proponents of such a rapid reaction force (RRF) differ in their estimates of the numbers needed—proposals range from 5,000 to 55,000 soldiers and police. We are persuaded, however, by MIT professors Carl Kaysen and George W. Rathjens that the optimum size of an RRF would be about 15,000, of which 10,600 would be deployable troops and 4,400 headquarters, logistics, and training staff. An RRF of 15,000 would permit the simultaneous deployment of two peacekeeping forces, with one such force in reserve.

The annual U.N. peacekeeping budget now stands at $2–3 billion. The cost of a 15,000-person RRF, as calculated by Kaysen and Rathjens, would be on the order of $1.5 billion annually. But a good portion of the cost of the proposed RRF would be offset by savings realized from the revamping of the current peacekeeping system.

The most recent endorsement of the idea of a rapid reaction force comes from the prestigious Carnegie Commission on Preventing Deadly Conflict. The commission, cochaired by former U.S. secretary of state Cyrus Vance, recommended the "establishment of a rapid reaction force of some 5,000 to 10,000 troops.... The Commission offers two arguments for such a capability. First, the record of international crises points out the need in certain cases to respond rapidly and, if necessary, with force; and second, the operational integrity of such a force requires that it not be assembled in pieces or in haste. A standing force may well be a necessity to effective prevention."

What would a rapid reaction force do? First, it would be available to reinforce long-term U.N. peacekeeping missions on an emergency basis. For example, if events turned sour in Cyprus or Macedonia, a battalion or two from the RRF could be sent out to reinforce the existing U.N. peacekeeping forces in those countries. RRF deployments would be temporary, not to exceed six months in most cases. Either the crisis would be resolved during those six months or a long-term peacekeeping force would be assembled. The elite troops of the RRF should not end up walking the Green Line [that divides the Greek-Cypriot and Turkish-Cypriot communities] in Cyprus for 20 years.

Lost Opportunities

Equally important, the RRF would respond to fast-breaking crises. Going back to the example of Rwanda, there were three situations in three years in which such a force could have been deployed to assist in the resolution of a crisis that called for armed intervention.

The first was during the genocide of April to July 1994, when reinforcements of several thousand tough, well-trained, well-equipped soldiers and police could have saved hundreds of thousands of lives by protecting noncombatants. (One of the hazards of peacekeeping, however, is that if a U.N. peacekeeping force had succeeded in holding down the number of murdered civilians to, say, 100,000, the operation would likely have been regarded as a failure.)

A second opportunity for the deployment of a rapid reaction force came when the teeming refugee camps of Zaire—housing more than a million Rwandan refugees—were formed in July and August 1994. Armed Hutu militia took over the camps and imposed their will. The unarmed representatives of U.N. civilian agencies were helpless in the face of the armed militiamen.

As the U.N. High Commissioner for Refugees, Sadako Ogata, noted, "The Rwandan refugee camps in Zaire and Tanzania were controlled by armed men, many of whom were probably guilty of genocide. We asked for international help in getting these people out of the camps. No country offered to get involved. My staff had to continue feeding criminals as the price for feeding hundreds of thousands of innocent women and children."

Boutros-Ghali strongly recommended that the Security Council assemble a multinational force of up to 7,000 troops to disarm the militia and remove them from the camps. The Security Council members greeted his proposal with thundering silence. The United Nations, consequently, was unable to do anything to wrest control of the camps from the Hutu militia. Had a standing rapid reaction force existed, it could have been deployed to the camps to disarm the militia and free the refugees from their control.

A third opportunity came in November 1996, when Laurent Kabila's ADFL [Alliance of Democratic Forces for the Liberation of Congo/Zaire] rebel forces in Zaire broke up the refugee camps. Most of the refugees returned home to Rwanda, but hundreds of thousands were unwilling or unable to do so and were forced deep into the interior of the country where they have suffered excruciating hardships and thousands have been systematically murdered by ADFL forces. In November 1996, an RRF could have made a quick excursion into Zaire to set up a safe transport corridor, thereby permitting the United Nations and private humanitarian agencies to bring aid to and repatriate the refugees. An intervention of this limited scope and duration would not have affected the outcome of the civil war raging at that time in eastern Zaire/Congo between Kabila's forces and long-time dictator Sese Seko Mobutu.

A multinational rescue was proposed by Canada to aid the refugees lost in the forests of Congo. Initially, the United States went along with the plan, then quickly backtracked when some reports suggested and Washington chose to believe that there were few refugees in eastern Congo except Hutu militia who did not want to return to Rwanda anyway. Since, Washington believed, there were few refugees, there was no need for a multinational rescue force.

This bit of extraordinary self-deception by the United States and others cost tens of thousands of legitimate refugees their lives. The existence of a rapid reaction force would have permitted the quick dispatch of an early rescue mission, saved lives, and probably saved money. In the end, the U.N. High Commissioner for Refugees airlifted many of the surviving refugees back to Rwanda in a lengthy, high-cost operation.

The international community thus struck out three times in quick succession with respect to genocide and its aftershocks in Rwanda and Congo. (Moreover, if an intervention had been carried out successfully on the first occasion, the opportunity for interventions two and three would not have arisen. The lesson is do it right the first time.)

Getting Big Daddy on Board

Canada, Denmark, and the Netherlands have taken these failures to heart in proposing means by which the United Nations can deploy peacekeepers more rapidly and efficiently than at present. All the rhetoric in the world, however, is not going to result in the creation of a rapid reaction force unless the big daddy on the international scene, the United States of America, gets behind the idea.

Penuriousness, neo-isolationism, and hostility toward the United Nations are holding it back.

Yet, a rapid reaction force has much to recommend itself to the United States. First, if a competent, international peacekeeping force existed, the need for U.S. bilateral deployment, as in Somalia and Haiti would decrease, thereby reducing America's costs and casualties. Second, the anguished political debate that arises at the prospect of U.S. soldiers being sent in harm's way would be stilled. (American volunteers, we foresee, might serve in an RRF, but they would be outside the jurisdiction and responsibility of the Department of Defense.) And, third, with such a force under the control of the Security Council, the United States would always be able to use its veto if it did not approve of a proposed deployment.

U.S. intelligence, logistics, and emergency airlift support would clearly be essential for a rapid reaction force to be feasible. Yet, the cost to the United States in providing these services to an RRF would not necessarily be high. The United States could negotiate with the United Nations to be reimbursed for any expenses exceeding the 25 percent share of peacekeeping costs that it sees as its fair share—and the repayment of U.S. arrears could give a strong boost to a new initiative in peacekeeping. Early-warning measures and fast deployment of a rapid reaction force might save the United States more money than they would cost. They would certainly save lives and contribute to America's national security and well-being.

This post–Cold War period has left America groping for a definition of its interests and role in the world. In 1992, in the euphoric aftermath of the Gulf War, President George Bush lauded the United Nations. "[N]ever before has the United Nations been so ready and so compelled to step up to the task of peacekeeping." A year later—after Somalia—Americans were talking not about a New World Order but of a New World Disorder, and confidence in the United Nations had plummeted.

The occasional necessity for international peacekeeping forces is doubted by virtually nobody. With the states of Central Africa in turmoil and the Bosnian situation far from settled, to name just two areas of concern, the question we must ask ourselves is whether the present ad hoc system of international peacekeeping is the best possible mechanism. The answer is an emphatic no. The creation of a rapid reaction force would give the international community the means to prevent and contain conflicts and to protect noncombatants that it now sadly lacks.

The United States should promote the creation of a rapid reaction peacekeeping force. It is in America's own interest to quiet the brushfires of distant conflicts before they burn out of control.

United Nations Peacekeeping Missions and Their Proliferation

I will make some short remarks here on the strategy of UN military operations —that is, the level at which the political and military dimensions of peace-keeping meet. In the course of my work I studied some 50 UN and other multinational peacekeeping and peace enforcement operations. The lessons learned from those missions give us a fairly good idea of the challenges of these missions and the institutional competence and capabilities of the UN itself.

...[T]oday we sit on the cusp of a periodic upswing in the size, character, and ambitions of UN peacekeeping operations. [Recently] the UN has mandated three large and complex peacekeeping operations—in East Timor, Sierra Leone, and the Democratic Republic of the Congo—in which the UN itself will direct significant military forces operating in some difficult environments. In addition, of course, there is the fairly new UN mission to Kosovo, but in that mission NATO [North Atlantic Treaty Organization] is handling the military tasks while the UN restricts itself to policing, administrative, and other basic governmental functions.

I say periodic upswing because a survey of the 52-year history of UN peacekeeping shows that it goes in cycles. I'd like briefly to discuss these cycles in order to better understand where we might be headed now. My study shows that UN peacekeeping goes through recurrent phases—and the pattern has been repeated several times in the past half-century. In the first phase small peacekeeping successes lead an emboldened international community to give the UN larger, more complex, and ambitious military operations in more belligerent environments. In the second phase these sorts of operations quickly overwhelm the capabilities of the UN itself, which tries unsuccessfully to improvise in operations for which it has no institutional structure, authoritative management systems, or military competency. In the third phase, burned and discredited, the UN pulls back to a more traditional peacekeeping role that suits the institution. Finally, with time healing some of these wounds and challenges to the international community continuing to mount, short memories compel the international community to thrust the UN back onto the international security stage in a more ambitious and central role than before. The lessons of each of these cycles are clear. The UN itself has never had, nor was it ever intended to

From U.S. Senate. Committee on Foreign Relations. Subcommittee on International Operations. *United Nations Peacekeeping Missions and Their Proliferation.* Hearing, April 5, 2000. Washington, D.C.: Government Printing Office, 2000. (S.Hrg 106-573.)

have, the authority, institutions, and procedures needed to successfully manage complex military operations in dangerous environments. Conversely, the UN—the world's most accepted honest broker—has exactly the characteristics needed to manage some peacekeeping operations undertaken in supportive political environments. Even then, the UN has struggled to competently direct even small and innocuous operations. But the real problems for all involved have come when the international community puts the UN in a military role for which it is neither politically suited nor strategically structured. My book goes into great detail on exactly why the UN has shown—in almost 50 missions —that there are strict limits to its military role. Quite simply, the UN should not be in the business of running serious military operations. It has neither the legitimacy, authority, nor systems of accountability needed to build the means necessary to direct significant military forces.

Authoritative, specifically structured, and well-rehearsed military alliances or coalitions of the willing better manage multinational military operations of the sort we've recently seen in the former Yugoslavia, Somalia, and Africa led by a major military power. These sorts of organizations are specifically structured —legally, politically, and organizationally—to direct complex and coercive military operations in uncertain environments. The model we've seen in Kosovo and East Timor recently may work best. An alliance like NATO or a multinational coalition such as that Australia led in East Timor can do the heavy lifting before turning it over to the UN.

. . . [L]et me briefly summarize how these cycles have occurred and in particular the U.S. and UN role in them. In my full testimony I have the complete story of the most recent cycle—that of Somalia and Bosnia—and perhaps in questioning we can discern from those episodes lessons for these new missions on the horizon. In 1948/49, UN peacekeeping started with relatively innocuous missions to Palestine and India-Pakistan—missions which, we should note, are still in existence today. A largely successful peacekeeping mission in the Sinai in the 1950's encouraged the UN to mount a very ambitious mission to the Congo in 1960. That mission ended very badly, taking the life of some 234 Blue Helmets [UN soldiers who traditionally wear blue helmets with the UN emblem on them] and the Secretary-General [Dag Hammarskjöld]. It is still referred to by many as "the UN's Vietnam."

Chastened, the international community returned to what was emerging as a more tried and true formula for UN peacekeeping. Small, lightly armed, and relatively unambitious missions deployed after a peace was concluded. These Blue Helmets did best when they followed the so-called principles of peacekeeping: strict neutrality, passive military operations, and the use of force only in self-defense. Importantly, the UN recognized that the Blue Helmets were only supporting players, there to help belligerents that had agreed to the UN presence. UN peacekeeping was never intended to be a coercive military instrument —one that could force a solution on one side or another to a conflict. This role for the UN, which is not specifically referred to in the Charter (nor envisaged by the UN's founders) evolved over time, the nature of the technique (peacekeeping) uniquely suiting the character and management abilities of the institution (the UN).

By the late 1980's, the UN's ability to manage a small number of peace-keeping operations was not in doubt. In fact, in 1988 the Blue Helmets were awarded the Nobel Peace Prize. We should remember that in 1988 UN peace-keeping represented a rather small and unambitious enterprise in the grand scheme of global security. In January of 1988 the UN was managing less than 10,000 troops in five long-running peacekeeping missions and on an annual peacekeeping budget of some $230 million. The U.S. then, as now, picked up about [one-third] the cost of those missions.

Things changed quickly, though, after the fall of the Berlin Wall. The thawing of the Cold War and the unprecedented cooperation shown by the Se-curity Council during the Persian Gulf War presaged a new era of UN-sponsored collective security. The enthusiasm for more and newer forms of UN peacekeep-ing was quickly manifested in a series of ambitious, expensive, dangerous, and militarily complex missions.

By 1993, the UN was managing almost 80,000 peacekeepers in eighteen different operations, including large and heavily armed missions to Cambodia, Somalia, and the former Yugoslavia. The annual peacekeeping budget grew to $3.6 billion.

Less than two years on from that peak however, UN peacekeeping had been thoroughly discredited. The Blue Helmets' failure to halt political vio-lence in Somalia, Rwanda, Haiti, and the former Yugoslavia was reinforced by images of peacekeepers held hostage in Bosnia, gunned down in Mogadishu, or butchered along with thousands in Kigali. The UN quickly retreated—turning a nascent peacekeeping mission in Haiti over to a U.S.-led coalition, passing Bosnia off to NATO, and leaving Somalia to slip back into chaos. By 1997, UN peacekeeping was down to a more manageable level of some 15,000 Blue Hel-mets operating in more mundane environments and on a budget of around $1.2 billion. All has been relatively quiet on the UN front until this past fall [1999], when Kosovo, East Timor, Sierra Leone, and the Congo sprang onto the scene. If those missions go forward as planned, they will add over 25,000 Blue Helmets and some $700 million–$1 billion in costs to the UN's plate. More important, several of these new missions, especially Sierra Leone and the Congo, look cer-tain to take place in very uncertain and belligerent environments—the sort in which the UN rarely if ever succeeds. . . . [A] word on the U.S. role in this latest cycle in the rise and fall of UN peacekeeping in the six years after the end of the Cold War. This message I believe is critical for the U.S. policy community because our own actions drive these episodes as much as anything else. More coherence in U.S. policy could have prevented many of the recent disasters in places such as Somalia and Bosnia. While a broad range of observers drew the same basic conclusion from peacekeeping's recent past—that the UN should not be in the business of managing complex, dangerous, and ambitious military op-erations—most are split on how it happened and whom to blame. Conservatives in the United States charge the UN itself and especially a fiendishly ambitious Boutros Boutros-Ghali who tried openly to accrue more and more military le-gitimacy and power for the UN itself. Liberal internationalists blame a parochial U.S. Congress that pulled the U.S. out of Somalia at the first sign of trouble, and is now holding America's UN dues hostage to its provincial agenda.

Both views are off base. Ironically, those who put UN peacekeeping through the wringer and hung the organization and its last Secretary-General out to dry were those American internationalists most likely to promote a larger collective security role for the United Nations. Over the past seven years, American officials sought for the UN a much greater role in international security affairs. But even though they were philosophically amenable to that goal, they choose to propel the UN into uncharted waters more out of political expediency rather than as a carefully crafted manifestation of their predisposition towards collective security. In many cases a new role for the UN was not so much a matter of policy, but a way of avoiding hard policy decisions such as those concerning the former Yugoslavia and Somalia. In essence, we used the UN as an excuse, not a strategy.

Either way, American officials, especially in the first Clinton administration, pushed a reluctant UN into much greater military roles than it could hope to handle. Once its failures were manifest, the same officials joined in the conventional wisdom that the UN itself "tried to do too much." Because of this, any post–Cold War "advances" in collective security were negated by those very internationalists who were so keen to champion the UN. As [professors] Paul Kennedy and Bruce Russett warned, UN operations such as those to Bosnia and Somalia "far exceed the capabilities of the system as it is now constituted, and they threaten to overwhelm the United Nations and discredit it, perhaps forever, even in the eyes of its warmest supporters." What they did not consider was that some of the UN's "warmest supporters" were those who were most responsible for putting it in desperate straits in the first place.

Patterns of Abuse

Advocates of collective security were almost giddy in the months immediately following the Gulf War. As David Henrickson noted, the end of the Cold War and the Security Council's role in the Gulf War "have produced an unprecedented situation in international society. They have persuaded many observers that we stand today at a critical juncture, one at which the promise of collective security, working through the mechanism of the United Nations, might at last be realized." Think tanks, conferences, workshops, and task-force reports trumpeting a proactive military role for the UN proliferated. In January 1992, the first ever Security Council summit declared that "the world now has the best chance of achieving international peace and security since the foundation of the UN." The heads-of-state asked Secretary-General Boutros-Ghali to prepare a report on steps the UN could take to fulfill their expectations of a more active military role.

In Boutros-Ghali's subsequent *An Agenda for Peace*, he outlined a series of proposals that could take the UN well beyond its traditional military role of classic peacekeeping. The Secretary-General called not only for combat units constituted under the long moribund Article 43 of the UN Charter, but for "peace-enforcement" units "warranted as a provisional measure under Article 40 of the Charter." Although these were largely theoretical and untested ideas, by the time they were published in July 1992, the Security Council had already implemented a similar agenda. A few months prior to *An Agenda for Peace*, large and ambitious UN missions to the former Yugoslavia and Cambodia were already approved and underway.

This initial episode reflected a pattern that would develop over the next several years. The UN, many times reluctantly so, would be thrust into an ambitious and dangerous series of missions and operations by a Security Council that was enthusiastic about new and enlarged mandates for UN peacekeepers —but not so keen on providing the support necessary to make them a success. In 1992, while the Secretary-General was (at the request of the world's most powerful leaders) preparing a draft report on possible new departures in peacekeeping, a series of international crises plunged the organization into what UN official Shashi Tharoor called "a dizzying series of peacekeeping operations that bore little or no resemblance in size, complexity, and function to those that had borne the peacekeeping label in the past."

In the former Yugoslavia, it soon became painfully obvious that despite the deployment of almost 40,000 combat troops, the UN was in over its head. Among American leaders, it was fashionable in both political parties to bemoan the ineffectiveness of the UN peacekeepers. This America was as responsible for what the UN was attempting to do in the former Yugoslavia as any other state or the organization itself. Between September 1991 and January 1996, the Security Council passed 89 resolutions relating to the situation in the former Yugoslavia, of which the United States sponsored one-third. While Russia vetoed one resolution and joined China in abstaining on many others, the United States voted for all 89 to include those twenty resolutions that expanded the mandate or size of the UN peacekeeping mission in the Balkans.

Far from the notion that the UN was pulling the international community into Bosnia, the U.S.-led Security Council was pushing a reluctant UN even further into a series of missions and mandates it could not hope to accomplish. Boutros-Ghali warned the members of the Security Council that "the steady accretion of mandates from the Security Council has transformed the nature of UNPROFOR's [United Nations Protection Force's] mission to Bosnia-Herzegovina and highlighted certain implicit contradictions. The proliferation of resolutions and mandates has complicated the role of the Force." His Undersecretary-General for peacekeeping, Kofi Annan, was more direct. Attempts to further expand the challenging series of missions being given to the UN were "building on sand."

This did not seem to deter the U.S.-led Security Council however, which was happy to expand the mission further while volunteering few additional resources to the force in Bosnia. A June 1993 episode demonstrating this pattern is instructive. Then, the UN field commander estimated he would need some 34,000 more peacekeepers to protect both humanitarian aid convoys and safe areas in Bosnia. The Security Council, having given him these missions in previous resolutions, instead approved a "light option" of 7,600 troops, of whom only 5,000 had deployed to Bosnia some nine months later. Quitting his post in disgust, the Belgian general in command remarked, "I don't read the Security Council resolutions anymore because they don't help me."

The Clinton administration, which had shown unbounded enthusiasm for UN peacekeeping in the first months of the administration, began to sour slightly on its utility by September 1993. By then Ambassador Madeleine Albright's doctrine of "assertive multilateralism" had given way to President Clinton beseeching the UN General Assembly to know "when to say no." But it was the United States and its allies on the Security Council who kept saying yes for the United Nations. Even after that speech, Mrs. Albright voted for all five subsequent resolutions (and sponsored two) that again expanded the size or mandate of the UN peacekeeping mission to the former Yugoslavia. All the while, until the fall of 1995, the U.S. steadfastly resisted participating in the UN mission or intervening itself with military forces through some other forum.

In Somalia, there was an even more direct pattern. There the United States pushed an unwilling UN into a hugely ambitious nation-building mission. In its waning days the Bush administration had put together a U.S.-led coalition that intervened to ameliorate the man-made famine in Somalia. From the very beginning of the mission it had been the intention of the U.S. to turn the operation over to a UN peacekeeping force. Conversely, Boutros Boutros-Ghali, an Egyptian well acquainted with the challenge of nation-building in Somalia, wanted no part of the mission for the UN Ambassador Robert Oakley, the U.S. envoy to Somalia, noted that in a meeting with the Secretary-General and his assistants on 1 December 1992, "the top UN officials rejected the idea that the U.S. initiative should eventually become a UN peacekeeping operation."

The U.S. kept up the pressure on the Secretary-General, who was powerless to resist the idea if it gained momentum in the Security Council. The debate resembled what [Assistant Secretary of State for Africa] Chester Crocker called "bargaining in a bazaar" and "raged out of public view" while the U.S. and the UN negotiated over the follow-[up] mission. For his part, Boutros-Ghali wanted the U.S.-led coalition to accomplish a series of ambitious tasks before the UN would take over. These included the establishment of a reliable cease-fire, the control of all heavy weapons, the disarming of lawless factions, and the establishment of a new Somali police force. For its part, the United States just wanted to leave Somalia as soon as possible. It was now time to put assertive multilateralism to the test. Madeline Albright shrugged off the challenge to the world body and wrote that the difficulties that the UN was bound to encounter in Somalia were "symptomatic of the complexity of mounting international nation-building operations that included a military component."

The debate, with Boutros-Ghali resisting up to the last, effectively ended on 26 March 1993 with the passage of Security Council resolution 814 establishing a new UN operation in Somalia. The resolution authorized, for the first time, Chapter VII enforcement authority for a UN-managed force. More importantly, the resolution greatly expanded the mandate of the UN to well beyond what the American force had accomplished. Former Ambassador T. Frank Crigler called the UN mandate a "bolder and broader operation intended to tackle underlying social, political, and economic problems and to put Somalia back on its feet as a nation." In the meantime, the U.S. withdrew its heavily armed 25,000 troop force and turned the baton over to a lightly armed and still arriving UN force. The transition, set for early May 1993, was so rushed that on the day the UN took command its staff was at only 30 percent of its intended strength. The undermanned and underequipped UN force was left holding a bag not even of its own making.

The travails of the UN mission in Somalia need no further elucidation here. Suffice it to say that the U.S., although no longer a direct player in Somalia, continued to lead the Security Council in piling new mandates on the UN mission there. The most consequential of these was the mandate to apprehend those Somali's responsible for the June 1993 killing of 24 Pakistani peacekeepers. The U.S. further complicated this explosive new mission with an aggressive campaign of disarmament capped by the deployment of a special operations task force that was to lead the manhunt for [Somalian leader] Mohammed Farah Aideed. This task force was not under UN command in any way and when it became engaged in the tragic Mogadishu street battle of 3 October 1993 the UN commanders knew nothing of it until the shooting started. Even MG [Major General] Thomas Montgomery, the American commander and deputy UN commander, was told of the operation only 40 minutes before its launch. A U.S. military report afterward noted that the principal command problems of the UN mission in Somalia were "imposed on the U.S. by itself."

This fact, that the UN was not involved in the deaths of eighteen American soldiers in Mogadishu, was buried by the administration. Even more cynically, several top-level administration officials charged in 1995 with selling the Dayton Peace Accords to a skeptical U.S. public constantly noted that U.S. soldiers in the NATO mission to Bosnia would not be in danger because the UN would not be in command, as it was in Somalia. Few single events have been as damaging to the UN's reputation with the Congress and American public as the continued perception that it was the United Nations that was responsible for the disaster in Somalia. Not only has this myth been left to fester, it was indirectly used, along with the UN's many other U.S.-initiated problems, to call for Boutros Boutros-Ghali's head during the 1996 Presidential campaign. Then, for the first time in several years, the U.S. used its veto to stand alone against the Security Council and bring down the Secretary-General who had resisted the U.S.-led events that so discredited him and his organization.

Conclusion—Friends Like These

After those particular episodes, UN peacekeeping is now happy to be, as a UN official recently told me, in "a bear market." Congress and the administration are happy as well with a low profile for UN military operations—especially as Clinton officials try to get Congress to pay America's share of the unprecedented peacekeeping debt. Fittingly, Madeleine Albright, as Secretary of State, is now chiefly responsible for convincing Congress to pay the bill that she is tacitly accountable for because of her votes during that busy time on the Security Council. Albright also played a central role as the official, more than any other in the Bush and Clinton administrations, who epitomized the keen hopes of liberal internationalists advocating a greater security role for the UN. In early 1993, her speeches were laced with talk of "a renaissance for the United Nations" and ensuring that "the UN is equipped with a robust capacity to plan, organize, lead, and service peacekeeping activities." By 1994, however, after it became obvious that the inherent limitations of a large multinational organization would not allow it effectively to manage complex military operations, Albright stated that "the UN has not yet demonstrated the ability to respond effectively when the risk of combat is high and the level of local cooperation is low." Left unsaid was that the U.S., more than any other member state, was responsible for giving the UN much to do in Somalia and Bosnia and little to do it with. It appeared, as Harvey Sicherman has written, that "the assertive multilateralists of 1992–3 placed more weight upon the UN than it could bear, while ignoring NATO and other regional coalitions."

Regional coalitions or more narrowly focused military alliances were ignored both for reasons of philosophy and political expediency. Philosophically, legitimacy could be gained for collective security in general and the UN in particular by having it directly manage the more dynamic military operations of the post–Cold War era. Thomas Weiss typified this school of thought and wrote, "the UN is the logical convenor of future international military operations. Rhetoric about regional organizations risks slowing down or even making impossible more timely and vigorous action by the UN, the one organization most likely to fulfill adequately the role of regional conflict manager." This appealed in particular to the officials of the Clinton administration who had developed and published many similar thoughts while in academia or the think-tank world.

But for the most part the U.S. promoted unprecedented UN missions to conflicts such as Bosnia and Somalia because they did not want the U.S. or its alliances to be principally responsible for difficult and protracted military operations in areas of limited interest. As Shashi Tharoor wrote, "it is sometimes argued that the peacekeeping deployment to Bosnia-Herzegovina reflected not so much a policy as the absence of policy; that [UN] peacekeeping responds to the need to 'do something' when policy makers are not prepared to expend the political, military, and financial resources required to achieve the outcome that the press and opinion leaders are clamoring for."

The final irony is that the UN's adventurous new role in 1993–1995 and peacekeeping's subsequent demise came about not necessarily by the well intentioned but unsupported design of collective security's most ardent proponents. Instead, it came about by default as these same supporters thrust upon the UN difficult missions they would rather not have addressed more directly. Given the recent and renewed enthusiasm for more missions of the sort that will greatly challenge the UN, the international community would do well to keep this lesson in mind.

POSTSCRIPT

Should the United Nations Be Given Stronger Peacekeeping Capabilities?

The increase in the use of UN peacekeeping forces is partly the result of the changes from the cold war to the post–cold war era, which can be explored in Steven R. Ratner, *The New UN Peacekeeping: Building Peace in Lands of Conflict After the Cold War* (St. Martin's Press, 1996). Within this larger context, the debate over creating a potentially permanent international police force (even army) is heating up in many forums. A good place to begin exploring this topic further is the report issued by Boutros Boutros-Ghali, *An Agenda for Peace: Preventive Diplomacy, Peacemaking, and Peacekeeping* (United Nations, 1992). It is also worthwhile to look into the Internet site for UN peacekeeping, which can be found at http://www.un.org/Depts/dpko/.

Recent events throughout the world have done even more to convince those who advocate a UN standing military force that it is important to create a force that can respond quickly to crises and to have the military power to intervene effectively when necessary. The events in Kosovo, the grisly border war between Ethiopia and Eritrea, and the clashes that occurred in May 1999 between India and Pakistan—both of which have nuclear weapons—are just a few examples of the continued fighting that some hope a UN force could prevent or stop. Moreover, advocates argue that the fluid, post–cold war international system presents an opportunity to establish such a force that should not be missed.

It is certainly arguable that UN peacekeeping forces have had limited effectiveness. They have often been late to arrive because of the political difficulties of getting a force authorized by the Security Council. UN forces are also lightly armed and often have severe restrictions on their missions. These and other reasons for UN peacekeeping failures (amid successes in other instances) are taken up in Dennis C. Jett, *Why Peacekeeping Fails* (St. Martin's Press, 2000).

Other analysts are skeptical of the possibility or wisdom of a standing UN force and its possible uses. To delve more extensively into Hillen's views, read his *Blue Helmets: The Strategy of UN Military Operations* (Brassey's, 2000). Some of these concerns are based on such narrow factors as cost. The entire UN peacekeeping operation comes approximately to a mere one-tenth of 1 percent of what the world's countries spend on their national military establishments. More substantively, there are worries that a more powerful, proactive UN might undermine the sovereignty of the less developed countries (LDCs), with the UN Security Council serving as a tool of the five big powers that control the council through their veto power. From this perspective, UN intervention carries the danger of neo-colonial control. Other opposition comes from those who believe that a UN force will undermine the national sovereignty of even larger countries. They object, for instance, to the possibility that U.S. troops could be placed under UN command without the authorization of Congress. They worry that there might someday even be an international draft. Such concerns seem far-fetched, but then so once did the very existence of international security forces. For a look to the future, read Olara A. Otunnu and Michael W. Doyle, eds., *Peacemaking and Peacekeeping for the Next Century* (Rowman & Littlefield, 1998).

Did the NATO Military Action Against Yugoslavia Violate Just War Theory?

YES: William T. DeCamp III, from "The Big Picture: A Moral Analysis of Allied Force in Kosovo," *Marine Corps Gazette* (February 2000)

NO: Bill Clinton, from Interview With Dan Rather, *CBS News,* April 5, 1999, and Interview With Jim Lehrer, *NewsHour,* June 21, 1999, *Weekly Compilation of Presidential Documents* (vol. 35, nos. 13 and 24, 1999)

ISSUE SUMMARY

YES: William T. DeCamp III, a lieutenant colonel in the United States Marine Corps Reserves, argues that what occurred during the military campaign against Yugoslavia demonstrates that it would serve civilian and military leaders well to revisit just war theory.

NO: Bill Clinton, former president of the United States, explains his view that both the reasons that the United States and other countries intervened militarily in Yugoslavia and the tactics that they used there were justified politically and morally.

Anumber of factors came together in the last decade or so of the twentieth century that have changed the military activities of the United States and other countries. Classic wars, with one country attacking another, have declined. "Interventions" have increased dramatically. Interventions occur when an outside power intervenes in a civil war or in some other form of internal crisis in another country.

The number of interventions have increased for a variety of reasons associated with changing politics, technology, and values. The end of the superpower confrontation between the United States and the Soviet Union made it possible for individual countries, or international organizations such as the United Nations, to intervene without the risk that the decision to intervene would be blocked by a veto in the UN Security Council or the danger that a superpower would support one side of the contending forces and cause an escalation of the conflict.

Technology is another factor that has promoted interventions. Television, especially with live satellite feeds, has had a dramatic impact on politics. Civil unrest has led to horrific scenes for as long as humans have clashed. What is different is that those bloody images are now projected almost instantaneously into our living rooms, bedrooms, and wherever else we watch television. Norms are also changing. World opinion is less willing to tolerate injustices, whether they are suppression of democracy in Haiti, starvation amid civil war in Somalia, or ethnic cleansing in Bosnia or Kosovo.

Americans were at the forefront of four interventions (Somalia, Haiti, Bosnia, and Kosovo) in the 1990s. The U.S. administration made strategic arguments for some of these interventions, especially those in Bosnia and Kosovo. Humanitarianism was also cited as a reason to act. In November 1995, when President Bill Clinton went on television to justify to the American people his decision to commit U.S. troops in Bosnia, he told them that for strategic and humanitarian reasons, "It is the right thing to do."

The use of multinational military force in Kosovo four years later was, in some ways, an extension of the events in Bosnia. The ethnic cleansing and other tragedies only ended in Bosnia after a UN-authorized intervention led by the United States. But the trouble was not over. The Yugoslav province of Kosovo was populated mostly by ethnic Albanians. They sought autonomy from the Serb-dominated government. Soon, stories began to be aired that the Yugoslav army and informal (but officially tolerated) Serbian death squads were terrorizing the ethnic Albanian population in Kosovo and perhaps even attempting to ethnically cleanse the province of its Albanian population by killing some and driving the rest of the terrorized Albanians over the border into Albania. Prolonged negotiations in 1998 and 1999 failed to bring an end to what much of the outside world viewed as excesses, even atrocities, by Serbian forces in Kosovo.

The details of these negotiations are not as important as their result: failure. On March 14, 1999, led by the United States, the North Atlantic Treaty Organization (NATO) launched air strikes on Serb military positions in Kosovo and throughout Yugoslavia. Soon strikes on transportation, power, and other infrastructure targets in the country were added. The air war went on for nearly three months until mid-June, when the Serbs finally gave way and let an international force (NATO plus Russian troops) enter Kosovo.

In the following selections, William T. DeCamp III measures against just war theory both the reasons behind the U.S.-led NATO air war against Yugoslavia and the way it was conducted. He finds that both failed to meet the test of morality. Taking a very different view, President Clinton refers to the intervention as a noble undertaking.

William T. DeCamp III  **YES**

The Big Picture: A Moral Analysis of Allied Force in Kosovo

Unless we take and keep the moral high ground, our military superiority will ultimately fail us.

"That's the trouble, you know," Yossarian mused sympathetically. "Between me and every ideal I always find Scheisskophs, Peckhams, Korns, and Cathcarts. And that sort of changes the ideal."

"You must try not to think of them," Major Danby advised affirmatively. "And you must never let them change your values. Ideals are good, but people are sometimes not so good. You must try to look up at the big picture."

— Catch-22, *Joseph Heller (1955)*

There were plenty of Scheisskophs, Peckhams, Korns, and Cathcarts stifling efforts to achieve an ideal in Kosovo. U.S. policymakers failed miserably to master the ABCs of policy and strategy. They changed the ideal of intervention in Kosovo, which was to save Kosovar Albanian lives, and managed to transform a just cause into an unjust war, and an unjust war into a feeble, protracted, and Pyrrhic peace. After the bombing of the Chinese Embassy in Belgrade on 7 May [1999], the U.S. charge d'affaires at the United Nations (U.N.) said:

> It's very important, despite this, to keep our eye on the big picture, and the big picture is that Slobadan Milosevic is responsible for what's going on in Yugoslavia now.

This is the same morally bankrupt reasoning that we use to justify continued bombing and sanctions of Iraq, as if immoral actions can be made moral by placing the burden of cessation of the killing on the leader of the people killed by the bombing and sanctions. Seen through a moral or practical prism, the unfortunate consequences of our performance in the Balkans will last well into the next century.

It would serve our civilian and military leaders well to revisit just war theory, as articulated by St. Thomas Aquinas, among others, apply it to the North Atlantic Treaty Organization (NATO) intervention in Kosovo, and recalibrate their moral compasses accordingly, as they grapple with modern dilemmas pitting suffering against sovereignty, and contemplate the United States' role in the U.N., and the U.N.'s role in the world. Morality is not only the prerogative of statesmen; it is also the province of generals, and lately, far too few of them seem capable or willing to enter the moral arena. We are tasked with fighting a different kind of war and enforcing a different kind of peace these days and we must be prepared morally, mentally, and physically to meet the challenges they present. The most important of these challenges is the moral one.

According to Harvard ethicist Reverend J. Bryan Hehir, the presumption against the use of force in just war theory demands specific exceptions based on stringent moral criteria, particularly if force is to be used to intervene in a conflict within a sovereign nation. The moral criteria are considered in response to three basic questions. The first two questions relate to jus ad bellum, justice of the war; the third question to jus in bello, justice in the war.

The first question is why, or for what purpose, can force be used?

The answer is to defend human life and human rights or to preserve political order. Serbian "ethnic cleansing," intent on destroying the Albanian majority, which could only be called genocide as defined by the 1951 U.N. Convention, was justification enough for NATO's use of force. Serbian and Russian chicken and egg arguments about whether Serbs or NATO caused the suffering are specious. When Milosevic sought to preserve Yugoslav sovereignty and political order, first through ultranationalist rhetoric and rabble-rousing, and ultimately through the expulsion and murder of Kosovar Albanians, he completely forfeited the precarious justice of his cause. NATO's cause was just, and everyone, including Mirjana Markovic knew it; however, when we pose the second and third questions, we find that a just cause, while necessary, can be insufficient to guarantee the justice of the use of force.

The second question is when, and under what conditions, can force be used?

The answer is when the action is characterized by the following: right intention, proper authority, last resort, moral probability of success, and proportionality. In the case of Kosovo, preventing genocide was a right intention, and far more credible justification than say, saving NATO. NATO could have been called a proper authority under Chapter VIII of the U.N. Charter, but was less legitimate acting on its own, outside the Charter. Assuming that they would not be successful in obtaining a Security Council resolution approving the use of force, the United States and NATO chose not to pursue it. That choice eroded the moral criterion of last resort; in lieu of a resolution, the United States and NATO satisfied themselves with the coerced cooperation of the Kosovar Albanians at Rambouillet and the preordained failure of Richard Holbrooke in Belgrade.

Up until the first bombs were dropped on 24 March, U.S. and NATO policy and diplomacy seemed designed to lead to a war rather than avoid one; yet once NATO aggression was underway, President Clinton, himself, in announcing the start of airstrikes that he said were designed to prevent a wider war, stated emphatically, I don't intend to put our troops in Kosovo to fight a war." So much for Sun Tzu and surprise. The means chosen to wage the war, that is, by airpower alone, and broadcasting this message to the enemy reduced the probability of success. Recalling the haunting words of a soldier in Vietnam, "We had to destroy the village in order to save it," NATO, in the face of Milosevic's intransigence, destroyed the Former Republic of Yugoslavia (FRY) from the air, but whether it saved Kosovo remains to be seen. NATO's use of force, by limiting itself to airpower alone, produced evils and disorders greater than the evil it intended, but failed, to eliminate. While a ground war may have caused more "collateral damage" initially, combined with air-power, it would have been a more credible deterrent. Then, had that deterrent failed, what the Department of Defense calls "Full Spectrum Dominance" could have been applied to achieve our objectives. But the United States was worried about casualties and American public support, so we went with air alone. Milosevic was right when he told a reporter on 29 April that NATO miscalculated. "You are not willing to sacrifice lives to achieve our surrender. But we are willing to die to defend our rights as a sovereign nation." The United States and NATO were more willing to kill than to die for their cause, and Milosevic called our bluffs. Unfortunately for him, he was wrong about his own peoples' willingness to die to defend their rights as a sovereign nation.

The third question is how, or by what means, can force be used?

The answer is that force can be used by means proportional to the threat that take into account noncombatant immunity. The nature and timing of the application of means matters. Kosovo presented the United States and NATO with a curious paradox arising from the choice to use airpower alone that became escalatory, among other reasons, to prove their commitment; when in fact, as retired Marine [Lieutenant General] Bernard E. Trainor has pointed out, the litmus test of that commitment would have been the fielding of ground troops. United States' willingness to kill but not to die in the Balkans was at least partly attributable to the United States equating our peripheral or vital interests to NATO's survival interests—NATO should have been first to offer ground troops to fight in Kosovo. This willingness-to-kill-but-not-to-die disconnect causes the United States to resort to coercive diplomacy without a viable deterrent and, when that fails, to turn to military force where it is compelled to use its technological power to advantage to defeat the enemy without risking casualties. But American and Allied unwillingness to risk casualties increases the courage and resolve of the enemy, which, in Kosovo, caused the United States to escalate the only means in its kit—airstrikes. Former Secretary of State Henry Kissinger said, "I've never seen a period in which obligations were defined so readily and spread around so recklessly."

In Kosovo, our resolve was greater than the resources we were willing to commit to the action; means were unequal to undefined ends. Immorality resided in the mismatch. Unsubstantiated claims by the FRY indicated that

NATO airstrikes killed thousands of noncombatants and wounded thousands more. Whether one believes the statistics is moot. The train, the convoy, the bus, the hospital, the embassy, the houses, the human shields—the catastrophic consequences of our bombing—flashed across television screens around the world. The American people and Congress decided not to support the President's air war and not to use "any means necessary" to stop Milosevic because, in simple terms, they did not believe that two wrongs made a right, and they saw no evidence that bombing was bringing an end to the evil; in fact, many believed that the bombing added its own evil. The Germans had second thoughts about the bombing as the coalition began to unravel, dismayed like Mary Robinson, [UN] High Commissioner for Human Rights, that "warmaking [had] become the tool of peacemaking." Of course, it has always been that way, but the fact remains that bad war makes bad peace. After the war, the Albanians and Serbs continued to play musical murder under the peacekeeping forces' noses, but this time it was the Albanians' turn to kill.

[Nineteenth century military strategist Karl von] Clausewitz warned that no one in his right senses ought to start a war without being clear in his mind what he intends to achieve by that war and how he intends to fight it—don't take the first step without considering the last. What President Clinton and company didn't get ... is the imperative connection between ends and means. If the end of U.S. policy was to save the Kosovar Albanians, and airpower alone was not achieving that end, then something had to give; add ground troops, or adjust the ends. Clinton's answer was to keep on bombing. The United States and NATO, having had no clear vision of an end state, and suffering self-inflicted subtraction of their means, took the first step, bombing, without considering the next, or the last. We bombed until such time as we could declare victory, one that can only be described, and projected, in retrospect as Pyrrhic. Rather than strengthen our negotiating position, bombing weakened it, and angered and alienated China and Russia, whose veto power in the U.N. Security Council threatened a peaceful resolution favorable to the United States and NATO, and whose relationships with the United States are relatively more important to U.S. foreign policy than NATO.

The United States and NATO had a policy-strategy mismatch that brought us to a military and moral culminating point—a point where the air war had failed to defeat Milosevic and its escalation or initiation of a ground war caused us to lose our moral superiority regardless of the final outcome, which remains to be played out. Our situation was reminiscent of the "peace with honor" dilemma the United States found itself in more than 25 years ago, and ironically, Clinton's instrument of choice in the Balkans was the same as Nixon's was in Vietnam—bombing. [The Reverend] Jesse Jackson, [U.N. Secretary-General] Kofi Annan, and the Pope, among others, were all right. From an admittedly ideal moral point of view, the United States and NATO should have stopped the bombing and gotten back to doing what we unfortunately do worst—diplomacy.

The more important moral point is that the United States had the opportunity to take the moral high ground and reestablish order from the beginning by exercising preventive diplomacy in the U.N. Security Council before the fact. But this would have required listening instead of talking, cooperation instead of coercion, sharing power rather than abusing it. Ironically, in the aftermath of the Kosovo war, the United States faces reengagement with the Russians, the Chinese, and the U.N. from a morally disadvantageous position. The State Department has no clue how to corral Albanians whose goal is a greater Albania, or how to muzzle Kofi Annan who is intent on defenestrating the definition of sovereignty. They have no idea how the United States should look after our national interests in the U.N.

Who cares how many tanks our airplanes did or did not kill? We should have worked harder and longer to obtain consensus in the U.N. We should have used ground forces and combined arms as part of a joint combined task force to defeat the FRY sooner. I would even go so far as to say that assassinating Milosevic would have been a more moral means than bombing his people. Once we failed to do those things, whether we like it or not, our lack of moral authority diminished our military might, as our highest civilian and military leaders continued to bomb even as they passed through the moral culminating point where small snapshots like Korisa turned into a big picture where our killing looked no better than Milosevic's murder.

We need to get the big picture. Killing is a *last* resort. The United States needs the U.N. as much as the U.N. needs the United States. If we are not willing to die for a cause, we should not be too willing or anxious to kill for it. Means matter as much as ends. Doing right is as important as being right.

Interviews With President Bill Clinton

[Reasons for NATO Airstrikes in Serbia]

Mr. Rather: As Commander in Chief, you've sent some of our best to fly every day, every night, through the valley of the shadow of death in a place far away. Why? For what?

President Clinton: For several reasons. First and most important, because there are defenseless people there who are being uprooted from their homes by the hundreds of thousands and who are being killed by the thousands; because it is not an isolated incident but, in fact, a repeat of a pattern we have seen from [Yugoslavia's president, Slobodan] Milosevic in Bosnia and Croatia. So there is a compelling humanitarian reason.

Secondly, we haven't been asked to do this alone. All of our NATO [North Atlantic Treaty Organization] allies are doing it with us. They all feel very strongly about it, and we are moving together. Thirdly, we do not want to see the whole region destabilized by the kind of ethnic aggression that Mr. Milosevic has practiced repeatedly over the last 10 years, but he's been limited. This is, in some ways, the most destabilizing area he could be doing it in. And fourthly, we believe we can make a difference.

And so for all those reasons, I believe we should be doing this.

Mr. Rather: Why now, and why this place? The Russians, in a somewhat similar situation in Chechnya, had maybe 100,000 casualties. We've had Rwanda, Sudan—you didn't go into those places. As a matter of fact, the Serbians argue the Croatians did the same thing with the Serbians in part of Croatia. So why this place? Why right now?

President Clinton: Well, first of all, if you go back to Yugoslavia, we never supported any kind of ethnic cleansing by anybody. And the circumstances under which we went into Bosnia and ended the Bosnian war were designed to guarantee safety and security for all the ethnic groups, not just the Muslims but also the Croats and the Serbs. And the peace agreement that the Kosovar Albanians agreed to would have brought in an international peacekeeping force under NATO that would have guaranteed security to the Serbs, as well as to the Albanians.

From Bill Clinton, Interview With Dan Rather, *CBS News,* April 5, 1999, and Interview With Jim Lehrer, *NewsHour,* June 21, 1999, *Weekly Compilation of Presidential Documents,* vol. 35, nos. 13 and 24 (1999).

So the United States and NATO believe that there should be no ethnic cleansing and no people killed or uprooted because of their ethnic background.

Secondly, we're doing it now because now it's obvious that Mr. Milosevic has no interest in an honorable peace that guarantees security and autonomy for the Kosovar Albanians, and instead he is practicing aggression. We might have had to do it last fall, but we were able to head it off. Remember, he created a quarter of a million refugees last year. And NATO threatened to take action, and we worked out an agreement, which was observed for a while, which headed this off.

When we agreed to take action was when he rejected the peace agreement and he had already amassed 40,000 soldiers on the border and in Kosovo, with about 300 tanks. So that's why we're doing it now.

And you asked about other places. In the Rwanda case, let's remember what happened. In Rwanda, without many modern military weapons, somewhere between 500,000 and 800,000—we may never know—people were killed in the space of only 100 days. I think the rest of the world was caught flat-footed and did not have the mechanisms to deal with it. We did do some good and, I think, limited some killing there. But I wish we'd been able to do more there. And I would hope that that sort of thing will not ever happen again in Africa. And that's one of the reasons we worked hard to build up a cooperative relationship with African militaries through the Africa Crisis Response Initiative.

So I believe there are lots of reasons. But if you look at Kosovo, we have a history there in Europe. We know what happens if you have ethnic slaughter there. We know how it can spread. And the main thing is, there is this horrible humanitarian crisis. And because of NATO, because of our allied agreement and because we have the capacity, we believe we can do something about it there. And I think we have to try....

[President's Feelings About Situation in Kosovo]

Mr. Rather: Mr. President, as you always try to do, we're talking in measured tones. As President of the United States, you have to be careful of what you say. But I'm told by those who are close to you that you have a lot of pent-up feelings about what's happening in the Balkans, what we're doing there. Can you share some of that with us?

President Clinton: Well, I guess I do have a lot of pent-up feelings, and I think the President is supposed to keep a lot of those feelings pent up. But let me say, I think throughout human history one of the things that has most bedeviled human beings is their inability to get along with people that are different than they are, and their vulnerability to be led by demagogues who play on their fears of people who are different than they are.

You and I grew up in a part of the country where that was a staple of political life during our childhood. That's why this race issue has always been so important to me in America. And here we are at the end of the cold war; we're [beginning] the 21st century; our stock market went over 10,000 [recently]; we see the Internet and all this technology with all this promise for all these people, not just the United States but all over the world. And what is the dominant problem of our time? From the Middle East to Northern Ireland to Bosnia to central Africa, people still wanting to kill each other because of their racial and religious, their ethnic, their cultural differences.

This is crazy. And it is embodied in the policies of Mr. Milosevic. He became the leader of the Serbs by playing on their sense of grievance, which may have had some justification—their sense of ethnic grievance—and made them believe that the only way they could fulfill their appropriate human destiny was to create a Serbs-only state, even if it meant they had to go in and go to war with the Bosnian Muslims, and they had to go to war with the Croatian Catholics; they had to go to war with Kosovar Albanian Muslims and clean them all out.

And to be doing it in a place where World War I began, which has been the source of so much heartache, where so much instability can occur in other neighboring countries in the last year of the 20th century, I think is a tragedy.

And I had hoped—he's a clever man, you know, Mr. Milosevic, not to be underestimated. He's tough; he's smart; he's clever. I told all of our people that. The worst thing you can ever do in life is underestimate your adversary. But underneath all that, for reasons that I cannot fathom, there is a heart that has turned too much to stone, that believes that it's really okay that they killed all those people in Bosnia, and they made a quarter of a million refugees there— or millions, probably 2 million by the time it was over, dislocated from their home; and a quarter million people died—and it's really okay what they're doing in Kosovo, that somehow non-Serbs on land that they want are less than human.

And I guess I've seen too much of that all my life. And I have all these dreams for what the modern world can mean. When I'm long gone from here, I hope that there will be a level of prosperity and opportunity never before known in human history, not just for Americans but for others. And it's all being threatened all over the world by these ancient hatreds.

We're working, trying to bring an end to the Northern Ireland peace process now. We're trying to keep the Middle East peace process going. All of this stuff, it's all rooted in whether people believe that their primary identity is as a member of the human race that they share with others who are different from them, or if they believe their primary identity is as a result of their superiority over people who may share the same village, the same neighborhood, and the same high-rise apartment. But they don't belong to the same ethnic group or racial group or religious group, so if they have to be killed, it's just fine.

I mean, I think that is the basis of Milosevic's power. And that is the threat to our children's world. That's what I believe.

[Air Strikes in Belgrade]

Mr. Rather: Mr. President, there are reports that . . . there will be air attacks in Belgrade, itself, that you've gotten NATO to authorize it. Is that correct? Is that accurate?

President Clinton: It is accurate that we are attacking targets that we believe will achieve our stated objective, which is either to raise the price of aggression to an unacceptably high level so that we can get back to talking peace and security, or to substantially undermine the capacity of the Serbian Government to wage war.

Mr. Rather: Does that include attacks now in Belgrade? In the vernacular of the military, have you authorized them to go downtown?

President Clinton: I have authorized them to attack targets that I believe are appropriate to achieve our objectives. We have worked very hard to minimize the risks of collateral damage. I think a lot of the Serbian people are—like I said, the Serbs, like other people, are good people.

They're hearing one side of the story. They've got a state-run media. They don't have anybody that can talk about Mr. Milosevic the way you get to talk about me from time to time. And that's too bad. And some of those targets are in difficult places. But I do not believe that we can rule out any set of targets that are reasonably related to our stated objective....

[Ground Troops]

Mr. Rather: I want to discuss ground troops. In the context of speaking as directly as you possibly can, when you say you have no intention to commit ground troops to accomplishing the mission in Kosovo, does that mean we are not going to have ground troops in there—no way, no how, no time?

President Clinton: It means just what it says.... I have used those words carefully. I am very careful in the words I use not to mislead one way or the other. And the reason is, I think I have embraced a strategy here that I believe has a reasonable, good chance—a reasonably good chance of succeeding—maybe even a better chance than that as long as we have more and more steel and will and determination and unity from all of our NATO allies. And I want to pursue that strategy. And I believe that all these discussions about, well, other strategies and should we do this, that, or the other thing do not help the ultimate success of the strategy we are pursuing. That is why I have used the words I have used; why I have said the words I have said.

Now, on the merits of it, the thing that bothers me about introducing ground troops into a hostile situation—into Kosovo and into the Balkans—is the prospect of never being able to get them out. If you have a peace agreement, even if it's difficult and even if you have to stay a little longer than you thought you would, like in Bosnia, at least there is an exit strategy and it's a manageable situation. If you go in a hostile environment in which you do not believe in ethnic cleansing and you do not wish to see any innocent civilians killed, you could be put in a position of, for example, creating a Kosovar enclave that would keep you there forever. And I don't believe that is an appropriate thing to be discussing at this time....

[Possible Scenarios in the Balkans]

[President Clinton's interview with Jim Lehrer comes after Yugoslavia has agreed to withdraw its troops from Kosovo.—Ed.]

Mr. Lehrer: Mr. President, were you surprised that Milosevic hung in there as long as he did, for 78 days?

President Clinton: Not after the beginning. When we started this, I thought there would be one of three possible scenarios. First of all, I absolutely reject the theory that some people have advanced that what he did was worse than he would have done if we hadn't bombed as early as we did. I just simply don't believe that. He had this plan laid out; he was going to carry it into effect last October [1999]. He didn't do it because of the threat of bombing. So what I knew was that if he decided to behave as he had in Bosnia, that there would be a day or two of bombing; then we'd make this agreement that we made . . . , and it would be over, but that there was a strong chance that it would not, because in the mind of Mr. Milosevic there was a big difference between Bosnia and Kosovo. Bosnia was something that he wanted badly that he didn't have; Kosovo was something that he had that he wanted to take absolute control of by running people out of. So once he decided to take the bombing, I was not surprised that he took it for quite a long while, because he kept looking for ways to break the unity of NATO. He kept looking for ways to turn someone against what we were doing. Of course, the third scenario was that the bombing never worked, and we had to take even more aggressive measures. But I always thought there was a much better than 50-50 chance that this bombing campaign would work. And I am gratified that it has achieved our objectives.

[Decision on Airstrikes]

Mr. Lehrer: What was it, or who was it, that convinced you that bombing alone would work?

President Clinton: Well, you know, when I talked to the American people about this in the beginning, I made it clear that there was no way that any bombing campaign could literally physically extract every Serbian soldier and paramilitary operative and put them back out of Kosovo. But I knew that our people had made dramatic progress in the last few years, even since Desert Storm [in the Persian Gulf War of 1991], in precision-guided weapons and in the capacity of our planes to deliver them and to avoid even fairly sophisticated anti-aircraft operations. And I just felt that if we worked at it and we could hold the coalition together, that we'd be able to do enough damage that we could do it. And Secretary [of Defense William] Cohen and General [Henry] Shelton [chairman of the Joint Chiefs of Staff] felt there was a better than 50-50 chance we could do it. . . .

I've been dealing with Mr. Milosevic now a long time, you know, more than 6 years, and I think I have some understanding of the politics and the environment in Serbia. And I just felt if we kept pounding away that we could raise the price to a point where it would no longer make any sense for him to go on and where he could no longer maintain his position if he did.

And I regret that he required his people to go through what they have gone through, to lower their incomes as much as they've been lowered and to erode their quality of life as much as it's been eroded and even to have the civilian casualties which have been sustained, although they're far, far less than they were in Desert Storm after the bombing, for example. Still, I hate it. But what we did miraculously resulted in no combat air losses to our people—we did lose two fine Army airmen in training—and minimized the losses to their people, to their civilians. But it did a terrible amount of damage. And finally, they couldn't go on, it didn't make any sense.

Mr. Lehrer: Mr. President, as I'm sure you're aware, the fact of no casualties by NATO has been used as a criticism of the whole approach here, that: yes, ethnic cleansing was bad in Kosovo; yes, we needed to do something; but it wasn't worth risking any American lives to do so.

President Clinton: Well, now, first of all, I never said that—that it wasn't worth risking any lives. We did risk lives. And I think the American people should know that. Our pilots, particularly the pilots in our A-10's [warplanes], they were quite frequently fired upon by people holding these shoulder missiles, and they would deliberately position themselves in populated areas where there were civilians living. And over and over again, our pilots risked their lives by avoiding firing back, when they could easily have taken those people out who were firing at them. But to do so would have killed civilians. So there was risk to the lives. I remind you, we lost two airplanes and had to go in there and rescue two pilots. So that's not true.

Secondly, if we had put a ground force in for an invasion, it still wouldn't be done today. That is, all this bombing we did, we would have had to do anyway. Let me take you back to Operation Desert Storm, where we deployed a half-million people in the theater, took, as I remember, $4\frac{1}{2}$ or 5 months to do it, bombed for 44 days there, but because of the terrain and the weather, they dropped more ordnance in 44 days than we did in our 79-day campaign [against Yugoslavia].

So we would have had to do everything we have done to do this. I told the American people at the time that we could not have mounted and executed an invasion that would have stopped this ethnic cleansing, because at the time the Rambouillet [peace] talks broke down, when the Kosovars accepted it and the Serbs didn't, keep in mind, he already had 40,000 troops in and around Kosovo, and nearly 300 tanks. So no force—there was no way to mobilize and implant a force quick enough to turn it back.

And somehow the suggestion that our moral position would have been improved if only a few more Americans had died, I think is wrong. Believe me, fewer Serbs died than would die if we had had to invade. We would have had to deploy a force of about 200,000. We would have put them at great risk just getting them into the country. That was actually the biggest risk. I don't think the combat, once in the country, was nearly as big a risk as the problems of deploying into Kosovo.

But I just don't accept that. I don't think that—we moved aggressively. We were criticized by some people in the Congress and elsewhere for starting the bombing too soon. And those who say that we should have used ground forces, even if we had announced on day one we were going to use ground forces, it would have taken as long as this bombing campaign went on to deploy them, probably longer.

[Ground Forces]

Mr. Lehrer: What about just the threat of ground forces? You were criticized—you and your fellow NATO leaders were criticized for taking it off the table at the very beginning, telling Milosevic all he had to do was hunker down.

President Clinton: I was afraid that I had done that when I said to the American people that I did not intend to use ground forces. And shortly thereafter in an interview, I made it clear that I did not do that. And then repeatedly I said that, and I said I thought we ought to be planning for ground forces.

So I think the differences, for example, between the British position and ours and others were somewhat overstated, because we had done quite a lot of planning for a ground force, and we had made it explicit that we weren't taking the option off the table. And Chancellor [Gerhard] Schroeder from Germany was reported as having done so. When I talked to him and examined the German text of what he'd said, it was obvious that there had been a little bit [of an] overstatement there.

So I don't think—I think that the NATO—my own view is if this had not worked, NATO would have put ground forces in there and that we were determined not to lose this thing, that we were determined to reverse the ethnic cleansing. I think the Europeans were especially sensitive, as I was, to the fact that it took 4 years to mobilize an action against Bosnia and that there were all kinds of arguments used about it, including the fact that U.N. peacekeepers were there, diplomacy was going on, any action would have upset all that, and they didn't want that to happen this time.

So the truth is that this action against ethnic cleansing was hugely more rapid and more responsive than what was done in Bosnia. And that's why there won't be nearly as many lost lives....

Mr. Lehrer: Since, just in the last 24 hours, since this thing [the Kosovo military action] has come to this critical concluding point, people who were criticizing this action, not just Republicans but pundits and people in foreign policy establishment, they're still criticizing you. They—does that surprise you?

President Clinton: Gosh, no. I find that in Washington, in this sort of, what Professor Deborah Tannen has called this culture of critique, if I make a mistake, people want me to admit that I made a mistake.... But if they turn out to be wrong, they just change the subject or just keep insisting that it was, you know, just a fluke. I think the most important thing is, were we right to take a stand in Kosovo against ethnic cleansing? Were we right to do it more quickly than we did in Bosnia? Should we set up—have a principle that guides us which says: Okay, in a world where people are fighting all the time over racial or ethnic or religious problems, we can't tell everybody they've got to get along; we can't stop every fight, like the fight between Eritrea and Ethiopia, or the struggles in Chechnya; but where we can, at an acceptable cost—that is, without risking nuclear war or some other terrible thing—we ought to prevent the slaughter of innocent civilians and the wholesale uprooting of them because of their race, their ethnic background, or the way they worship God?

I think that's an important principle, myself. I think it's a noble thing. I think the United States did a good thing. Now, they may argue that I did it—went about it in the wrong way. They may—I've answered that, I hope. At least I'm confident that I did the right thing in the right way. And that's what—historians can judge that based on the long-term consequences of this. But I believe what we did was a good and decent thing. And I believe that it will give courage to people throughout the world, and I think it will give pause to people who might do what Mr. Milosevic has done throughout the world....

Now, it seems to me if we're going to reap the promise of the 21st century, if we don't want to go to Europe or some other place and have a bunch of Americans die in a bloody war, where we can nip this stuff in the bud, we ought to do it. And that's what I've tried to do. And I think it was the right thing to do....

[As I reflect on criticism of my actions,] I think—you know, differences are good. Nobody's got the whole truth. But you've got to get the rules of engagement right. And I think what we did in Kosovo was profoundly important.

POSTSCRIPT

Did the NATO Military Action Against Yugoslavia Violate Just War Theory?

The clash of views between DeCamp and Clinton with regard to the war against Yugoslavia as related to Kosovo raises many troubling questions. These are taken up further in Ivo H. Daalder and Michael E. O'Hanlon, *Winning Ugly: NATO's War to Save Kosovo* (Brookings Institution Press, 2000).

Some of the questions in this debate surely involve the specific circumstances of and actions taken during the crisis with Yugoslavia over its rebellious province. There are, however, larger controversies that extend to all interventions everywhere, and these fall under the category of *jus ad bellum* (just cause of war). The conflict in Kosovo was a civil war, and that is true whatever one may think of the respective causes and actions of the Serbs and the Kosovo Liberation Army and whether or not one thinks that the conflict threatened to spread and destabilize the region. The crises in Somalia and Haiti, where the United States intervened in the 1990s, were also clearly internal. The conflict in Bosnia was all or mostly a civil war in what was, depending on one's view, either a secessionist country or a rebellious Yugoslav province. This leads to the question, What right do outside powers, even acting collectively through the UN or a regional organization, have to intervene in another country's internal affairs? One commentary on the increase in and the changing rules of intervention can be found in Michael J. Glennon, "The New Interventionism," *Foreign Affairs* (May 1999).

The charges leveled by DeCamp also raise concerns about *jus in bello* (just conduct of war). Of particular note is the tension between the moral standard of discrimination, which requires an effort to minimize noncombatant casualties, and what is arguably another moral imperative on a leader—to limit the casualities to the troops of the leader's country. Perhaps the ultimate example, at least so far in turbulent human history, was the decision of President Harry Truman to drop atomic bombs on the Japanese cities of Hiroshima and Nagasaki, neither of which had much value as a military target per se. Essentially, say many, what Truman did was to use a technological advantage to kill some 340,000 Japanese civilians in order to avoid having to invade Japan and suffer casualties, which were unknowable but estimated to potentially reach 1 million killed or wounded.

A related line of thought is that the possibility of seemingly "antiseptic" war (for the technologically superior powers that deal death for others while suffering few casualties) may tempt such advanced countries to become increasingly interventionist. For such a view, read Michael Ignatieff, *Virtual War: Kosovo and Beyond* (St. Martin's Press, 2001).

ISSUE 15

Should the United States Ratify the International Criminal Court Treaty?

YES: Lawyers Committee for Human Rights, from Statement Before the Committee on International Relations, U.S. House of Representatives (July 25, 2000)

NO: John R. Bolton, from Statement Before the Committee on International Relations, U.S. House of Representatives (July 25, 2000)

ISSUE SUMMARY

YES: The Lawyers Committee for Human Rights, in a statement submitted to the U.S. Congress, contends that the International Criminal Court (ICC) is an expression, in institutional form, of a global aspiration for justice.

NO: John R. Bolton, senior vice president of the American Enterprise Institute in Washington, D.C., contends that support for an international criminal court is based largely on naive emotion and, thus, adhering to its provisions is not wise.

Historically, international law has focused primarily on the actions of and relations between states. More recently, the status and actions of individuals has become increasingly subject to international law.

The first significant step in this direction was evident in the Nuremberg and Tokyo war crimes trials after World War II. In these panels, prosecutors and judges from the victorious powers prosecuted and tried German and Japanese military and civilian leaders for waging aggressive war, for war crimes, and for crimes against humanity. Most of the accused were convicted; some were executed. There were no subsequent war crimes tribunals through the 1980s and into the mid-1990s. Then, however, separate international judicial tribunals' processes were established to deal with the Holocaust-like events in Bosnia and the genocidal massacres in Rwanda.

The 11-judge tribunal for the Balkans sits in The Hague, the Netherlands. The 6-judge Rwanda tribunal is located in Arusha, Tanzania. These tribunals have indicted numerous people for war crimes and have convicted and imprisoned a few of them. These actions have been applauded by those who believe that individuals should not escape punishment for crimes against humanity that they commit or order. But advocates of this increased and forceful application of international law also feel that the ad hoc tribunals are not enough.

Such advocates are convinced that the next step is the establishment of a permanent International Criminal Court (ICC) to prosecute and try individuals for war crimes and other crimes against humanity. The move for an ICC was given particular impetus when President Bill Clinton proposed just such a court in 1995. Just a year later, the United Nations convened a conference to lay out a blueprint for the ICC. Preliminary work led to the convening of a final conference in June 1998 to settle the details of the ICC. Delegates from most of the world's countries met in Rome, where their deliberations were watched and commented on by representatives of 236 nongovernmental organizations (NGOs.) The negotiations were far from smooth. A block of about 50 countries informally led by Canada, which came to be known as the "like-minded group," favored establishing a court with broad and independent jurisdiction.

Other countries wanted to narrowly define the court's jurisdiction and to allow it to conduct only prosecutions that were referred to it by the UN Security Council (UNSC). The hesitant countries also wanted the court to be able to prosecute individuals only with the permission of the accused's home government, and they wanted the right to file treaty reservations exempting their citizens from prosecution in some circumstances. Somewhat ironically, given the impetus that President Clinton had given to the launching of a conference to create the ICC, the United States was one of the principal countries favoring a highly restricted court. U.S. reluctance to support an expansive definition of the ICC's jurisdiction and independence rested on two concerns. One was the fear that U.S. personnel would be especially likely targets of politically motivated prosecutions. The second factor that gave the Clinton administration pause was the requirement that the Senate ratify the treaty. Senate Foreign Relations Committee chairman Jesse Helms has proclaimed that any treaty that gave the UN "a trapping of sovereignty" would be "dead on arrival" in the Senate.

In the following selections, the Lawyers Committee for Human Rights and John R. Bolton present their markedly differing views of the wisdom of founding an ICC. Both analyses agree that, if it works the way that it is intended to, the International Criminal Court will have a profound impact. Where they differ is on whether that impact would be positive or negative.

 **YES**

Statement of the Lawyers Committee
for Human Rights

The United States has compelling reasons to remain open to eventual co-operation with the International Criminal Court (ICC). United States interests may dictate such cooperation, even while the U.S. remains a non-party to the Rome Statute.... The following paper describes the U.S. interest in supporting the ICC.

I. A strong and independent International Criminal Court serves important national interests of the United States.

At the end of World War Two, with much of Europe in ashes, some allied leaders urged that the leaders of the defeated Third Reich be summarily executed. The United States disagreed. U.S. leaders insisted that a larger and more valuable contribution to the peace could be made if the Nazis were individually charged and tried for violations of international law. The International Criminal Court is an expression, in institutional form, of an aspiration for justice with which the United States had been deeply identified ever since World War Two. It was created to advance objectives that are totally consistent with the long-term U.S. national interest in a peaceful, stable, democratic and integrated global system. And the Rome Treaty, in its final form, promised to advance that interest in the following ways:

- *First,* the treaty embodies deeply held American values. The establishment of the Court responds to the moral imperative of halting crimes that are an offense to our common humanity. The ICC promises to promote respect for human rights; advance the rule of law around the world, both domestically and internationally; reinforce the independence and effectiveness of national courts; and uphold the principle of equal accountability to international norms.

From U.S. House of Representatives. Committee on International Relations. *The International Criminal Court: A Threat to American Military Personnel?* Hearing, July 25, 2000. Washington, D.C.: Government Printing Office, 2000.

- *Second,* the ICC will help to deter future gross violations. It will not halt them completely, of course. But over time, its proceedings will cause prospective violators to think twice about the likelihood that they will face prosecution. This deterrent effect is already apparent in the former Yugoslavia. Even though leading architects of ethnic cleansing, such as Radovan Karadzic and Ratko Mladic, have not been brought to trial, their indictment has limited their ability to act and has allowed more moderate political forces to emerge, reducing the risk to U.S. and other international peacekeepers still in Bosnia.

- *Third,* through this deterrent effect the ICC will contribute to a more stable and peaceful international order, and thus directly advance U.S. security interests. This is already true of the Yugoslav Tribunal, but it will be much more true of the ICC, because of its broader jurisdiction, its ability to respond to Security Council referrals, and the perception of its impartiality. The court will promote the U.S. interest in the preventing [of] regional conflicts that sap diplomatic energies and drain resources in the form of humanitarian relief and peacekeeping operations. Massive human rights violations almost always have larger ramifications in terms of international security and stability. These include widening armed conflict, refugee flows, international arms and drug trafficking, and other forms of organized crime, all of which involve both direct and indirect costs for the United States.

- *Fourth,* the ICC will reaffirm the importance of international law, including those laws that protect Americans overseas. For many people in the United States, "international law" is seen either as a utopian abstraction, or an unwelcome intrusion into our sovereign affairs. But as Abram Chayes, former Department of State Legal Adviser, remarked shortly before his death [in 2000], there is nothing utopian about international law in today's world. On the contrary, it is a matter of "hard-headed realism." Many nations who voted for the Rome Treaty had similar misgivings about its potential impact on their sovereignty. But they recognized that this kind of trade-off is the necessary price of securing a rule-based international order in the 21st century. France, for example, which participates extensively in international peacekeeping operations, made this calculation, joined the consensus in Rome and ... ratified the treaty. The United States, likewise, should see the ICC as an integral part of an expanding international legal framework that also includes rules to stimulate and regulate the global economy, protect the environment, control the proliferation of weapons of mass destruction, and curb international criminal activity. The United States has long been a leading exponent, and will be a prime beneficiary, of this growing international system of cooperation.

II. The risks posed by the ICC to U.S. servicemen and officials are negligible in comparison to the benefits of the Court to United States' interests.

In assessing the U.S. government's concerns, it is important to bear in mind some basic threshold considerations about the ICC. Most fundamentally, it will be a court of last resort. It will have a narrow jurisdiction, and is intended to deal with only the most heinous crimes. The ICC will step in only where states are unwilling or unable to dispense justice. Indeed, that is its entire purpose: to ensure that the worst criminals do not go free to create further havoc just because their country of origin does not have a functioning legal system. The Court was designed with situations like Rwanda and Cambodia and Sierra Leone in mind, not to supplant sophisticated legal systems like those of the United States. Furthermore, there are strict guidelines for the selection of ICC judges and prosecutors, as well as a set of internal checks and balances, that meet or exceed the highest existing international standards. The legal professionals who staff the Court will not waste their time in the pursuit of frivolous cases.

Second, the Court will only deal with genocide, war crimes and crimes against humanity, all of which are subject to a jurisdiction narrower than that available to domestic courts under international law. It will not be concerned with allegations of isolated atrocities, but only with the most egregious, planned and large-scale crimes.

Could a member of the U.S. armed forces face credible allegations of crimes of this magnitude? Genocide would seem to be out of the question. War crimes and crimes against humanity are more conceivable. The My Lai massacre in Vietnam revealed the bitter truth that evil knows no nationality: American soldiers can sometimes be capable of serious crimes. If such a crime were committed today, it would appear self-evident that the U.S. military justice system would investigate and prosecute the perpetrators, as it did at My Lai, whether or not an ICC existed. And if it were an isolated act, not committed in pursuit of a systematic plan or policy, it would not meet the threshold for ICC concern in any case.

Benign support by the United States for the ICC as a non-party to the Treaty would reaffirm the standing U.S. commitment to uphold the laws of war and could be offered in the knowledge that the Court would defer to the U.S. military justice system to carry out a good faith investigation in the unlikely event that an alleged crime by an American was brought to its attention. The marginal risk that is involved could then simply be treated as part of the ordinary calculus of conducting military operations, on a par with the risk of incurring casualties or the restraints imposed by the laws of war. The preparation and conduct of military action is all about risk assessment, and the marginal risk of exposure to ICC jurisdiction is far outweighed by the benefits of the Court for U.S. foreign policy.

III. The ICC provides an opportunity for the United States to reaffirm its leadership on the issue of international justice, which for so long has been a central goal of U.S. policy.

We urge the United States to develop a long-term view of the benefits of the ICC. Such an approach would open the door to cooperation with the Court as a non-state party, and eventually to full U.S. participation. This policy shift should be based on the following five premises:

- **The creation of new international institutions requires concessions from all the participants.** As an international agreement, the Rome Statute bears the marks of many concessions to sovereign states—not least the United States. As such, the ICC will have a twofold virtue: it will be imbued with the flexibility of an international institution as well as with the rigor of a domestic criminal court. The risks involved in supporting the present ICC Treaty are more than outweighed by the expansion of an international legal framework that is congenial to U.S. interests and values.
- **The risks of U.S. exposure to ICC jurisdiction are in fact extremely limited, as a result of the extensive safeguards that are built into the Rome Treaty.** Those safeguards are there in large part because the United States insisted on their inclusion. The modest risks that remain can never be fully eliminated without compromising the core principles established at Nuremberg and undermining the basic effectiveness of an institution that can do much to advance U.S. interests. The best way to minimize any residual risk is to remain engaged with others in helping to shape the Court. The risks, in fact, will only be aggravated if the United States decides to withdraw from the ICC process. Joining the ICC, on the other hand, would allow the United States to help nominate, select and dismiss its judges and prosecutors, and so ensure that it operates to the highest standards of professional integrity. More broadly, the ICC's Assembly of States Parties would provide an ideal setting for the United States to demonstrate its leadership in the fight against impunity for the worst criminals.
- **The Pentagon's views, while important, should be balanced among other U.S. policy interests in reference to the ICC.** The U.S. military has an institutional interest in retaining the maximum degree of flexibility in its operational decisions. But this must be put in proper perspective by civilian authorities as they weigh the pros and cons of the ICC. Legislators and others who have so far remained on the sidelines of the ICC debate will have an important part to play in helping the Administration develop a broader approach to the ICC, one that puts long-term stewardship of the national interest into its proper perspective.
- **U.S. leadership requires working in close cooperation with our allies around the world.** It is tempting to believe that U.S. economic and military supremacy is now so absolute that the United States can go it alone and impose its will on the rest of the world. But the evolution of the ICC is a reminder that this kind of unilateralism is not possible in today's more complex world. The United States has tried to impose its will on the ICC negotiations, and it has failed. In its repeated efforts to find a "fix," the United States has succeeded only in painting itself into a corner. Worse, it has disregarded one of the cardinal rules of

diplomacy, which is never to commit all your resources to an outcome that is unattainable. Unable to offer credible carrots, decisive sticks, or viable legal arguments, the United States finds itself on what one scholar has called a "lonely legal ledge," able neither to advance nor to retreat. Asking for concessions it cannot win, in a process it can neither leave nor realistically oppose, the United States has so far resisted coming to terms with the limits of its ability to control the ICC process.

- **The costs of opposition to the Court are too high and would significantly damage the U.S. national interest.** Once the ICC is up and running, it seems highly unlikely that the United States would refuse to support the principle of accountability for the worst international crimes simply because the Court was the only viable means of upholding that principle. It is far more likely that a future U.S. administration will see the advantage in supporting the Court, if only as a matter of raw political calculus. Opposition to a functioning Court would undermine faith in a world based on justice and the rule of law and would shake one of the foundation stones on which the legitimacy of U.S. global leadership has rested since World War Two.

For the last half century, U.S. foreign policy has sought to balance military strength with the nurturing of an international system of cooperation based on democracy and the rule of law. It would be a serious mistake to imagine that victory in the Cold War means that the institutional part of this equation can now be abandoned, and that ad hoc applications of force should prevail over the consistent application of law.

NO ↩

John R. Bolton

Statement of John R. Bolton

Unfortunately, support for the ICC [International Criminal Court] concept is based largely on emotional appeals to an abstract ideal of an international judicial system, unsupported by any meaningful evidence, and running contrary to sound principles of international crisis resolution. Moreover, for some, faith in the ICC rests largely on an unstated agenda of creating ever-more-comprehensive international structures to bind nation states in general, and one nation state in particular. Regrettably, the Clinton Administration's naïve support for the concept of an ICC... left the U.S. in a worse position internationally than if we had simply declared our principled opposition in the first place.

Many people have been led astray by analogizing the ICC to the Nuremberg trials, and the mistaken notion that the ICC traces its intellectual lineage from those efforts. However, examining what actually happened at Nuremberg easily disproves this analysis, and demonstrates why the ICC as presently conceived can never perform effectively in the real world. Nuremberg occurred after complete and unambiguous military victories by allies who shared juridical and political norms, and a common vision for reconstructing the defeated Axis powers as democracies. The trials were intended as part of an overall process, at the conclusion of which the defeated states would acknowledge that the trials were prerequisites for their readmission to civilized circles. They were not just political "score settling," or continuing the war by other means. Moreover, the Nuremberg trials were effectively and honorably conducted. Just stating these circumstances shows how different was Nuremberg from so many contemporary circumstances, where not only is the military result ambiguous, but so is the political and where war crimes trials are seen simply as extensions of the military and political struggles under judicial cover.

Many ICC supporters believe simply that if you abhor genocide, war crimes and crimes against humanity, you should support the ICC. This logic is flatly wrong for three compelling reasons.

First, all available historical evidence demonstrates that the Court and the Prosecutor will not achieve their central goal—the deterrence of heinous crimes —because they do not (and should not) have sufficient authority in the real world. Beneath the optimistic rhetoric of the ICC's proponents, there is not a

From U.S. House of Representatives. Committee on International Relations. *The American Service-members' Protection Act of 2000.* Hearing, July 25, 2000. Washington, D.C.: Government Printing Office, 2000. Notes omitted.

shred of evidence to support their deterrence theories. Instead, it is simply a near-religious article of faith. Rarely, if ever, has so sweeping a proposal for restructuring international life had so little empirical evidence to support it. Once ICC advocate said in Rome that: "the certainty of punishment can be a powerful deterrent." I think that statement is correct, but, unfortunately, it has little or nothing to do with the ICC.

In many respects, the ICC's advocates fundamentally confuse the appropriate role of political and economic power; diplomatic efforts; military force and legal procedures. No one disputes that the barbarous actions under discussion are unacceptable to civilized peoples. The real issue is how and when to deal with these acts, and this is not simply, or even primarily, a legal exercise. The ICC's advocates make a fundamental error by trying to transform matters of international power and force into matters of law. Misunderstanding the appropriate roles of force, diplomacy and power in the world is not just bad analysis, but bad and potentially dangerous policy for the United States.

Recent history is unfortunately rife with cases where strong military force or the threat of force failed to deter aggression or gross abuses of human rights. Why we should believe that bewigged judges in The Hague will prevent what cold steel has failed to prevent remains entirely unexplained. Deterrence ultimately depends on perceived effectiveness, and the ICC is most unlikely to be that. In cases like Rwanda, where the West declined to intervene as crimes against humanity were occurring, why would the mere possibility of distant legal action deter a potential perpetrator? . . .

Moreover, the actual operations of the existing Yugoslav and Rwanda ("ICTR") tribunals have not been free from criticism, criticism that foretells in significant ways how an ICC might actually operate. A UN experts' study (known as the "Ackerman Report," after its chairman) noted considerable room for improvement in the work of the tribunals. . . .

[For example], ICC opponents have warned that it will be subjected to intense political pressures by parties to disputes seeking to use the tribunal to achieve their own non-judicial objectives, such as score-settling and gaining advantage in subsequent phases of the conflict. The Ackerman Report, in discussing the ICTY's quandary about whether to pursue "leadership" cases or low-level suspects, points out precisely how such political pressures work, and their consequences: "[u]navoidable early political pressures on the Office of the Prosecutor to act against perpetrators of war crimes . . . led to the first trials beginning in 1995 against relatively minor figures. And while important developments . . . have resulted from these cases, the cost has been high. Years have elapsed and not all of the cases have been completed." In short, political pressures on the Tribunals, to which they respond, are not phantom threats, but real. . . .

Second, the ICC's advocates mistakenly believe that the international search for "justice" is everywhere and always consistent with the attainable political resolution of serious political and military disputes, whether between or within states, and the reconciliation of hostile neighbors. In the real world, as opposed to theory, justice and reconciliation may be consistent—or they may not be. Our recent experiences in situations as diverse as Bosnia, Rwanda,

South Africa, Cambodia and Iraq argue in favor of a case-by-case approach rather than the artificially imposed uniformity of the ICC.

For example, an important alternative is South Africa's Truth and Reconciliation Commission. After apartheid, the new government faced the difficulty of establishing truly democratic institutions, and dealing with earlier crimes. One option was certainly widespread prosecutions against those who committed human rights abuses. Instead, the new government decided to establish the Commission to deal with prior unlawful acts. Those who had committed human rights abuses may come before the Commission and confess their past misdeeds, and if fully truthful, can, in effect, receive pardons from prosecution.

I do not argue that the South African approach should be followed everywhere, or even necessarily that it is the correct solution for South Africa. But it is certainly a radically different approach from the regime envisioned by the ICC. . . .

Efforts to minimize or override the nation state through "international law" have found further expression in the expansive elaboration of the doctrine of "universal jurisdiction." Until recently an obscure, theoretical creature in the academic domain, the doctrine gained enormous public exposure (although very little scrutiny) during the efforts [of a Spanish judge] to extradite General Augusto Pinochet of Chile from the United Kingdom [to Spain].

Even defining "universal jurisdiction" is not easy because the idea is evolving so rapidly. . . . The idea was first associated with pirates. . . . Because pirates were beyond the control of any state and thus not subject to any existing criminal justice system, the idea developed that it was legitimate for any aggrieved party to deal with them. Such "jurisdiction" could be said to be "universal" because the crime of piracy was of concern to everyone, and because such jurisdiction did not comport with more traditional jurisdictional bases, such as territoriality or nationality. In a sense, the state that prosecuted pirates could be seen as vindicating the common interest of all states. (Slave trading is also frequently considered to be the subject of universal jurisdiction, following similar reasoning.)

. . . [This sense of universal jurisdiction] is a far cry from what "human rights" activists, NGOs [nongovernmental organizations], and academics . . . have in mind today. From a very narrow foundation, theorists have enlarged the concept of universal jurisdiction to cover far more activities, with far less historical or legal support, than arose earlier in the context of piracy. At the same time, they have omitted reference to the use of force, and substituted their preferred criminal prosecution. The proscribed roster of offenses now typically includes genocide, torture, war crimes and crimes against humanity, which are said to vest prosecutorial jurisdiction in all states.

Announcing his decision in the November 25, 1998 decision of *Ex parte Pinochet,* Lord Nicholls described the crimes of which the General stood accused by saying, "International law has made it plain that certain types of conduct . . . are not acceptable conduct on the part of anyone." Although that decision . . . did not actually rest on universal jurisdiction, Lord Nicholls in fact stated the doctrine's essential foundation.

The worst problem with universal jurisdiction is not its diaphanous legal footings but its fundamental inappropriateness in the realm of foreign policy. In effect (and in intention), the NGOs and theoreticians advocating the concept are misapplying legal forms in political or military contexts. What constitutes "crimes against humanity" and whether they should be prosecuted or otherwise handled—and by whom—are not questions to be left to lawyers and judges. To deal with them as such is, ironically, so bloodless as to divorce these crimes from reality. It is not merely naïve, but potentially dangerous, as Pinochet's case demonstrates.

Morally and politically, what Pinochet's regime did or did not do is primarily a question for Chile to resolve. Most assuredly, Pinochet is not, unlike a pirate or a slave trader, beyond the control of any state. Although many people around the world intensely dislike the solution that Chile adopted in order to restore constitutional and democratic rule in 1990, especially the various provisions for amnesty, the terms and implementation of that deal should be left to the Chileans themselves. They (and their democratically elected government) may continue to honor the deal, or they may choose to bring their own judicial proceedings against Pinochet. One may accept or reject the wisdom or morality of either course (and I would argue that they should uphold the deal), but it should be indisputable that the decision is principally theirs to make. The idea that Spain or any other country that subsequently filed extradition requests in the United Kingdom has an interest superior to that of Chile—and can thus effectively overturn the Chilean deal—is untenable. And yet, if the British had ultimately extradited Pinochet to Spain, that is exactly what would have happened. A Spanish magistrate operating completely outside the Chilean system will effectively have imposed his will on the Chilean people. One is sorely tempted to ask: Who elected him? If that is what "universal jurisdiction" means in practice (as opposed to the theoretical world of law reviews), it is hopelessly flawed.*

Spain *does* have a legitimate interest in justice on behalf of Spanish citizens who may have been held hostage, tortured, or murdered by the Pinochet regime. And the Spanish government may take whatever steps it ultimately considers to be in the best interest of Spanish citizens, but its recourse lies with the government of Chile, and certainly not with that of the United Kingdom. . . .

Because of the substantial publicity surrounding the Pinochet matter, we can expect copycat efforts covering a range of other "crimes against humanity" in the near future. But adding purported crimes (shocking though they may be) to the list of what triggers universal jurisdiction does not make the concept any more real. Nor does a flurry of law review articles (and there has been far more than a flurry) make concrete an abstract speculation. In fact, "universal jurisdiction" is conceptually circular: universal jurisdiction covers the most dastardly offenses; accordingly, if the offense is dastardly, there must be universal jurisdiction to prosecute it. Precisely because of this circularity, there is absolutely

---

* [Pinochet was ultimately returned to Chile, where he was charged with crimes and awaits trial. —Ed.]

no limit to what creative imaginations can enlarge it to cover, and we can be sure that they are already hard at work. . . .

Third, tangible American interests are at risk. I believe that the ICC's most likely future is that it will be weak and ineffective, and eventually ignored, because [it was] naïvely conceived and executed. There is, of course, another possibility: that the Court and the Prosecutor (either as established now, or as potentially enhanced) will be strong and effective. In that case, the U.S. may face a much more serious danger to our interests, if not immediately, then in the long run.

Although everyone commonly refers to the "Court" created at the 1998 Rome Conference, what the Conference actually did was to create not just a Court, but also a powerful and unaccountable piece of an "executive" branch: the Prosecutor. Let there be no mistake: our main concern from the U.S. per-spective is not that the Prosecutor will indict the occasional U.S. soldier who violates our own laws and values, and his or her military training and doc-trine, by allegedly committing a war crime. Our main concern should be for the President, the Cabinet officers on the National Security Council, and other senior leaders responsible for our defense and foreign policy. They are the real potential targets of the ICC's politically unaccountable Prosecutor.

One problem is the crisis of legitimacy we face now in international organ-izations dealing with human rights and legal norms. Their record is, to say the least, not encouraging. The International Court of Justice and the UN Human Rights Commission are held in *very* low esteem, and not just in the U.S. ICC supporters deliberately chose to establish it independently of the ICJ to avoid its baggage.

Next is the overwhelming repudiation by the Rome Conference of the American position supporting even a minimal role for the Security Council. Alone among UN governing bodies, the Security Council does enjoy a signifi-cant level of legitimacy in America. And yet it was precisely the Council where the U.S. found the greatest resistance to its position. The Council has primacy in the UN for "international peace and security," in all their manifestations, and it is now passing strange that the Council and the ICC are to operate virtually independently of one another. The implicit weakening of the Security Council is a fundamental *new* problem created by the ICC, and an important reason why the ICC should be rejected. The Council now risks both having the ICC interfer-ing in its ongoing work, and even more confusion among the appropriate roles of law, politics and power in settling international disputes.

The ICC has its own problems of legitimacy. Its components do not fit into a coherent international structure that clearly delineates how laws are made, adjudicated and enforced, subject to popular accountability, and structured to protect liberty. Just being "out there" in the international system is unaccept-able, and, indeed, almost irrational unless one understands the hidden agenda of many NGOs supporting the ICC. There is real vagueness over the ICC's sub-stantive jurisdiction, although one thing is emphatically clear: this is *not* a court of limited jurisdiction. . . .

Examples of vagueness in key elements of the Statute's text include:

- "Genocide," as defined by the Rome Conference is inconsistent with the Senate reservations attached to the underlying Genocide Convention, and the Rome Statute is not subject to reservations.
- "War crimes" have enormous definitional problems concerning civilian targets. Would the United States, for example, have been guilty of "war crimes" for its WWII bombing campaigns, and use of atomic weapons, under the Rome Statute?
- What does the Statute mean by phrases like "knowledge" of "incidental loss of life or injury to civilians"? "long-term and severe damage to the natural environment"? "clearly excessive" damage?

Apart from problems with existing provisions, and the uncertain development of customary international law, there are many other "crimes" on the waiting list: aggression, terrorism, embargoes (courtesy of Cuba), drug trafficking, etc. The Court's potential jurisdiction is enormous. Article 119 provides: "any dispute concerning the judicial functions of the Court shall be settled by the decision of the Court."

Consider one recent example of the use of force, the NATO air campaign over former Yugoslavia. Although most Americans did not question the international "legality" of NATO's actions, that view was not uniformly held elsewhere. During the NATO air war, Secretary General Kofi Annan expressed the predominant view that "unless the Security Council is restored to its pre-eminent position as the sole source of legitimacy on the use of force, we are on a dangerous path to anarchy." ...

Implicitly, therefore, in Annan's view, NATO's failure to obtain Council authorization made its actions illegitimate, which is what those pursuing the hidden agenda want to hear: while one cannot stop the United States from using force because it is so big and powerful, one can ensure that it is illegitimate absent Security Council authorization, *and thus a possible target of action by the ICC Prosecutor.* . . .

Many hope to change [U.S. military] behavior as much as the international "rules" themselves, through the threat of prosecution. They seek to constrain military options, and thus lower the potential effectiveness of such actions, or raise the costs to successively more unacceptable levels by increasing the legal risks and liabilities perceived by top American and allied civilian and military planners undertaking military action.

... Amnesty [International] asserted ... that "NATO forces violated the laws of war leading to cases of unlawful killing of civilians." The NGO complained loudly about NATO attacks on a "civilian" television transmitter in Belgrade, even though it served the Milosevic regime's propaganda purposes. Similarly, Human Rights Watch ... concluded that NATO violated international law, but stopped short of labeling its actions as "war crimes." In another recent report, this NGO announced its opposition to the sale of American air-to-ground missiles to Israel because of the Israeli "war crime" of attacking Lebanese electrical power stations. Of course, much the same could also be said about American air attacks during the Persian Gulf War, aimed at destroying critical communications and transportation infrastructure inside Iraq, in order to deny it to Saddam's military. If these targets are now "off limits," the American military will be far weaker than it would otherwise be....

·⟨◉⟩·

What to do next is obviously the critical question. Whether the ICC survives and flourishes depends in large measure on the United States. We should not allow this act of sentimentality masquerading as policy to achieve indirectly what was rejected in Rome. We should oppose any suggestion that we cooperate, help fund, and generally support the work of the Court and Prosecutor. We should isolate and ignore the ICC.

Specifically, I have long proposed for the United States a policy of "Three Noes" toward the ICC: (1) no financial support, directly or indirectly; (2) no collaboration; and (3) no further negotiations with other governments to "improve" the Statute. ... This approach is likely to maximize the chances that the ICC will wither and collapse, which should be our objective. The ICC is a fundamentally bad idea. It cannot be improved by technical fixes as the years pass.... We have alternative approaches and methods consistent with American national interests, as I have previously outlined, and we should follow them.

POSTSCRIPT

Should the United States Ratify the International Criminal Court Treaty?

The ICC treaty is, in part, an American product. The United States was a major force behind convening a conference to draft a treaty, with President Clinton issuing a clarion call during one commencement address for a permanent court that could try and punish those who committed war crimes and other abominations. Once at the conference in Rome, however, the United States retreated from the president's rhetorical position and sought to limit virtually any possibility that an American civilian or military leader would ever stand before the ICC's bar of justice. The debate yielded compromises that met many a reservation of the United States and some other countries. In the end, however, the conference opted to create a relatively strong court by a vote of 120 yes, 7 no (including China, India, and the United States), and 21 abstentions. UN Secretary General Kofi Annan told the delegates in Rome, "Two millennia ago one of this city's most famous sons, Marcus Tullius Cicero, declared that 'in the midst of arms, law stands mute.' As a result of what we are doing here today, there is real hope that that bleak statement will be less true in the future than it has been in the past." Annan's speech and other material related to the ICC can be found on the Internet at http://www.un.org/law/icc/index.html. Another very useful Internet site is http://www.iccnow.org/.

Some of the basic provisions of the ICC are

1. The court's jurisdiction includes genocide and a range of other crimes committed during international and internal wars. Such crimes must be "widespread and systematic" and committed as part of "state, organization, or group policy," not just as individual acts.
2. Except for genocide and complaints brought by the United Nations Security Council (UNSC), the ICC will not be able to prosecute alleged crimes unless either the state of nationality of the accused or the state where the crimes took place has ratified the treaty.
3. Original signatories will have a one-time ability to "opt out" of the court's jurisdiction for war crimes, but not genocide, for a period of seven years.
4. The UNSC can delay one prosecution for one year. The vote to delay will not be subject to veto.
5. The ICC will only be able to try cases when national courts have failed to work.

Once the treaty was adopted by the conference, it was opened to the world's countries for signature and ratification. The treaty will be open for accession (signature) by the world's countries until sometime in 2001. Once 60 countries have signed and ratified it, the treaty will go into effect. As of May 2001, representatives of 139 countries had signed the ICC treaty, and it had been ratified by 32 states, including such important countries as Canada, France, and Germany.

In the waning days of his administration, President Clinton directed a State Department representative to sign the ICC treaty on behalf of the United States. That act was mostly symbolic, however, and even Clinton warned that the "United States should have the chance to observe and assess the functioning of the Court, over time, before choosing to become subject to its jurisdiction. Given these concerns, I will not, and do not recommend that my successor [George W. Bush] submit the Treaty to the Senate for advice and consent until our fundamental concerns are satisfied." That caution was also symbolic, many believe, because President Bush's approach to international relations made it very unlikely that he would soon support the ICC, whatever Clinton would have recommended.

Technically, U.S. ratification of the ICC treaty and support of the ICC once it begins is not necessary for the court to function. But, in reality, the United States is the world's hegemonic power, and U.S. opposition to the court will almost certainly hinder its operations and could abort the full establishment of the ICC.

For further reading to help put the proposed ICC in the context of international law, see Geoffrey Robertson, *Crimes Against Humanity: The Struggle for Global Justice* (New Press, 2000) and Yves Beigbeder, *Judging War Criminals: The Politics of International Justice* (St. Martin's Press, 1999).

Worldwide Guide to Women in Leadership

This site is an excellent compilation of women who have served as party, legislative, and executive political leaders.

http://hjem.get2net.dk/Womeningovernments/

Centre for Economic and Social Studies on the Environment

The Centre for Economic and Social Studies on the Environment, which is located in Brussels, conducts multidisciplinary research on the qualitative and quantitative evaluation of sustainable development (economic-environmental interactions).

http://www.ulb.ac.be/ceese/

Exercising Your Rights of Political Protest in Washington, D.C.

This document, prepared by the Washington, D.C., chapter of the National Lawyer's Guild, provides commentary about what are and are not legal forms of protest in the United States.

http://www.nlg.org/manuals/protest_manual_dc.htm

PART 6

Normative, Social, and Environmental Issues

*W*hen all is said and done, policy is, or at least ought to be, about values. That is, how do we want our world to be? There are choices to make about what we want to do. It would be easy if these choices were clearly good versus evil. But things are not usually that simple, and the issues in this part present a series of conundrums related to human rights, social tolerance, and the environment.

- Would World Affairs Be More Peaceful If Women Dominated Politics?

- Is Violence as a Form of Protest on International Political Issues Always Wrong?

- Is Dangerous Global Warming Occurring?

ISSUE 16

Would World Affairs Be More Peaceful If Women Dominated Politics?

YES: Francis Fukuyama, from "Women and the Evolution of World Politics," *Foreign Affairs* (September/October 1998)

NO: Mary Caprioli, from "The Myth of Women's Pacifism," An Original Essay Written for This Volume (August 1999)

ISSUE SUMMARY

YES: Francis Fukuyama, the Hirst Professor of Public Policy at George Mason University, contends that a truly matriarchal world would be less prone to conflict and more conciliatory and co-operative than the largely male-dominated world that we live in now.

NO: Professor of political science Mary Caprioli contends that Fukuyama's argument is based on a number of unproven assumptions and that when women assume more political power and have a chance to act aggressively, they are as apt to do so as men are.

$\mathbf{P}$olitical scientists are just beginning to examine whether or not gender makes a difference in political attitudes and the actions of specific policymakers and whether or not any gender differences that may exist as a result have a biological origin or are a product of the divergent ways in which males and females are socialized. The ultimate question is whether or not an equal representation of women among policymakers—or, even more radically, a reversal of tradition that would put women firmly in charge of foreign and defense policy—would make an appreciable difference in global affairs. That is what this debate is about.

Certainly there is good evidence that women in the mass public are less likely to countenance war than men. In the United States, for example, polls going back as far as World War II and extending to the present have indicated that women are less ready than men to resort to war or to continue war. Examining the difference between males and females in their opinions about the use of force against Iraq during the Persian Gulf crisis yields some fascinating results. Polls of men and women in 11 countries found that in 10 of the countries

(Belgium, France, Germany, Great Britain, Israel, Italy, Japan, Mexico, Nigeria, and Russia), men were more likely than women to favor using force against Iraq. Only in Turkey were women more bellicose than men. The pro-war average across the 11 societies was 55 percent for men and 47 percent for women. In the United States, 69 percent of the men thought that the benefits of war would be worth the cost in lives; only 49 percent of the women agreed.

Yet the attitudes of women who are in positions of authority may be much different from those of other women. So far only about two dozen women have been elected to lead countries, although that number is slowly growing. Yet the relative scarcity of female international leaders makes comparisons with their male counterparts difficult. There can be no doubt, though, that able, sometimes aggressive leadership has been evident in such modern female heads of government as Israel's Golda Meir and India's Indira Gandhi.

Moreover, it would be grossly inaccurate to say, "Men are apt to favor war, women are not." The reality is that favoring or not favoring war in each of the 11 countries in the study noted above was much more associated with the country itself. There were some countries in which both men and women strongly favored war. In Israel, which was threatened, then attacked, by Iraq, an overwhelming majority of both men and women favored force. In other countries, a majority of both men and women opposed using force.

In a more extended sense, the following readings are also about equal political opportunity for men and women. There are two reasons to favor equal opportunity. The first is more philosophical and rests on justice. This argument holds that equity demands that women have the same ability as men to achieve political office. In most societies these days there are few people who would disagree, at least publicly, with this view.

The second argument in support of political gender equality is more controversial and at the heart of this debate. This is the disagreement over whether or not women would make a policy difference because they are inherently apt to have a different view of politics than men do. Many scholars, feminist and otherwise, agree that there is a deep-seated difference. Feminist scholar Betty Reardon suggests that "from the masculine perspective, peace for the most part has meant the absence of war and the prevention of armed conflict." She terms this "negative peace." By contrast, Reardon maintains that women think more in terms of "positive peace," which includes "conditions of social justice, economic equity and ecological balance." The implication of this is that in a world run much more by women than is now the case, military budgets would go down and budgets for social, educational, and environmental programs would go up. Even though he is not a feminist scholar, as such, Francis Fukuyama, author of the first of the following selections, would fit in with this school of thought.

There are other scholars, feminist and otherwise, who do not think that women and men have "hard-wired" political differences. For them, a matriarchal society would run generally the same as a patriarchal society, no matter what the issue. Mary Caprioli adheres to this line of thought in the second selection, and so the debate is joined.

Francis Fukuyama

 **YES**

Women and the Evolution
of World Politics

Chimpanzee Politics

In the world's largest captive chimp colony at the Burger's Zoo in Arnhem, Netherlands, a struggle worthy of Machiavelli unfolded during the late 1970s. As described by primatologist Frans de Waal, the aging alpha male of the colony, Yeroen, was gradually unseated from his position of power by a younger male, Luit. Luit could not have done this on the basis of his own physical strength, but had to enter into an alliance with Nikkie, a still younger male. No sooner was Luit on top, however, than Nikkie turned on him and formed a coalition with the deposed leader to achieve dominance himself. Luit remained in the background as a threat to his rule, so one day he was murdered by Nikkie and Yeroen, his toes and testicles littering the floor of the cage.

Jane Goodall became famous studying a group of about 30 chimps at the Gombe National Park in Tanzania in the 1960s, a group she found on the whole to be peaceful. In the 1970s, this group broke up into what could only be described as two rival gangs in the northern and southern parts of the range. The biological anthropologist Richard Wrangham with Dale Peterson in their 1996 book *Demonic Males* describes what happened next. Parties of four or five males from the northern group would go out, not simply defending their range, but often penetrating into the rival group's territory to pick off individuals caught alone or unprepared. The murders were often grisly, and they were celebrated by the attackers with hooting and feverish excitement. All the males and several of the females in the southern group were eventually killed, and the remaining females forced to join the northern group. The northern Gombe chimps had done, in effect, what Rome did to Carthage in 146 B.C.: extinguished its rival without a trace.

There are several notable aspects to these stories of chimp behavior. First, the violence. Violence within the same species is rare in the animal kingdom, usually restricted to infanticide by males who want to get rid of a rival's offspring and mate with the mother. Only chimps and humans seem to have a

From Francis Fukuyama, "Women and the Evolution of World Politics," *Foreign Affairs*, vol. 77, no. 5 (September/October 1998). Copyright © 1998 by The Council on Foreign Relations, Inc. Reprinted by permission of *Foreign Affairs*.

proclivity for routinely murdering peers. Second is the importance of coalitions and the politics that goes with coalition-building. Chimps, like humans, are intensely social creatures whose lives are preoccupied with achieving and maintaining dominance in status hierarchies. They threaten, plead, cajole, and bribe their fellow chimps to join with them in alliances, and their dominance lasts only as long as they can maintain these social connections.

Finally and most significantly, the violence and the coalition-building is primarily the work of males. Female chimpanzees can be as violent and cruel as the males at times; females compete with one another in hierarchies and form coalitions to do so. But the most murderous violence is the province of males, and the nature of female alliances is different. According to de Waal, female chimps bond with females to whom they feel some emotional attachment; the males are much more likely to make alliances for purely instrumental, calculating reasons. In other words, female chimps have relationships; male chimps practice realpolitik.

Chimpanzees are man's closest evolutionary relative, having descended from a common chimp-like ancestor less than five million years ago. Not only are they very close on a genetic level, they show many behavioral similarities as well. As Wrangham and Peterson note, of the 4,000 mammal and 10 million or more other species, only chimps and humans live in male-bonded, patrilineal communities in which groups of males routinely engage in aggressive, often murderous raiding of their own species. Nearly 30 years ago, the anthropologist Lionel Tiger suggested that men had special psychological resources for bonding with one another, derived from their need to hunt cooperatively, that explained their dominance in group-oriented activities from politics to warfare. Tiger was roundly denounced by feminists at the time for suggesting that there were biologically based psychological differences between the sexes, but more recent research, including evidence from primatology, has confirmed that male bonding is in fact genetic and predates the human species.

The Not-So-Noble Savage

It is all too easy to make facile comparisons between animal and human behavior to prove a polemical point, as did the socialists who pointed to bees and ants to prove that nature endorsed collectivism. Skeptics point out that human beings have language, reason, law, culture, and moral values that make them fundamentally different from even their closest animal relative. In fact, for many years anthropologists endorsed what was in effect a modern version of Rousseau's story of the noble savage: people living in hunter-gatherer societies were pacific in nature. If chimps and modern man had a common proclivity for violence, the cause in the latter case had to be found in civilization and not in human nature.

A number of authors have extended the noble savage idea to argue that violence and patriarchy were late inventions, rooted in either the Western Judeo-Christian tradition or the capitalism to which the former gave birth. Friedrich Engels anticipated the work of later feminists by positing the existence of a primordial matriarchy, which was replaced by a violent and repressive patriarchy only with the transition to agricultural societies. The problem with this theory is, as Lawrence Keeley points out in his book *War Before Civilization,* that the most comprehensive recent studies of violence in hunter-gatherer societies suggest that for them war was actually more frequent, and rates of murder higher, than for modern ones.

Surveys of ethnographic data show that only 10–13 percent of primitive societies never or rarely engaged in war or raiding; the others engaged in conflict either continuously or at less than yearly intervals. Closer examination of the peaceful cases shows that they were frequently refugee populations driven into remote locations by prior warfare or groups protected by a more advanced society. Of the Yanomamö tribesmen studied by Napoleon Chagnon in Venezuela, some 30 percent of the men died by violence; the !Kung San of the Kalahari desert, once characterized as the "harmless people," have a higher murder rate than New York or Detroit. The sad archaeological evidence from sites like Jebel Sahaba in Egypt, Talheim in Germany, or Roaix in France indicates that systematic mass killings of men, women, and children occurred in Neolithic times. The Holocaust, Cambodia, and Bosnia have each been described as a unique, and often as a uniquely modern, form of horror. Exceptional and tragic they are indeed, but with precedents stretching back tens if not hundreds of thousands of years.

It is clear that this violence was largely perpetrated by men. While a small minority of human societies have been matrilineal, evidence of a primordial matriarchy in which women dominated men, or were even relatively equal to men, has been hard to find. There was no age of innocence. The line from chimp to modern man is continuous.

It would seem, then, that there is something to the contention of many feminists that phenomena like aggression, violence, war, and intense competition for dominance in a status hierarchy are more closely associated with men than women. Theories of international relations like realism that see international politics as a remorseless struggle for power are in fact what feminists call a gendered perspective, describing the behavior of states controlled by men rather than states per se. A world run by women would follow different rules, it would appear, and it is toward that sort of world that all postindustrial or Western societies are moving. As women gain power in these countries, the latter should become less aggressive, adventurous, competitive, and violent.

The problem with the feminist view is that it sees these attitudes toward violence, power, and status as wholly the products of a patriarchal culture, whereas in fact it appears they are rooted in biology. This makes these attitudes harder to change in men and consequently in societies. Despite the rise of women, men will continue to play a major, if not dominant, part in the governance of postindustrial countries, not to mention less-developed ones. The realms of war and international politics in particular will remain controlled by men for longer than many feminists would like. Most important, the task of resocializing men to be more like women—that is, less violent—will run into limits. What is bred in the bone cannot be altered easily by changes in culture and ideology.

The Return of Biology

We are living through a revolutionary period in the life sciences. Hardly a week goes by without the discovery of a gene linked to a disease, condition, or behavior, from cancer to obesity to depression, with the promise of genetic therapies and even the outright manipulation of the human genome just around the corner. But while developments in molecular biology have been receiving the lion's share of the headlines, much progress has been made at the behavioral level as well. The past generation has seen a revival in Darwinian thinking about human psychology, with profound implications for the social sciences.

For much of this century, the social sciences have been premised on Emile Durkheim's dictum that social facts can be explained only by prior social facts and not by biological causes. Revolutions and wars are caused by social facts such as economic change, class inequalities, and shifting alliances. The standard social science model assumes that the human mind is the terrain of ideas, customs, and norms that are the products of man-made culture. Social reality is, in other words, socially constructed: if young boys like to pretend to shoot each other more than young girls, it is only because they have been socialized at an early age to do so.

The social-constructionist view, long dominant in the social sciences, originated as a reaction to the early misuse of Darwinism. Social Darwinists like Herbert Spencer or outright racists like Madsen Grant in the late nineteenth and early twentieth centuries used biology, specifically the analogy of natural selection, to explain and justify everything from class stratification to the domination of much of the world by white Europeans. Then Franz Boas, a Columbia anthropologist, debunked many of these theories of European racial superiority by, among other things, carefully measuring the head sizes of immigrant children and noting that they tended to converge with those of native Americans when fed an American diet. Boas, as well as his well-known students Margaret Mead and Ruth Benedict, argued that apparent differences between human groups could be laid at the doorstep of culture rather than nature. There were, moreover, no cultural universals by which Europeans or Americans could judge other cultures. So-called primitive peoples were not inferior, just different. Hence was born both the social constructivism and the cultural relativism with which the social sciences have been imbued ever since.

But there has been a revolution in modern evolutionary thinking. It has multiple roots; one was ethology, the comparative study of animal behavior. Ethologists like Konrad Lorenz began to notice similarities in behavior across a wide variety of animal species suggesting common evolutionary origins. Contrary to the cultural relativists, they found that not only was it possible to make important generalizations across virtually all human cultures (for example, females are more selective than males in their choice of sexual partners) but even across broad ranges of animal species. Major breakthroughs were made by William Hamilton and Robert Trivers in the 1960s and 1970s in explaining instances of altruism in the animal world not by some sort of instinct towards species survival but rather in terms of "selfish genes" (to use Richard Dawkins' phrase) that made social behavior in an individual animal's interest. Finally, advances in neurophysiology have shown that the brain is not a Lockean tabula rasa waiting to be filled with cultural content, but rather a highly modular organ whose components have been adapted prior to birth to suit the needs of socially oriented primates. Humans are hard-wired to act in certain predictable ways.

The sociobiology that sprang from these theoretical sources tried to provide a deterministic Darwinian explanation for just about everything, so it was perhaps inevitable that a reaction would set in against it as well. But while the term sociobiology has gone into decline, the neo-Darwinian thinking that spawned it has blossomed under the rubric of evolutionary psychology or anthropology and is today an enormous arena of new research and discovery.

Unlike the pseudo-Darwininsts at the turn of the century, most contemporary biologists do not regard race or ethnicity as biologically significant categories. This stands to reason: the different human races have been around only for the past hundred thousand years or so, barely a blink of the eye in evolutionary time. As countless authors have pointed out, race is largely a socially constructed category: since all races can (and do) interbreed, the boundary lines between them are often quite fuzzy.

The same is not true, however, about sex. While some gender roles are indeed socially constructed, virtually all reputable evolutionary biologists today think there are profound differences between the sexes that are genetically rather than culturally rooted, and that these differences extend beyond the body into the realm of the mind. Again, this stands to reason from a Darwinian point of view: sexual reproduction has been going on not for thousands but hundreds of millions of years. Males and females compete not just against their environment but against one another in a process that Darwin labeled "sexual selection," whereby each sex seeks to maximize its own fitness by choosing certain kinds of mates. The psychological strategies that result from this never-ending arms race between men and women are different for each sex.

In no area is sex-related difference clearer than with respect to violence and aggression. A generation ago, two psychologists, Eleanor Maccoby and Carol Jacklin, produced an authoritative volume on what was then empirically known about differences between the sexes. They showed that certain stereotypes about gender, such as the assertion that girls were more suggestible or had lower self-esteem, were just that, while others, like the idea that girls were less competitive, could not be proven one way or another. On one issue, however, there was virtually no disagreement in the hundreds of studies on the subject: namely, that boys were more aggressive, both verbally and physically, in their dreams, words, and actions than girls. One comes to a similar conclusion by looking at crime statistics. In every known culture, and from what we know of virtually all historical time periods, the vast majority of crimes, particularly violent crimes, are committed by men. Here there is also apparently a genetically determined age specificity to violent aggression: crimes are overwhelmingly committed by young men between the ages of 15 and 30. Perhaps young men are everywhere socialized to behave violently, but this evidence, from different cultures and times, suggests that there is some deeper level of causation at work.

At this point in the discussion, many people become uncomfortable and charges of "biological determinism" arise. Don't we know countless women who are stronger, larger, more decisive, more violent, or more competitive than their male counterparts? Isn't the proportion of female criminals rising relative to males? Isn't work becoming less physical, making sexual differences unimportant? The answer to all of these questions is yes: again, no reputable evolutionary biologist would deny that culture also shapes behavior in countless critical ways and can often overwhelm genetic predispositions. To say that there is a genetic basis for sex difference is simply to make a statistical assertion that the bell curve describing the distribution of a certain characteristic is shifted over a little for men as compared with women. The two curves will overlap for the most part, and there will be countless individuals in each population who will have more of any given characteristic than those of the other sex. Biology is not destiny, as tough-minded female leaders like Margaret Thatcher, Indira Gandhi, and Golda Meir have proven. (It is worth pointing out, however, that in male-dominated societies, it is these kinds of unusual women who will rise to the top.) But the statistical assertion also suggests that broad populations of men and women, as opposed to exceptional individuals, will act in certain predictable ways. It also suggests that these populations are not infinitely plastic in the way that their behavior can be shaped by society.

Feminists and Power Politics

There is by now an extensive literature on gender and international politics and a vigorous feminist subdiscipline within the field of international relations theory based on the work of scholars like Ann Tickner, Sara Ruddick, Jean Bethke Elshtain, Judith Shapiro, and others. This literature is too diverse to describe succinctly, but it is safe to say that much of it was initially concerned with understanding how international politics is "gendered," that is, run by men to serve male interests and interpreted by other men, consciously and unconsciously, according to male perspectives. Thus, when a realist theorist like Hans Morganthau or Kenneth Waltz argues that states seek to maximize power, they think that they are describing a universal human characteristic when, as Tickner points out, they are portraying the behavior of states run by men.

Virtually all feminists who study international politics seek the laudable goal of greater female participation in all aspects of foreign relations, from executive mansions and foreign ministries to militaries and universities. They disagree as to whether women should get ahead in politics by demonstrating traditional masculine virtues of toughness, aggression, competitiveness, and the willingness to use force when necessary, or whether they should move the very agenda of politics away from male preoccupations with hierarchy and domination. This ambivalence was demonstrated in the feminist reaction to Margaret Thatcher, who by any account was far tougher and more determined than any of the male politicians she came up against. Needless to say, Thatcher's conservative politics did not endear her to most feminists, who much prefer a Mary Robinson [President of Ireland] or Gro Harlem Brundtland [first female prime minister of Norway] as their model of a female leader, despite—or because of—the fact that Thatcher had beaten men at their own game.

Both men and women participate in perpetuating the stereotypical gender identities that associate men with war and competition and women with peace and cooperation. As sophisticated feminists like Jean Bethke Elshtain have pointed out, the traditional dichotomy between the male "just warrior" marching to war and the female "beautiful soul" marching for peace is frequently transcended in practice by women intoxicated by war and by men repulsed by its cruelties. But like many stereotypes, it rests on a truth, amply confirmed by much of the new research in evolutionary biology. Wives and mothers can enthusiastically send their husbands and sons off to war; like Sioux women, they can question their manliness for failing to go into battle or themselves torture prisoners. But statistically speaking it is primarily men who enjoy the experience of aggression and the camaraderie it brings and who revel in the ritualization of war that is, as the anthropologist Robin Fox puts it, another way of understanding diplomacy.

A truly matriarchal world, then, would be less prone to conflict and more conciliatory and cooperative than the one we inhabit now. Where the new biology parts company with feminism is in the causal explanation it gives for this difference in sex roles. The ongoing revolution in the life sciences has almost totally escaped the notice of much of the social sciences and humanities, particularly the parts of the academy concerned with feminism, postmodernism, cultural studies, and the like. While there are some feminists who believe that sex differences have a natural basis, by far the majority are committed to the idea that men and women are psychologically identical, and that any differences in behavior, with regard to violence or any other characteristic, are the result of some prior social construction passed on by the prevailing culture.

The Democratic and Feminine Peace

Once one views international relations through the lens of sex and biology, it never again looks the same. It is very difficult to watch Muslims and Serbs in Bosnia, Hutus and Tutsis in Rwanda, or militias from Liberia and Sierra Leone to Georgia and Afghanistan divide themselves up into what seem like indistinguishable male-bonded groups in order to systematically slaughter one another, and not think of the chimps at Gombe.

The basic social problem that any society faces is to control the aggressive tendencies of its young men. In hunter-gatherer societies, the vast preponderance of violence is over sex, a situation that continues to characterize domestic violent crime in contemporary postindustrial societies. Older men in the community have generally been responsible for socializing younger ones by ritualizing their aggression, often by directing it toward enemies outside the community. Much of that external violence can also be over women. Modern historians assume that the Greeks and Trojans could not possibly have fought a war for ten years over Helen, but many primitive societies like the Yanomamö do exactly that. With the spread of agriculture 10,000 years ago, however, and the accumulation of wealth and land, war turned toward the acquisition of material goods. Channeling aggression outside the community may not lower societies' overall rate of violence, but it at least offers them the possibility of domestic peace between wars.

The core of the feminist agenda for international politics seems fundamentally correct: the violent and aggressive tendencies of men have to be controlled, not simply by redirecting them to external aggression but by constraining those impulses through a web of norms, laws, agreements, contracts, and the like. In addition, more women need to be brought into the domain of international politics as leaders, officials, soldiers, and voters. Only by participating fully in global politics can women both defend their own interests and shift the underlying male agenda.

The feminization of world politics has, of course, been taking place gradually over the past hundred years, with very positive effects. Women have won the right to vote and participate in politics in all developed countries, as well as in many developing countries, and have exercised that right with increasing energy. In the United States and other rich countries, a pronounced gender gap with regard to foreign policy and national security issues endures. American women have always been less supportive than American men of U.S. involvement in war, including World War II, Korea, Vietnam, and the Persian Gulf War, by an average margin of seven to nine percent. They are also consistently less supportive of defense spending and the use of force abroad. In a 1995 Roper survey conducted for the Chicago Council on Foreign Relations, men favored U.S. intervention in Korea in the event of a North Korean attack by a margin of 49 to 40 percent, while women were opposed by a margin of 30 to 54 percent. Similarly, U.S. military action against Iraq in the event it invaded Saudi Arabia was supported by men by a margin of 62 to 31 percent and opposed by women by 43 to 45 percent. While 54 percent of men felt it important to maintain superior world wide military power, only 45 percent of women agreed. Women, moreover, are less likely than men to see force as a legitimate tool for resolving conflicts.

It is difficult to know how to account for this gender gap; certainly, one cannot move from biology to voting behavior in a single step. Observers have suggested various reasons why women are less willing to use military force than men, including their role as mothers, the fact that many women are feminists (that is, committed to a left-of-center agenda that is generally hostile to U.S. intervention), and partisan affiliation (more women vote Democratic than men). It is unnecessary to know the reason for the correlation between gender and antimilitarism, however, to predict that increasing female political participation will probably make the United States and other democracies less inclined to use power around the world as freely as they have in the past.

Will this shift toward a less status- and military-power-oriented world be a good thing? For relations between states in the so-called democratic zone of peace, the answer is yes. Consideration of gender adds a great deal to the vigorous and interesting debate over the correlation between democracy and peace that has taken place in the past decade. The "democratic peace" argument, which underlies the foreign policy of the Clinton administration as well as its predecessors, is that democracies tend not to fight one another. While the empirical claim has been contested, the correlation between the degree of consolidation of liberal democratic institutions and interdemocratic peace would seem to be one of the few nontrivial generalizations one can make about world politics. Democratic peace theorists have been less persuasive about the reasons democracies are pacific toward one another. The reasons usually cited—the rule of law, respect for individual rights, the commercial nature of most democracies, and the like—are undoubtedly correct. But there is another factor that has generally not been taken into account: developed democracies also tend to be more feminized than authoritarian states, in terms of expansion of female franchise and participation in political decision-making. It should therefore surprise no one that the historically unprecedented shift in the sexual basis of politics should lead to a change in international relations.

The Reality of Aggressive Fantasies

On the other hand, if gender roles are not simply socially constructed but rooted in genetics, there will be limits to how much international politics can change. In anything but a totally feminized world, feminized policies could be a liability.

Some feminists talk as if gender identities can be discarded like an old sweater, perhaps by putting young men through mandatory gender studies courses when they are college freshmen. Male attitudes on a host of issues, from child-rearing and housework to "getting in touch with your feelings," have changed dramatically in the past couple of generations due to social pressure. But socialization can accomplish only so much, and efforts to fully feminize young men will probably be no more successful than the Soviet Union's efforts to persuade its people to work on Saturdays on behalf of the heroic Cuban and Vietnamese people. Male tendencies to band together for competitive purposes, seek to dominate status hierarchies, and act out aggressive fantasies toward one another can be rechanneled but never eliminated.

Even if we can assume peaceful relations between democracies, the broader world scene will still be populated by states led by the occasional [bloody dictator]. Machiavelli's critique of Aristotle was that the latter did not take foreign policy into account in building his model of a just city: in a system of competitive states, the best regimes adopt the practices of the worst in order to survive. So even if the democratic, feminized, postindustrial world has evolved into a zone of peace where struggles are more economic than military, it will still have to deal with those parts of the world run by young, ambitious, unconstrained men. If a future Saddam Hussein is not only sitting on the world's oil supplies but is armed to the hilt with chemical, biological, and nuclear weapons, we might be better off being led by women like Margaret Thatcher than, say, Gro Harlem Brundtland. Masculine policies will still be required, though not necessarily masculine leaders. . . .

Living Like Animals?

In Wrangham and Peterson's *Demonic Males*..., the authors come to the pessimistic conclusion that nothing much has changed since early hominids branched off from the primordial chimp ancestor five million years ago. Group solidarity is still based on aggression against other communities; social cooperation is undertaken to achieve higher levels of organized violence. Robin Fox has argued that military technology has developed much faster than man's ability to ritualize violence and direct it into safer channels. The Gombe chimps could kill only a handful of others; modern man can vaporize tens of millions.

While the history of the first half of the twentieth century does not give us great grounds for faith in the possibility of human progress, the situation is not nearly as bleak as these authors would have us believe. Biology, to repeat, is not destiny. Rates of violent homicide appear to be lower today than during mankind's long hunter-gatherer period, despite gas ovens and nuclear weapons. Contrary to the thrust of postmodernist thought, people cannot free themselves entirely from biological nature. But by accepting the fact that people have natures that are often evil, political, economic, and social systems can be designed to mitigate the effects of man's baser instincts.

... [To that end,] liberal democracy and market economies work well because, unlike socialism, radical feminism, and other utopian schemes, they do not try to change human nature. Rather, they accept biologically grounded nature as a given and seek to constrain it through institutions, laws, and norms. It does not always work, but it is better than living like animals.

Mary Caprioli

The Myth of Women's Pacifism

In a recent article in *Foreign Affairs,* Francis Fukuyama asserts that a more feminized world run by women would be more peaceful. Indeed, he concludes that biology is not destiny and that it is better not to live like animals. Presumably, this means that men can learn to be more peaceful in their behavior, and this new pacifism on the part of men would translate into a more peaceful world. What Fukuyama seems to eliminate from his analysis is that if men change their behavior, then so too would women. If a more egalitarian world would change men's behavior, then it would most likely change women's behavior, too. If men were to become more peaceful, women would potentially become more aggressive.

Fukuyama's argument is based on a number of assumptions. In order to conclude that a future world would be more peaceful if only men acted more like women, one must assume that a gender gap exists in support for the use of force. Furthermore, an acceptance of a gender gap assumes a dichotomy based on gender. Not only must there exist only two genders divided by sex, but there must also be a universality of experience for women and men across cultures. In order to understand Fukuyama's argument, it is necessary to have an understanding of gender and to explore the evidence for proclaiming the existence of a gender gap. Any prediction characterizing a future world must be made only after acquiring such understandings.

Gender

Gender is crucial to any study supporting and explaining the meaning of gender, in which gender is found to be a cause of state bellicosity. Is gender a function of genital-type, to each person's level of testosterone, or the extent to which each individual had been socialized into accepting standards of feminine and masculine attitudes, which would be a cultural measure of gender?

Gender is the crux of any argument based on the existence of a difference between men and women—the existence of a gender gap. We must, therefore, examine whether or not gender is a useful category of analysis. The literature on gender, especially within anthropology, is prolific yet surprisingly monolithic.

All define gender as a culturally construed category. If a definition of gender is based on culture, then gender is not a universal category of analysis.

Indeed, the term "gender" is used to designate socially constructed roles attributed to women and men. These gender roles are learned, change over time, and vary both within and between cultures. Gender issues, therefore, have to do with differences in how women and men are supposed to act. In other words, gender definitions control and restrict behaviors. As Klaus Theweleit highlights in his 1993 piece "The Bomb's Womb and the Genders of War" in the edited volume *Gendering War Talk,* women traditionally have not had the power to act violently, which might explain the identified gender gap in support for war. The culturally proscribed role of women based on gender determines women's alternatives. In this instance, the use of violence is simply not an option for women. Women, therefore, are not necessarily choosing not to act violently but do not have the choice to act violently—a very important distinction.

Indeed, women who have obtained the power to act violently have done so. These leaders include prime ministers Margaret Thatcher (Great Britain), Indira Gandhi (India), Golda Meir (Israel), Khalida Zia (Bangladesh), Maria Liberia-Peters (Netherlands-Antilles), Gro Harlem Brundtland (Norway), and Benazir Bhutto (Pakistan). Using Stuart Bremer's 1996 Militarized Interstate Dispute (MID) data set, which covers the time period from 1816 until 1992, it is possible to examine the level of violence sanctioned by female leaders in comparison to male leaders.

Only twenty-four states have placed a female leader in office since 1900, with the first female leader obtaining power in 1960. In this instance, a female leader is defined as a president, prime minister, or any other decision-maker who is essentially the 'decision-maker of last resort' on decisions to use force and other high-level international decisions. Edith Cresson, who was premier of France in 1991–1992, is therefore not considered a leader in this discussion because that position is one of significantly lesser importance than that of the French president, who was a male.

We can compare the behavior of female and male leaders from 1960 until 1992 using MID. MID includes a variable for the level of hostility used during the crisis. Hostility level is divided into five levels coded as follows: 1) no militarized action, 2) threat to use force, 3) display of force, 4) use of force, and 5) war. Both female and male leaders rely on the fourth category, the use of force, most frequently. Furthermore, both female and male leaders' average use of violence is equal. According to this evidence, female leaders are no more peaceful than their male counterparts.

Of course, critics would argue that female leaders in a male world must act more aggressively in order to prove themselves. According to this argument women are still considered to be by nature more pacific than men are. Because women must operate in a social and political environment that has been defined, structured and dominated by men for centuries, they must recondition themselves to act more violently in order to gain power in a "man's world." On the other hand, women's assent to power and growing equality in relation to men may free women from gender stereotypes restricting their behavior. In

Table 1

States With Female Leaders Since 1900–1994

STATE	LEADER	YEARS IN OFFICE
Argentina	Isabel Perón	1974–1976
Bangladesh	Khalida Zia	1991–1996
Bolivia	Lidia Gueiler Tejada	1979–1980
Burundi	Sylvie Kingi	1993–1994
Canada	Kim Campbell	1993
Central African Republic	Elisabeth Domitien	1975–1976
Dominica	Mary Eugenia Charles	1980–1995
Haiti	Ertha Pascal-Trouillot	1990–1991
India	Indira Gandhi	1966–1977
		1980–1984
Israel	Golda Meir	1969–1974
Lithuania	Kazimiera Prunskiene	1990–1991
Malta	Agatha Barbara	1982–1987
Netherlands Antilles	Maria Liberia-Peters	1984–1985
		1988–1994
Nicaragua	Violeta Chamorro	1990–1997
Norway	Gro Harlem Brundtland	1981
		1986–1989
		1990–1996
Pakistan	Benazir Bhutto	1988–1990
		1993–1996
Philippines	Corazon C. Aquino	1986–1992
Poland	Hanna Suchocka	1993
Portugal	Maria de Lourdes Pintasilgo	1979
Rwanda	Agathe Uwilingiyimana	1993–1994
Sri Lanka	Sirimavo Bandaranaike	1960–1965
		1970–1977
Turkey	Tansu Ciller	1993–1996
United Kingdom	Margaret Thatcher	1979–1990
Yugoslavia	Milka Planinc	1982–1986

this more equal world, women become free to exercise different alternatives, including the option of using violence.

The power and role of women varies across cultures because power is based on these culturally dependent gender roles. Because all people are born into, and socialized to a particular culture, the argument for biological determinism becomes impossible to prove. The only way to prove conclusively that women are more peaceful would be to raise a number of baby girls from birth in a cultural vacuum. Such an experiment would be unethical at best. Scholars, therefore, must speculate as to the 'nature' of women. For example, do women in power ignore and overcome inherent gender-based characteristics in order to gain and maintain power? Did Margaret Thatcher have to keep her natural tendency to be peaceful in constant check? Conversely, do people who are attracted to power share basic characteristics regardless of gender? Is Thatcher's biological tendency toward violence no different from a 'normal' tendency of any human's tendency toward violence?

The adoption of gender as a category of analysis implies a universality of experience across cultures and over time. This assumption, especially when espoused by educated and predominantly Western and European women, is as biased as some men's assumption of a universal human experience based on a male perspective. Placing women at the center of analysis is no less biased than focusing on men. Furthermore, the acceptance of this dichotomy between the only two recognized genders implies the acceptance that there do exist biological behavioral differences between the genders—an assumption that remains unproven.

Recognizing the exclusion of the female gender, as culturally defined, in most international relations literature is important to understanding the assumptions within existing research. To assume that including two genders or that taking the female-gender perspective will rectify the problems in current research and society is problematic, for both assume a universality of experience. As Third World feminists have clearly detailed, the experience of women is not universal. As scholars we must, therefore, recognize that the absence of a gendered analysis or conversely, the exclusive reliance on gendered analyses is a bias within research. We must understand that classifying an individual's behavior on the basis of gender is not a valid assumption.

Beyond the scope of this discussion, but important to note, is the argument that there are more than two genders. Arguments identifying a gender gap associate gender with sexuality. Furthermore, gender is assumed to include only two genders: the mythical male and female. If gender is equated with sexuality then children, the aged, especially post-menopausal women, gays, and lesbians would all constitute different genders. And, how would hermaphrodites —those 'sexless' people according to definitions of gender as male/female who are 'assigned' a sex at birth—be categorized?

Following a definition of gender based on sex or at least male and female sex organs, gender/sex differences should be the genesis of power inequality between women and men. These gender differences would necessarily have to be universal both between and within cultures. Yet, research conclusively demonstrates that gender changes over time within cultures and is not consistent among different cultures. Nonetheless, scholars continue to attempt to show a gender gap in the support for the use of force.

Often, this feminine pacifism is linked to women's maternal qualities and more specifically to their ability to have children. This argument is prejudiced in that it discounts men's 'maternal' instincts toward their children. As with the argument for two sexes, there exists a gray area in this argument about women's maternal instincts. For example, how would a single man who adopts a child be classified—or women who are infertile—or women who choose never to have children? Would the single dad not have any 'maternal' characteristics while assuming that women who choose not to have children possess 'maternal' characteristics by virtue of being female?

After examining the numerous gray areas surrounding much of the argument in support for women's pacifism, the argument seems rather thin. Yet, some studies do show that women seem to be less supportive of the use of violence than men. Of course, other groups of people including African Americans are also less supportive of the use of violence than are white men.

Gender Gap

All evidence in support for the existence of a gender gap comes from public opinion surveys of the Western world and in particular of the United States and the United Kingdom. The women of these countries can hardly be representative of women worldwide. In addition, the size of this identified gender gap varies from study to study. Another shortcoming of public opinion surveys is that women are more likely to indicate no opinion in public opinion surveys or merely fail to voice support for war. Little mention is made of political scientist John Mueller's admonition that not voicing support for a war is not the same as opposing it. In this instance, women might be constrained for voicing support for the use of force by gender stereotypes, so they offer no opinion.

Beyond the problems associated with public opinion surveys lie other challenges to a gender-gap theory for the support of violence. For instance, Nancy E. McGlen and Meredith Reid Sarkees in their 1993 book *Women in Foreign Policy: The Insiders* find varying degrees of a gender gap amongst the masses but none with women working within the State Department or the Defense Department. Some scholars might argue that women in the State and Defense Departments are not representative of women in general, or that these women might be forced to act violently to prove themselves in a predominantly male arena, or that they must adhere to traditional, institutional roles. Such arguments may be countered by the idea that these women are free to act violently —they have the opportunity to act violently and they do.

Not only do scholars challenge the existence of a gender gap but also the reasons for a gender gap. Some scholars suggest that the gender gap is created only by those women who identify with the women's movement. This argument suggests that it is not some inherent quality of women that creates a gender gap in support for the use of force but that women who happen to adhere to a feminist ideology of pacifism are more pacifist much in the same way that Democrats tend to be more pacific than Republicans. In keeping with Fukuyama's argument, it would be prudent, therefore, to encourage people to be Democrats in order to ensure world peace. This task should be less difficult than changing every culture of the world to have men change their behavior to act in the way women supposedly do—by not acting violently—and for women's supposed behavior to remain unchanged—to remain pacific.

A parallel discussion to the argument of women's nature would be asking whether or not people are born Democrat. Are party ideologies an inherent characteristic of some individuals, or are some individuals socialized into accepting the ideology of the Democrats? This is similar to questioning whether pacifism is an inherent quality of women or if women are socialized into being more pacific.

Others argue that any current gender gap associated with support for the commitment of armed forces or for war would be eradicated by the inclusion of more women in active duty within the armed forces. This argument follows the one outlined above in that women are not able to act violently and are traditionally excluded from activities and professions that include violence. Once women are included in active duty within the armed forces, they will not only achieve a certain level of equality but will also be free to act violently and support the use of violence.

Indeed, a group's relative position of power within society may determine its proclivity toward peaceful conflict resolution rather than some inherent quality. For example, John Mueller in his numerous research and public opinion surveys found that African Americans were more pacifistic in that as a group, African Americans were largely against escalation and for withdrawal in their general support for World War II, the Korean War, the Vietnam War, and the Persian Gulf War. According to this logic, one's placement in the hierarchy of power would best predict one's support for war as evidenced by women's and African Americans' more dovish nature.

Mark Tessler and Ina Warriner in an article in the January 1997 issue of *World Politics* argue that there is no evidence to show that women are less militaristic than men are. They do, however, find that individuals who are more supportive of equality between women and men are also less supportive of violence as a means of resolving conflict. This argument suggests that the relationship between more pacifist attitudes and international conflict rests upon the degree of gender equality that characterizes a society. Those who express greater concern for the status and role of women, and particularly for equality between women and men, are more likely than other individuals to believe that the international disputes in which their country is involved should be resolved through diplomacy and compromise. In other words, societies that have values that are less gender-based should be more pacific in their international behavior.

This argument that more gender-neutral societies are less internationally bellicose is similar to the theory outlined above that argues that people are more pacifist based on their position in society. In either situation, a society that is hierarchical in nature because it is based on prejudice against such classifications as gender and race will be more internationally bellicose. Once the social hierarchy is abolished in that all people gain the freedom to act as they choose, then differences among separate classifications of people will be eliminated. For instance, women and African Americans may become more aggressive as they gain more equality, more power. So too, may men become more pacific as they are freed from gender stereotypes that demand men to be aggressive.

Admittedly, I am no expert on chimpanzees. I can, however, speculate that female chimps might be more aggressive if they had the opportunity to act aggressively. Within the animal kingdom, power is often based on size. With humans, the base of power varies from physical size, to the size of one's bank account, to the size of one's intellect. Women, therefore, have an increasingly greater opportunity to act violently, an opportunity that her chimpanzee sisters may not enjoy.

The Future

The future may not be as rosy as Fukuyama suggests, at least not in terms of a global pacifism brought about by the increasing equality of women. Of course, equality in itself seems to be a positive force if only in freeing individuals to act according to their desires rather than by being restricted by cultural stereotypes related to, and defined by gender. This new freedom to act, however, does not necessarily translate into a global peace.

Fukuyama fleetingly mentions that the number of women incarcerated for violent crimes is increasing in proportion to that of men. The important question remains unanswered: Why are more women committing violent crimes? As American society becomes more egalitarian with regard to the sexes, women are gaining more power. This power may not be directed toward pacifist, nurturing ideals. Lord Acton wrote, "Power tends to corrupt, and absolute power corrupts absolutely." Perhaps he was correct.

POSTSCRIPT

Would World Affairs Be More Peaceful If Women Dominated Politics?

Studies of biopolitics, ethology, gender genetics, and other related approaches are just beginning to probe the connection between biology and politics. Also, the so-called nature-versus-nurture debate continues and presents some fascinating questions. Bear in mind that neither Fukuyama nor Caprioli (nor, for that matter, any other serious scholar) argues that "biology is destiny." Rather, all scholars recognize that human behavior is a mix of socialization and genetic coding. It is the ratio of that mix and its manifestations that are the points of controversy. Fukuyama clearly believes that genetics plays a strong role. Caprioli assigns a much greater role to socialization than Fukuyama does in accounting for the fact that women seem less aggressive than men.

There are a number of good books on the general topic of women and gender as they relate to world politics. These books include Vivienne Jabri and Eleanor O'Gorman, eds., *Women, Culture, and International Relations* (Lynne Rienner, 1998); J. Ann Tickner, *Gender in International Relations: Feminist Perspectives on Achieving Global Security* (Columbia University Press, 1994); Jill Sterns, *Gender and International Relations: An Introduction* (Rutgers University Press, 1998); and V. Spike Peterson, ed., *Gendered States: Feminist (Re)Visions of International Relations Theory* (Lynne Rienner, 1992).

Fukuyama suspects that males tend to act like males and females tend to act like females largely because of evolutionary biology. For a classic ethological view, read Desmond Morris, *The Naked Ape* (Dell, 1976) and Robert Ardrey, *The Territorial Imperative* (Atheneum, 1966). This line of thinking has many critics, some of whom directly dispute what Fukuyama has argued. More on this perspective can be found in Barbara Ehrenreich and Katha Pollitt, "Fukuyama's Follies," *Foreign Affairs* (January 1999).

Whatever the reality may be, its implications are important because women are increasingly coming to play leading roles. More on this change can be found in Jane S. Jaquette, "Women in Power: From Tokenism to Critical Mass," *Foreign Policy* (Fall 1997). During the past few decades, women have led such important countries as Great Britain, India, and Israel. Just a few short years ago a first was reached when, in Bangladesh, the choice for a country's prime minister came down to two women. Another breakthrough occurred when Madeleine Albright became the first female secretary of state for the United States. For studies of women in foreign policy leadership positions, read Nancy E. McGlen and Meredith Reid Sarkees's *The Status of Women in Foreign Policy* (Headline Series, 1995) and *Women in Foreign Policy* (Routledge, 1993).

ISSUE 17

Is Violence as a Form of Protest on International Political Issues Always Wrong?

YES: Satish Kumar, from "Can the Use of Violence Ever Be Justified in the Environmental Struggle?" *The Ecologist* (November 2000)

NO: Jake Bowers, from "Can the Use of Violence Ever Be Justified in the Environmental Struggle?" *The Ecologist* (November 2000)

ISSUE SUMMARY

YES: Satish Kumar, editor of *Resurgence* magazine and director of Schumacher College in the United Kingdom, argues that it is inherently wrong to try to overcome wrong—even wrong backed by violence—with violence or counterviolence.

NO: Jake Bowers, an activist on behalf of the Romani people, commonly known as Gypsies, argues that sometimes violence against objects, rather than people, is justified.

I t is doubtful that anyone, at least anyone without a deep authoritarian streak, would take a stand against citizen activism in politics at every level—local, national, and international. Indeed, from political leaders, academics, and many other sources, there is a constant clarion call to all to get active in politics instead of staying on the sidelines. "We must be more than an audience, more even than actors. We must be authors of the history," Madeleine K. Albright told Americans as she began her tenure as U.S. secretary of state.

There are even those who condemn bystanders as facilitators of the continuation or advent of evil. The Reverend Martin Luther King, Jr., in his "Letter from Birmingham Jail," wrote, "We will have to repent in this generation not merely for the vitriolic words and actions of bad people, but for the appalling silence of the good people." Similarly, President John F. Kennedy told Peace Corps volunteers, "Dante once said that the hottest places in hell are reserved for those who in a period of moral crisis maintain their neutrality."

There can be little doubt that citizen activism can be effective. In a democracy, voting for candidates is the most common way for citizens to affect policy. Working on a candidate's behalf, donating money to campaigns, and other election-related activities are also important. Certainly, it is the case that elected leaders do not always follow through with their campaign promises. Nevertheless, it is also true that once in office, elected leaders do often practice what they preached during the campaign. Thus, who gets elected does influence policy, no matter what the cynics might say.

This connection between citizen voting and policy is being made even more important by the growth of democracy worldwide. Since 1972 one organization, Freedom House, has been rating national governments as free (democratic), partly free, and not free. In that time both the number of democratic governments and their percentage of all national governments globally have increased steadily. This likely means that not only does democratic activism work but it is available to more people in more countries than it was not long ago.

Beyond activity connected with elections, there is a wide array of other actions that individuals and groups can take to try to influence policy. Sit-ins, marching, boycotts, and other demonstrations can often be effective. Students have often been important agents of political change through direct action. The sum of millions of individual actions—ranging from burning draft cards, to holding massive demonstrations in front of the White House, to students' protesting on U.S. campuses—helped end American involvement in Vietnam. Consumer boycotts can also play a part in influencing policy. Individuals have made a difference by refusing to eat tuna fish that does not bear the "dolphin safe" label, for example.

At some point, these efforts usually move to a point of confrontation with others. During the Vietnam War, some war protestors took relatively mild actions, like sitting in the offices of campus administrators. There was also a whole range of violent actions, ranging from hurling rotten fruit at offending politicians to setting off bombs that destroyed property and sometimes lives. For example, four antiwar activists, two of whom were students at the University of Wisconsin, Madison, set off a huge homemade bomb in 1970 at the site of the Army Math Research Center on campus. A graduate student died in the blast, and three other students were injured. At the extreme, protests can become open, armed rebellion seeking to topple the government. The Vietnam protests never approached that level, but protests in other countries on other issues have brought governments down.

This issue addresses the proper boundaries of political activity. When, if ever, is it appropriate to take the kind of direct action that is at some level illegal, whether that means trespassing to paint antiwar slogans on an Army recruiting station or planting a bomb that demolishes the recruiting center and perhaps kills recruiters or even innocent bystanders?

The debate between Satish Kumar and Jake Bowers in the following selections should stimulate your thoughts on this matter of limits. Violence is never the answer, Kumar argues. Bowers disagrees; violence should be a last resort, he grants, and should not be directed against people. But, he concludes, there is a point at which the ends justify violent means.

Satish Kumar

 **YES**

Can the Use of Violence Ever Be Justified in the Environmental Struggle?

[Jake Bowers] and I probably agree that our industrial, technological and capitalist society is a violent society. It is inflicting dreadful destruction on nature. Modern society behaves as if it is at war against nature. Soil, forests, oceans and animals are treated as if they have no integrity and no meaning. All this, we agree.

But where I part company with [Mr. Bowers] is in the methods used to deal with this violence. People like [him] at Earth First! in the UK and in the USA seem to think that [they] can overcome violence with more violence. [The] actions [of those people] give the impression that by inflicting destruction on people, or the property of people, who are violent to nature, [they] will be able to transform the situation. I disagree with this position entirely.

I disagree on practical as well as philosophical grounds. Let us start with the practical. The forces [Mr. Bowers is] fighting against are much more powerful, better trained and have greater resources than a small band of militant, radical activists can ever muster. The police, army and the courts have years of experience in the field of law and order—they are fully equipped to suppress your actions. Police can handle violent protesters more easily, because they are trained to do it, whereas they don't know how to handle non-violent protesters. Therefore, the success of violent methods is doubtful.

[Mr. Bowers] may enjoy short-term TV exposure and media headlines, but even the media are pillars of the polluting society. They will sensationalise [his] actions and present [his] case with distortions. Furthermore, only a small number of people are ever going to feel able to use violent methods. So [Mr. Bowers is] limiting the number of participants who can join [his] actions. If non-violent techniques of protest were used, many more people would be able to join [him.] So, by resorting to violence, [he is] reducing the scope of people's participation.

There is no real distinction between violence to people and violence to property. Violence is ultimately violence. [Mr. Bowers's] opponents are inflicting violence on nature; they might also claim that [he is] using violence to natural property. But even if [he] were successful in [his] violent methods, it is, in my view, philosophically, morally and ethically wrong. Fire cannot extinguish fire. Violence cannot bring an end to violence, in fact violence breeds more violence.

The ends do not justify the means. In conventional thinking, the police and army use violence because they believe that the ultimate ends are right. Also, industrial and technological society uses an unecological means of extraction, production and consumption because they believe that, in the end, this will benefit humanity. So it is very easy to have lofty aims and use unecological or violent means to achieve those aims. That, in my view, is flawed. The means must be compatible with the ends. If we are critical of the industrial society using the wrong means, destructive means and unecological means, then how can [Mr. Bowers] justify violent actions to create a more ecologically sustainable society?

All wars have been justified by their perpetrators on the grounds that they were acting for the greater good, and for peace. But that greater good or peace is hardly ever achieved. In the meantime, terrible atrocities are committed. Therefore I believe that Earth First! and other militant green groups who are fighting for animal rights, or the rights of the Earth, should declare their total adherence and commitment to non-violence. That will earn them a greater number of supporters and followers and they will also be more effective.

We have precedents to prove that non-violent actions are effective. Take the example of Mahatma Gandhi. His non-violent, non-co-operation with the British became so popular and powerful that in the end, the British had to end their colonial rule in India. A similar example was set by Martin Luther King [Jr.] and the movement for civil rights. Because of that movement, a number of new laws and regulations were enacted to reduce racialism.

Similar non-violent actions in our time should be able to create pressure on governments, businesses and industry to reduce their obsession with economic growth.

This kind of non-violent action requires a campaign to educate the masses, so that large numbers of people are prepared to participate in consumer boycotts and even court arrest. The non-violent way is a good practical tactic, as well as a good philosophy, but above all, non-violence is a way of life. We cannot merely use non-violence as a means of protest—we have to learn to live non-violently, even if we are not able to practise non-violence 100 per cent, our commitment to non-violence must be unconditional.

I hope [Mr. Bowers] will consider the use and practice of non-violence in a more creative and positive way, rather than dismiss it as mere idealism.

⁕

... I am pleased to note that [Mr. Bowers] accept[s] non-violence as a tactical and practical way of campaigning. My point is that non-violence is not something which one can use when it suits.

I would accept that if there was something harmful to people or nature, removing that obstacle is part of non-violent action. For example, Greenpeace believed that GM crops would contaminate and pollute neighbouring farms, therefore with transparency and compassion, they removed the crops. I would consider this within the definition of non-violent action. Similarly, inspiring non-violent action was demonstrated by Julia 'Butterfly' Hill who camped in a redwood tree in California for two years, taking upon herself the pain and inconvenience of being there. However, I feel that a number of actions taken by EarthFirst!, in the US particularly, don't have a similar commitment to non-violence. Most people in the world, like [Mr. Bowers], will give qualified and conditional support to non-violence. Most people would be non-violent to those who are non-violent to them. What [Mr. Bowers] mean[s] is that [he] will practise non-violence when it suits [him]—this is not a very big deal.

[He] propose[s] that something must feel violated before we can say that violence has been used against it. My point here is that the people who commit violence are violating themselves.

[Mr. Bowers] say[s] that Gandhi's India and King's America do not follow the path of non-violence. Is that the fault of Gandhi and King? Pacifists during the war became conscientious objectors, even though that did not stop the war. Was that the fault of the pacifists? If we can create a culture of non-violence, if large numbers of people are educated and trained in the practice of non-violence, if the educational establishments, the media and the general social ethos were in favour of non-violence, and if the nations of the world agreed that they would resolve their differences through non-violence, then a huge amount of suffering, destruction and ecological genocide would come to an end. Even if this lofty aim cannot be achieved tomorrow, our efforts should be directed towards that goal.

'Self-defence' is a feeble excuse. All warmongers and dictators use this excuse. The real purpose of violence is that one side wishes to control the other side.

Of course I agree that in human nature both violence and non-violence exist. We harbour a certain amount of hate and love in our hearts. The question is, which side do we wish to cultivate and enhance. At the moment, violence gets the upperhand because we as a society spend an enormous amount of resources on violent techniques.

[Mr. Bowers is] making a very weak defence of violence when [he] say[s] that nature is violent. Predators prey to survive. Humans prey for greed and control. . . . When hunters and gatherers killed for their survival, they did it with humility and respect. Whereas in modern society, violence has become a way of life.

If humans used as little violence as nature does, I would not complain. It is the organised and premeditated violence committed by modern society which is totally unnatural and cause for concern. I am sure [Mr. Bowers] will be against the violence of the established order, but my point is that we cannot pick and choose non-violence. Even though my sympathies are with the oppressed, with the victims and with the natural world, I will stand up for their rights and fight through non-violent means, and I would like [Mr. Bowers] to join me in creating that kind of non-violent world order.

... I did not [argue] that the destruction of property is justified—I [contend] that if there was something harmful to people or nature, removing that obstacle is part of non-violent action. There is a profound difference between the two statements. I disapprove of the violent actions which took place in Prague, even though I am in support of protesters against globalisation.

Nelson Mandela is more non-violent than violent. The way he has shown forgiveness is exemplary, but I did not agree with him when he advocated armed struggle. It is not just a question of one place like South Africa—we have oppressed people all over the world. I would like to see all movements against oppression oppose oppression without violence. If the oppressed use the means applied by the oppressors, then when the oppressed come to power they are likely to continue to use violence.

Self-defence is no excuse. The real problem is not such small spontaneous acts of self-defence; the real problem is organised and institutionalised violence which is used in the name of self-defence and ulitarianism.

Somewhere we have to break the chain of violence and create a new culture of non-violence, so that people are trained in schools and colleges to use non-violent techniques to resolve differences. It may be a long journey, but a journey of a thousand miles begins with one step.

[Mr. Bowers's] comparison with violence and power is not quite accurate. 'Power over' is violent, 'empowerment within' is non-violent. Power over other people will always corrupt; in the same way, violence to others will always diminish our humanity. We need to move away from the culture of war heroes and even from green warriors, and stop 'fighting' for peace. One cannot fight fire with fire—or violence with violence.

" Is Violence As a Form of Protest on International Political Issues Always wrong?" (handwritten)

Jake Bowers

⬅ **NO**

Source " Ecologist " (handwritten)

Can the Use of Violence Ever Be Justified in the Environmental Struggle?

I would never dismiss non-violence as mere idealism. I think it is a good and beautiful path to follow. It is, in fact, one that I still follow up to a point, and I will come to that point later. I agree with the practical arguments [Mr. Kumar has] given for non-violent activism. We can never challenge the state on a physical level; we would be demonised by the media, as well as physically destroyed. Any attempt to challenge the state's monopoly on violence would, quite literally, be suicide. All this is true for contemporary Britain. We live in an imperfect democracy where people can still persuade business and government, if they slog long enough and hard enough.

I disagree with [Mr. Kumar], however, on philosophical grounds, as well as with [his] definition of violence. But first, I'd like to set [him] straight on a few facts about Earth First! [EF!] We have never advocated or engaged in any form of violence. Ever since it was started in this country, Earth First! has been a movement based upon non-violent direct action and civil disobedience. We have attracted thousands of people to engage in non-violent direct action in defence of the Earth and never injured a single person.

I believe that violence can only be committed towards living, feeling things. Surely, something must feel violated before we can say that violence has been used against it. Machines that are built for the sole purpose of raping nature cannot feel pain. Swords do not weep as they are turned into ploughshares. Their owners may feel aggravated and inconvenienced but I doubt that they feel pain. Property should only be destroyed if no living thing is going to be hurt. The friction that ecological sabotage causes within that great abusive machine we call progress is not only needed, it is great therapy for tired and weary environmentalists. A society which values property more than life may define sabotage as violence, but it, and [Mr. Kumar] are wrong to do so.

I cannot make an unconditional commitment to non-violence. On a personal level, as an unashamed meat eater, it would be hypocritical. On a political level, I can't do it because I think it has limitations. I once believed, like Gandhi, that allowing myself to be physically hurt by my opponents would provoke respect and humanity in them. A few good kickings later I quickly forgot that idea! There are people in this world whose humanity is buried so deep that it would take a millennium for it to come to the surface. I therefore retain my right to defend myself. It is a right that each and every one of us has.

[Mr. Kumar is] right that means and ends must be compatible. Violent struggle does indeed create a violent society. But the same, sadly, cannot be said of non-violence for one very important reason: humans are naked apes who, by nature, are prone to being violent and domineering. Nuclear weapons in Gandhi's India, and Martin Luther King [Jr.]'s America, with its death penalty, racial violence and gun culture are hardly what I would call long-term campaign successes. Nature itself, for all its symbiosis and beauty, is often a very violent thing and human nature reflects it. Predators eat prey, and prey animals defend themselves—that's just the way it is. We, too, are part of that world, not above or below it. We follow the same natural laws, and those laws also apply to political struggle.

Predatory capitalism sees nature as its prey. Indigenous peoples, the human component of the ecosystem, are also often targets of abuse and resisters to the attack. Native resistance in the 'wild west', or armed Zapatistas in Mexico, are examples of violent self-defence that are entirely justified. I hope I am never forced to do it, but I cannot condemn anybody that does. Crazy Horse may not have beaten the US cavalry, but I cannot condemn his actions, just as I cannot condemn the Mohawk of Oka in Quebec, who violently and successfully defended their sacred white pines in more recent times.

As a Romani [Gypsy] activist, I believe that the struggle for cultural diversity is intimately linked to the fight for biological diversity. 500,000 of my people died in Nazi death camps. Nazi forces had detailed intelligence about the location of British Gypsy encampments prior to the Battle of Britain, and had there been a German invasion, my grandparents would have been on one of the first cross-channel shipments to Auschwitz. As much as I hate war, I for one am glad that British forces violently defended Britain at that time. I am equally indebted to the thousands of Romani partisans who used their knowledge of stealthy living to fight and wear down the Nazi war machine. Environmentalists, ultimately, have always got somewhere to go to when the bulldozers win the day. We have the luxury of choosing when to fight. But when you, personally, are the object of annihilation, when you are the hunted, non-violence is a luxury that cannot be afforded.

❧❦❧

... I'm glad [Mr. Kumar] accept[s] that the destruction of property can sometimes be justified. A similar view prevails when juries acquit activists charged with criminal damage. Thankfully, those jury members possess a sense of justice many judges often seem to lack.

I practice non-violence when it suits the situation. A person once attacked me with a knife. To my surprise, for I was a committed pacifist then, I reacted with an instinctive punch that put that person on the floor long enough for me to take the knife from [his] hands. This also is not a very big deal and I doubt that Mike Tyson would have been impressed. But just as I do not wish to compete with the sadism of a boxer, I have no wish to compete with the disturbing masochism that some pacifists possess. [Mr. Kumar's] talk of taking pain and inconvenience on reminds me of this. Describing self-defence as a 'feeble excuse' is a kind of inverse machismo, where those [whose] suffering and martyrdom are greatest come highest in the pecking order. I have no desire to break my back on the wheels of capitalism, or prostrate myself before it. I'd rather break those wheels than be broken upon them. Enduring all the suffering they willingly dispense may make [Mr. Kumar] feel better, it might even result in sainthood, but I doubt that it will actually change anything.

Of course Gandhi and Martin Luther King [Jr.] are not responsible for the violent states of their respective countries. I was merely reflecting upon the depressing fact that the love they talked of does not seem to be as contagious as the hatred they fought. I agree with [Mr. Kumar] that non-violence is something that must be cultivated in a society. It is a seed of hope within what [he] rightly describe[s] as a society based upon violence. I'm just not absolutist enough to think it has a universal application. Gandhi and King are examples to us all. But they stand alongside advocates of armed resistance like Crazy Horse, Nelson Mandela, Geronimo and Malcolm X in my personal opinion.

To equate the plight of the oppressed with the empire building of dictators is not only insulting to their struggle, it is naïve. Such reasoning places Nelson Mandela on a par with Hitler and Stalin. Similarly, is a woman who kicks a rapist in the groin in an attempt to preserve her dignity as evil as the rapist? I think not. [Mr. Kumar] hint[s] that violence for survival is acceptable and that: 'If humans used as little violence as nature does, I would not complain'. This is my point entirely! In survival situations, when genocide or personal destruction is about to occur, violent self-defence is the only course of action. If [he] agree[s] with this, [his] commitment to non-violence is actually no more unequivocal than my own.

'Violence is violence', may be a nice phrase, but it is as simplistic as saying that 'power is power'. Power is often used to oppress, but power from above is totally different from the power that comes from within. Personal empowerment is something that transforms the world rather than impoverishing it. I still believe that violence can be used defensively without mutating into an expansive, predatory urge to control and ultimately destroy everything in its path. With great discipline this is possible. There has, for example, been no large-scale lynching of white South Africans since the ANC [African National Congress] came to power; instead a process of forgiveness and reconciliation has begun. By exchanging the bullet for the ballot box, they are helping to create a better world order that all of us dream of. The fact that violence played a role in their struggle does not make their victory a hollow one.

⋅⊙⋅

... I agree with a lot of what [Mr. Kumar] say[s], particularly about the culture of hero worship. One of the reasons we started Earth First! was to encourage ordinary people to use non-violent direct action (NVDA) to save the planet. It was a direct response to the ultimately disempowering images of corporate environmentalists in uniforms heroically buzzing around in ships and helicopters. Earth First! has trained thousands of people, from school kids to pensioners, in NVDA and has always promoted the Gandhian philosophy you believe in. I'd like to state that EF! does not support violence. The support I've given for self-defence is based upon my own personal opinions formed during a decade of grassroots activism.

Fire cannot be fought with fire. Resistance should be like water, and always seek the lowest path. If dialogue is possible, that's great. Why fight when talking may achieve your aims. Most exploiters or oppressors, however, will not engage in dialogue until they see the need to. This is when creative conflict is best used. The greatest advances in democracy have always been made when marginalised people force their participation in processes that deliberately exclude them. If this can be achieved non-violently, that too is wonderful. The velvet revolutions in Eastern Europe prove that it can be done.

But sadly, there are times when non-violence is not enough. Especially when the will of the powerful is simply to exterminate the powerless. Such pressure forces violent action to ensure survival, just as water eventually turns to hot, expanding steam when put in a pressure cooker. The nature of a political struggle must match the conditions that surround it. Malcolm X articulated this well when he said we must liberate ourselves by any means necessary. I hope we never find it necessary to be violent, but let's not be dogmatic enough in our relative good fortune to condemn those who have no choice.

POSTSCRIPT

Is Violence as a Form of Protest on International Political Issues Always Wrong?

One of the difficult aspects of debating violence as a form of political protest is remaining objective when formulating standards governing the subject of the protest. On the general topic of protest, consult Dieter Rucht, Ruud Koopmans, and Friedhelm Neidhardt, eds., *Acts of Dissent: New Developments in the Study of Protest* (Rowman & Littlefield, 2000) and Ekkart Zimmermann, *Protest, Revolt, and Revolution: New Developments in Conflict Research* (Westview Press, 2000).

To most of us, the Oklahoma bomber, Timothy McVeigh, was a heinous criminal. But he thought he was justified. In a statement, he referred to those he killed as collateral damage. In wars that kill innocent people, these people are often considered collateral damage, too. The point here is not to say that McVeigh and the U.S. and other allied military forces participating in military actions are the same; they are not. Rather, it is to say that what is just is often a matter of perspective, and the line between terrorists' planting bombs and pilots' dropping bombs is hazy.

Apart from the matter of tactics, it is important to ask at what point, if any, does violence become acceptable. The Weathermen and many other anti–Vietnam War groups were convinced that the United States was waging an immoral war that was killing tens of thousands of innocent people in Vietnam. Some of the antiwar activists did not feel they could stop the war in time, if at all, through peaceful means. So they took action. Buildings were burned; others were blown up. People died. For more on the Vietnam War protests, read Margot Fortunato Galt, *Stop This War! American Protest of the Conflict in Vietnam* (Lerner, 2000).

Even if one agrees with Bowers's view that violence should not be directed at individuals, there is always the chance that any form of violence can escalate. The protestors at the University of Wisconsin did not intend to kill anyone, but it happened. In another incident students at Ohio's Kent State University hurled rocks and empty tear gas canisters at the national guardsmen, who had been sent to the campus because of the antiwar violence there. Sadly, the soldiers opened fire on the crowd, killing four students and wounding eight others. President Richard Nixon publicly condemned the actions of the guardsmen but added, "When dissent turns to violence it invites tragedy."

Americans should be reminded that their government was born in violent protest. Indeed, the Declaration of Independence was a radical document that proclaimed, "Whenever any Form of Government becomes destructive of these ends, it is the Right of the People to alter or to abolish it, and to institute new Government." The patriots did institute a new form of government, and they accomplished their goal through violence. More on the patriots as radicals can be found in Gordon S. Wood, *The Radicalism of the American Revolution* (Vintage Books, 1993).

ISSUE 18

Is Dangerous Global Warming Occurring?

YES: Robert T. Watson, from Presentation at the Sixth Conference of Parties to the United Nations Framework Convention on Climate Change (November 13, 2000)

NO: Jerry Taylor, from "Global Warming: The Anatomy of a Debate," Presentation Before the Johns Hopkins University Applied Physics Laboratory (January 16, 1998)

ISSUE SUMMARY

YES: Robert T. Watson, chair of the UN's Intergovernmental Panel on Climate Change (IPCC) and senior scientific adviser for environment at the World Bank, argues that human-induced climate change, or global warming, is among the number of environmental problems that threaten our ability to meet basic human needs.

NO: Jerry Taylor, director of natural resource studies at the Cato Institute, contends that the debate over global warming is overdrawn and has become less a discussion of scientific and economic issues than an exercise in political theater.

W e live in an era of almost incomprehensible technological boom. In a very short time—less than a long lifetime in many cases—technology has brought some amazing things. But these advances have had by-products. A great deal of prosperity has come about through industrialization, electrification, the burgeoning of private and commercial vehicles, and a host of other inventions and improvements that, in order to work, consume massive amounts of fossil fuel (mostly coal, petroleum, and natural gas). The burning of fossil fuels sends carbon dioxide (CO_2) into the atmosphere. The discharge of CO_2 from burning wood, animals exhaling, and some other sources is nearly as old as Earth itself, but the twentieth century's advances have rapidly increased the level of discharge. Since 1950 alone, global CO_2 emissions have increased 278 percent, with more than 26 billion tons of CO_2 now being discharged annually. There are now almost 850 billion tons of CO_2 in the atmosphere.

Many analysts believe that as a result of this buildup of CO_2, we are experiencing a gradual pattern of global warming. The reason, according to these scientists, is the *greenhouse effect*. As CO_2 accumulates in the upper atmosphere, it creates a blanket effect, trapping heat and preventing the nightly cooling of the Earth. Other gases, especially methane and chlorofluorocarbons (CFCs, such as freon), also contribute to the thermal blanket.

Many scientists and others believe that global warming is evident in changing climatological data. It is estimated that in the last century the Earth's average temperature rose about 1.1 degrees Fahrenheit. In fact, of the 10 warmest years since global record keeping began in 1856, 9 of those years occurred in the 19 years between 1980 and 1998. Many weather experts also see an increase in the number and intensity of hurricanes and other catastrophic weather events, and they attribute these to global warming.

Not everyone believes that global warming caused by a CO_2 buildup is occurring or worries about it. Some scientists do not believe that future temperature increases will be significant, either because they will not occur or because offsetting factors, such as increased cloudiness, will ease the effect. Others believe that recent temperature increases reflect natural trends in the Earth's warming and cooling process.

Whatever the reality may be, the 1990s has seen efforts to constrain and cut back CO_2 emissions. The Earth Summit held in Rio de Janeiro in 1992 was the first of these efforts. At Rio, most of the economically developed countries (EDCs) signed the Global Warming Convention and agreed to voluntarily stabilize emissions at their 1990 levels by the year 2000. They also resolved to reconvene in 1997 to review progress under the agreement. However, five years later many of the EDCs, including the United States, had made no progress toward meeting the goals set in 1992.

The 1997 meeting was held in Kyoto, Japan. The negotiations were too complex to detail here, but the proposed treaty that resulted seeks to stem global warming through a series of provisions that have proven controversial. Because EDCs have put and continue to put the greatest amount of greenhouse gases in the atmosphere, the treaty calls on them to reduce CO_2 and other greenhouse gas emissions by 6 to 8 percent below their respective 1990 levels by 2012. The United States' cut would be 7 percent, Europe's cut would be 8 percent, and Japan's cut would be 6 percent. The treaty urges the less developed countries (LDCs), including China and India, to adopt voluntary goals but exempts them from binding standards. The arguments for this exemption are, first, that the LDCs have been and remain relatively minor contributors to the problem, and second, that the LDCs need to build up their economies and cannot afford to meet emissions quotas.

In the following selections, Robert T. Watson and Jerry Taylor address whether or not the kind of strong actions contained in the Kyoto Treaty are justified. If the problem is "man-made" and as threatening as Watson reports, then the requirements outlined in the Kyoto Treaty, and perhaps more, are in order. If, however, Taylor's argument is valid, then drastic action would do more harm than good.

Robert T. Watson    **YES**

Presentation of Robert T. Watson

Introduction

One of the major challenges facing humankind is to provide an equitable standard of living for this and future generations: adequate food, water and energy, safe shelter and a healthy environment (e.g., clean air and water). Unfortunately, human-induced climate change, as well as other global environmental issues such as land degradation, loss of biological diversity and stratospheric ozone depletion, threatens our ability to meet these basic human needs.

The overwhelming majority of scientific experts, whilst recognizing that scientific uncertainties exist, nonetheless believe that human-induced climate change is inevitable. Indeed, during the last few years, many parts of the world have suffered major heat waves, floods, droughts, fires and extreme weather events leading to significant economic losses and loss of life. While individual events cannot be directly linked to human-induced climate change, the frequency and magnitude of these types of events are predicted to increase in a warmer world.

The question is not whether climate will change in response to human activities, but rather how much (magnitude), how fast (the rate of change) and *where* (regional patterns). It is also clear that climate change will, in many parts of the world, adversely affect socio-economic sectors, including water resources, agriculture, forestry, fisheries and human settlements, ecological systems (particularly forests and coral reefs), and human health (particularly diseases spread by insects), with developing countries being the most vulnerable. The good news is, however, that the majority of experts believe that significant reductions in net greenhouse gas emissions are technically feasible due to an extensive array of technologies and policy measures in the energy supply, energy demand and agricultural and forestry sectors. In addition, the projected adverse effects of climate change on socio-economic and ecological systems can, to some degree, be reduced through proactive adaptation measures. These are the fundamental conclusions, taken from already approved/accepted IPCC [Intergovernmental Panel on Climate Change] assessments, of a careful and objective

From Robert T. Watson, Presentation at the Sixth Conference of Parties to the United Nations Framework Convention on Climate Change (November 13, 2000).

analysis of all relevant scientific, technical and economic information by thousands of experts from the appropriate fields of science from academia, governments, industry and environmental organizations from around the world.

Decision-makers should realize that once carbon dioxide, the major anthropogenic greenhouse gas, is emitted into the atmosphere, it stays in the atmosphere for more than a century. This means that if policy formulation waits until all scientific uncertainties are resolved, and carbon dioxide and other greenhouse gases are responsible for changing the Earth's climate as projected by all climate models, the time to reverse the human-induced changes in climate and the resulting environmental damages would not be years or decades, but centuries to millennia, even if all emissions of greenhouse gases were terminated, which is clearly not practical.

This presentation, which briefly describes the current state of understanding of the Earth's climate system and the influence of human activities; the vulnerability of human health, ecological systems, and socio-economic sectors to climate change; and approaches to mitigate climate change by reducing emissions and enhancing sinks, is based on accepted and approved conclusions from the IPCC Second Assessment Report (SAR) and a series of Technical Papers and Special Reports... and supplemented by recent information that is being assessed in the draft IPCC Third Assessment Report (TAR)....

Part I: The Earth's Climate System: The Influence of Human Activities

The Earth's climate is changing: The Earth's climate has been relatively stable since the last ice age (global temperature changes of less than 1 degree Centigrade over a century during the past 10,000 years). During this time modern society has evolved, and, in many cases, successfully adapted to the prevailing local climate and its natural variability. However, the Earth's climate is now changing. The Earth's surface temperature this century is clearly warmer than any other century during the last thousand years, i.e., the climate of the 20th century is clearly atypical. The Earth has warmed by between 0.4 and 0.8 degree centigrade over the last century, with land areas warming more than the oceans, and with the last two decades being the hottest this century. Indeed, the three warmest years during the last one hundred years have all occurred in the 1990s and the twelve warmest years during the last one hundred years have all occurred since 1983. In addition, there is evidence that precipitation patterns are changing, that sea level is increasing, that glaciers are retreating world-wide, that Arctic sea ice is thinning, and that the incidence of extreme weather events is increasing in some parts of the world.

The atmospheric concentrations of greenhouse gases are changing due to human activities: The atmospheric concentrations of greenhouse gases have increased because of human activities, primarily due to the combustion of fossil fuels (coal, oil and gas), deforestation and agricultural practices, since the beginning of the pre-industrial era around 1750: carbon dioxide by nearly 30%, methane by more than a factor of two, and nitrous oxide by about 15%. Their concentrations are higher now than at any time during the last 420,000 years, the period for which there are reliable ice-core data, and probably significantly longer. In addition, the combustion of fossil fuels has also caused the atmospheric concentrations of sulfate aerosols to have increased. Greenhouse gases tend to warm the atmosphere and, in some regions, primarily in the Northern Hemisphere, aerosols tend to cool the atmosphere.

The weight of scientific evidence suggests that the observed changes in the Earth's climate are, at least in part, due to human activities: Climate models that take into account the observed increases in the atmospheric concentrations of greenhouse gases, sulfate aerosols and the observed decrease in ozone in the lower stratosphere, in conjunction with natural changes in volcanic activity and in solar activity, simulate the observed changes in annual mean global surface temperature quite well. This, and our basic scientific understanding of the greenhouse effect, suggests that human activities are implicated in the observed changes in the Earth's climate. In fact, the observed changes in climate, especially the increased temperatures since around 1970, cannot be explained by changes in solar activity and volcanic emissions alone.... [T]he observed changes in temperature, especially those since around 1970, can be simulated quite well by a climate model that takes into account human-induced changes in greenhouse gases and aerosols. Not only is there evidence of a change in climate at the global level consistent with climate models, but there is observational evidence of regional changes in climate that are consistent with those predicted by climate models. For example, climate models predict an increase in intense rainfall events over the United States of America consistent with the observations.

Emissions of greenhouse gases are projected to increase in the future due to human activities: Future emissions of greenhouse gases and the sulfate aerosol precursor, sulfur dioxide, are sensitive to the evolution of governance structures world-wide, changes in population and economic growth, the rate of diffusion of new technologies into the market place, energy production and consumption patterns, land-use practices, energy intensity, and the price and availability of energy. While different development paths can result in quite different greenhouse gas emissions, most projections suggest that greenhouse gas concentrations will increase significantly during the next century in the absence of policies specifically designed to address the issue of climate change. Some projections suggest that an initial increase in emissions could be followed by a decrease after several decades if there was a major transition in the world's energy system due to the pursuit of a range of sustainable development goals. The SRES [IPCC Special Report on Emission Scenarios] reported, for example, carbon dioxide emissions from the combustion of fossil fuels are projected to range from about 5 to 35 GtC per year in the year 2100: compared to current emissions of about 6.3 GtC per year. Such a range of emissions would mean that the atmospheric concentration of carbon dioxide would increase from today's level of about 365 ppmv (parts per million by volume) to between about 550 and 1000 ppmv by 2100.

Latest projections of carbon dioxide emissions are consistent with earlier projections, but projected sulfur dioxide emissions are much lower: While the SRES reported similar projected energy emissions for carbon dioxide to the 1992 projections, it differed in one important aspect from the 1992 projections, in-so-far-as the projected emissions of sulfur dioxide are much lower, because of structural changes in the energy system and because of concerns about local and regional air pollution (i.e., acid deposition). This has important implications for future projections of temperature changes, because sulfur dioxide emissions lead to the formation of sulfate aerosols in the atmosphere, which as stated earlier can partially offset the warming effect of the greenhouse gases.

Global mean surface temperatures are projected to increase by about 1.5 to 6.0°C by 2100.   Based on the range of climate sensitivities and the plausible ranges of greenhouse gas and sulfur dioxide emissions reported in the SRES, a number of climate models project that the global mean surface temperature could increase by about 1.5 to 6.0°C by 2100. This range compares to that reported in the IPCC SAR of 1.0–3.5°C. The revised higher estimates of projected warming arise because the lower projected emissions of sulfur dioxide result in less offset of the warming effect of the greenhouse gases. These projected global-average temperature changes would be greater than recent natural fluctuations and would also occur at a rate significantly faster than observed changes over the last 10,000 years. Temperature changes are expected to differ by region with high latitudes projected to warm more than the global average, and during the next century land areas are projected to warm more than the oceans, and the northern hemisphere is projected to warm more than the southern hemisphere. However, the reliability of regional scale predictions is still low.

Seasonal and latitudinal shifts in precipitation with arid and semi-arid areas becoming drier: Model calculations show that evaporation will be enhanced as the climate warms, and that there will be an increase in global mean precipitation and an increase in the frequency of intense rainfall. However, not all land regions will experience an increase in precipitation, and even those land regions with increased precipitation may experience decreases in run-off and soil moisture, because of enhanced evaporation. Seasonal shifts in precipitation are also projected. In general, precipitation is projected to increase at high latitudes in winter, while run-off and soil moisture is projected to decrease in some mid-latitude continental regions during summer. The arid and semi-arid areas in Southern and Northern Africa, Southern Europe, the Middle East, parts of Latin America and Australia are expected to become drier.

Sea level projected to rise about 15–95 cms by 2100:   Associated with changes in temperature, sea level is projected to increase by about 15–95 cm by 2100, caused primarily by thermal expansion of the oceans and the melting of glaciers. The revised temperature projections are not likely to result in significantly different projections of changes in sea level over the next century because of the large thermal inertia of the oceans, i.e., the temperature of the oceans responds very slowly to a change in greenhouse gas concentrations. However, recent more advanced models are tending to project somewhat lower values of sea level rise. It should be noted that even when the atmospheric concentrations of greenhouse gases are stabilized, temperatures will continue to increase by another 30–50% over several decades, sea level will continue to rise over hundreds of years and ice sheets will continue to adjust for thousands of years....

The frequency and magnitude of ENSO [El Niño-Southern Oscillation] events may increase: Long-term, large-scale, human-induced changes in climate are likely to interact with natural climate variability on time-scales of days to decades (e.g., the El Niño-Southern Oscillation [ENSO] phenomena). Recent trends in the increased frequency and magnitude of ENSO events, which lead to severe floods and droughts in regions of the tropics and sub-tropics, are projected to continue in many climate models.

Incidence of some extreme events projected to increase: While the incidence of extreme temperature events, floods, droughts, soil moisture deficits, fires and pest outbreaks is expected to increase in some regions, it is unclear whether there will be changes in the frequency and intensity of extreme weather events such as tropical storms, cyclones, and tornadoes. However, even if there is no increase in the frequency and intensity of extreme weather events there may be shifts in their geographic location to places less prepared and more vulnerable to such events.

Part II: The Vulnerability of Water Resources, Agriculture, Natural Ecosystems, and Human Health to Climate Change and Sea Level Rise

The IPCC has assessed ... and is continuing to assess ...the potential consequences of changes in climate for socio-economic sectors, ecological systems and human health for different regions of the world at the regional and global scale. Because of uncertainties associated with regional projections of climate change, the IPCC assesses the vulnerability of these natural and social systems to changes in climate, rather than attempting to provide quantitative predictions of the impacts of climate change at the regional level. Vulnerability is defined as the extent to which a natural or social system is susceptible to sustaining damage from climate change, and is a function of the magnitude of climate change, the sensitivity of the system to changes in climate and the ability to adapt the system to changes in climate. Hence, a highly vulnerable system is one that is highly sensitive to modest changes in climate and one for which the ability to adapt is severely constrained.

Most impact studies have assessed how systems would respond to a climate change resulting from an arbitrary doubling of atmospheric carbon dioxide concentrations. Very few studies have considered the dynamic responses to steadily increasing greenhouse gas concentrations; fewer yet have been able to examine the consequences of increases beyond a doubling of greenhouse gas concentrations or to assess the implications of multiple stress factors. Thus there is a need for the increased development and use of time-dependent integrated assessment models.

The IPCC SAR concluded that human health, terrestrial and aquatic ecological systems, and socioeconomic systems (e.g., agriculture, forestry, fisheries, water resources, and human settlements), which are all vital to human development and well-being, are all vulnerable to changes in climate, including the magnitude and rate of climate change, as well as to changes in climate variability. Whereas many regions are likely to experience the adverse effects of climate change—some of which are potentially irreversible—some effects of climate change are likely to be beneficial. Hence, different segments of society can expect to confront a variety of changes and the need to adapt to them.

There are a number of general conclusions that can be easily drawn: (i) human-induced climate change is an important new stress, particularly on ecological and socio-economic systems that are already affected by pollution, increasing resource demands, and non-sustainable management practices; (ii) the most vulnerable systems are those with the greatest sensitivity to climate change and the least adaptability; (iii) most systems are sensitive to both the magnitude and rate of climate change; (iv) many of the impacts are difficult to quantify because existing studies are limited in scope; and (v) successful adaptation depends upon technological advances, institutional arrangements, availability of financing and information exchange, and that vulnerability increases as adaptation capacity decreases. Therefore, developing countries are more vulnerable to climate change than developed countries.

The range of adaptation options for managed systems such as agriculture and water supply is generally increasing because of technological advances, thus reducing the vulnerability of these systems to climate change. However, some regions of the world, i.e., developing countries, have limited access to these technologies and appropriate information. The efficacy and cost-effectiveness of adaptation strategies will depend upon cultural, educational, managerial, institutional, legal and regulatory practices that are both domestic and international in scope. Incorporation of climate change concerns into resource-use and development decisions and plans for regularly scheduled investments in infrastructure will facilitate adaptation.

The issues of climate variability and climate change need to be integrated into resource use and development decisions: Many sectors are currently not optimally managed with respect to today's natural climate variability because of the choice of policies, practices and technologies. Decreasing the vulnerability of socio-economic sectors and ecological systems to natural climate variability through a more informed choice of policies, practices and technologies will, in many cases, reduce the long-term vulnerability of these systems to climate change. For example, use of seasonal climate forecasts into management decisions can reduce the vulnerability of the water and agricultural sectors to floods and droughts caused by the ENSO phenomena.

Let me now briefly discuss the implications of climate change for a representative number of systems: water resources, agricultural productivity and food security, natural ecosystems (forests and coral reefs), human health and sea level rise.

Water Resources

Climate change could exacerbate water stress in arid and semi-arid areas, and most regions will experience an increase in floods: Currently 1.3 billion people do not have access to adequate supplies of safe water, and 2 billion people do not have access to adequate sanitation. Today, some nineteen countries, primarily in the Middle East and Africa, are classified as water-scarce or water-stressed. Even in the absence of climate change, this number is expected to double by 2025, in large part because of increases in demand from population and economic growth. Unfortunately in many regions of the world a significant fraction of water is wasted, largely through inefficient irrigation in the agricultural sector.... [C]limate change could further exacerbate the frequency and magnitude of droughts in some places, in particular central Asia, northern and southern Africa, the Middle East, the Mediterranean and Australia where droughts are already a recurrent feature. Developing countries are highly vulnerable to climate change and increased water stress because many are located in arid and semi-arid areas. In addition, it should be recognized that the frequency and magnitude of floods in most regions of the world are expected to increase because of the projected increase in heavy precipitation events.

Agricultural Productivity and Food Security

Agricultural productivity is projected to decrease in many countries in the tropics and sub-tropics: Currently, 800 million people are malnourished; as the world's population increases and incomes in some countries rise, food demand is expected to double over the next three to four decades. Studies show that on the whole, global agricultural production might be relatively unaffected by small changes in climate, i.e., global mean surface temperature changes of less than 2 degrees Centigrade, but is projected to decrease with greater warming. Crop yields and changes in productivity due to climate change will vary considerably across regions and among localities, thus changing the patterns of production. In general, productivity is projected to increase in middle to high latitudes, depending on crop type, growing season, changes in temperature regime, and seasonality of precipitation. However, in the tropics and subtropics, where some crops are near their maximum temperature tolerance and where dryland, non-irrigated agriculture dominates, yields are likely to decrease for even small changes in climate, especially in Africa and Latin America, where decreases in overall agricultural productivity of up to 30% are projected during the next century. Therefore, there may be increased risk of hunger in some locations in the tropics and subtropics where many of the world's poorest people live.

Natural Ecosystems

Biological systems have already been affected by changes in climate during the last several decades: There are a number of instances where changes in biological systems, e.g., earlier flowering of trees and egg-laying in birds, lengthening of the growing season, and the pole-ward and altitudinal shifts in insect ranges, have been associated with regional changes in climate. While these biological systems are subject to numerous stresses that can alter their behavior, it should be noted that in many cases these observed changes in biological systems are consistent with well-known biological responses to climate.

Climate change is projected to alter the structure and functioning of ecological systems and decrease biological diversity: The structure, composition and geographic distribution of many ecosystems will shift as individual species respond to changes in climate and disturbance regimes, but these ecological changes are likely to lag behind the changes in climate by decades to centuries. There will likely be reductions in biological diversity and in the goods ecosystems provide society, e.g., sources of food, fiber, medicines, recreation and tourism, and ecological services such as controlling nutrient cycling, waste quality, water run-off, soil erosion, pollination services, detoxification and air quality.

Forests are vulnerable to projected changes in climate: The distribution of forests and forest species are projected to change in response to changes in temperature, precipitation, extreme events, pest outbreaks and fires, altering the ecosystem goods and services provided. Boreal systems are the most vulnerable, primarily due to changes in fire regime and pest outbreaks, leading to forest die-back, a change in age structure and a decrease in carbon content. The global terrestrial biosphere is currently sequestering about 0.7 Gt C per year, the difference between a global uptake of 2.3 Gt C per year and an emission of about 1.6 Gt C per year from tropical deforestation.... The majority of the uptake is estimated to occur in the temperate forests (about 1–2 Gt C per year, in response to management practices, carbon dioxide fertilization, nitrogen deposition and climate change), with little net uptake in Boreal regions. This terrestrial uptake will likely diminish with time and forest ecosystems may even become a source of carbon emissions. Net carbon emissions are very sensitive to the El Niño-Southern Oscillation phenomena, with the terrestrial biosphere being a net source during ENSO years to a net sink in non-ENSO years, albeit with large regional variations.

Coral reefs are threatened by increases in temperature: Coral reefs, which are the most biologically diverse marine ecosystems, are important for fisheries, coastal protection, erosion control and tourism. Coral reef systems, which are already being threatened by pollution, unsustainable tourism and fishing practices, are very vulnerable to changes in climate. While these systems may be able to adapt to the projected increases in sea level, sustained increases in water temperatures of 3–4 degrees Centigrade above long-term average seasonal maxima over a 6-month period can cause significant coral mortality; short-term increases on the order of only 1–2 degrees Centigrade can cause shorter-term "coral bleaching".

Human Health

Human health is sensitive to changes in climate because of its impact, in particular, on changes in food security, water supply and quality, and the functioning and range of ecological systems.   These impacts are likely to be mostly adverse, and in many cases would cause loss of life. Direct health effects would include increases in heat-related mortality and illness resulting from an anticipated increase in heatwaves, although offset to some degree in temperate regions by reductions in winter mortality. Indirect effects would include extensions of the range and season for vector organisms (e.g., mosquito, water snails, black and tsetse flies), often increasing the likelihood of transmission of vector-borne infectious diseases (e.g., malaria, dengue, yellow fever and encephalitis). Projected changes in climate could lead to an increase in the number of people at risk of malaria of the order of tens of millions annually, primarily in tropical, subtropical, and less well protected temperate-zone populations. Some increases in non-vector-borne infectious diseases such as salmonellosis, cholera and other food- and water-related infections could also occur, particularly in tropical and subtropical regions, because of climatic impacts on water distribution and temperature, and on micro-organism proliferation. The impacts of climate change on food production within food-insecure regions and the consequences of economic dislocation and demographic displacement (e.g., sea level rise) would have wide-ranging health impacts.

Sea Level Rise

Sea-level rise is projected to have negative impacts on human settlements, tourism, freshwater supplies, fisheries, exposed infrastructure, agricultural lands and wetlands, causing loss of land, economic losses and the displacement of tens of millions of people: It is currently estimated that about half of the world's population lives in coastal zones. Changes in climate will affect coastal systems through sea-level rise and an increase in storm-surge hazards and possible changes in the frequency and/or intensity of extreme events. Impacts may vary across regions, and societal costs will greatly depend upon the vulnerability of the coastal system and the economic situation of the country. Sea-level rise will increase the vulnerability of coastal populations to flooding. An average of about 50 million people per year currently experience flooding due to storm surges; a 50 cm sea-level rise could double this number. The estimates will be substantially higher if one incorporates population growth projections. A number of studies have shown that small islands and deltaic areas are particularly vulnerable to a one-meter sea-level rise. In the absence of mitigation actions (e.g., building sea walls), land losses are projected to range from 1.0% for Egypt, 6% for Netherlands, 17.5% for Bangladesh, to about 80% of the Marshall Islands, displacing tens of millions of people, and in the case of low-lying Small Island States, the possible loss of whole cultures. Many nations face lost capital value in excess of 10% of GDP. While annual adaptation/protection costs for most of these nations would be relatively modest (about 0.1% GDP), average annual costs to many small island states could be as high as several percent of GDP, assuming adaptation is possible.

Part III: Approaches to Mitigate Climate Change by Reducing Emissions and Enhancing Sinks

Significant reductions in net greenhouse gas emissions are technically, and economically, feasible: Cost-effective reductions in greenhouse gases can be achieved by utilizing an extensive array of technologies:

- *energy supply*—more efficient conversion of fossil fuels; switching from high to low carbon fossil fuels; decarbonization of flue gases and fuels, coupled with carbon dioxide storage; increased use of modern renewable sources of energy (e.g., plantation biomass, micro-hydro, wind, and solar); and increasing the use of nuclear energy (subject to addressing safety, environmental and other concerns);
- *energy demand*—industry, transportation, and residential/commercial buildings;
- *agricultural and forestry*—afforestation, reforestation, slowing deforestation, improved forest, cropland and rangeland management, including restoration of degraded agricultural lands and rangelands, promoting agroforestry, and improving the quality of the diet of ruminants; and
- *waste management and reductions in halocarbon emissions.*

Policy instruments can be used to facilitate the penetration of lower carbon intensive technologies and modified consumption patterns. By the year 2100, the world's commercial energy system will be replaced at least twice because of the natural lifetime of energy systems offering opportunities to change the energy system without premature retirement of capital stock. However, full technical potential is rarely achieved because of a lack of information and cultural, institutional, legal and economic barriers. The optimum mix of policies to facilitate the penetration of lower carbon intensive technologies and encourage the efficient use of energy will vary from country to country as policies need to be tailored for local situations and developed through consultation with stakeholders. Policies include: energy pricing strategies (e.g., carbon taxes and reduced energy subsidies); reducing or removing subsidies that increase greenhouse gas emissions (e.g., agricultural and transport sub-sidies); internalization of environmental extranalities (e.g., incorporating the health costs associated with particulates caused by the combustion of coal into the price of coal); incentives such as provisions for accelerated depreciation and reduced costs for the consumer; domestic and international tradable emis-sions permits and joint implementation; voluntary programs and negotiated agreements with industry; utility demand-side management programs; regula-tory programs including minimum energy efficiency standards; market pull and demonstration programs that stimulate the development and application of advanced technologies; and product labeling.

Energy services are critical to poverty alleviation and economic development: It is quite clear that increased energy services in developing countries are critical in order to alleviate poverty and underdevelopment, where 1.3 billion people live on less than $1 per day, 3 billion people live on less than $2 per day, and 2 billion people are without electricity. Hence the challenge is to assist develop-ing countries expand their production and consumption of energy in the most efficient and environmentally benign manner.

Co-benefits can lower the cost of climate change mitigation: The long term chal-lenge of stabilizing the atmospheric concentrations of greenhouse gas concen-trations will . . . eventually require global emissions of greenhouse gases to be significantly lower than today. . . . Given the challenges of improving indoor and outdoor air quality in many parts of the world, and the goals to reduce acid deposition, land degradation and protect biodiversity, policies, practices and technologies that can simultaneously address these local and regional envi-ronmental issues, while reducing net greenhouse gas emissions, are particularly attractive. Estimates of the costs of mitigating climate change should take into account the co-benefits of switching from a fossil fuel based economy to a lower-carbon intensity energy system. Co-benefits from energy sector inter-ventions could include lower levels of local and regional pollution, including particulates, surface ozone and acid rain. Such interventions would have both social and economic benefits. [Evidence] show[s] the high levels of pollution in many developing country cities and the health costs associated with total suspended particulates in China. Co-benefits from the agricultural and forestry sector could include increased soil fertility and reduced loss of biodiversity.

Significant reductions in greenhouse gases can be accomplished by pursuing sus-tainable development goals.   A future world with greenhouse gas emissions comparable to those of today can either be achieved through the adoption of specific polices, practices and technologies to limit greenhouse gas emissions or through the adoption of a range of policies, practices and technologies to achieve other sustainable development goals. It should be noted that a major oil company, Shell, has suggested that the mix of energy sources could change radically during the next century. Non-fossil energy sources (solar, wind, mod-ern biomass, hydropower, geothermal and nuclear) could account for as much as half of all energy produced by the middle of this century. Such a future would be consistent with the lower projections of greenhouse gas emissions and would clearly eliminate the highest projections of greenhouse gases from being realized. However, an energy efficient and low-carbon energy world is considered by many to be unlikely to occur without significant policy reform, technology transfer, capacity-building and enhanced public and private sector energy R&D [research and development] programs.

Technology transfer is a critical issue: The recent IPCC Special Report on Methodological and Technological Issues in Technology Transfer examined the flows of knowledge, experience and equipment among governments, private sector entities, financial institutions, NGOs [nongovernmental organizations], and research and education institutions, and the different roles that each of these stakeholders can play in facilitating the transfer of technologies to address climate change in the context of sustainable development. The report concluded that the current efforts and established processes, i.e., business-as-usual, will not be sufficient to meet this challenge. The report concluded that enhanced capacity is required in developing countries and that additional government actions can create the enabling environment for private sector technology transfers within and across national boundaries. Government actions could include *inter-alia*, reforming legal systems, protecting intellectual property rights and licenses, encouraging financial reforms, promoting competitive and open markets for environmentally sound technologies, and knowledge sharing....

Summary

Without action to limit greenhouse gas emissions the Earth's climate will warm at a rate unprecedented in the last 10,000 years: If actions are not taken to reduce the projected increase in greenhouse gas emissions, the Earth's climate is projected to change at a rate unprecedented in the last 10,000 years with adverse consequences for society, undermining the very foundation of sustainable development.

Policymakers are faced with responding to the risks posed by anthropogenic emissions of greenhouse gases in the face of significant scientific uncertainties. They may want to consider these uncertainties in the context that climate-induced environmental changes cannot be reversed quickly, if at all, due to the long time scales (decades to millennia) associated with the climate system. Decisions taken during the next few years may limit the range of possible policy options in the future because high near-term emissions would require deeper reductions in the future to meet any given target concentration. Delaying action would increase both the rate and the eventual magnitude of climate change, and hence adaptation and damage costs.

Policymakers will have to decide to what degree they want to take precautionary measures to limit anthropogenic climate change by mitigating greenhouse gas emissions and enhancing the resilience of vulnerable systems by means of adaptation.

Uncertainty does not mean that a nation or the world community cannot position itself better to cope with the broad range of possible climate changes or protect against potentially costly future outcomes. Delaying such measures may leave a nation or the world poorly prepared to deal with adverse changes and may increase the possibility of irreversible or very costly consequences. Options for mitigating change or adapting to change that can be justified for other reasons today and make society more flexible or resilient to anticipated adverse effects of climate change appear particularly desirable.

NO ←

Jerry Taylor

Global Warming: The Anatomy of a Debate

Introduction

The national debate over what to do, if anything, about the increasing concentration of greenhouse gases in the atmosphere has become less a debate about scientific or economic issues than an exercise in political theater. The reason is that the issue of global climate change is pregnant with far-reaching implications for human society and the kind of world our children will live in decades from now.

Introducing nuance and clear-headed reason to this debate is something of a struggle. As Cato Institute chairman William Niskanen has noted, for any international action to merit support, all of the following propositions must be proven true:

- A continued increase in the emission of greenhouse gases will increase global temperature.
- An increase in average temperature will generate more costs than benefits.
- Emissions controls are the most efficient means to prevent an increase in global temperature.
- Early measures to control emissions are superior to later measures.
- Emissions controls can be effectively monitored and enforced.
- Governments of the treaty countries will approve the necessary control measures.
- Controlling emissions is compatible with a modern economy.

The case for any one of those statements is surprisingly weak. The case for a global warming treaty, which depends on the accuracy of all those statements, is shockingly weak.... [I] will concentrate on a few of the most important of those propositions.

From Jerry Taylor, "Global Warming: The Anatomy of a Debate," Presentation Before the Johns Hopkins University Applied Physics Laboratory (January 16, 1998). Copyright © 1998 by The Cato Institute. Reprinted by permission.

A Continued Increase in the Emission of Greenhouse Gases Will Increase Global Temperature

First off, this subject is terribly complex; the 2nd Assessment Report of the International Panel on Climate Change [IPCC] is 500 pages long with 75 pages of references. As Ben Santer, author of the key IPCC chapter that summarized climate change science, has noted, there are legions of qualifications in those pages about what we know and what we don't. But, unfortunately, those qualifications get lost in the journalistic and political discourse.

I will dispense with an introductory discussion of the rudimentary elements of greenhouse theory.... Largely on the basis of computer models, which attempt to reflect what we know, what we assume, and what we can guess, many people believe that continued emissions of anthropogenic greenhouse gasses will increase global temperatures anywhere from 1 to 3.5 degrees Celsius.

At this point, I should note that those estimates have been coming down over time. The 1990 IPCC report predicted a little more than twice this amount of warming, and projections have been declining ever since as better models have been constructed. One wonders, at this rate, whether the models will continue to predict increasingly smaller amounts of warming until even the upper bound forecasts become so moderate as to be unimportant.

What We Know—And What We Don't Know

Here's what the data say, about which there is little debate; ground-based temperatures stations indicate that the planet has warmed somewhere between .3 and .6 degrees Celsius since about 1850, with about half of this warming occurring since WWII. Moreover:

- Most of the warming occurs over land, not over water;
- Most of the warming occurs at night; and
- Most of the warming moderates wintertime low temperatures.

But even here, we have uncertainties. Shorter sets of data collected by far more precise NASA satellites and weather balloons show a slight cooling trend over the past 19 years, the very period during which we supposedly began detecting the greenhouse signal. Those data are generally more reliable because satellite and balloons survey 99% of the earth's surface, whereas land-based data (1) only unevenly cover the three-quarters of the earth's surface covered by oceans and (2) virtually ignore polar regions.

While some of that cooling was undoubtedly a result of Mt. Pinatubo [a volcano that erupted in the Philippines in 1991] and the increased strength of the El Niño southern oscillation, those events fail to explain why the cooling occurred both before and after those weather events were played out and why, even correcting for those events, the temperature data show no significant warming during the 19-year period.

While it is true, as critics point out, that the satellite and weather balloons measure temperatures in the atmosphere and not on the ground,

- where ground-based measurements are most reliable—over the North American and European landmasses, the correlation coefficient between satellite and surface measurements is 0.95—close to perfect agreement, and
- the computer models predict at least as much warming in the lower atmosphere as at the surface, so if warming were occurring, it should be detectable by the satellites and weather balloons.

Even assuming that ground-based temperature data are more reflective of true climate patterns, that still leaves us with a mystery. When fed past emissions data, most of the computer models predict a far greater amount of warming by now than has actually occurred (the models that are reasonably capable of replicating known conditions are a tale unto themselves to which I'll return in a moment). Notes the IPCC, "When increases in greenhouse gases only are taken into account... most climate models produce a greater mean warming than has been observed to date, unless a lower climate sensitivity is used." Indeed, the most intensive scientific research is being done on why the amount of warming that has occurred so far is so low. After all, a .3–.6 degree Celsius warming trend over the last 150 years all but disappears within the statistical noise of natural climate variability.

There are three possibilities:

- something's wrong with the temperature data;
- something's masking the warming that would otherwise be observed; or
- the atmosphere is not as sensitive to anthropogenic greenhouse gases as the models assume.

Indirect Evidence of Global Temperature

Scientists who argue the first possibility cite the largely incompatible, imprecise, and incomplete nature of even recent land-based temperature records. Those observations, of course, are absolutely correct. Instead, these scientists concentrate on indirect evidence suggesting that the planet has been warming and has been warming significantly over the relatively recent past. They typically point to precipitation trends, glacial movement, sea level increases, and increased extreme temperature variability as suggestive of a significant warming trend. Let's take each of these issues in turn.

Precipitation Trends
According to the IPCC, global rainfall has increased about 1% during the 20th century, although the distribution of this change is not uniform either geographically or over time. Evidence gleaned from global snowfall is definitely mixed. Still, measuring either rain or snowfall is even more difficult than measuring simple temperature. As the IPCC notes, "Our ability to determine the

current state of the global hydropologic cycle, let alone changes in it, is hampered by inadequate spatial coverage, incomplete records, poor data quality, and short record lengths."

Recent evidence from climatologist Tom Karl that the incidence of 2-inch rainfalls has increased in the U.S. received sensational coverage but even according to Karl amounts to "no smoking gun." Why? Because he found only one additional day of such rainfall every two years—well within statistical noise —and that most of those days occurred between 1925 and 1945, a time period that does not coincide with major increases in emissions of anthropogenic greenhouse gases.

Glacial Movement

The data here are contradictory. Glaciers are expanding in some parts of the world and contracting in others. Moreover, glacial expansion/contraction is a long-running phenomenon and trends in movement do not appear to have changed over the past century.

Sea Level

While there is some evidence that sea levels have risen 18 cm over the past 100 years (with an uncertainty range of 10-25 cm), there is little evidence that the rate of sea level rise has actually increased during the time that, theoretically, warming has been accelerating. Says the IPCC, "The current estimates of changes in surface water and ground water storage are very uncertain and speculative. There is no compelling recent evidence to alter the conclusion of IPCC (1990) that the most likely net contribution during the past 100 years has been near zero or perhaps slightly positive."

Concerning both ice and sea level trends, the IPCC reports that "in total, based on models and observations, the combined range of uncertainty regarding the contributions of thermal expansion, glaciers, ice sheets, and land water storage to past sea level change is about −19 cm to +37 cm."

Extreme Weather Variability

Again, the data here are mixed. Reports the IPCC, " . . . overall, there is no evidence that extreme weather events, or climate variability, has increased, in a global sense, through the 20th century, although data and analyses are poor and not comprehensive. On regional scales, there is clear evidence of changes in some extremes and climate variability indicators. Some of these changes have been toward greater variability; some have been toward lower variability."

The Masking Theory

The second theory is more widely credited. The most likely masking culprit according to the IPCC are anthropogenic aerosols, primarily sulfates, that reflect some of the sun's rays back into space and thus have a cooling effect on the climate. That aerosols have this affect is widely understood. But as ambient concentrations of anthropogenic aerosols continue to decline (yes, global pollution is on the decline, not on the rise), the argument is that this artificial cooling effect will be eliminated and the full force of anthropogenic greenhouse gas loading will be felt in short order.

This theory becomes particularly attractive when the details of temperature variability are considered. The warming, as noted a moment ago, is largely a nighttime, winter phenomenon; patterns, which suggest increased cloud cover, might have something to do with the temperature records.

The best evidence marshaled thus far in support of the masking theory was published in *Nature* in the summer of 1996. The study... used weather balloon temperature data from 1963 to 1987 to determine temperature trends in the middle of the Southern Hemisphere, where virtually no sulfates exist to counter greenhouse warming. The article, which caused a sensation in the scientific world, showed marked warming and seemed to confirm the argument that, when sulfates were absent, warming was clearly evident. The article was featured prominently in the 1995 IPCC report as strong evidence that artificial sulphate masking was behind the dearth of surface warming.

Yet it turns out that, if one examines a fuller set of data from the Southern Hemispheric (1958–95, 13 years' worth of data that [the study] did not use), no warming trend is apparent. Moreover, if we carefully examine the land-based temperature records, we discover that it is the regions most heavily covered by sulfates—the midlatitude land areas of the Northern Hemisphere—that have experienced the greatest amount of warming. That, of course, is the exact opposite of what we should discover if the masking hypothesis were correct.

Climate Sensitivity

As I noted a few moments ago, a few of the climate models come reasonably close to replicating past and present climatic conditions when historical data are entered. Those models, interestingly enough, predict the least amount of future warming based on present trends. The two most prominent of those models, those of the National Center for Atmospheric Research and the U.K. Meteorological Organization, predict warming of only 1.2 degrees Celsius and 1.3 degrees Celsius over the next 50 years; the lower-bound estimates reported by the IPCC.

The argument for moderate climate sensitivity to anthropogenic greenhouse gas emissions largely rests on three observations:

- First, there appear to be carbon sinks that continue to absorb more carbon dioxide than can be explained. While most models assume that those sinks are presently or nearly beyond their carrying capacity, we have no way of knowing that.
- Second, 98% of all greenhouse gases are water vapor, and many atmospheric physicists, most notably Richard Lindzen of MIT, doubt that a doubling of anthropogenic greenhouse gases would have much climate effect absent a significant change in the concentration of atmospheric water vapor.

- Finally, a warming planet would probably lead to increased cloud cover, which in turn would have uncertain effects on climate. Concedes the IPCC, "The single largest uncertainty in determining the climate sensitivity to either natural or anthropogenic changes are clouds and their effects on radiation and their role in the hydrological cycle... at the present time, weaknesses in the parameterization of cloud formation and dissipation are probably the main impediment to improvements in the simulation of cloud effects on climate."

The Anatomy of the "Consensus"

Despite all the uncertainty, we are constantly told that there is a "consensus" of scientific opinion that human-induced climate changes are occurring and that they are a matter of serious concern. That belief is largely due to the weight given the IPCC report, where this consensus is supposedly reflected. Here is the talismanic sentence in the executive summary of that report, a summation of the 500 pages written not by the scientists who produced that report but by a small, politically appointed executive committee: "the balance of the evidence suggests" that human influences explain some of the detected warming. Now, compare that statement with this, which appears on p. 439 of the report:

> Finally, we come to the difficult question of when the detection and attribution of human-induced climate change is likely to occur. The answer to this question must be subjective, particularly in the light of the large signal and noise uncertainties discussed in this chapter. Some scientists maintain that these uncertainties currently preclude any answer to the question posed above. Other scientists would and have claimed, on the basis of the statistical results presented in Section 8.4, that confident detection of significant anthropogenic climate change has already occurred.

On p. 411, the statement is even clearer:

> Although these global mean results suggest that there is some anthropogenic component in the observed temperature record, they cannot be considered as compelling evidence of clear cause-and-effect link between anthropogenic forcing and changes in the Earth's surface temperature.

Counterbalancing IPCC's note of cautious concern are other, far harsher judgements about the scientific evidence for global climate change:

> 4,000+ scientists (70 of whom are Nobel Prize winners) have signed the so-called Heidelberg Appeal, which warns the industrialized world that no compelling evidence exists to justify controls of anthropogenic greenhouse gas emissions.

> A recent survey of state climatologists reveals that a majority of respondents have serious doubts about whether anthropogenic emissions of greenhouse gases present a serious threat to climate stability.

> Of all the academic specialists, climatologists (only about 60 of
> whom hold Ph.d.'s in the entire U.S.) and atmospheric physicists
> are those most qualified to examine evidence of climate change.
> It is those professions that are most heavily populated by the
> so-called "skeptics."

A recent joint statement signed by 2,600 scientists under the auspices
of the environmental group Ozone Action is less than compelling. A survey
of those signatories by Citizens for a Sound Economy concludes that fewer
than 10% of them had any expertise at all in any scientific discipline related
to climate science.

An Increase in Average Temperature Will Generate More Costs Than Benefits

How costly might global warming prove to be 100 years hence? Well, that
largely depends on the distribution of warming through time and space. It also
depends on how much warming occurs; will it be the upper bound or lower
bound estimate that comes to pass?

Benign Warming Patterns

For what it's worth, I tend to agree with the IPCC's summary statement that the
"balance of the evidence suggests" that anthropogenic greenhouse gas emissions explain some of the detected warming observed thus far over the past 100
years. But as noted earlier, that warming has been extremely moderate, has been
largely confined to the northern latitudes during winter nights, and has exhib-
ited no real detrimental effects thus far. I expect those trends to continue and
that's the main reason why I doubt that the costs of warming will be particularly
consequential.

The present observed warming pattern is certainly consistent with our
understanding both of atmospheric physics, which indicates the following:

- The driest airmasses will warm faster and more intensely than moister
  airmasses. The driest airmasses are the coldest; i.e., those in the northern latitudes during the night.
- Increased warming will increase the amount of water evaporation,
  which will in turn result in greater cloud cover. Cloud cover during the
  daytime has a cooling effect; during the nighttime, a warming effect.

Virginia state climatologist Pat Michaels concludes that

> If warming takes place primarily at night, the negative vision of future cli-
> mate change is wrong. Evaporation rate increases, which are a primary cause
> of projected increases in drought frequency, are minimized with nighttime,
> as opposed to daytime, warming. The growing season is also longer because
> that period is primarily determined by night low temperatures. Further,
> many plants, including some agriculturally important species, will show

enhanced growth with increased moisture efficiency because of the well-known "fertilizer" effect of CO_2. Finally, terrestrial environments with small daily temperature ranges, such as tropical forests, tend to have more biomass than those with large ones (i.e., deserts and high latitude communities) so we should expect a greener planet.

Nighttime warming also minimizes polar melting because mean temperatures are so far below freezing during winter that the enhanced greenhouse effect is sufficient to induce melting.

Indeed, this warming scenario predicts benign, not deleterious, effects on both the environment and the economy.

But what if the warming turns out to be more serious than this? What if the median estimate reported by the climate models comes to pass: a 2.5 degree Celsius warming over the next 100 years?

There have been six particularly comprehensive or prominent serious studies undertaken to estimate the macroeconomic consequences of such a warming. None of them gives us much reason for alarm. The main reason is that most modern industries are relatively immune to weather. Climate affects principally agriculture, forestry, and fishing, which together constitute less than 2 percent of U.S. gross domestic product (GDP). Manufacturing, most service industries, and nearly all extractive industries remain unaffected by climate shifts. A few services, such as tourism, may be susceptible to temperature or precipitation alterations: a warmer climate would be likely to shift the nature and location of pleasure trips.

1974 Department of Transportation [DOT] Study

Back when the world was more concerned with global cooling than global warming, the DOT brought together the most distinguished group of academics ever assembled before or after to examine the economic implications of both cooling and warming. In 1990 dollars, the DOT study concluded that a .9 degree Fahrenheit warming would save the economy $8 billion a year. Only increases in electricity demand appeared on the "cost" side of the warming ledger. Gains in wages, reduced fossil fuel consumption, lower housing and clothing expenses, and a slight savings in public expenditures appeared on the "benefit" side. The amount of warming examined by DOT is roughly equivalent to what the ground-based monitors suggest the planet has experienced over the last 100 years.

1986 EPA [Environmental Protection Agency] Study

Crafted mostly by internal staff (not one of whom had any economics training), the EPA produced few figures, and no quantitative estimates of costs or benefits, failed to even refer to the DOT study of only 12 years earlier, and was littered with qualifications like "could" and "might." While conceding that global warming would reduce mortality slightly, the report nonetheless concluded impressionistically that warming would probably cost the economy.

1991 Nordhaus Study

Perhaps the most prominent academic study of the economic consequences of warming was produced by Yale economist William Nordhaus, an informal adviser to the Clinton administration. Nordhaus calculates that a doubling of atmospheric carbon dioxide concentrations would cost the economy approximately $14.4 billion in 1990 dollars, or about 0.26% of national income. On the "cost" side, Nordhaus places increased electricity demand, loss of land due to flooding, coastal erosion, and the forced protection of various threatened seaboard properties. On the "benefits" side, Nordhaus places reductions in demand for nonelectric heat. He concludes that agricultural implications are too uncertain to calculate but estimates that losses could be as great as $15 billion annually while gains could reach $14 billion annually. Finally, Nordhaus assumes that unmeasured impacts of warming could dwarf his calculations, so he arbitrarily quadruples his cost estimates to produce an estimate of warming costs somewhere around 1% of GDP.

1992 Cline Study

One of the most extensive treatments of the economic consequences of climate change and climate change abatement was produced by economist William Cline of the Institute for International Economics. Instead of assuming a median—4.5 degree Fahrenheit—estimate of warming a century hence (as all other studies tend to do), he assumes 18 degree Fahrenheit warming by 2300 and works back from there. Moreover, Cline includes an extremely low "social" discount rate to calculate the value of future investment. Despite all this, his preliminary calculations reveal that, for every $3 of benefits to be gained by emission restrictions, $4 of costs is incurred. Only by applying arbitrary adjustments after his initial calculations are performed does he find that the benefits of control exceed their cost; but that won't occur, even according to Cline, for at least a century.

Even more controversial are Cline's allocations of costs and benefits of warming. He finds no benefits whatsoever. Costs are found not only in the traditional places (sea level rise, species loss, and moderately increased hurricane activity) but also in areas where most economists have found benefits: agricultural productivity, forest yields, overall energy demand, and water demand. His net estimate is that, spread out over 300 years, the costs of warming will be approximately $62 billion annually.

Unfortunately, it is the Cline study that receives the lion's share of attention from the IPCC. The existence of contrary studies is often simply ignored in the document.

1997 Mendelsohn Study

Robert Mendelsohn of the Yale School of Forestry and Environmental Studies calculated late last year that a temperature hike of 2.5 degrees Celsius would lead to a net benefit of $37 billion for the U.S. economy. Farming, timber, and commercial energy sectors all benefit, with agriculture enjoying "a vast increase in supply from carbon fertilization."

1998 Moore Study

Economist Thomas Gale Moore of Stanford University might be termed the "anti-Cline." Whereas Cline has reported the steepest potential costs of warming, Moore's review of the literature this year in addition to his own investigation pegs net annual benefits of the median warming scenario at $105 billion. While Moore too finds costs in species loss, sea level rise, increased hurricane activity, and increased tropospheric ozone pollution, he finds moderate benefits in agricultural productivity, forest yields, marine resource availability, and transportation. Moreover, he argues that major benefits will accrue from reduced energy demand, improved human morbidity, an increase from miscellaneous amenity benefits, lower construction costs, greater opportunities for leisure activities, and increased water supplies.

Historical Evidence

There is some historical precedent for optimism regarding the consequences of the median computer model warming scenario. The period 850 AD–1350 AD experienced a sharp and pronounced warming approximately equivalent to that predicted by the median warming scenario; 2.5 degrees Celsius. That period is known to climate historians as the Little Climate Optimum. While there were some climatic dislocations such as coastal flooding, there were marked increases in agricultural productivity, trade, human amenities, and measurable improvements in human morbidity and mortality.

Only when the climate cooled off at the end of the Little Climate Optimum did trade drop off, harvests fail, and morbidity and mortality rates jump largely due to an increase in diseases, particularly the plague.

The reason for optimism here is that human civilization was far more weather dependent a millennia ago than it is today. And even our more primitive, weather dependent ancestors appeared to do fairly well during their episodic warming.

Early Measures to Control Emissions Are Superior to Later Measures

Assuming even the worst about the consequences of unabated anthropogenic greenhouse gas emissions and their economic consequences does not necessarily imply that emissions controls today make more sense than emissions controls tomorrow.

There is no compelling need to act now. According to a recent study by Wigley et al. in *Nature*, waiting more than 20 years before taking action to limit anthropogenic greenhouse gas emissions would result in only about a .2 degree Celsius temperature increase spread out over a 100-year period.

Why might we want to wait a couple of decades before acting? First, we might profitably "look before we leap." There are a tremendous number of uncertainties that still need to be settled before we can be reasonably sure that action is warranted. Second, we can't anticipate what sorts of technological advances might occur in the intervening period that might allow far more efficient and less costly control or mitigation strategies than those before us today. Given the low cost of waiting, it would seem only prudent to continue to try to answer the open questions about climate change before making major changes to Western civilization.

Controlling Emissions Is Compatible With a Modern Industrialized Economy

The restrictions on greenhouse gas emissions agreed to in Kyoto are not in any way minor or insubstantial. Reducing U.S. emissions 7% below what they were in 1990 by the year 2012 means reducing emissions almost 40% below what they would be absent the agreement. Adjusted for expected population growth, this means a 50% reduction per capita in greenhouse gas emissions. Virtually everyone agrees that these targets can be met only by reducing fossil fuel consumption, the main source of virtually all anthropogenic emissions.

Environmentalists argue that such reductions can occur relatively painlessly, that we can cut the amount of fuel we use by 50% and actually produce even more economic growth as a result. Virtually no mainstream academic economist shares that opinion. The two most prominent and well respected academic specialists—Robert Stavins of the John F. Kennedy School of Government at Harvard and William Nordhaus of Yale—maintain that only the functional equivalent of a $150 per ton carbon tax can accomplish this, which they calculate would reduce GDP by 3%, or, as Stavins puts it, "approximately the cost of complying with all other environmental regulations combined." A recent survey in *Forbes* summarizing the recent macroeconomic modeling that's been done on the subject broadly agrees with Stavins's and Nordhaus's estimates.

Then there is the matter of whether the emissions cuts presently on the table are even worth the bother. According to the best computer model from the National Center for Atmospheric Research, the Kyoto agreement, even if signed by all the nations of the world, would reduce global warming by an infinitesimal .18 degrees Celsius over the next 50 years. That's not much bang for the global warming buck.

The reason is that, according to all observers, actually stopping any further global warming from occurring (assuming the median predictions of present climate models) would require a 70% reduction of present emissions, roughly the equivalent of completely abandoning the use of fossil fuels. This, according to Jerry Mahlman, director of the Geophysical Fluid Dynamics Laboratory at Princeton, "might take another 30 Kyotos over the next century." Indeed, environmentalists are frequently quoted as saying that, ultimately, we will need to completely restructure society around the objective of energy efficiency and sustainability, the economic and political costs of which we can only imagine.

Unless we're prepared to see that journey to its completion, there's little point in even bothering to sign the Kyoto agreement because, in and of itself, it will make virtually no difference to our planetary climate.

Conclusion: A Matter of Perspective

Let me wind up my comments on a provocative note. We are constantly urged to act because "we shouldn't be gambling with our children's future." In fact, our kids are marshaled endlessly to shame us into planning for the worst... for their sake. But even assuming the absolute worst case about future planetary climate change and the most extreme estimates about what that climate change will ultimately cost society, conservative estimates are that our grandchildren 100 years hence will not be 4.4 times wealthier than we are—as they would be absent global warming—but will instead be only 3.9 times wealthier than we are at present.

I ask you, would you have been comfortable had your grandmother impoverished herself so that you could be 4.4 times wealthier than she rather than 3.9 times wealthier than she? Remember also that increased energy costs are borne most directly by the poor, who spend a greater portion of their income on energy than do the wealthy. Moreover, the poor who will pay the highest price of greenhouse gas abatement will be those in the developing world who will be denied the opportunity to better their lifestyle and standard of living. They will be "saved" from the fate of industrialization and experiencing even the most rudimentary comforts of Western consumer societies.

We're not really gambling with the lives of our grandchildren. They'll be just fine regardless of how the climate plays itself out. We're gambling with the lives of today's poor, who stand to lose the most if we act rashly.

POSTSCRIPT

Is Dangerous Global Warming Occurring?

T he provisions of the Kyoto Treaty include the requirement that the treaty will not go into effect until it is ratified by at least 55 countries representing at least 55 percent of the world's emissions of greenhouse gases. Since the United States is the source of approximately 25 percent of the world's carbon dioxide emissions, the U.S. stand on the treaty is of great importance.

Like most environmental problems, the negative impacts of global warming have been and will be slow to build up and, therefore, are somewhat hard to see. If the projections of the UN panel and others are correct, average temperatures will rise most years in small fractions of degrees. Patterns of storms, rain, and other weather factors that strongly govern the climate of any region will also change slowly. Many predict that some coastal cities may disappear and that some now-fertile areas may become deserts, but that may be many years in the future. However, other regions may benefit. Marginal agricultural areas in northern regions may someday flourish, for example. To make matters more confusing, the Earth warms and cools in long cycles, and some scientists believe that to the degree there is a general warming, it is all or mostly the result of this natural phenomenon. If that is true, cutting back on greenhouse gases will have little or no effect.

There is a major "but," though. That is, if we ignore global warming there will only be an escalating buildup of greenhouse gases, and EDCs will continue to emit them just as emissions from LDCs will rise as part of their modernization efforts. If those who are alarmed about global warming are correct, and we ignore it, there will be many devastating effects on large portions of the globe.

In the end, the question is, Should the United States and other countries bet trillions in economic costs that emissions-driven global warming is occurring? For now, at least, the answer for the United States is no. President George W. Bush termed the Kyoto treaty "deeply flawed" and decided not to submit it to the U.S. Senate for ratification on the grounds that the treaty "exempts the developing nations around the world, and ... is not in the United States' economic best interests." You can further explore the difficulties by reading David Victor, *The Collapse of the Kyoto Protocol and the Struggle to Slow Global Warming* (Princeton University Press, 2001).

For more on the overall issues, go to the interactive Internet site on global warming at http://www.edf.org/pubs/Brochures/GlobalWarming/. For a somewhat skeptical review of the evidence behind the claims about global warming problems, consult S. George Philander, *Is the Temperature Rising? The Uncertain Science of Global Warming* (Princeton University Press, 2000).

Contributors to This Volume

EDITOR

JOHN T. ROURKE, Ph.D., is a professor of political science at the University of Connecticut for campuses in Storrs and Hartford, Connecticut. He has written numerous articles and papers, and he is the author of *Congress and the Presidency in U.S. Foreign Policymaking* (Westview Press, 1985); *The United States, the Soviet Union, and China: Comparative Foreign Policymaking and Implementation* (Brooks/Cole, 1989); and *International Politics on the World Stage,* 8th ed. (McGraw-Hill/Dushkin, 2001). He is also coauthor, with Ralph G. Carter and Mark A. Boyer, of *Making American Foreign Policy,* 2d ed. (Brown & Benchmark, 1996). Professor Rourke enjoys teaching introductory political science classes—which he does each semester—and he plays an active role in the university's internship program as well as advising one of its political clubs. In addition, he has served as a staff member of Connecticut's legislature and has been involved in political campaigns at the local, state, and national levels.

STAFF

Theodore Knight   List Manager
David Brackley   Senior Developmental Editor
Juliana Gribbins   Developmental Editor
Rose Gleich   Administrative Assistant
Brenda S. Filley   Director of Production/Design
Juliana Arbo   Typesetting Supervisor
Diane Barker   Proofreader
Richard Tietjen   Publishing Systems Manager
Larry Killian   Copier Coordinator

AUTHORS

MICHAEL W. BELL is a staff member of the International Monetary Fund.

NICHOLAS BERRY is a senior analyst at the Center for Defense Information. Berry also served as a lieutenant in the U.S. Navy as a diver in explosive ordnance disposal (EOD). He is the author of *War and the Red Cross* (St. Martin's Press, 1997). He holds M.A. and Ph.D. degrees from the University of Pittsburgh.

JOHN R. BOLTON is the senior vice president of the American Enterprise Institute. During the presidential administration of George Bush he served as the assistant secretary of state for international organization affairs. A Yale-educated lawyer, Bolton has held a variety of posts in both the Reagan and Bush administrations.

SOPHIE BOUKHARI is a journalist for the *UNESCO Courier.*

JAKE BOWERS, a Romany activist and writer, cofounded Earth First! UK in 1991. He recently completed a three-year journey around Europe in a traditional Romany wagon in order to trace his Roma ancestry.

MICHEL CAMDESSUS served as managing director and chairman of the Executive Board of the International Monetary Fund from January 1987 to February 2000. Camdessus was educated at the University of Paris and earned postgraduate degrees in economics at the Institute of Political Studies of Paris and the National School of Administration.

JAMES K. CAMPBELL is an expert on terrorism and serves as a commander in the U.S. Navy. He is also the author of *Weapons of Mass Destruction Terrorism* (Interpact Press, 1997).

MARY CAPRIOLI is an assistant professor of political science at the University of Massachusetts–Dartmouth.

JOHN CAVANAGH is director of the Institute for Policy Studies in Washington, D.C. He is coauthor, with Sarah Anderson and Thea Lee, of *Field Guide to the Global Economy* (New Press, 2000).

BILL CLINTON served as the 42d president of the United States from 1993 to 2001. Clinton graduated from Georgetown University and in 1968 won a Rhodes scholarship to Oxford University. He received a law degree from Yale University in 1973 before entering politics in Arkansas. He became Arkansas state attorney general in 1976 and was elected governor of Arkansas in 1978. Clinton is the author of *My Plans for a Second Term* (Carol Publishing Group, 1995) and coauthor, with Al Gore, of *Putting People First: How We Can All Change* (Times Books, 1992).

ARIEL COHEN is a leading authority on Russian and Eurasian affairs. Currently, he is the research fellow in Russian and Eurasian studies at the Heritage Foundation. Cohen frequently testifies before committees of the U.S. Congress and regularly appears on CNN, NBC, BBC-TV, and other major radio and TV networks. He also writes as a guest columnist for the *Washington Post, USA Today,* the *Wall Street Journal,* the *Washington Times,* and other newspapers. He is the author of *Russian Imperialism: Development and Crisis* (Praeger, 1996).

CARL CONETTA is codirector of the Project on Defense Alternatives at the Commonwealth Institute in Cambridge, Massachusetts. He is coauthor, with Charles Knight, of *Defense Sufficiency and Cooperation: A U.S. Military Posture for the Post-Cold War Era* (Commonwealth Institute, 1998).

WILLIAM T. DECAMP III served as deputy military adviser to the United States ambassador to the United Nations prior to his retirement in June 1999. He retired from the United States Marine Corps with the rank of lieutenant colonel.

BILL EMMOTT has been editor in chief of *The Economist* since 1993. Emmott has written several books, including *Japanophobia: The Myth of the Invincible Japanese* (Crown, 1993) and *The Sun Also Sets* (DIANE, 1998). He is a keynote speaker on the new global organization, European affairs and the currency debate, business practices throughout the world, and future economic trends.

AARON L. FRIEDBERG is a professor of politics and international affairs in the Woodrow Wilson School at Princeton University. He is also director of the Research Program in International Security. He is the author of *The Weary Titan: Britain and the Experience of Relative Decline, 1895–1905* (Princeton University Press, 1988). He has been a fellow at the Woodrow Wilson Center and a recipient of the Helen Dwight Reid Award and the Edgar S. Furniss National Security Book Award. In 1998 he was awarded a senior fellowship at the Norwegian Nobel Institute.

FRANCIS FUKUYAMA, a former deputy director of the U.S. State Department's policy planning staff, is a senior researcher at the RAND Corporation in Santa Monica, California. He is also a fellow of the Johns Hopkins University School for Advanced International Studies' Foreign Policy Institute and director of its telecommunications project. He is the author of *The Great Disruption* (Simon & Schuster, 1999).

JOHN HILLEN is a policy analyst for defense and national security policy at the Heritage Foundation and the author of *Blue Helmets in War and Peace: The Strategy of UN Military Operations* (Brassey's, 1997).

ROBERT KAGAN is senior associate at the Carnegie Endowment for International Peace and a member of the Council on Foreign Relations. He is the author of *A Twilight Struggle: American Power and Nicaragua, 1977–1990* (Free Press, 1996). He has also written for *Foreign Affairs, Foreign Policy, Commentary,* the *New York Times,* the *New Republic,* the *Wall Street Journal,* the *Washington Post,* and other publications.

HERBERT C. KELMAN is the Richard Clarke Cabot Professor of Social Ethics at Harvard University. He is also director of the Program on International Conflict Analysis and Resolution at the Weatherhead Center for International Affairs and cochair of Harvard's Middle East Seminar. He is the author of *Crimes of Obedience: Toward a Social Psychology of Authority and Responsibility* (Yale University Press, 1990).

STEPHEN D. KRASNER is the Graham H. Stuart Professor of Political Science at Stanford University. Krasner earned his Ph.D. from Harvard University. He served as editor for *International Organization* from 1987 to 1992, and he is the author of *Sovereignty: Organized Hypocrisy* (Princeton University Press, 1999).

SATISH KUMAR is the editor of *Resurgence* magazine and director of Schumacher College. He is a former Jain monk and peace activist. He is the author of *Path Without Destination* (Morrow/Avon, 2000).

LAWYERS COMMITTEE FOR HUMAN RIGHTS is a New York–based civil rights advocacy group. The committee seeks to influence the U.S. government to promote the rule of law in both its foreign and domestic policy and presses for greater integration of human rights into the work of the UN and the World Bank. The committee works to protect refugees through the representation of asylum seekers and by challenging legal restrictions on the rights of refugees in the United States and around the world.

MARK LEONARD is director of the Foreign Policy Centre, an independent think tank launched by British Prime Minister Tony Blair and Foreign Secretary Robin Cook to revitalize debate on global issues. Educated at Cambridge University, Leonard has previously worked as a journalist at *The Economist*, as political adviser to Calum Macdonald MP (Minister of State for Scotland), and as a stagiaire in the legal service of the European Council of Ministers in Brussels, Belgium.

ANATOL LIEVEN, a British journalist, writer, and historian, joined the Carnegie Endowment in March 2000 as senior associate for foreign and security policy in the Russia and Eurasia Center. He was previously the editor of *Strategic Comments* and also an expert on the former Soviet Union and aspects of contemporary warfare at the International Institute for Strategic Studies (IISS) in London. Lieven is the author of *Chechnya: Tombstone of Russian Power* (Yale University Press, 1998).

SCOTT MARSHALL is vice chairman of the Communist Party and a contributing editor of *Political Affairs.*

CHARLES WILLIAM MAYNES has been president of the Eurasia Foundation since April 1997. Previously he was the editor of *Foreign Policy* magazine.

DANIEL PIPES is director of the Middle East Forum and a columnist for the *Jerusalem Post*. He has taught at the University of Chicago, Harvard University, and the U.S. Naval War College, and he has served in the State and Defense Departments. He is the author of several books, including *Conspiracy* (Free Press, 1999).

SIMON RETALLACK is the managing editor of *The Ecologist's* Special Issues.

LIONEL ROSENBLATT is president emeritus of Refugees International, a Washington-based advocacy organization.

HENRY H. SHELTON became the 14th chairman of the Joint Chiefs of Staff on October 1, 1997, and was reconfirmed by the Senate for a second two-year term in 1999. Prior to becoming chairman, he served as commander in chief of the United States Special Operations Command. His military education includes completion of studies at the Air Command and Staff College and the National War College. He holds the rank of general in the United States Army.

VANDANA SHIVA is a writer and science policy advocate. She directs the Research Foundation for Science, Technology, and Natural Resource Policy in New Delhi, India. Her current work centers on biodiversity and sustainable agriculture. Shiva is a contributing editor of the *People-Centered Development Forum* and a member of the Third World Network. She is the author of *Earth Work* (Feminist Press at the City University of New York, 2001).

WALTER B. SLOCOMBE was nominated by President Bill Clinton to be undersecretary of defense for policy on July 13, 1994, and confirmed by the Senate on September 14, 1994. Prior to this appointment, he had served as principal deputy undersecretary of defense for policy since June 1, 1993. He received his law degree from Harvard Law School.

JERRY TAYLOR is director of the Cato Institute's Natural Resources Studies. He formerly served as an editor for the *Environmental Monitor*.

MARC A. THIESSEN serves on the majority staff of the U.S. Senate Committee on Foreign Relations under Senator Jesse Helms.

LARRY THOMPSON is director of advocacy for Refugees International, a Washington-based advocacy organization.

JONATHAN B. TUCKER is director of the Chemical and Biological Weapons Nonproliferation Program for the Center of Nonproliferation Studies at the Monterey Institute of International Studies. He is the editor of *Toxic Terror: Assessing Terrorist Use of Chemical and Biological Weapons* (MIT Press, 2000).

ROBERT T. WATSON is the associate director for environment in the Office of Science and Technology Policy (OSTP). Prior to joining OSTP, he was director of the science division and chief scientist for the Office of Mission to Planet Earth at the National Aeronautics and Space Administration. Watson received his Ph.D. from London University.

KIMBERLY WEIR is a doctoral student and an assistant in the Department of Political Science at the University of Connecticut.

CAROL WELCH is an international policy analyst at Friends of the Earth USA.

Index